BK 192. N883D
DAVID HUME, COMMON-SENSE MORALIST, SCEPTICAL
METAPHYSICIAN NORTON DA
C1982 25.00 FV

3000 625404
St. Louis Community College

D0146715

192 N883d
NORTON
 DAVID HUME, COMMON-SENSE
 MORALIST, SCEPTICAL
 METAPHYSICIAN   25.00

St. Louis Community College

Library

5801 Wilson Avenue
St. Louis, Missouri 63110

« DAVID HUME »

« DAVID HUME »

Common-Sense Moralist, Sceptical Metaphysician

DAVID FATE NORTON

Princeton University Press
Princeton, New Jersey

Copyright © 1982 by Princeton University Press

Published by Princeton University Press,
41 William Street, Princeton, New Jersey
In the United Kingdom: Princeton University Press, Guildford, Surrey

All Rights Reserved

Library of Congress Cataloging in Publication Data will be
found on the last printed page of this book

Publication of this book has been aided by a grant from
the Paul Mellon Fund of Princeton University Press

This book has been composed in Linotron Goudy

Clothbound editions of Princeton University Press books
are printed on acid-free paper, and binding materials are
chosen for strength and durability

Printed in the United States of America by Princeton
University Press, Princeton, New Jersey

FOR MARY
WITHOUT DOUBT

Contents

Preface

THIS BOOK presents a general interpretation of Hume's philosophy, an interpretation that reveals this philosophy to be significantly more complex than many earlier interpreters have thought. The traditional view that Hume is a purely negative sceptic who dogmatically denies the existence of many fundamental things which the plain man believes to exist constitutes at best a Procrustean bed into which his philosophy has been forced. Hume does not deny that there are substances, causes, or values, although he does raise fundamental questions about the grounds of our beliefs in these things. On the other hand, the more recent naturalistic interpretation of Hume—the interpretation of Kemp Smith and his followers, to be more precise—seems merely to stretch and trim at different places in order to fit Hume into a nonsceptical mold. About some matters Hume was a sceptic. About these he thought himself sceptical; he says that he is sceptical; he offers sceptical analyses and conclusions that run counter to and overturn deep-seated and widely held "natural beliefs." Hume's philosophy is not characterized by the thorough subordination of reason to feeling, instinct, or natural belief.

In contrast to these one-sided interpretations I argue that Hume was both sceptic and nonsceptic. There is nothing paradoxical or necessarily inconsistent about this interpretation. I show that Hume was, in his terms, a "speculative sceptic." However, this scepticism took, roughly speaking, the form of pre-Cartesian scepticisms, or the form of those scepticisms in which doubting and denying are not only thought to be quite different activities, but fundamentally antithetical activities as well. I also show that Hume did not think of himself as a moral sceptic, but as a moral realist, and that he himself distinguished between speculative philosophy and practical philosophy (or between epistemology-metaphysics and morals, we might say). Further, I show that he explicitly and systematically resisted the idea that we should make sentiment the standard of truth in speculative philosophy, even though he did assign it that role in practical philosophy or morals.

I claim here, in short, that Hume is a sceptical metaphysician but a common-sense moralist. To give meaning and plausibility to this claim I provide historical context as well as detailed textual and philosophical analysis of Hume and of those of his contemporaries who provide the relevant historical context. To illustrate, there is a chapter on Frances Hutcheson, who is known to have been an influence on Hume, while another chapter is concerned with George Turnbull and Henry Home, Lord Kames, two relatively obscure Scottish metaphysician-moralists who are Hume's philosophical foils. There are also detailed expositions of Hume's views on the roles of reason and sentiment in morals and metaphysics, and of several kinds of scepticism (for example, moral, religious, Cartesian, Pyrrhonian, and Academic). These expositions are interspersed with analyses or reconstructions of other relevant aspects of Hume's thought. My primary concern has been to make my general view of Hume clear and plausible, even convincing. Nevertheless, this has not prevented me from attempting to contribute to our understanding of specific aspects of his philosophy. Thus those who are unconvinced by the general interpretation I offer may yet find this book of use for understanding Hume's moral theory, his views on the importance of reason in the affairs of life and philosophy alike, and his views on the nature and causes of belief and doubt.

I should perhaps add that I have made far greater efforts to understand and explain Hume's positions than to criticize them. This should not be thought to mean that I suppose these positions are beyond criticism or even that I accept any given conclusion I attribute to Hume. However, I do think that Hume has suffered more than most philosophers from premature criticism—from being criticized before being understood—and I am generally content to attempt to redress this situation. I also wish to note that although I say relatively little about the particular speculative debates that influenced Hume—and almost nothing about Locke and Berkeley—I do not intend to suggest these debates and philosophers had little influence on him. Indeed, despite the claim (see chapter 1) that historians of philosophy have emphasized speculative issues at the expense of moral ones, the interpretation I put forward makes little sense unless it is supposed that speculative matters were of great importance to Hume.

IN PREPARING this study over a period of several years, I have incurred numerous philosophical debts. I would happily acknowledge each of these were that possible. But as it clearly is not, I can only acknowledge all of them and give my special thanks to those whose aid and encouragement have been most prominent.

I wish first to express my special appreciation to Richard H. Popkin, who first interested me in philosophical scepticism, and who never failed to stimulate and respond to my continuing interest in this topic. I also wish to thank Harry M. Bracken and Richard A. Watson for equally unfailing encouragement and critical concern. More specifically, I am indebted to these friends for reading and commenting on the penultimate draft of this work.

It has also been my good fortune to have had this earlier draft read in its entirety by Páll S. Árdal, John Bricke, Vere Chappell, George Davie, James Noxon, Wade Robison, David Stove, and David Yalden-Thomson, while Tom Beauchamp, John Biro, James Moore, and Terence Penelhum read substantial portions of it. There is no significant part of this book that has not been clarified or improved as a consequence of the comments and suggestions resulting from this extraordinary display of scholarly goodwill on the part of these members of the Hume Society. I am indeed grateful for this help. I wish also to thank Anil Gupta, James McGilvray, and John Trentman, colleagues at McGill University whose help has taken less specific forms, but was nonetheless real, and Sanford Thatcher of Princeton University Press for choosing readers whose critical acumen forced me to clarify my aims and my arguments. Mrs. Margaret Dunnett typed the manuscript, and Shirin Rajabalee assisted in the many ways that a good secretary does; I am grateful to both. The index was prepared by Diana Witt.

I have dedicated the book to still another friend, Mary Norton.

Her contributions to this scholarly effort were as exceptional as she herself is.

I have also had support of another kind from McGill University and the Canada Council (now the Social Sciences and Humanities Research Council of Canada). These institutions combined to provide me with an uninterrupted stretch of time that enabled me to complete a first draft of the main body of my text. In addition, both contributed toward the costs of preparing various versions of the manuscript. It is a pleasure to acknowledge this aid.

I also wish to thank the several editors who have first published materials that appear here in an altered form, and James R. Groves for permission to use an article that was first published by Austin Hill Press. These articles and places of publication are:

"Shaftesbury and Two Scepticisms." *Filosofia*, Supplemento al fascicolo 4 (1968): 713-724.
"Hutcheson's Moral Sense Theory Reconsidered." *Dialogue* 13 (1974): 3-23.
"George Turnbull and the Furniture of the Mind." *Journal of the History of Ideas* 35 (1975): 701-716.
"Hume's Common Sense Morality." *Canadian Journal of Philosophy* 5 (1975): 523-543.
"Hutcheson on Perception and Moral Perception." *Archiv für Geschichte der Philosophie* 59 (1977): 181-197.
"Hume and His Scottish Critics." In *McGill Hume Studies*. San Diego: Austin Hill Press, 1979.

« DAVID HUME »

Introduction

> I cannot agree to your Sense of *Natural*. Tis founded on
> final Causes; which is a Consideration, that appears to me
> pretty uncertain & unphilosophical. For pray, what is the
> End of Man? Is he created for Happiness or for Virtue? For
> this Life or for the next? For himself or for his Maker? Your
> Definition of *Natural* depends on solving these Questions,
> which are endless, & quite wide of my Purpose.
>   David Hume to Francis Hutcheson,
>   September 17, 1739

I.   David Hume's philosophy has been exciting responses for
nearly 250 years. The overwhelming majority of these responses
have been negative, based on the understanding that Hume's
philosophy is itself negative, a dogmatically sceptical denial of
man's knowledge of truth and value. The earliest known published
description of his *Treatise of Human Nature*, for example, describes
the book as the work of a "new free-thinker" with "evil intentions." Subsequent reviewers saw the *Treatise* as denying that we
can have any knowledge of causes, and as the work of a paradoxical and dogmatic Pyrrhonist who confidently asserted "that
it is false that everything that exists must necessarily have a cause
of existence."[1] A few years later, when Hume applied for the
Chair of Moral Philosophy at Edinburgh, he was charged with,
among other things, universal scepticism, downright atheism, and
sapping the foundations of morality by denying the real distinction
between good and evil.[2] In 1751 his friend and kinsman Henry
Home (later Lord Kames) published a book-length attack on
moral and epistemological scepticism, and there accused Hume

[1] For an account of the early notices and reviews of the *Treatise*, see E. C.
Mossner, *The Life of David Hume* (Edinburgh: Thomas Nelson, 1954), pp. 116-
132.
[2] The charges were made by the Rev. William Wishart, Principal of Edinburgh
University. See *A Letter from a Gentleman to his friend in Edinburgh*, ed. E. C.
Mossner and J. V. Price (Edinburgh: The University Press, 1967), pp. xv-xvii.

3

of being only too pleased to continue a procession of doubts begun by Berkeley: Hume doubted not only the reality of external objects, but also that of our own perceptions and even that of our own existence.[3] Thomas Reid elaborated this historical account, but he reached essentially the same conclusion: Hume, having accepted the theory of ideas bequeathed by Descartes and Locke, followed it to its logical conclusion, or, that is, to the point that he denied genuine knowledge, basic realities (for example, causes, a substantial self), and real values. Hume, he said, was a dangerous sceptic who represented mankind as mere Yahoos and undermined both natural and moral philosophy.[4] James Beattie spread this representation across the learned world, where it became the entrenched orthodoxy. Throughout the nineteenth century and much of the twentieth, Hume as philosopher was Hume the universal sceptic who dogmatically denied the existence of knowledge, causes, substances, freedom, values, and God.

There have always been some readers who questioned the adequacy of this picture. In response to the charges of Wishart, for example, Hume and his friends published the *Letter from a Gentleman*. This work, while still showing admiration for some forms of scepticism, contends that the *Treatise* had been misrepresented and misunderstood, that its aim was not universal and dogmatic doubt, but modesty and humility. Kant, although he clearly thought Hume was a sceptic, appears to recognize that his scepticism was neither so radical nor so simplistic as his common-sense critics supposed.[5] Thomas Brown no doubt startled his nineteenth-century Scottish audience with the heretical suggestion that Hume the great sceptic and Reid his stalwart opponent differed more in tone than substance.[6] In the middle of the same century

[3] See Part 2 of the *Essays on the Principles of Morality and Natural Religion* (Edinburgh: Kincaid and Donaldson, 1751). This work was published anonymously, but the third edition, published in 1778, was signed by Kames.

[4] Reid's criticisms of Hume are found throughout his *Inquiry into the Human Mind on the Principles of Common Sense*, 1764, and his *Essays on the Intellectual Powers of Man*, 1785. Citations of Reid here are from *The Works of Thomas Reid*, ed. Sir William Hamilton, 2 vols., 7th ed. (Edinburgh: Maclachan and Stewart, 1872). The remark about Yahoos is from 1: 102b.

[5] Kant's remark is found in the Introduction to his *Prolegomena to Any Future Metaphysics*.

[6] Brown's interesting remark is cited in full, p. 195 below.

G. H. Lewes noted that much "stupid ridicule and frivolous objection" have been brought against Hume, particularly by the so-called common-sense philosophers whose view that our belief in the existence of matter is instinctive is not appreciably different from Hume's own.[7] Such comments were little heeded, however, amid the widespread acceptance of T. H. Green's updated version of the Kames-Reid interpretation of Hume's role: Hume built his philosophy upon the philosophical principles that were provided by Locke and Berkeley, and he rigorously developed these principles to their logical—that is, to their sceptical, entirely negative—conclusions.[8] It is only in recent years that there has been a sustained challenge to the time-honored view of Hume as the great destructive sceptic.

Most of the credit for this challenge must go to Norman Kemp Smith. He does not deny that scepticism is an essentially negative philosophical force, but he does deny that Hume is a sceptic. Further, Kemp Smith did not attack the venerable thesis that Hume accepted the fundamental principles of his empiricist predecessors only to reveal the inadequacies of these principles, but he did deny that Hume's aim in doing this was sceptical. Rather, he says, Hume's goal was to challenge the widely accepted assumption that assurance rests on direct insight or evidence, an assumption he wished to challenge because he had a novel positive theory of belief to offer in its place. This positive theory is a naturalistic one, or one in which belief is accounted for by reference to specific natural features of the human mind—that is, to instincts, propensities, passions, or sentiments—and one in which, most importantly, reason is reduced to an entirely subsidiary role as the slave of the passions.[9] Hume's overriding aim was positive; it was to explain how certain fundamental beliefs (in necessary connection and substance, for example) arise. The particular approach he takes could not be less like that of the

[7] A *Biographical History of Philosophy*, 4 vols. (London: Charles Knight, 1845-1846), 4: 36-37.

[8] Green's version of this account is to be found in his Introduction to *David Hume: The Philosophical Works*, ed. T. H. Green and T. H. Grose, 4 vols. (1886; reprint ed., Darmstadt: Scientia Verlag Aalen, 1964).

[9] Kemp Smith (then Norman Smith) initially presented this interpretation in "The Naturalism of Hume," *Mind*, n.s. 14 (1905): 149-173; 335-347.

sceptics, for they rely on argument and evidence, on reason, while Hume's philosophy is characterized by the "thorough subordination of reason to feeling and instinct."[10] Hume may seem sceptical when he argues that we have neither rationally nor empirically founded knowledge of necessary connection or external objects, but he is not, for he is simply trying to show that in all respects (not just in morals) reason is and ought to be subservient to our natural beliefs: "The maxim which is central in [Hume's] ethics—'Reason is and ought to be the slave of the passions'—is no less central in his theory of knowledge, being there the maxim: 'Reason is and ought to be subordinate to our natural beliefs.' "[11] In addition, Hume's "doctrine of the primacy of the vulgar consciousness," or his fundamental thesis, namely, "that feeling has primacy over reason," shows that he had come to the positive conclusion that "in all the really ultimate issues" we can and must rely upon "Nature's guidance, operating . . . not through reason but by way of feeling (inclusive of belief). . . ."[12]

To some, this interpretation of Hume seems scarcely credible. David Stove, for example, writes that some of "the great philosophers are makers, others are breakers." He then goes on to say that Spinoza, Leibniz, and Kant are taken to be makers and that most of us would name David Hume as the breaker *par excellence*, the sceptical philosopher "whose *forte* consists in casting doubt on accepted beliefs by exposing the weakness of accepted inferences." Or at any rate, he suggests, most philosophers think of Hume in this way despite the fact that Hume specialists have, following the lead of Kemp Smith, adopted the opposite interpretation of Hume's philosophy: "According to this interpretation, Hume was no sceptic: his philosophy was as affirmative as any, and was in fact just a kind of naturalism or positivism. Hume

[10] "The Naturalism of Hume," p. 150.

[11] *The Philosophy of David Hume* (1941; reprint ed., London and New York: Macmillan, 1964), p. 11. Hereafter referred to as Kemp Smith.

[12] Kemp Smith, pp. 543, 545. To avoid the ambiguities that arise upon any use of the term *naturalistic*, I have generally refrained from referring to Kemp Smith's view as the "naturalistic interpretation" of Hume—despite the fact that this terminology is now standard among Hume scholars. I refer instead to the "subordination thesis," or the claim, cited here, that Hume's philosophy is characterized by the "thorough subordination" of reason to feeling, instinct, or natural belief. This thesis is described more fully in Sec. III of this chapter.

was so far from intending to subvert 'natural' or accepted beliefs, according to Kemp Smith, that his philosophy was in fact principally intended to *endorse* certain natural beliefs. . . . "[13] In contrast, Stove takes it as evident that those who have been impressed with the sceptical, negative, or destructive character of Hume's philosophy are in fact correct.[14]

Stove's claim about the Hume specialists, unqualified as it is, is an overstatement. Nevertheless, Kemp Smith's central claims are widely accepted. His suggestion that Hume's philosophy is no less common sensical than that of Thomas Reid and James Beattie has been repeated by Richard H. Popkin, who has also said that on Hume's view, a man "believes whatever nature leads him to believe, no more and no less."[15] Nicholas Capaldi suggests that "Hume's pretense at skepticism was a literary device" and that there are "several senses in which Hume may be said to be a common sense philosopher."[16] R. J. Butler suggests that Hume considered even belief in God a justified "natural belief."[17] Robert Paul Wolff, in acknowledging Kemp Smith's "brilliant paper" on Hume's naturalism, goes on to suggest that the *Treatise* propounds a proto-Kantian theory of mental activity which accounts for "all the puzzling features of empirical knowledge."[18] Barry Stroud acknowledges the same master before claiming that Hume's arguments "show that reason, as traditionally understood, has no role in human life."[19]

And so it is now, as Terence Penelhum has put it, that the

---

[13] D. C. Stove, "Hume, Kemp Smith, and Carnap," *Australasian Journal of Philosophy*, 55 (1977): 189.

[14] See also, for example, Stove's "The Nature of Hume's Scepticism," in *McGill Hume Studies*, ed. D. F. Norton, N. Capaldi, and W. Robison (San Diego: Austin Hill Press, 1979), pp. 203-226.

[15] See *The Encyclopedia of Philosophy*, ed. Paul Edwards, 8 vols. (New York: Macmillan and Free Press, 1967), s.v. "Skepticism," and "David Hume: His Pyrrhonism and His Critique of Pyrrhonism," in *Hume*, ed. V. Chappell (New York: Doubleday, 1966), p. 95.

[16] *David Hume: The Newtonian Philosopher* (Boston: Twayne, 1975), pp. 30, 200-203.

[17] "Natural Belief and the Enigma of Hume," *Archiv für Geschichte der Philosophie* 42 (1960): 73-100. Butler's claim is discussed more fully below, pp. 248-249.

[18] "Hume's Theory of Mental Activity," in Chappell, *Hume*, pp. 99-100.

[19] *Hume* (London: Routledge & Kegan Paul, 1978), p. 14.

"most vexed problem" in the study of Hume is that of his scepticism: one asks whether he is a sceptic, and, if so, what kind of
sceptic he is.[20] The issue is not, of course, simply that of determining whether Hume is or is not to be called a sceptic. Indeed,
if that were the issue one would justifiably shrug and go on to
something more interesting, for in some sense it matters little
what we call Hume or even how we characterize his philosophy,
especially given the ambiguity of the terms (*sceptic, naturalist*)
which we must use. It is important, however, to see more clearly
Hume's own resolution of the profound tensions that existed
between his critical intellectual activities and his beliefs as a more
or less ordinary person, or between his rational, sceptical doubts,
and his affective, naturalistic beliefs. If we are to learn from Hume
himself and not from some preconception of him, it is important
to address ourselves to the question of his scepticism.

In this study I do address this question, and I offer a comprehensive and definitive answer to it. This is not to say that I expect
in this book to end the debate about Hume's scepticism, but I
do place this debate in a broader and more rewarding context. I
do not accept the traditional view of Hume as a purely negative
sceptic. Nor do I accept Kemp Smith's totally naturalistic interpretation of him. I argue instead that while some of Hume's views
were from the beginning sceptical, yet they were directed toward
a positive end. I also argue that his moral theory, although a
common-sense theory, nonetheless includes a central role for
reason in one of its traditional forms.

I believe that Hume is a sceptical metaphysician and a common-sense moralist, but I also believe that the assertion of such
a belief outside a particular and ample context is largely pointless
and the claim itself virtually meaningless. Consequently, I pro-

---

[20] "Hume's Scepticism and the *Dialogues*," *McGill Hume Studies*, p. 253. Penelhum
is among those who see that Hume's philosophy may quite consistently include
both sceptical and naturalistic elements. Others who recognize this fact include
Wade Robison in "Hume's Scepticism," *Dialogue* 12 (1973): 87-99, and "David
Hume: Naturalist and Meta-sceptic," in *Hume: A Re-evaluation*, ed. D. Livingston
and J. King (New York: Fordham University Press, 1976), pp. 23-49; and, sometimes and in some senses, R. H. Popkin in the second of the two articles mentioned
in n. 15 above.

vide just such a context: I have broadened the historical perspective from which Hume's work is to be viewed, and I have provided detailed commentary on his extensive discussions of the roles of reason and sentiment in morals and metaphysics, and on his characterizations of diverse forms of scepticism. As a result, it will be clear why I accept neither the traditional negativistic view of Hume nor Kemp Smith's naturalistic view, and why it is that I claim Hume is a sceptical metaphysician and a common-sense moralist.

II.   Seen from a somewhat different perspective, this book may be taken to be an extended argument to support the following claims:

1. Hume's philosophy developed in response to two quite distinguishable philosophical crises, a speculative crisis and a moral crisis, or, as may be preferable, in response to two kinds of scepticism, epistemological and moral.
2. Hume's responses to these distinct scepticisms, his metaphysics and his theory of morals, respectively, differed significantly in method and substance.
3. Hume was fully cognizant of the differences between his sceptical speculative position and his common-sensical moral theory, and in fact he gave reasonably clear (although not always convincing) reasons for supposing metaphysics and moral theory to be distinct and (partially) different philosophical enterprises.

To these claims one could add a fourth of a different sort, but one which brings together this perspective and the interpretative disagreements that were sketched in Section I: Philosophers and scholars have found it difficult to appreciate fully Hume's philosophy because they have uniformly overlooked or underestimated important differences between his metaphysics and his moral theory. In the eighteenth century Hume was taken to be an epistemological sceptic and assumed to be, consequently, a moral sceptic. In our own century some have noted that he is not a moral sceptic and have assumed that he is, consequently, no sceptic at all. There is, in short, a certain either-or mentality about our interpretation of Hume: either he is a destructive, negative sceptic, or he is a constructive positive naturalist.

Neither of these exclusivist interpretations is correct. In order to see why and how they fail to be correct we must overcome the conceptual framework that governs our view of Hume and early modern British philosophy. To this end, I will here make only two brief remarks.

First, I note that most contemporary philosophers and scholars appear to operate with the conception of scepticism that was sketched out by Hume's contemporary opponents. According to this conception the sceptic is, to all intents and purposes, a negative dogmatist who pronounces that those matters that are not certainly true are false, or that those things not certainly known are nonexistent. Insofar, then, as Hume cast doubt on such philosophical fundamentals as necessary connection, material and immaterial substance, or God, he is taken to have denied that these things exist, or to have claimed that propositions asserting their existence are false. Of course, Hume's eighteenth-century opponents thought that to strike thus at philosophical fundamentals was a very dangerous—socially as well as morally dangerous—thing to do, and so their recognition that Hume had raised sceptical doubts was simultaneous with their vilification of him as destructive. Presently, we are more inclined to suppose that sceptical denials are destructive and absurd, but the Reid-Beattie conception of the sceptic as a negative dogmatist still prevails. It was because Kemp Smith conceived of scepticism in this fashion, I suggest, that he was led to the extreme and indefensible view that Hume is not a sceptic.[21]

Second, I note that the overwhelming majority of contemporary philosophers view seventeenth- and eighteenth-century British philosophy, and hence Hume, from a predominantly epistemological (as contrasted to moral) perspective. The most common account of this philosophy presents Hume's philosophical efforts as the logical and negative outcome of the empiricism

[21] It is only in chap. 6 that I return to a systematic discussion of scepticism and of Hume's scepticism.

initiated by Bacon and Hobbes and embraced by Locke and Berkeley. This view of Hume as the entirely negative and sceptical conclusion of a logical-historical development (Locke, Berkeley, Hume, empiricism-to-its-logical-conclusion) was sketched out as early as 1750, and it continues to provide the fundamental perspective on the philosophy of the period. It is certainly true that this particular account has been challenged. It has been said, in contrast, that the impetus for the philosophical developments of the period is to be found in a competition between reason and experience as they sought to replace the church as the basic philosophical authority.[22] It has been said that this impetus was the rise of the new science and the need to provide epistemological and metaphysical theories commensurate with the discoveries of this science.[23] It has also been said that the crucial impetus came from a *crise pyrrhonienne* and the ensuing epistemological battle waged between dogmatists and sceptics.[24] But no matter how different these more recent interpretations may be, they bear a fundamental likeness to the older view: each

[22] It might be said that this is the standard, comprehensive account of post-Renaissance philosophy before Kant. However, it is given an interesting turn by Sir Karl Popper. After suggesting that the "birth of modern science and technology was inspired by [the] epistemological optimism" of Bacon and Descartes, Popper goes on to note that these philosophers and their followers "taught that there was no need for any man to appeal to authority in matters of truth because each man carried the sources of knowledge in himself; either in his power of sense perception . . . or in his power of intellectual intuition. . . ." The central philosophical debate, it is implied, is over which of these internal authorities is in fact authoritative. See *Conjectures and Refutations* (New York: Basic Books, 1962), pp. 4-5.

[23] Consider, for example, the still important work of E. A. Burtt, *The Metaphysical Foundations of Modern Physical Science* (London: Kegan Paul, 1925; rev. ed., 1932); A. N. Whitehead, *Science and the Modern World* (New York: Macmillan, 1926); or the more recent attempt of J. H. Randall to account for early modern philosophy as the outcome of an attempt to place the "new wine" of seventeenth-century science in the "old bottles" of classical-medieval epistemology and metaphysics: *The Career of Philosophy. From the Middle Ages to the Enlightenment* (New York: Columbia University Press, 1962).

[24] This interpretation of the rise of early modern philosophy is explicit in R. H. Popkin, *A History of Skepticism from Erasmus to Descartes* (New York: Humanities Press, 1964). D. D. Raphael has noted the tendency of early modern epistemology to overshadow the moral philosophy of the period in *The Moral Sense* (London: Oxford University Press, 1947), p. 1.

assumes that the central motivating concern of early modern British philosophy was *speculative* rather than *practical*, to use Locke's terms, or *epistemological* rather than *moral*, to use our own.[25] We have taken it for granted that the history of early modern philosophy is just the history of epistemological theories. In point of fact, however, in the hundred years from Hobbes to Hume British philosophers were intensely concerned with moral theory, and highly motivated to refute what they saw as, and called, "moral scepticism."[26] Our epistemological interpretations

[25] "That it is impossible for the same thing to be, and not to be" is a *speculative* principle, according to Locke. "That one should do as he would be done unto" is a *practical* one. Hume follows this usage (see below, p. 102, for example), and so I sometimes use *speculative* as a synonym for *metaphysical*. However, the distinction marked by this terminology is at best a general one; morals may well include epistemological and metaphysical components, and certainly does for both Hume and the other philosophers who will be discussed in detail in the chapters which follow.

[26] The moral scepticism in question took specifiably different forms. These agreed insofar as they denied (in effect, at least) that moral distinctions are founded in objective (independent, publicly available) features of the world (in contrast to observers). Marcus Singer, noting that there are many varieties of moral or ethical scepticism, suggests that these "agree in maintaining, in one way or another, that there can be no such thing as a good reason for a moral judgment, that there are no valid moral arguments, that morality has no rational basis, and that the difference between right and wrong is merely a matter of taste, opinion, or convention" (*Generalization in Ethics*, 2d ed. [New York: Atheneum, 1971], pp. 7-8).

Many of those who opposed this moral scepticism (Cudworth, Shaftesbury, Hutcheson, Hume, and Turnbull, to name those here discussed in some detail) are appropriately called "moral realists," and are generally so denominated in this study. The moral realists agreed in thinking that moral distinctions are objective, or that such claims as "That was an evil act" or "Cook is a good person" are assertions of moral fact whose truth or falsity depends upon objective (independent, publicly available) features of the world (in contrast to observers), and whose truth or falsity may be known (at least to those who have observed the act or person in question). These philosophers took what C. D. Broad describes as the common-sense view of morals, namely, that certain actions, persons, or things are or would be good/right, and others are or would be evil/wrong "whether the contemplation of them did or did not call forth emotions of approval or disapproval in all or most men," or that moral approbation arises in beings having certain constitutions *because* some actions, persons, or things are morally good. Broad, incidentally, claims that Hume exactly reverses this common-sense view, a claim that is shown to be false in chap. 3. See *Five Types of Ethical Theory* (London: Routledge & Kegan Paul, 1930; reprint ed., Littlefield, Adams, 1959), pp. x, 85-86.

of this period are not without genuine value, but the almost unbroken attention we have given to the *crise pyrrhonienne* or *crise spéculative* has all but obscured the fact that these early philosophers were faced with a *crise morale* of equal proportions. The complexities of Hume's philosophy cannot be appreciated until the effects of this moral heritage have been taken into account.

Chapters 1 and 2 of this work present the required consideration of this moral heritage. In chapter 1, I outline the features of Hobbes's philosophy that made him the so-called Terror of Malmesbury, as well as those of the widely accepted Cartesian metaphysics that made such moral scepticism difficult to rebut, and thus contributed in no small way to the *crise morale* I have posited. In the remaining sections of chapter 1, I present first two typical responses to this crisis in moral theory, and then I begin the arguments in support of the three related claims that were just made. To establish a prima facie case for supposing that Hume thought there were important differences between morals and metaphysics (differences important enough to allow him to be a common-sense moralist while remaining a sceptical metaphysician), I rely on an exchange of letters between Hume and his close friend Gilbert Elliot of Minto. That Hume was opposed to moral scepticism can be readily shown, however, by reference to his published philosophical works, a reference that is also made in chapter 1.

In subsequent chapters I examine more closely Hume's distinction between the domains of morals and metaphysics, but not before I have in chapter 2 offered a detailed exposition of the

---

It should also be noted that this moral realism or common-sense morality includes, but is not identical with, what is sometimes called "ethical objectivism," or the view that ethical utterances are objective in that "the truth of what is asserted by some ethical sentence is independent of the person who uses this sentence, the time at which he uses it, and the place where he uses it" (Jonathan Harrison, *The Encyclopedia of Philosophy*, ed. Paul Edwards, 8 vols. [New York: Macmillan and Free Press, 1967], s.v. "Ethical Objectivism"). One could hold that an action is right because its agent approved of it (a form of ethical subjectivism), yet consistently hold that it is objective in the above sense. The moral realists reject subjectivism, emotivism, ethical relativism, and ethical positivism.

moral theory of Francis Hutcheson. In chapter 3, I show that Kemp Smith was clearly correct to say that Hutcheson's moral sense theory greatly influenced Hume, but that Hume, nonetheless, made very significant modifications to that theory, even in morals. Chapter 4 is devoted to George Turnbull and Henry Home, Lord Kames, two Scottish contemporaries of Hume whose metaphysical and epistemological thought does appear to represent the extension of Hutcheson's moral theory into the speculative domain, and hence does appear to be of that naturalistic sort that Kemp Smith has attributed to Hume.

In chapter 5, I show that Hume simply does not accept the primacy of sentiment (or "natural belief") in the speculative domain, or in what he calls metaphysics and natural theology. I show, in other words, that Hume's nonmoral epistemology is not one in which sentiment or natural belief is given primacy over reason, or one marked by the "thorough subordination of reason to sentiment." On the contrary, reason is there described as a principle that can turn or even quell the most natural of sentiments, as a force in its own right and one that makes possible a critical, sceptical metaphysics which Hume thinks to be of genuine value. Thus if in chapter 3, I show Hume defending one form of sentimentalist moral theory, in chapter 5, I show him to have defended a form of rational metaphysics. The two chapters together contain the main ground for my contention that while Hume is a common-sense moralist he is nevertheless a sceptical metaphysician.

Chapter 6 constitutes an extensive discussion of scepticism and of the relationship of doubt and belief in several forms of scepticism. Its main concern, obviously, is to outline the manner in which Hume attempts to reconcile these apparently disparate features of his thought. If the work as a whole has been successful, then it will have convinced the reader that Hume is not a thoroughgoing naturalist who has subordinated reason to instinct and feeling, but a critical philosopher who, although offering a naturalistic theory of mind, carefully preserves an independent role for reason.

III.   Before pursuing further the argument I have sketched, it is necessary to attempt some clarification of the naturalistic inter-pretation of Hume that I oppose. That there is a debate about Hume and naturalism is at least mildly ironic, for Hume was, after all, one of the first philosophers to note just how ambiguous the term *natural* is. It is clearly a relative term, but one with such an array of correlatives that we may well wonder what sense, if any, could be said to constitute its semantic core. In a three-paragraph discussion in the *Treatise*, Hume specifically suggests that what is *natural* may be contrasted to that which is *miraculous*, *rare* and *unusual*, *artificial*, *civil* and *moral*, while elsewhere in the same work he contrasts *natural* and *philosophical* relations, and also *natural* and *original* causes.[27] In short, *natural* is contrasted to at least seven separate and different terms. The moral here is obvious: one who would dispute about Hume's naturalism needs to specify precisely what it is that is or is not being disputed.

Among the different meanings that we ourselves assign to the term *naturalistic* there are several that seem descriptive of Hume's intentions or achievements. If naturalism is thought to be the view "that the whole of the universe or experience may be ac-counted for by a method like that of the physical sciences,"[28] then Hume must certainly be called a naturalist because of his efforts to extend the "experimental Method of Reasoning into moral Subjects," or for, that is, attempting to explain mental phenomena by use of the principles and techniques (suitably modified) of the natural philosophers of his time. We would also be inclined to say that Hume is a naturalist in that he sought to produce coherent philosophical explanations without the slightest recourse to supernatural entities or transcendental principles. His

[27] *Treatise*, pp. 474-475, 13, 280-281. In his Analytical Index to the *Treatise*, Selby-Bigge suggests that Hume (at p. 226) also opposes *natural* to *normal*, a suggestion that is of interest in the present context: An illness, says Hume, "tho' it be contrary to health, the most agreeable and most natural situation of man," can be said to be natural insofar as it arises "from natural causes." In short, the meanings of *natural* are so various that it is on occasion in opposition to itself.
[28] This definition of *naturalism* is offered by John Dewey in the *Dictionary of Philosophy and Psychology*, ed. J. M. Baldwin, 3 vols. (1925; reprint ed., Glouces-ter, Mass.: Peter Smith, 1960), 2: 137-138.

Natural History of Religion is an obvious example of this kind of naturalism. Another example is his attempt to explain moral values as derived from human nature or from, that is, human beings as constituted and active in the world. It is not, then, so far as I am concerned, the fact of Hume's naturalism that is in dispute. The dispute is instead about the role that Hume assigns to reason in the formulation of belief. It is about this that we must be clear if we are to characterize or understand correctly Hume's philosophy.

I have granted that there are senses in which it may be appropriately said that Hume is a naturalist. I also grant that his explanation of belief could appropriately (although perhaps not helpfully) be called naturalistic. Hume does, for example, attempt to explain belief within the methodological framework which we call naturalistic, and the explanation that results is one that eschews reliance on supernatural or transcendental causes in favor of appeals to the principles of human nature. I deny, however, that Hume holds the theory of belief that has been ascribed to him by Kemp Smith and his followers, namely, the theory that belief is not only natural, but also essentially irrational.[29] In Hume's own terms, belief is natural in that it is not miraculous, unusual, or, speaking generally, unavoidable. However, each individual belief is unnatural in that it is not original or connatural. Nor does Hume ever seem to suggest that there is an original principle or faculty of belief.[30] Even more importantly, belief may be, in Hume's terms, artificial. Belief generally may be unavoidable (a human who believed nothing whatsoever is as impossible as one who did not breathe), but specific beliefs are partly constituted or often enough modified by the activity of reason or the

[29] On Kemp Smith's interpretation of Hume, belief is always irrational for, although reason may lead to the same beliefs to which sentiments lead, these beliefs no more depend on reason than do those that are in conflict with reason.

[30] This is not surprising, for Hume hypothesizes very few original principles or faculties; indeed, he appears to suppose that there are the understanding and the passions. Kemp Smith argues that belief is entirely the product of the passions, but I contend that he is mistaken and that the understanding has a central role in the formation of belief. Subsequently, I outline the more important ways in which these two aspects of our nature interact, according to Hume, to produce belief.

understanding.[31] We may wish to say that for Hume belief arises naturally, but the activities of reason constitute one of its determining influences or causes.[32]

To summarize, in challenging Kemp Smith's claim that Hume is a naturalist I am disputing a limited but centrally important set of claims made by Kemp Smith and his followers. These are claims about the roles that are assigned to reason and to sentiment in Hume's philosophy, claims that either constitute or derive from what I call the "subordination thesis," or the thesis that *Hume's philosophy is characterized by the thorough subordination of reason to feeling, instinct, or natural belief.* Representative of these claims are assertions of the following sort:

[31] Hume's discussion of *artificial* actions and virtues elucidates this claim. Actions, he says, which are appropriately called virtuous or vicious are themselves artificial in that they "are perform'd with a certain design or intention." Later, he explains that in calling justice an artificial virtue he means that it does not proceed from "original principles, without the intervention of thought or reflextion." He also suggests that "our natural uncultivated ideas of morality" are inadequate because they conform to the biases of our affections, and that the remedy of this deficiency "is not deriv'd from nature, but from *artifice*; or more properly speaking, nature provides a remedy in the judgment and understanding, for what is irregular and incommodious in the affections" (*Treatise*, pp. 475, 484, 489). Applied to belief, such an outlook would be consistent with granting that a specific belief is indeed natural (not arbitrary, but normal, even necessary) and yet that it is the consequence of the operation of the understanding or that the belief is significantly determined by thought and reflection, the result of consciously chosen intellectual activities.

[32] Hume says as much: "Our reason must be consider'd as a kind of cause, of which truth is the natural effect; . . ." (*Treatise*, p. 180). Kemp Smith does not deny that reason has this role for Hume (see *The Philosophy of David Hume*, pp. 68, 100, 447), but he attempts to limit the scope of reason to the demonstrative sciences in which alone, according to Hume's terminology, knowledge is produced. In arguing, as I am, that reason may for Hume play a significant role in the formation of belief, I am directly contradicting Kemp Smith on the matter of the scope of reason. It should be noted, however, that Hume's use of *reason* is ambiguous, and that I am not restricting myself to the claim that demonstrative reason can play a role in the formation of belief. Rather, I am arguing that Hume supposes our beliefs to come under the influence of thought and reflection—or consciously chosen intellectual activities—whatever form these may take. For a specification of several of the senses in which Hume uses *reason*, see chap. 3, n. 4. A related discussion that will stimulate all serious readers of Hume is Páll S. Árdal, "Some Implications of the Virtue of Reasonableness in Hume's *Treatise*," in *Hume: A Re-evaluation*, pp. 91-106. Árdal places a great deal of emphasis on reason as the "discovery of truth."

1. In respect of matters of fact and existence, reason, Hume accordingly teaches, is the blindest of guides.[33]

2. In all questions which concern matters of fact and existence, it is not knowledge but belief, i.e., not reason but feeling—in Hume's terminology, the passions, inclusive of belief—which is in supreme control.[34]

3. Man, no less than the animals, lives under the tutelage of Nature, and must find in *its* dictates, not in any programme which has to justify itself to reason, the ultimate criteria alike of belief and of action.[35]

4. Hume's reflexions in the study have, in his view, been effectual; and on issuing from the study he is acting on the principles to which they have committed him. Have not these reflexions taught him that it is upon Nature's guidance, operating in all the really ultimate issues not through reason, but by way of feeling (inclusive of belief), that we have to rely?[36]

5. In the field of matters of fact and existence, on the other hand, the term "reason," if still held to, is a name only for certain fundamental beliefs to which we are instinctively and irrevocably committed. Such reflective thinking as may be possible in this domain has to operate in subordination to, and in conformity with, them. In this field, as in the narrower field of morals, reason operates, as it ought to operate, only in the service of our instinctively determined propensities.[37]

6. When Hume says "ought," he means, of course, an "ought" which he interprets in a sheerly naturalistic manner; it is a hypothetical, not a categorical "ought." The beliefs which ought to be accepted are, he teaches, beliefs that Nature itself marks out for us. In their fundamental forms,

[33] Kemp Smith, p. 46.
[34] Kemp Smith, p. 447.
[35] Kemp Smith, p. 45.
[36] Kemp Smith, p. 545.
[37] Kemp Smith, p. 68.

anthropocentrism of the old cosmology. Galile...
established that the heavens are no more perfe...
while his experiments or reflections on falling...
clined planes helped to establish that rest is no mor...
motion, thus together making all but untenable be...
erarchy of values intrinsic in the natural world itself...
doctrine that every part of nature has an intrinsic *telos* an...
place. Nature, Galileo also argued, could be genuinely...
stood—its effects actually predicted—by eliciting its mathe...
ical structure. But as a consequence, he went on to suggest t...
"real" existence pertains only to qualities of a mathematical sor...
The remaining qualities, so-called, he argued, are without such
real existence; they are mere affections, secondary qualities, "mere
names" masquerading as "primary phenomena."[1] In this manner
were those qualities of particular interest to moral philosophers,
qualities such as goodness or virtue, evil or vice, banished from
the primary or real world. In the Scholastic scheme fact and value
had been intertwined in such a way that moral qualities were
supposed to be as objective and real as any others. In the reconstructed world of the new metaphysics they were found to be of
only secondary status, mere affections of the mind.

Those who found the new natural philosophy compelling could
adopt one of several alternative moral theories. One such alternative was the rigorous naturalism of Hobbes. Hobbes not only
rejected the Scholastic tendency to explain the natural world in
the anthropomorphic terms of human psychology and valuation
(appetite and perfection, for example), but, making a complete
turn from the old conceptions, he went on to explain the moral
and human world in terms of a revived atomism (as, at both the
microcosmic and macrocosmic levels, bodies or atoms in motion).
To him, it seemed reasonable to reject as unfounded all attempts
to find substantive qualitative distinctions among the various
aspects of the physical world. And it seemed equally reasonable
to suppose that man himself is simply another part of this physical

[1] Galileo's remarks on what have come to be known as primary and secondary
qualities are from *The Assayer*. See *The Discoveries and Opinions of Galileo*, trans.
and ed. Stillman Drake (Garden City, N.Y.: Doubleday, 1957), pp. 273-278.

---

as "natural" beliefs, we have no choice but to accept
them; they impose themselves upon the mind.[38]

These assertions leave little doubt about Kemp Smith's fundamental thesis. On his view, Hume makes reason thoroughly
subordinate to the passions not only in morals, but in all matters
of fact and existence, and in all matters of importance. There is
some question, however, regarding the precise position that is
ascribed to Hume. Sometimes it seems to be what might be called
"Providential Naturalism," sometimes a "normative naturalism,"
and sometimes merely the theory that we simply must accept the
dictates of nature. When it is said that man in Hume's opinion
is "under the tutelage of Nature" or must rely on "Nature's guidance," Kemp Smith makes Hume sound very much like his Scottish contemporaries who were, avowedly, just such Providential
Naturalists. As Kemp Smith correctly reports, Hutcheson, whose
work influenced Hume, thought that human nature had been "so
providentially ordered" that our "instinctively determined, common-sense judgments" constitute a reliable source of information
about reality. To this, Kemp Smith also adds that Hume refused
to indulge in such unverifiable hypotheses. Nevertheless, he goes
on to say that Hume saw us as dependent upon the tutelage of
"Nature," whereas Hume himself restricts his references to "nature." This difference may be small, but it arouses at least the
suspicion that Kemp Smith sometimes attributes to Hume a theistic outlook that surely cannot be sustained after careful attention
has been given to Hume's work.[39]

But for that matter, Hume does not subscribe to the normative

[38] Kemp Smith, p. 388. Tom L. Beauchamp has pointed out to me that Kemp
Smith sometimes seems to take a rather different view, such as, for example,
when he says (p. 153) that "Hume might well have named the artificial virtues
the rational virtues, and so, without giving up the primacy of feeling, have more
completely recognised the regulating power of reason in determining our specifically moral approbation." However, on the following page Kemp Smith goes on
to repeat his claim about the subordination of reason in the clearest of terms:
"Hume's principle of the subordination of reason to the passions thus runs through
his whole philosophy."

[39] Kemp Smith's views on Hutcheson are discussed in more detail in chap. 2,
Hume's views on Providential Naturalism in chaps. 2, 4, and 5.

naturalism asserted by citation 5, nor even to the view that we simply must accept the dictates of nature. Hume's naturalistic theory of belief constitutes a direct challenge to Descartes's thoroughly voluntaristic view of belief. For him, belief is not, as Descartes claims, an act of the will to be performed, ideally, only at the instigation and with the sanction of reason. But the fact that Hume took such an antivoluntaristic stance did not necessarily commit him to a radically involuntarist account of belief, or to the view that reason is "thoroughly subordinate" to the passions or sentiments in all matters of fact and existence. Nor does Hume choose such a radical position. Instead, he adopts the more moderate view that belief, while not voluntary or the result of an act of the will, is nonetheless subject to the influence of reason or voluntary acts of thought. What we believe may at the moment of belief be in the control of our natural propensities, but there is, nonetheless, a time and manner in which the activities of reason may produce a significant influence upon our beliefs—so much so that some natural or common-sense beliefs are actually altered or even discarded. Hume is far from thinking that we must passively accept all that nature leads us to believe, or that there is no role for reason in human affairs. On the contrary, he believes in the efficacy of reason even against the forces of nature and finds that in its highest form, that is, in critical philosophy, reason has a profound role in human affairs.

« 1 »

Hume and the
Crise Morale

It requires but very little knowledge of human affairs to perceive, that a sense of morals is a principle inherent in the soul, and one of the most powerful that enters into the composition.

David Hume,
A Treatise of Human Nature

I. The reconstruction of a viable moral theory, I have suggested, was the most urgent concern of British philosophy in the hundred years following the publication of the major works of Thomas Hobbes. To be sure, the intellectual upheaval occasioned by the voyages of exploration, the Reformation, and the new science shook the foundations of all philosophy, speculative as much as practical, especially given that fact and value were inextricably intertwined in the theoretically stable world of Scholasticism. Clearly, the metaphysical upheaval of the late Renaissance was of staggering proportions and of deep concern to such sensitive speculative thinkers as Descartes. Soon enough, however, metaphysician natural philosophers began to put their world back together; soon enough there was the grandly successful science of Galileo, Newton, and a host of others, and a growing consensus about the nature of nature herself and how to learn about her.

For the moral theorists there were no such grand successes, and little consensus. Indeed, the very success of natural philosophy seemed to compound the problems of moral theory. The revolutionary hypothesis of Copernicus provided eventually a clear understanding of the heavens, but it destroyed the comforting

world. Nature he took to be constituted of material bodies in
motion. Man he took to be similarly constituted, equally susceptible to scientific explanation although the only natural science
is that of bodies in motion.[2]

Given this initial commitment, Hobbes found it reasonable to
think of every man as entirely self-regarding (that is, as buffeted
by other bodies, including other men, but concerned only to
maintain his power of movement, or ability to, in turn, desire
and fulfill desire) and equally reasonable to erect both moral and
political theories that unabashedly proclaim the selfishness of
man. *Goodness* or *virtue*, Hobbes appears to be arguing, have no
more application to the actions (motions) of a human being than
they have to the actions of an animal: they are merely names for
what is pleasant or satisfying to creatures with desires, where
desire itself is represented as no more than a response (complex
though it may be) to the forces which act on the desiring individual. Further, there is nothing essentially different in this respect between animate and inanimate creation, for although animate creation is capable of self-locomotion in response to stimuli,
this represents only a difference in complexity of response. *Desire*
is not the name for a distinctive psychological activity; rather,

[2] I recognize that this understanding of Hobbes and of the relation of his views
regarding the natural world to his morals, politics, and psychology is not universal,
and that in the past century it has been challenged by such diverse writers as G.
C. Robertson, Leo Strauss, Michael Oakeshott, A. E. Taylor, and Howard War-
render. However, I am here concerned far more with a historical conception of
Hobbes than with his views per se, and it seems fair to claim not only that
"Hobbes's own contemporaries reacted to his thought with virtually unanimous
horror" (Thomas Spragens, *The Politics of Motion* [Lexington: University Press of
Kentucky, 1973], p. 21), but also that the more philosophical of these contemporaries said the sorts of things I have here outlined. Some evidence that they
did so is found in the following sections of this chapter, and further evidence
may be found in Spragens and in S. I. Mintz, *The Hunting of the Leviathan*
(Cambridge: At the University Press, 1962). Spragens (pp. 22-35) gives a helpful
survey of the principal interpretations of Hobbes that have been offered more
recently, then goes on to discuss (guided by Kuhn's model of scientific revolutions)
the manner in which the new science of the seventeenth century displaced the
older cosmology, and the implications of this displacement on Hobbes's conceptions of morals and politics. Perhaps I should note that for a number of reasons,
I find the older view of Hobbes, now restated by Spragens, more convincing than
the more recent views of Robertson et al.

it is the name we apply to entirely physical activity (bodies in motion) at the microcosmic or submacrocosmic level. *Desire* is a term entirely analogous to *impetus* or *pressure* as these are applied to solids or fluids.

Gone from Hobbes's philosophy, then, is a distinctively moral domain. There is no *summum bonum*, there is no realm of objective (independent and intersubjective) values or ends, there is no disinterested desire for the good of another, there is no free, immaterial soul to direct man's impulses. Man is a part of nature; there is no transcendental nature. The physiocentrism of his position is complete, and by its completeness intrinsic moral character is eliminated from man and the world. Granted, Hobbes allows for the apparently moral (always at bottom, however, a form of self-regard), and he can speak of natural right (of each to all) and of the natural law (our "obligation" to preserve ourselves), but there is here no relenting from the reduction of value to fact. Granted, he allows for a fundamental human goal, but this is no more than the desire to be able to continue to desire and to satisfy our desires. There are no specific principles that could or should guide our behavior in any and all circumstances, and if there are laws they are only the unavoidably arbitrary commands of the sovereign or God.

One would scarcely expect such a theory of value to alleviate a *crise morale*. Nor did it. Indeed, Hobbes's bold materialistic hypothesis might well be said to have turned, in Britain at least, merely serious difficulty into grave crisis. It is not immediately clear, however, how the immeasurably more popular Cartesian or dualistic metaphysics made the life of the moral realist that much easier than had Hobbes's materialism. Descartes, after all, appears to have marched to the measured tones of Galileo's drum. He too proclaimed that nature, the physical world, was essentially mathematical, and hence that those apparent qualities of things that are not mathematical cannot be located in nature. Of course, given Descartes's metaphysics, this meant that these qualities must be ideas in the mind. It meant, in other words, that certain qualities (most notably colors, sounds, smells, or those qualities that have since become known as secondary qualities) that had by earlier philosophers been taken to be in the physical world itself were now understood to be merely modifications of the mind, ideas, or, at most, ideas for which there were in principle no resembling qualities in objects. There was, in short, an ontological gulf between objects and a great many qualities, all those, namely, except the primary qualities.

This theory led to well-known epistemological problems. Having noticed that all ideas are in the mind, Simon Foucher and Pierre Bayle, followed by Berkeley and Hume, asked how we could be sure that the ideas of primary qualities accurately represent the qualities of bodies. In fairness to Descartes, it must be said that he had offered an answer to this objection. He had said that the ideas of primary qualities are clear, distinct, and provided innately by God himself. Furthermore, they are easily recognizable because they are mathematical in form. That this answer was also found inadequate did not necessarily lead to the dismissal of the Cartesian ontology but, often enough, to attempts at more satisfactory epistemological theories, a great many of which accepted the distinction between primary and secondary qualities, and to the implicit mathematization of objective reality which seems to accompany that distinction. In short, some ideas, those adapted to quantitative expression, were taken to be representative of reality; other ideas, although presumably caused by qualities in objects, were only psychological reactions to such qualities, and not representative of them.

These philosophical developments have been widely discussed, of course, but much less attention has been given to the fact that moral qualities were among those displaced by the Cartesian revolution. Given a world that is either extended, figured, and subject to motion and rest, or unextended mind, it seems that any moral qualities that might previously have been thought to be objective, or in the world itself, can only be ideas in the mind. Furthermore, they are just those kinds of ideas that fail to be informative about any publicly available features of the world. In the dualistic Cartesian world—Cartesian dualism dominated Western thought in the late seventeenth and early eighteenth centuries—moral qualities became, in the generic sense, secondary, of diminished reality, or, in the now common parlance, subjective. At the same time that Hobbes was presenting a powerful case for the view that our moral ideas have no genuine moral reference, the only viable alternative among the new metaphysics left the status of these same presumably moral ideas very much in doubt, unsettled, and even seriously challenged.

II.   Descartes and the other dualists may have contributed to the *crise morale* of the late seventeenth century, but in Britain at least it was the bold materialist hypothesis of Hobbes that served as the focus of this crisis. Certainly, the breadth and profundity of the outcry against him sufficiently confirms that there was such a crisis. The problem, it should be appreciated, was not merely to refute the dogmatic scepticism of Hobbes and the moral agnosticism (if that it was) of Descartes. The problem was to accomplish these ends while granting, even applauding, the very scientific advances that seemed to fuel the metaphysical claims that led in the first place to doubts about the objectivity of morals or the possibility of moral knowledge. It would not do to ignore or minimize modern man's finest intellectual achievements in an effort to buttress or reestablish the objectivity of moral distinctions. Scholastic physics and cosmology had been overturned; if moral scepticism were to be refuted, it would need to be on some other foundation.

Typically, those who strove to formulate new but realistic theories of morals are divided into rationalists and empiricists, an imperfect but usable distinction. Or, put in more detailed terms, the responses to moral scepticism tended to follow one of two forms: a modified Platonism (or expanded Cartesianism) which could incorporate the new science into a dualistic metaphysics and thus attempt to represent moral reality as analogous to mathematical and scientific truths, and, consequently, be on a par with the representative primary qualities of which the new philosophy was so confident. Alternatively, there developed an empiricism which, while accepting this same dualistic metaphysics, insisted that moral differences are objectively real, but are made known to us through "affections" of the mind, affections which

resemble the ideas of secondary qualities. The moral philosophy
of Ralph Cudworth (1617-1688) is a paradigm of the first kind
of response, while that of Anthony Ashley Cooper, Lord Shaftesbury (1671-1713), often taken to be the founder of the moral
sense school, is an example of the second approach. For all their
differences, these philosophers represent a single tradition, an
antisceptical tradition that leads to Hume's antisceptical, common-sense theory of morals, and hence a brief résumé of their
moral theories is in order.[3]

III. That Ralph Cudworth was adamantly opposed to Hobbes's
moral philosophy is well known. He was not, however, opposed
to the "atomical philosophy" per se, or to that revival of this
ancient view to which Hobbes (along with Descartes and Gassendi, he thought) had contributed. Indeed, Cudworth forthrightly embraced the physics of this revived philosophy and had
little patience for those who might resist the new science. It
is "absurd and ridiculous," he writes, to suppose that "all the
new celestial phenomena, as of the jovial planets, and the moun-
tains in the moon, and the like, are no real things; but that the
clear diaphanous crystal of the telescopes may be so artificially
cut, ground, and polished, as to make all those, and any other
phenomena, clearly to appear to sense, when there is no such

[3] Although it is not my intention to claim any direct intellectual link between
Cudworth and Shaftesbury, Prof. James Moore has reminded me that there may
well have been such a link: Shaftesbury was the pupil of Locke, who was on
intimate terms with Lady Masham, who, in turn, was Cudworth's daughter. This
link is at least suggested by Ernst Cassirer in *The Platonic Renaissance in England*,
trans. F.C.A. Koelln and J. P. Pettegrove (Austin: University of Texas Press,
1953), chap. 6, and John Passmore, in *Ralph Cudworth: An Interpretation* (Cambridge: At the University Press, 1951), p. 98, explicitly speculates on the matter,
saying that "Lady Masham certainly lent Shaftesbury books and not improbably
[Cudworth's] manuscripts." Subsequently, however, Passmore was only willing to
say that "Locke and Shaftesbury may have had access to [Cudworth's manuscripts]
by way of Lady Masham" (*Encyclopedia of Philosophy*, s.v. "Cudworth, Ralph").
Shaftesbury's interest in the Cambridge Platonists is established by the fact that
he edited and published some of Whichcote's sermons in 1698. There is yet much
to be learned about the origins of the moral sense school, as was some years ago
made clear by R. S. Crane; see n. 30 to this chapter.

thing. . . ."[4] In contrast, he argues, the atomical physics has in this "last age" been "so successfully restored by the writings of some learned authors, and the truth thereof so convincingly evidenced by many other experiments besides that of the glassy prism and rainbow, that there is little doubt left concerning it. And indeed unless this philosophy be acknowledged to be true, we must of necessity affirm, that the sensible and corporeal world is altogether unintelligible."[5]

But if, in Cudworth's view, "this old atomical philosophy be most solidly and substantially true," the further views that some philosophers—both ancient and modern—have tried to build upon it are false. They represent not consequences of the atomic physics, but the paradoxical, sceptical fantasies of those who would rather overturn knowledge itself than to grant that there are any real moral differences. The philosophy of Protagoras, for example, although uniformly sceptical regarding all kinds of knowledge, seemed to Cudworth "chiefly intended as a battery or assault against morality . . . against the absolute and immutable natures of good and evil, just and unjust. . . ."[6] Protagoras, then, was one of those old philosophers—and Hobbes one of the new— who "would not stick to shake the very foundations of all things, and to deny that there was any immutable nature . . . of anything, and by consequence any absolute certainty of truth or knowledge; maintaining this strange paradox, that both all being and knowledge was fantastical and relative only, and therefore that nothing was good or evil, just or unjust, true or false, white or black, absolutely and immutably, but relatively to every private person's humour or opinion."[7]

[4] *The True Intellectual System of the Universe: wherein all the Reason and Philosophy of Atheism is Confuted, and its Impossibility Demonstrated, with a Treatise concerning Eternal and Immutable Morality*, ed. J. L. Mosheim, trans. J. Harrison, 3 vols. (London: Thomas Tegg, 1845), 3: 637. All citations are from the *Treatise concerning Eternal and Immutable Morality* which is wholly contained in vol. 3 (hereafter cited as *Eternal Morality*).
[5] *Eternal Morality*, p. 552.
[6] *Eternal Morality*, pp. 552, 542.
[7] *Eternal Morality*, pp. 540-541. Richard Price offers much the same account: Protagoras, he says, noted particularly the relativity of our sensations or experience, and concluded that (1) all things are in perpetual flux; (2) nothing is true

In contrast, Cudworth believed that the atomical philosophy itself overturns any scepticism that is said to be consequent upon it, and were it not for the moral implications of such scepticism, he might well have spared himself the pains of an extensive refutation. Pointing out the paradoxical nature of Protagorean scepticism—if no claims are absolutely true, then that claim, too, is relative and false—would be sufficient were not there the necessity of showing that moral good and evil, just and unjust, are real and immutable aspects of reality, which in turn requires that we see that the human mind is not a mere *tabula rasa*, without "innate furniture or activity"; that matter is not the "first original and source of all things"; and that "it is not possible that there should be any such thing as morality" unless there is a God who is this first original and source of all things.[8]

To accomplish the needed refutation, Cudworth focuses on the true atomical philosophy, for an analysis of this reveals to his satisfaction that sense experience alone can never give us knowledge, not even of the physical world. Knowledge, for Cudworth, does not arise from particulars, but descends to them; our knowledge of general laws and our knowledge of individual things may be awakened or occasioned by sense experience, but its ultimate source is the intellect. Our senses do not perceive things themselves, but, presumably, certain "passions" that are traceable to local motions. These passions—ideas of secondary qualities, in effect—apprise us that there are individual objects existing in our vicinity, but, all in all, sense is essentially a practical, not an intellectual, faculty: "Sense is a kind of dull, confused, and stupid

---

or false; and (3) applied this scepticism to moral good and evil. Interestingly, Price sees Hume's speculative scepticism as the explicable outcome of earlier *moral* scepticism. "Modern scepticism," he writes, "has not stuck at" saying that all causal judgments are modifications of our own thoughts, not judgments of the understanding. He then goes on to say that it is "no inconsiderable apology for it [Hume's scepticism regarding causes], that in doing this, it has only extended further what some writers of the best moral character have contended for, with respect to moral rectitude" (A *Review of the Principle Questions in Morals*, ed. by D. D. Raphael [Oxford: Clarendon Press, 1948], pp. 54-55). However, Price is probably referring (by "some writers of the best moral character") to Hutcheson and Shaftesbury, not Hobbes.

[8] *Eternal Morality*, pp. 553, 640-645.

perception obtruded upon the soul from without, whereby it perceives the alterations and motions within its own body, and takes cognizance of individual bodies existing round about it, but doth not clearly comprehend what they are, nor penetrate into the nature of them, it being intended by nature . . . not so properly 'for knowledge' as for the 'use of the body.' "[9]

Knowledge, on the other hand, does comprehend the essences of things, and it is the result of an "inward and active energy of the mind itself," directed toward the "primary and immediate objects of intellection," namely, the reasons of things, or, that is, the ideas found within the mind itself. Just as hard or soft, hot or cold, and other similar qualities are modifications of matter, so the "several objective ideas of the mind [cause, effect, equality, inequality, whole, part, and so forth] in scientifical speculation" are "several modifications of the mind knowing."[10] These ideas, Cudworth argues, cannot have arisen from sense experience alone, for they function to order and arrange our sense experience. Furthermore, because our knowledge of the natures or essences of compound corporeal things always involves just such conceptions or ideas or relations, it can be seen that "the natures of no compounded corporeal things can possibly be known or comprehended by sense." Likewise, the simple and individual corporeal things which our senses reveal to us are also said to be "known and understood by the active power of the mind exerting its own intelligible ideas upon them."[11] If, for example, we identify an individual object as a white triangular surface, or as "a solid tetrahedron . . . included all within a triangular superficies," we find upon examination that it is not by sense that we know this object. The essence of a corporeal substance is its impenetrable extension, existing, and this particular object is further known through the conceptions of whiteness and triangularity. None of these ideas is obtained or learned through sense, which gives us only a bare, uncomprehending experience of things, or an experience analogous to that which an animal or illiterate might

[9] *Eternal Morality*, pp. 570, 561.
[10] *Eternal Morality*, pp. 577-580.
[11] *Eternal Morality*, pp. 595, 601-602.

have of a printed page, as compared to those who know the meanings of the printed symbols, and hence can understand what they have experienced. Sense experience may be the occasion of the mind's knowing activity, but that activity is, strictly speaking, inward and downward, whether it is individual things or "universal axiomatical truth, and scientific theorems" that are known.[12]

It remains only for Cudworth to draw his moral conclusions. Knowledge, even knowledge of individual physical objects, depends upon ideas or conceptions which cannot be obtained from experience, which must be prior to experience. And yet there is such knowledge. There must, then, be such ideas. But if man has innately such conceptions as cause, effect, substance, triangle, sphere, and equality, it will not seem extraordinary to claim that he has innately also such conceptions as "wisdom, folly, prudence, imprudence, knowledge, ignorance, verity, falsity, virtue, vice, honesty, dishonesty, justice, injustice," and so forth.[13] The mind of man is *not* a *tabula rasa*; rather, it is replete with innate tools or furnishings which enable us to know the world, and to know moral reality just as we know physical reality. There can be no question, either, of this moral reality being mutable, private, or conventional. Knowledge is, after all, of that which is unchangeable and public, and of the natures of things. Hence the Protagorean-Hobbesian suggestion that man is the measure of all things moral is simply nonsense and contradictory. If our moral terms have any significance, they must refer to the natures of things (for example, men's actions or souls) and cannot then be altered "by mere will or opinion."[14] Moral statements as much as those of physics make reference to reality, and are true or false as they

[12] *Eternal Morality*, pp. 603-617. A few pages later (p. 620), Cudworth concludes by saying: "Wherefore we conclude, that the immediate objects of geometrical science, properly so called, are not individual bodies or superficies, but the intelligible and universal ideas of a triangle, square, circle, pyramid, cube, sphere, actively exerted from the mind, and comprehended in it. For the mind doth not seek its objects of knowledge abroad without itself, but must needs actively comprehend them within itself: which also, as we shall show in the following chapter, are immutable things, and always the same."

[13] *Eternal Morality*, p. 586.

[14] *Eternal Morality*, p. 640.

reflect or fail to reflect that reality. What we prefer or decree has no more effect on that reality than it does on the shape of a triangle or the existence of the "jovial planets." In short, neither sense nor matter is the origin of knowledge, and thus there is no reason to suppose that our moral knowledge—or moral reality— is any less objective, any less fixed, than physics or mathematics.[15]

Cudworth also saw Hobbes as challenging the notion that the universe and man were ordered to any purpose or were more than constituent matter in motion. The fact alone, he says, that a philosopher should believe that knowledge arises from "sensible and material things" convicts him of "nothing else but downright atheism." For, if it is true that knowledge results from matter and sense, and is nothing more than their stamp upon us, then "it must needs follow that this corporeal world was not made or framed by any antecedent wisdom or knowledge, but that it sprang up of itself from the blind, fortuitous, and giddy motions of eternal atoms . . . Which is all one as to say that there is no God at all."[16] And, of course, nearly every claim of Cudworth contradicts this antiteleological perspective and emphasizes the design of a God who is concerned for man's well-being: the senses were given to us to apprise and warn us of the objects around us, and we are innately furnished with the intellectual apparatus that enables us not only to satisfy our natural curiosity and to effect a virtuous life, but also to see the goodness, wisdom, and design of our maker:

[15] Cf. Samuel Clarke and Price, two other rationalists, on this same point: "For, as the addition of certain numbers, necessarily produces a certain sum; and certain geometrical or mechanical operations, give a constant and unalterable solution of certain problems or propositions: so in moral matters, there are certain necessary and unalterable respects or relations of things, which have not their original from arbitrary and positive constitution, but are of eternal necessity in their own nature." Clarke, *A Discourse concerning the Unchangeable Obligations of Natural Religion,* . . . first printed in 1706, cited here from *British Moralists 1650- 1800,* ed. D. D. Raphael, 2 vols. (Oxford: Clarendon Press, 1969), 1: 213. "What I have hitherto aimed at has been, to prove that morality is a branch of *necessary truth,* and that it has the same foundation with it. If this is acknowledged, the main point I contend for is granted, and I shall be very willing that truth and morality should stand and fall together." Price, *Review,* p. 85.

[16] *Eternal Morality,* pp. 629-630.

The intellect doth not rest here, but upon occasion of those
corporeal things thus comprehended in themselves, naturally
rises higher to the framing and exciting of certain ideas from
within itself, of other things not existing in those sensible
objects, but absolutely incorporeal. For being ravished with
the contemplation of this admirable mechanism and artificial
contrivance of the material universe, forthwith it naturally
conceives it to be nothing else but the passive stamp, print
and signature of some living art and wisdom; as the pattern,
archetype and seal of it, and so excites from within itself an
idea of that divine art and wisdom [which] . . . are contrived
not only for the beauty of the whole, but also for the good
of every part in it, that is endued with life and sense, [for
these] it exerts another idea, viz. of goodness and benignity
from within itself, besides that of art and wisdom, [and these
ideas] . . . being looked upon as modes of some intellectual
being or mind in which they exist, it from hence presently
makes up an idea of God, as the author or architect of this
great and boundless machine; a mind infinitely good and
wise; and so as it were resounds and re-echoes back the great
Creator's name. . . .[17]

IV. Shaftesbury was equally adamant in his opposition to the
moral scepticism of Hobbes (and of Locke), so much so that his
moral sense theory is perhaps best presented as a critical analysis
and refutation of such scepticism—that is, of those moral theories
which deny the objectivity of moral distinctions, or which, as
the result of maintaining some epistemological or metaphysical
theory, undercut the basis of belief in the reality of these distinctions. Seen from this perspective, moral scepticism is in fact,
we would say, a form of dogmatism, for it results from a tendency
to rely narrow-mindedly upon a single method or insight. By
being dogmatic one becomes sceptical in the sense that one denies
or disbelieves all those views that appear to be contrary to one's
own. "There is," as Shaftesbury puts it,

[17] *Eternal Morality*, p. 597.

a faith which carries with it a . . . stubborn resolution to give everything the lie except the reason. The stubbornness of this faith is such as to contradict the very senses, the imaginations, the habitual and almost natural opinions of mankind . . . the plausible and in all appearances most innocent thoughts, unexceptional judgments, and warrantable fancies: as of what is good, what ill, what eligible, what ineligible, what indifferent and what of concern. If by reason be understood the reason of the world, this is indeed giving reason, and (if you will too) common sense the lie.[18]

Hobbes and Locke, Shaftesbury explains, had in just this way undercut reason and common sense. Granted, their reasoning had been careful, but they had been too insistent upon reasoning of a particular sort. As a result they had been led to contradict less esoteric experience and had in fact come to deny the existence of "real good" (or evil). Granted, Hobbes was an "able and witty philosopher," but he made the mistake of attempting to explain every human act according to a single principle, that of self-love. The moral system which results, Shaftesbury argues, has the signal characteristic of making apparent moral distinctions meaningless. Such words as *courage, friendship, love,* and *public interest,* words which seem to denote altruistic acts or tendencies, are found to mean, on Hobbes's view, nothing different from their apparent opposites, for all acts and tendencies are similarly motivated, and

---

[18] *The Life, Unpublished Letters, and Philosophical Regimen of Anthony Ashley Cooper, Earl of Shaftesbury,* ed. B. Rand (London and New York: Sonnenshein, 1900), pp. 37-38. Hereafter cited as *Life and Letters.* Shaftesbury's characterization of moral scepticism as a kind of negative dogmatism which denies, for a variety of reasons, the reality of moral distinctions and/or the possibility of genuinely altruistic or benevolent acts, is a paradigm eighteenth-century conception of that view. Thus when I later claim that Hume sought to refute moral or ethical scepticism, I shall be claiming that he also attempted to refute those negative, cynical views which he and others ascribed to Hobbes and Mandeville. There are important methodological similarities between moral scepticism and the methodic doubt or methodic negation that is now often called "Cartesian scepticism" and is found in Descartes's First Meditation, and other similarities between it and religious scepticism or atheism as (once) popularly conceived. How greatly moral scepticism and Cartesian scepticism differ from other forms of scepticism (Pyrrhonism, Academic scepticism) is discussed in chapter 6 of this book.

hence all are at bottom alike. Furthermore, Hobbes in effect denies that there is "any such thing as natural justice" and that there is in reality any such thing as virtue. To Shaftesbury, who called himself a "realist in morality," such conclusions constituted a "general scepticism" that was both misguided and genuinely dangerous.[19]

Locke, despite the fact that he had been Shaftesbury's tutor, comes in for even harsher criticism. What Hobbes began, Locke brought to fruition: "It was Mr. Locke that struck the home blow: for Mr. Hobbes's character and base slavish principles in government took off the poison of his philosophy. Twas Mr. Locke that struck at all fundamentals, threw all order and virtue out of the world. . . ." And again:

> Then comes the credulous Mr. Locke, with his Indian, barbarian stories of wild nations, that have no such idea (as travellers, learned authors! and men of truth! and great philosophers! have informed him), not considering that is but a negative upon a hearsay, and so circumstantiated that the faith of the Indian . . . may be as well questioned as the veracity or judgment of the relater; who [the travellers, and so forth] cannot be supposed to know sufficiently the mysteries and secrets of those barbarians: whose language they but imperfectly know; to whom we good Christians have by our little mercy given sufficient reason to conceal many secrets from us. . . .
>
> Thus virtue, according to Mr. Locke, has no other measure, law, or rule, than fashion and custom; morality, justice, equity, depend only on law and will. . . . And thus neither right nor wrong, virtue nor vice, are anything in themselves; nor is there any trace or idea of them naturally imprinted on human minds. Experience and our catechism teach us all! I suppose 'tis something of like kind which teaches birds their nests, and how to fly the minute they have full feathers.

[19] *Characteristics of Men, Manners, Opinions, Times*, ed. J. M. Robertson, Introduction by S. Grean, 2 vols. in one (New York: Bobbs-Merrill, 1964), 2: 203. This work was first published in 1711.

Your Theocles [of the *Moralists*], whom you commend so much, laughs at this, and, as modestly as he can, asks a *Lockist* whether the idea of *woman* (and what is sought after in woman) be not taught also by some catechism, and dictated to the man. Perhaps if we had no schools of Venus, nor such horrid lewd books, or lewd companions, we might have no understanding of this, till we were taught by our parents; and if the tradition should happen to be lost, the race of mankind might perish in a sober nation.—This is very poor philosophy.[20]

It is clear, then, that Shaftesbury looked upon the scepticism of Hobbes and Locke with more than mere distrust. He finds their views one-sided and ridiculous—they are absurd intellectual speculations—but he also finds them of great consequence. They are views that could easily have effects of the most disastrous sort. They are a threat to the whole fabric of morality; they threaten to undermine moral concern because they deny the objectivity of morals. For, says Shaftesbury, if virtue is not real, if there are not between acts objective moral differences, then no one need be concerned with the moral quality of his acts. In fact, to strive to act virtuously if virtue is mere appearance or fiction would be nothing more than play, and such behavior would more aptly be called absurd. To Shaftesbury, these are vicious principles which, if unanswered, threaten to corrupt mankind simply by being adopted and acted upon. Hence he undertook to refute them.

The most convincing refutation, Shaftesbury suggests, will not be merely to show that virtue is "really something in itself, and in the nature of things; not arbitrary . . . not . . . dependent on custom, fancy, or will," but first to discover what led Hobbes and Locke to such absurd and misleading conclusions. Then moral philosophy may be put on a reliable foundation that eliminates further absurdities of this sort.[21]

A key to this approach is Shaftesbury's conviction that the

[20] *Life and Letters*, pp. 403-405. Theocles is Shaftesbury's spokesman in the *Moralists*, a "philosophical rhapsody," which constitutes Treatise 5 of the *Characteristics*. (Unless indicated otherwise, all italics are in the text.)
[21] *Characteristics*, 2: 49-53; 285-287.

views of Hobbes and Locke are prima facie absurd and that they are unbelievable and contrary to common sense. Starting with this conviction, he sets out to discover what has led philosophers into these absurdities. Why, he asks, have philosophers repeatedly presented us with such "darker disquisitions and moonlight voyages"? Because, he says, they "renounce daylight and in a manner extinguish the bright visible outside world, by allowing us to know nothing beside what we can prove by strict and formal demonstration." Or, as he says elsewhere, philosophers have made their productions absurd and dangerous because they have been caught up by rational speculation and system-building.[22]

In contrast, Shaftesbury insists that philosophy must give up speculation in favor of observation; to counter the demonstrated but nonetheless absurd conclusions of the speculative moralists, we need only take notice of the way the world is. And if a philosopher seeks to understand what activates man (is it really only self-love?) he must begin by observing man's soul itself. He must learn to "proceed by the inward way," to "acquire a very peculiar and strong habit of turning [the] eye inwards in order to explore the interior regions and recesses of the mind. . . ." In fact, although Shaftesbury also relies upon observation of men's behavior, he seems to think that it is this introspective inquiry which is the more necessary and the more likely to be fruitful. In a passage reminiscent of Hume's call for an examination of human nature itself, we are told that, "How little regard soever may be shown to that moral speculation or inquiry which we call the study of ourselves, it must, in strictness, be yielded that all knowledge whatsoever depends upon this previous one, 'and that

---

[22] *Characteristics*, 2: 286-287. Shaftesbury also says: "The truth is, as notions stand now in the world with respect to morals, honesty is like to gain little by philosophy, or deep speculations of any kind," and, "The most ingenious way of becoming foolish is by a system." *Characteristics*, 1: 88, 189. His point is surely not unlike Butler's more elegant suggestion that the only way to comprehend what Hobbes has said about benevolence is to suppose that he "had a general hypothesis, to which the appearance of good-will could no otherwise be reconciled," or, in other words, that Hobbes put his hypothesis before the facts, and used it to interpret them. See sermon 1, *Fifteen Sermons*, first published in 1726, cited here from *British Moralists 1650-1800*, 1: 338. In the Preface to his *Sermons*, Butler reveals that he, too, thinks of Hobbes's moral views as "sceptical."

we in reality can be assured of nothing till we are first assured of what we are ourselves.' " Elsewhere, it is said, "A plain home-spun philosophy, of looking into ourselves, may do us wondrous service."[23]

So far as Shaftesbury is concerned, his own introspective observations did such a wondrous service: they provided proof that the moral sceptics were wrong. They did this by revealing that man does have a natural moral character and that his very nature leads him to recognize and react to moral distinctions. This in turn reveals that there are in fact real moral distinctions. The mistake of Locke, he says, was to make ideas of order and virtue

> *unnatural*, and without foundation in our minds. *Innate* is a word he poorly plays upon; the right word, though less used, is *connatural*. For what has birth or progress of the foetus out of the womb to do in this case? The question is not about the time the *ideas* entered, or the moment that one body came out of the other, but whether the constitution of man be such that, being adult and grown up, at such or such a time, sooner or later (no matter when), the idea and sense of order, administration, and a God, will not infallibly, inevitably, necessarily spring up in him.[24]

Shaftesbury counters the view that he ascribes to Locke by reminding his readers of the multitude of functions that animals, without example or instruction, are able to perform. Their females, for instance, even when carrying young for the first time "have a clear prospect or presentation of their state which is to follow." Consequently, they know what they must do for themselves and at what time to do it. Without the least experience, they know "the seasons of the year, the country, climate, place,

---

[23] *Characteristics*, 2: 286-287, 274-275; 1: 31. Hume's familiar remark, found in the Introduction to the *Treatise*, is that "the only expedient, from which we can hope for success in our philosophical researches [is] to leave the tedious lingring method, which we have hitherto followed, and instead of taking now and then a castle or village on the frontier, to march up directly to the capital or center of these sciences, to human nature itself; which being once masters of, we may every where else hope for an easy victory."

[24] *Life and Letters*, p. 403.

aspect, situation, the basis of their building, the materials, architecture; the diet and treatment of their offspring." Without the least need to reason, they understand "the whole economy of their nursery."[25] In addition, as those who are familiar with animals will testify, "To each species there belongs a several humour, temper, and turn of inward disposition, as real and peculiar as the figure and outward shape. . . ." But if the "natural habits and affections" of the inferior animals are known and admitted, why should one balk at admitting that man also has a natural disposition or nature? Thus, it is argued, man's weakness itself, his long and helpless infancy (which requires the close cooperation of parents if it is to be survived), his weak and defenseless form, his pressing need for choice provisions and shelter—all these things, being proper and natural to man, lead naturally to society. "In short," he says, "if generation be natural, if natural affection and the care and nurture of the offspring be natural, things standing as they do with man, and the creature being of that form and constitution he now is, 'it follows that society must also be natural to him.' "[26]

Furthermore, if society is natural to man, so must be those moral concerns which are necessary for the maintenance of society. Man is not only disposed by his nature to live in society, but he also has the "notions and principles of fair, just and honest" which make this possible. Whether or not we shall want to call them innate, these notions and principles are every bit as natural as the disposition they support. Anatomists tell us, says Shaftesbury, that certain principles of body are formed in the foetus before birth, and hence they call them innate. But so far as these moral principles are concerned, the time of their formation is only a curious speculation. The real question is whether these

[25] *Characteristics*, 2: 76-77. According to Shaftesbury, we have also a *natural* idea of what is *natural* or undeformed. "What [is] more certain than that the poorest ignoramus of our species, being kept from seeing anything but old males, and clothed bodies (as in a monkish cloister, or barbarous hermitage) would in a clear light when brought to see nudities, distinguish between the true and the natural, and the unnatural deformed kind." *Second Characters, or the Language of Forms*, ed. B. Rand (Cambridge: At the University Press, 1914), pp. 107-108.
[26] *Characteristics*, 2: 290, 83.

principles are merely learned or natural. The regularity and universality with which they accompany life indicate that they are from nature and nothing else, that they are instinctive moral principles which are a part of man's "natural moral sense" or natural "sense of right and wrong." They are a part of "our constitution and make," as "natural to us as natural affection itself."[27]

This discovery of natural principles essential to the well-being of the individuals who possess them is all that is necessary to show that Locke was mistaken. He had denied the existence of such affections; Shaftesbury shows that they do indeed exist; therefore, Locke was wrong. But in order to refute the even more vicious scepticism of Hobbes, it must not only be shown that there are natural affections, but that some of these are benevolent. Here Shaftesbury draws upon the implications of what he has already observed, namely, that society is natural to man. If this is the case, then whatever is necessary for the continuance and well-being of society must also be natural to man. And what could be more important, more necessary for the well-being of society, than benevolent dispositions among those who make it up? It is clear, then, that Hobbes's description of man and his motivations is erroneous. Indeed, far from being the naturally selfish egoist which Hobbes claimed, man is best described when he is made to appear most unselfish: The "most truly natural" of man's principles are those "which tend toward public service and the interest of society at large."[28] The essential positive aspect of Shaftesbury's moral sense philosophy is, then, just the combination of his refutations of Locke and Hobbes: just as there are animal natures, so is there a human nature, and just as animal behavior reveals specific instincts, so does human behavior reveal specific dispositions, including, most significantly, a disposition to act benevolently.

However, there is another significant feature of Shaftesbury's positive theory. If we say that, against Locke, Shaftesbury argues that we have a natural sensitivity to moral differences, and that,

[27] *Characteristics*, 2: 135; 1: 260-262.
[28] *Characteristics*, 2: 293-294.

against Hobbes, he argues that we have a natural inclination to behave morally by doing what is morally advantageous or benevolent, we can also say that he counters both philosophers by maintaining that we have a natural faculty by which we discover or apprehend right or wrong behavior.[29] Shaftesbury's investigations convinced him that man is equipped to discover the "eternal measures and immutable independent nature or worth of virtue," and that the apprehension of these moral objects is in many ways analogous to our apprehension of physical objects. Although Shaftesbury does not make clear just how this moral perceiving takes place, he does insist on the analogy with ordinary perception: "The case," he says, "is the same in the mental or moral subjects as in the ordinary bodies or common subjects of sense." Actually, though, he is more helpful when he suggests that moral perception is analogous to the perception of physical beauty, for both of these activities seem to be dependent upon a prior perception of physical objects (including events and actions), which are then, so to speak, reperceived by the moral sense or sense of beauty. When the shapes, motions, and colors of physical objects are perceived by the eye, the beauty of these is seen "according to the different measure, arrangement, and disposition of their several parts." When behavior and action are perceived, the moral worth of these is seen by the moral sense "according to the regularity or irregularity of the subjects." In short, the mind, too, has its senses, and is not without "eye and ear, so as to discern proportion, distinguish sound, and scan each sentiment or thought which comes before it. It can let nothing escape its censure. It feels the soft and harsh, the agreeable and disagreeable in the affections; and finds a foul and fair, a harmonious and a dissonant, as really and truly here as in any musical

[29] It is this second disposition, which has been described as "a kind of intellectual instinct" or an "intuitive faculty," that is most often identified as the moral sense. There is no need here to enter into debate on the appropriateness of these descriptions, or the tendency to suppose that "moral sense," as applied to Shaftesbury's views, refers only to a cognitive faculty. However, these issues are usefully discussed in D. D. Raphael, *The Moral Sense* (London: Oxford University Press, 1947), and in Grean's Introduction to the *Characteristics*.

numbers or in the outward forms or representations of sensible things."[30]

Shaftesbury also claims that this cognitive moral sense has a critical and reflective aspect, the conscience, by which we apprehend the evil of our own acts. Every rational creature, he says, is by his nature forced "to have representations of himself and his inward affairs constantly passing before him." Some of these reflections, those of "unjust action or behavior," are found by such a creature to be "horridly offensive and grievous," for the conscience enables this rational creature to sense the moral "deformity" of ill-deserving or unnatural acts as well as to know that punishment is due whenever such acts have been committed.[31]

To summarize, Shaftesbury's discovery, as he thought, of a cognitive moral sense seemed to him to remove all doubts about the refutation of moral scepticism. We have been found to have a faculty or sense by which real moral differences can be known, and each of us can easily confirm this discovery and witness the operation of this moral faculty. If questions are raised regarding the reliability of the moral sense, these can be eliminated by appeal to the source of this and other natural faculties. Each of these faculties comes, obviously, from nature, and it is both clear and well known that nature has provided for the welfare of man, has provided whatever is needed for us to become well adapted, successful parts of nature, and has equipped man for the pursuit of his own "natural and proper good."[32] We observe that we have a cognitive moral sense; we know it to operate and distinguish right from wrong; we know this sense to be reliable. Therefore, moral scepticism is unfounded, Hobbes and Locke are wrong, and the reality of virtue is proven beyond all doubt. Let us, he says,

---

[30] *Characteristics*, 1: 251-255. Although Shaftesbury is clearly representative of the moral sense school insofar as he attributes to feelings or affections of the mind a central role in the differentiation of objective right and wrong, virtue and vice, he was by no means the first British moralist to suppose our feelings fulfilled such a role. For a brief but enlightening account of his predecessors in this regard, see R. S. Crane, Review of William E. Alderman's "Shaftesbury and the Doctrine of Moral Sense in the Eighteenth Century," *Philological Quarterly* 11 (1932): 205-206.

[31] *Characteristics*, 1: 305-306.

[32] *Characteristics*, 1: 293-294.

carry scepticism ever so far, let us doubt, if we can, of everything about us, we cannot doubt of what passes within ourselves. Our passions and affections are known to us. They
are certain, whatever the objects may be on which they are
employed. Nor is it of any concern to our argument how
these exterior objects stand: whether they be realities or mere
illusions; whether we wake or dream. . . . In this dream of
life . . . our demonstrations have the same force; our balance
and economy hold good, and our obligation to virtue is in
every respect the same.[33]

V. Hume's moral theory, I submit, must be seen as a part of
this antisceptical moral tradition. For, although I shall be the
first to say that other aspects of his work must be seen as part of
another speculative tradition, and that his allegiance to the moral
sense school is far from total and had a far less comprehensive
effect on his philosophy than has been alleged by Kemp Smith,
Hume does undertake the joint tasks of refuting moral scepticism
and putting morals on a solid, objective foundation. Much as had
Shaftesbury (and later Hutcheson), Hume thought that there
were moral philosophers who accepted neither the reality of moral
distinctions nor the procedures proper to morality. These philosophers (Hobbes and Mandeville, primarily) he explicitly regards as moral sceptics; his rebuttal of them is nothing less than
an attempt, characteristically moderate, to refute moral scepticism.

One can easily understand that Hume's refutation of moral
scepticism, as it is presented in the *Treatise* alone, might be
overlooked. Not only does he, in one often quoted passage, appear
to champion a form of subjectivism in morals that would leave
him more akin to Hobbes than to Shaftesbury, but he himself
saw that he had not in that work shown much "Warmth in the
Cause of Virtue." But his explanation of this second fact reveals
that this deficiency was the result of his decision to proceed in
the *Treatise* as an anatomist rather than as a painter, to reveal

[33] *Characteristics*, 1: 336-337.

the underlying structure of morality, not portray its vivid surface, and not the result of any sceptical intentions. "I am much more ambitious," he wrote, "of being esteemed a Friend of Virtue," and then went on to announce his intention "to make a new Tryal, if it be possible to make the Moralist & Metaphysician agree a little better."[34]

This "new Tryal" was apparently attempted too late to make a concern with moral scepticism an obvious part of the *Treatise*. In fact, so far as I can determine, neither *sceptic* nor *scepticism*

---

[34] Hume to Hutcheson, 17 September 1739, in *The Letters of David Hume*, ed. J.Y.T. Greig (Oxford: Clarendon Press, 1932), 1: 32-33. Hume also suggests in this letter that one may consider virtue "either as an Anatomist or as a Painter; either to discover its most secret Springs & Principles or to describe the Grace & Beauty of its Actions. I imagine it impossible to conjoin these two Views. Where you pull off the Skin, & display all the minute Parts, there appears something trivial, even in the noblest Attitudes & most vigorous Actions. . . . An Anatomist, however, can give a very good Advice to a Painter or Statuary: and in like manner, I am perswaded, that a Metaphysician may be very helpful to a Moralist: tho' I cannot easily conceive these two Characters united in the same Work. Any warm Sentiment of Morals, I am afraid, wou'd have the Air of Declamation amidst abstract Reasonings, & wou'd be esteemed contrary to good Taste."

When William Wishart attacked the *Treatise* he charged that it sapped the "Foundations of Morality by denying the natural and essential Difference betwixt Right and Wrong, Good and Evil, Justice and Injustice; making the Difference only artificial, and to arise from Human Conventions and Compacts." Hume appears to have regarded this as the most severe of the six charges brought against his work, and was quick to ally himself with Hutcheson and to insist that he had made due allowance for the difference between virtue and vice, but had chosen to base that difference on instinct and feeling, rather than reason, although this principle, too, he granted, has a considerable role to play in morals. See *A Letter from a Gentleman*, pp. 18, 30-31. I suggest, however, that this particular piece in the Humean corpus must be used with some caution. In the first place, Hume claims that he did not write it for publication. "I am sorry," he wrote to Kames, "you shou'd have found yourself oblig'd to print the Letter I wrote to Mr Couts, it being so hastily compos'd that I scarce had time to revise it" (*New Letters of David Hume*, ed. Ernest C. Mossner and Raymond Klibansky [London: Clarendon Press, 1954], Letter of 13-15 June 1745, p. 15). The tenor of Hume's remarks also indicates that he did not see the *Letter* through the press, as would have been difficult for he was living near St. Albans at the time, while the *Letter* was published in Edinburgh. We cannot be certain, then, that Kames and some other of Hume's friends did not alter the text slightly or even significantly. Finally, leaving these problems aside, the text itself raises at least as many questions as it answers. See my "Hume's *A Letter from a Gentleman*: A Review Note," *Journal of the History of Philosophy* 6 (1968): 160-167.

appears in books II and III of that work; Hobbes, the premier
egoist and moral sceptic, is mentioned only in book I, in connection with his views on causality; and Mandeville is mentioned
only to be praised along with Locke, Shaftesbury, Hutcheson,
and Butler, as one of those late philosophers who have put their
subject on a sound observational footing.[35] To this, one should
add that it is only in the "Conclusion" of book III that Hume
reveals that he is defending the cause of virtue, and even then
his disclosure is put indirectly. Those who have resolved our
"sense of morals into original instincts of the human mind, may,"
he says, "defend the cause of virtue with sufficient authority; but
[they] want the advantage, which those possess, who account for
that sense by an extensive sympathy with mankind." It is, then,
only because we know that Hume accounted for our sense of
morals by means of an "extensive sympathy," as well as by reference to "original instincts of the mind," that we can see that
he did think of himself as defending the cause of virtue in the
Treatise.[36] But we can also see against whom he was defending
that cause, and that at least as early as 1738-1739 he was beginning to identify their views as sceptical. Thus in book III we find
that he has on several occasions challenged the views of those
philosophers who have alleged that all moral distinctions are the
result of "artifice and education" skillfully utilized by politicians
seeking to control the populace. He also challenges those who
in treating of the selfish aspect of man have exaggerated the facts
beyond recognition, supposing that we are quite incapable of
society or of any social behavior unless there is a government to
rule and control us, and whose descriptions of mankind "are as
wide of nature as any accounts of monsters, which we meet with
in fables and romances." These absurd conclusions can be attributed, Hume suggests, to an overzealous adherence to some
system—a central characteristic of moral scepticism as described

[35] *Treatise*, pp. 80, xxi. Mandeville became the third in the triumvirate of
British moral sceptics with the publication of the *Fable of the Bees* (1714).
[36] *Treatise*, p. 619. It is important to note that the title page of book 3 of the
Treatise bears the motto, from Lucan's *De bello civili:—Durae semper virtutis amator,
Quaere quid est virtus, et posce exemplar honesti.* [Lover always of hardy virtue, Ask
what virtue is and demand a model of goodness. (Trans. Gerald A. Press).]

by earlier moral sense philosophers—which results in the perversion of the judgment or good sense of the philosophers who construct the systems. As a result, these "moral sceptics," as Hume all but calls them, "scruple" over obvious moral distinctions or make the "utmost efforts to extirpate all sense of virtue from among mankind."[37]

Any doubts about Hume's concern with moral scepticism and the centrality of his opposition to it are surely removed when one turns to the *Enquiry concerning the Principles of Morals*. Hume begins that work by noting how irksome it is to dispute with disingenuous persons who do not really believe the opinions they defend, and who engage in controversy only in a spirit of opposition or through the desire to display their wit and ingenuity. Those philosophers who have denied the reality of moral distinctions must be considered such disingenuous controversialists, for it is simply not conceivable that any person could ever seriously maintain that all acts and persons are morally equivalent. The differences between men which nature has brought about, and the additional differences which are brought about by education and custom, are so great that "there is no scepticism so scrupulous" as to claim sincerely and absolutely that there are no moral distinctions. One can scarcely imagine a man so insensible and so prejudiced that he is never touched with the ideas of right and wrong, or never forced to admit that others are similarly affected. Thus it may be that the best manner of winning over such an extreme sceptic is to take no notice of him. Here the response to moral scepticism is similar to the advice given to the famous shepherdess who had lost not her morals but her sheep. Leave this sceptic alone, Hume says, and it is very probable that he will, in the end, "come over to the side of common sense and reason" of his own accord.[38]

However, Hume was unable to follow his own advice about such sceptics, for he goes on to point out that there is a hypothesis which is widely held and of the greatest consequence because it

[37] *Treatise*, pp. 500, 521; 579; 486, 547, 609; 500.
[38] *Second Enquiry*, pp. 169-170.

is "utterly incompatible with all virtue or moral sentiment," and can only have the effect of encouraging depravity. This is the theory that all "virtue" is only apparent virtue, that it is in fact only hypocrisy, cheat, fraud, or self-interested machination. Another variation on the hypothesis, one frequently maintained by philosophers and, consequently, the "foundation of many a system," is the theory that "whatever affection one may feel, or imagine he feels for others, no passion is, or can be disinterested." What appears to be generous friendship, it is said, is really self-love; however much we may be convinced that we have an unselfish interest in others, that interest is, "at bottom," indistinguishable from the most craven selfishness.[39]

That Hume thought each of these views sceptical is made clear in later sections of the *Enquiry*. In section 5 we are told that, because of the obvious "usefulness of the social virtues, it has been readily inferred by sceptics, both ancient and modern, that all moral distinctions arise from education, and were, at first, invented, and afterwards encouraged, by the art of politicians, in order to render men tractable, and subdue their natural ferocity and selfishness, which incapacitated them for society." Hume grants that education may have a great influence on our sentiments of approbation, even to the extent of creating new sentiments of this sort, as happens in the case of the superstitious notions we are taught. But, he continues,

> that *all* moral affection or dislike arises from this origin, will never surely be allowed by any judicious enquirer. Had nature made no such distinction, founded on the original constitution of the mind, the words *honourable* and *shameful*, *lovely* and *odious*, *noble* and *despicable*, had never place, in any language; nor could politicians, had they invented these terms, ever have been able to render them intelligible, or make them convey any idea to the audience. So that nothing can be more superficial than this paradox of the sceptics; and it were well, if, in the abstruser studies of logic and metaphysics, we could as easily obviate the cavils of that

[39] *Second Enquiry*, pp. 295-296.

sect, as in the more practical and more intelligible sciences of politics and morals.[40]

In section 6 Hume again discusses the moral sceptics, this time challenging the "sullen incredulity" of those who claim that the esteem or value we ascribe to others is entirely accounted for by the operation of our love for ourselves, an incredulity sometimes carried so far by these philosophers that they are led "absolutely to deny [the] existence and reality" of all "moral endowments." But there are, Hume counters, qualities which we praise in others—temperance, patience, constancy, and hundreds more—and which are never thought to be of use to anyone but the person possessing them. There are qualities, useful only to the possessor, which are praised by others. Let those, he says, who resolve morality into self-love manifest the most "peevish delicacy" or the "most de-termined scepticism." They will yet find that they "cannot for a moment refuse the tribute of praise and approbation" that goes to a man possessed of these qualities. The happiness and misery of others, it will be found, are not indifferent to us. Neither are the qualities which tend only to the advantage of their possessors. Once this has been conceded we can see that there is no foun-dation for such sceptical incredulity; consequently, we can hope that "a natural unforced interpretation of the phenomena of hu-man life will afterwards . . . prevail among all speculative en-quirers."[41]

VI. Perhaps it will be objected that much of this has already been said and that it is now almost commonplace. Even the Introduction to this work reveals that it has been four decades since Kemp Smith argued that the Reid-Beattie interpretation of Hume—that interpretation which sees him as the sceptical cul-mination of empiricist principles—is mistaken, that this inter-pretation constitutes a serious distortion of Hume's intentions and achievements. It may be that Kemp Smith does not suggest

[40] *Second Enquiry*, pp. 214.
[41] *Second Enquiry*, pp. 242-244. On p. 236 Hume announces his intention to "mention a few instances, in order to remove, if possible, all doubt and hesita-tion."

that one of Hume's central concerns was the refutation of moral scepticism, but this particular claim could be supposed implicit in his naturalistic interpretation of Hume. That is, Kemp Smith argued that Hume was not a sceptic, and not in basic disagreement with Hutcheson or Thomas Reid, two philosophers known for their opposition to, respectively, moral and speculative scepticism. It follows, then, that there is nothing essentially new in the suggestions that have just been made.

This objection fails. For all the debt which every careful reader of Hume owes to Kemp Smith (he more than anyone has caused us to look more closely at what Hume says), it must be said that the account of Hume which he gives suffers from two serious flaws. In the first place, Kemp Smith quite mistakenly supposes that Hutcheson's sentimentalist moral theory is noncognitivist and subjectivistic. Consequently, it cannot be correct to say that my account of Hume contra moral scepticism is implicit in his general interpretation, for moral subjectivism is one form of the moral scepticism that both Hutcheson and Hume attempt to refute. Secondly, Kemp Smith mistakenly supposes that Hume's theory of knowledge represents a wholesale extension of Hutcheson's moral theory into the speculative domain, and hence that Hume's moral and epistemological positions are entirely analogous, both essentially characterized by the thorough subordination of reason to sentiment or feeling. Or, in short, that Hume is a naturalist and not a sceptic. Both claims are wrong. Hutcheson is not a noncognitivist and subjectivist; Hume, while he opposes the moral sceptics, retains an epistemological scepticism.

Kemp Smith's other claims, that Hume is not a sceptic, and that his theory of knowledge is an adaptation of Hutcheson's subjectivist moral theory, are necessarily a central concern of this study. At the outset, I would like to suggest that they attribute to Hume what strikes me as intellectual behavior uncharacteristic of him, for if anything marks his thought as it has survived, it is his tendency to steer between philosophical extremes. Despite his claims regarding impressions and ideas in the opening sections of the *Treatise*, Hume does not adopt a radical empiricism. Nor does he succumb, despite an often iterated belief in propensities and tendencies of the mind, to the appeal of a full-fledged nativism. His moral philosophy, while critical of both the egoists and the rationalists, is nonetheless noticeably less optimistic than that of the sentimentalists who were such a significant influence on him.[42] He quite consciously intended his *History of England* and certain of his important political essays to be neither Whig nor Tory, but a nonpartisan analysis of the English constitution in its historical context, and he succeeded to the extent that he was able to criticize and agree with views of both parties, thus raising the ire of both. Even in religion his position, however difficult to ascertain in detail, is clearly neither of the two dogmatisms—theism and atheism—that were so readily available to a Scot of cosmopolitan experience. If these assessments of Hume's positions are correct, it would in fact have been uncharacteristic of him to adopt Hutcheson's moral epistemology in the wholesale, unmitigated fashion suggested by Kemp Smith.

However, my case does not rest on such *a priori* grounds. In a text just cited, for example, Hume suggests that one cannot deal with the speculative sceptic in the same manner as one deals with his moral counterpart: "It were well if, in the abstruser studies of logic and metaphysics," he says, "we could as easily obviate the cavils of that sect [the sceptics] as in the more practical and intelligible sciences of politics and morals." Or, to take a second example, there is Hume's important (although generally overlooked) reply to Gilbert Elliot's suggestion that man has the speculative equivalent of the moral sense. This exchange of letters was occasioned by the brief *Dialogue* included in the second *Enquiry*. Hume sent the manuscript of this work to Elliot during the second half of 1750, asking for comments and criticisms. Elliot replied in early 1751. He had read the piece carefully, he reports, and although always instructed by his friend's writings, he found this effort had given him a satisfaction even greater than usual. It first led him, he writes, into "the most disconsolate state of

---

[42] By *sentimentalist* I mean nothing pejorative, but only to characterize those ethical theories which claim that moral distinctions are founded in sentiments or feelings, in contrast to the *rationalists*, who claimed reason as the foundation of such distinctions.

doubt and uncertainty," but it did this only to reveal a clear path out of such doubt. "Why can't you always write in this manner?" Elliot asks. Set as many sceptical problems as you like, but show us that you have no less ability "to establish true principles, than subtlety to detect false ones." Then, only seeming to change the subject, Elliot admits to an "unphilosophical" or "lazy" disposition, and although he is willing to grant that "there is no writing or talking of any subject that is of importance enough to become the object of reasoning, without having recourse to some degree of subtlety or refinement," he suggests giving this unphilosophical disposition its head. Our reasoning ought and does have a stop: when or where it is stopped by nature, there we can, as philosophers and as ordinary men, rest:

> The only question is, where to stop,—how far we can go, and why no farther. To this question I should be extremely happy to receive a satisfactory answer. I can't tell if I shall rightly express what I have just now in my mind: but I often imagine to myself, that I perceive within me a certain instinctive feeling, which shoves away at once all subtle refinements, and tells me with authority, that these air-built notions are inconsistent with life and experience, and, by consequence cannot be true or solid. From this I am led to think, that the speculative principles of our nature ought to go hand in hand with the practical ones; and, for my own part, when the former are so far pushed, as to leave the latter quite out of sight, I am always apt to suspect that we have transgressed our limits. If it should be asked—how far will these practical principles go? I can only answer, that the former difficulty will recur, unless it be found that there is something in the intellectual part of our nature, resembling the moral sentiment in the moral part of our nature, which determines this, as it were, instinctively. Very possibly I have wrote nonsense. However, this notion first occurred to me at London, in conversation with a man of some depth of thinking; and talking of it since to your friend H. Home

[Lord Kames], he seems to entertain some notions nearly of the same kind, and to have pushed them much farther.[43]

Hume's reply was written from Ninewells in February 1751; in it he articulates clearly the distinction between *morals* and *metaphysics*, and he equally clearly suggests that these represent different domains with quite distinct standards of truth:

Dear Sir,

Your Notion of [the] correcting Subtility of Sentiment is certainly very just with regard to Morals, which depend upon Sentiment; & in Politics & natural Philosophy, whatever Conclusion is contrary to certain Matter of Fact must certainly be wrong, and there must some Error lie somewhere in the Argument, whether we be able to show it or not. But in Metaphysics or Theology, I cannot see how either of these plain & obvious Standards of Truth can have place. Nothing there can correct bad Reasoning but good Reasoning: and Sophistry must be oppos'd by Syllogism.[44]

---

[43] Elliot's letter is printed in J. H. Burton, *Life and Correspondence of David Hume*, 2 vols. (Edinburgh: William Tait, 1856), 1: 323-324.

[44] *Letters*, 1: 150-151. The balance of Hume's discussion is also noteworthy: "About seventy or eighty Years ago, I observe, a Principle like that which you advance prevail'd very much in France amongst some Philosophers & *beaux Esprits*. The Occasion of it was this. The famous Mons. Nicole of the Port Royal, in his *Perpetuité de la Foi*, push'd the Protestants very hard upon the Impossibility of the People's reaching a Conviction of their Religion by the way of private Judgement; which requir'd so many Disquisitions, Reasonings, Researches, Erudition, Impartiality, & Penetration, as not one of a hundred, even amongst Men of Education, is capable of. Monsr Claude & the Protestants answer'd him, not by solving his Difficulties (which seems impossible) but by retorting them (which is very easy). They show'd that to reach the Way of Authority, which the Catholics insist on, as long a Train of acute Reasoning & as great Erudition was requisite as woud be sufficient for a Protestant. We must first prove all the Truths of natural Religion, the Foundation of Morals, the divine Authority of the Scripture, the Deference which it commands to the Church, the Tradition of the Church &c. The Comparison of these controversial Writings begot an Idea in some, that it was neither by Reasoning nor Authority we learn our Religion, but by Sentiment. And certainly this were a very convenient Way, and what a Philosopher wou'd be very well pleas'd to comply with, if he coud distinguish Sentiment from Education. But to all Appearance the Sentiment of Stockholm, Geneva, Rome antient & modern, Athens, & Memphis, have [not] the same Characters. And no thinking man can implicitly assent to any of them; but from the general

I grant that it has now become fashionable to suppose that Hume follows Hutcheson, who was an avowed follower of Shaftesbury. It has also become fashionable to suppose that Hume's philosophy represents the extension of Hutcheson's sentimentalist views into the domain of epistemology and metaphysics. The first of these fashions is a well-founded anticipation of one aspect of the account I am offering. However, Hume did not effect the wholesale extension of Hutcheson's moral sense into the speculative domain. To his credit, and to the confusion of many of his readers, Hume responded to two sets of philosophical concerns, speculative and practical, metaphysical-epistemological and moral. And, as the letter to Elliot indicates (and I shall subsequently show in detail), Hume responded to these two sets of concerns in significantly different ways. Despite his clear and acknowledged debt to the older philosopher, Hume does not extend Hutcheson's moral epistemology into the domain of metaphysics, or become a naturalist in Kemp Smith's sense. On the contrary, Hume regularly, systematically, and consciously maintains the distinction between morals, which depends on feelings or sentiments, and a useful, valid metaphysics, which is dependent on, answerable to, reason or the understanding, the sometimes overwhelming strength of the sentiments notwithstanding. Furthermore, he maintains this distinction despite the fact that he does believe that sentiment, common sentiment, is the standard by which moral theories are to be judged.

In the simplest terms, my central thesis is that Hume maintains a common-sense morals, but at the same time he outlines and supports a sceptical metaphysics. This thesis is not, however, a simple one, and hence before it can be established it is necessary to give it a precise and detailed content. To this end one must examine carefully Hume's characterization of these two domains—morals and metaphysics—and his view of the relation-

Principle, that as the Truth in these Subjects is beyond human Capacity, & that as for one's own Ease he must adopt some Tenets, there is more Satisfaction & Convenience in holding to the Catechism we have been first taught. Now this I have nothing to say against. I woud only observe, that such a Conduct is founded on the most universal & determin'd Scepticism, join'd to a little Indolence. For more Curiosity & Research gives a direct opposite Turn from the same Principles."

ships holding between sentiment and reason in each. And even this task seems to be best approached obliquely, through a reexamination of the work of Francis Hutcheson, for this work has been said to hold the key to all of Hume's philosophy. As I have indicated, I do not accept this latter claim in the sense that it was made by Kemp Smith, but I do believe that a satisfactory understanding of Hume's philosophy depends in part upon an accurate reading of Hutcheson. Hence the following chapter includes a relatively detailed exposition of Hutcheson's moral sense theory. This exposition reveals that Hutcheson, far from being a subjectivist (as Kemp Smith claims) or an emotivist (as William Frankena claims), holds a version of moral realism in which affective states or sentiments function as cognitive elements in a system that is designed to refute the moral scepticism of Hobbes and Mandeville. Our moral sentiments, according to Hutcheson, inform us of real and objective moral characteristics, just as other affective states inform us of real and objective physical characteristics. On his view we have, thanks to the design of the Creator, natural faculties that give rise to certain sentiments, and these sentiments, when their ultimate source is taken into account, can be seen to be reliable guides to reality. By no stretch of the imagination can Hume be supposed to have borrowed this providential aspect of Hutcheson's thought, not even in morals. However, the discussion of this and other Humean modifications of Hutcheson's theory is taken up in the chapters that follow.

« 2 »

Hutcheson's Moral Realism

> The Quality approved by our moral Sense is conceived to
> reside in the Person approved, and to be a Perfection and
> Dignity in him. . . . The admired Quality is conceived as
> the Perfection of the Agent, and such a one as is distinct
> from the *Pleasure* either in the Agent or the Approver; tho'
> 'tis a sure Source of Pleasure to the Agent. The Perception
> of the Approver, tho' attended with Pleasure, plainly rep-
> resents something quite distinct from this Pleasure; even as
> the Perception of *external Forms* is attended with Pleasure,
> and yet represents something distinct from this Pleasure.
> This may prevent many Cavils upon this Subject.
>
> Francis Hutcheson
> *An Inquiry into the Original of*
> *our Ideas of Beauty and Virtue*

I.   By the middle of the eighteenth century, Scottish philosophers had attained a central, even dominant, importance in the
development of European philosophy. In the earlier decades of
the century, however, Scottish intellectuals looked beyond their
borders for philosophical enlightenment. If in these early days
their speculative concerns and fancies led them to Descartes or
Locke or Berkeley, their practical or moral interests did not. For
moral enlightenment they chose to attend to the nearly indige-
nous improvements and systematizations of Shaftesbury that Francis Hutcheson provided. Whether this choice of Hutcheson as
mentor in morals established or reflected a propensity of the
Scottish philosophical character (perhaps it did both), it was a
choice of considerable significance, given that in the Scottish
philosophy that developed in later decades, moral concerns far
outweighed speculative ones, as the work of Hume illustrates.[1]

---

[1] On the debt of Scottish philosophy to the Irish enlightenment provided by

55

That Hume's thought was profoundly shaped by his knowledge and appreciation of Hutcheson has been argued at some length by Norman Kemp Smith. It is a mistake, Kemp Smith argues, to interpret Hume as he is so often interpreted, that is, as providing merely a consistent and purely negative extension of the empirical principles of Locke and Berkeley. Rather, the famous analyses of causation, personal identity, and substance found in book I of the *Treatise* are best understood as the result of extending Hutcheson's moral philosophy, wherein reason is subjugated to feeling or sentiment, to the speculative domain. On this account, Hume did in fact recognize certain deficiencies in the theory of ideas propounded by Locke and Berkeley, but he did not choose to supplement that theory with either the Lockean doctrine of intuition or the Berkelean doctrine of notions. He chose instead to challenge the assumption "*that assurance ought always to rest on direct insight, or failing direct insight, on evidence,*" and he substituted a contrary view, namely, "the doctrine that the determining influence in human, as in other forms of animal life, is feeling, not reason or understanding, i.e. not evidence whether *a priori* or empirical. . . ." Belief, on Hume's theory, is one of the passions (his "general title for the instincts, propensities, feelings, emotions and sentiments, as well as for the passions ordinarily so called"); at the same time he is said to have resolutely reversed the roles previously assigned to reason and feeling, respectively, and to have modified his central ethical maxim, "Reason is and ought to be the slave of the passions," for use in his theory of knowledge. There the maxim becomes, "Reason is and ought to be subordinate to our natural beliefs."[2]

Kemp Smith had no difficulty gathering external evidence to make plausible the claim that Hume was influenced by Hutcheson. Then, to provide internal evidence he offers a brief account of key aspects of Hutcheson's moral theory, a theory he finds generally consonant with the relevant epistemological theory of the *Treatise*, thus making it plausible to say that Hume has put

Berkeley and Hutcheson, see George Davie, "Berkeley, Hume, and the Central Problem of Scottish Philosophy," *McGill Hume Studies*, pp. 43-62.

[2] Kemp Smith, pp. 10-11.

Hutcheson's doctrine of the moral sense to epistemological purposes.

Kemp Smith explicates Hutcheson's theory of the moral sense
by suggesting that it amounts to a modification of Locke's distinction between outer and inner senses. What Locke called "reflexion" Hutcheson sees as genuinely analogous to the outer senses;
hence he is said to maintain that there are "inner senses of a *non-
cognitive* character, namely, the aesthetic and moral senses." These
are distinguished from the outer senses by the fact that all of their
impressions are secondary impressions, or those that require "for
their occurrence the antecedent apprehension of impressions of
the outer senses." Otherwise, the inner senses (whose impressions
include the passions as well as aesthetic and moral sentiments)
function much like the outer senses. There is some mystery concerning both senses. We can no more give a rational account of
the connection between sugar and the sweetness we experience
than we can give a rational account of the connection between
an action, for example, and the secondary impression that results
from it. Here, too, says Kemp Smith, "the inner perceptions are
not linked to their antecedent conditions in any closer or more
rational manner. This, however, if true, carries far-reaching consequences in its train; and, as Hutcheson recognises, calls for
further argument."[3]

This argument, as Kemp Smith reconstructs it, begins by showing that the pleasures and pains consequent upon our experience
of natural, moral, or aesthetic objects are independent of our will.
Some things please us, some displease us, but the pleasure or
displeasure is immediate and involuntary. In this way, Hutcheson
is said to draw attention to the fact that all moral sentiments are
disinterested, for they are "determined for us by the very nature
of our human frame, and do not allow of being altered or modified
to suit what we may consider to be our selfish interests." Furthermore, if good or evil (that which is approved or disapproved)
is thus predetermined by our nature, it seems to follow that what
we consider useful is simply "a derivative type of the approved,"

[3] Kemp Smith, pp. 24-26.

or that which will serve as a means to a previously and naturally determined end, or good. Further, the only role available for calculation and reflection will be to determine what is useful, or the means to those ends that are set by human nature itself.[4]

These claims leave Hutcheson open to an objection based on the apparent variability of our moral sentiments: why, if these follow from human nature itself, do we find such variations in what is approved? Hutcheson in reply distinguishes the natural from the conventional, and he argues that while our sentiments could be modified by custom and education, these could never so much as affect us were we not provided with the sense which in the first place furnishes us with sentiments. He also points out that even the outer senses are subject to variations, and the mind to disorders. Yet no one doubts that these faculties are a part of our nature. Thus one can account for variations among moral impressions without giving up the claim that these impressions arise from our nature itself.

These considerations led Hutcheson, says Kemp Smith, to conclude that our sensory judgments are nonrational; that is, they are based exclusively on feeling. Such judgments as "This sugar is sweet," "This building is beautiful," and "This action is morally good" are alike in three fundamental respects: "first, they are *immediately* certain; secondly, they are *for us* necessary judgments; and thirdly, they are lacking in any kind of *rational* justification." When they are proclaimed, they reflect no more than sheer immediate experience, and further, they do not subsequently "turn out to have genuinely independent, objective, absolute grounds, of a kind discoverable by reason." There are in fact many theoretical, cognitive judgments that are grounded in reason, but they are of a different sort altogether. Further, when we proclaim something to be beautiful or morally good, we neither reflect on any related cognitive judgments before we make these proclamations, nor are we able later to derive with any certainty such cognitive judgments from our immediate, sensory judgments, for there is no necessary connection between things and the pleasure

[4] Kemp Smith, pp. 27-28.

58

they give us: "Possibly, the Deity could have form'd us so as to have receiv'd no Pleasure from such Objects, or connected Pleasure to those of a quite contrary Nature." At best, we have a presumption, based on the view that the Deity is benevolent, that the world is ordered in a rational way, and that things that are sweet taste sweet and that things approved (called "good") are good.[5]

Kemp Smith concludes his brief account by suggesting that Hutcheson's moral teaching rests on a twofold foundation: first, on the view that all exciting "reasons" (motives to action) "presuppose instincts and affections. . . . there is no exciting 'reason' previous to affection . . . [so that] Reason is in this relation the servant of the passions, occupying itself solely with the means to their fulfillment." The second part of the foundation is the doctrine of justifying "reasons." These presuppose a moral sense, Kemp Smith says, meaning that it is the moral sense, not reason, which determines "our *approbation* of this and that action, in ourselves and others. . . . It is this second doctrine which chiefly concerns us. The view which Hutcheson sets himself to refute is the view that moral judgments are rational judgments, and are approved in view of, and by reference to, their conformity to reason. All such alleged reasons, he proceeds to show, presuppose an end not thus justified."[6]

II. With Kemp Smith's most general claims (that Hume was profoundly influenced by Hutcheson, and that it is a mistake to see Hume as providing merely a sceptical extension of empiricism), I am in complete agreement. However, when he begins to explain how it was that Hutcheson influenced Hume, Kemp Smith goes badly astray for the very simple reason that he has misread Hutcheson, and hence missed much of the point of Hutcheson's moral philosophy. If we look at this philosophy with more care and in more detail, I believe we shall find it to be of genuine use in our efforts to understand important aspects of Hume's moral theory.

[5] Kemp Smith, pp. 28-33.
[6] Kemp Smith, pp. 37-38.

As a matter of fact, Hutcheson set himself to refute two views: those of the rationalists, to be sure, but also those of the morally sceptical egoists, Hobbes and Mandeville. Furthermore, Kemp Smith's noncognitivist interpretation notwithstanding, it can be shown that this opposition to the sceptical moralists led Hutcheson to adopt, perhaps necessarily, a cognitivist account of the moral sense.[7]

Hutcheson's concern over the views of the egoists is revealed in his earliest publication, a letter which previewed the first edition of his *Inquiry into the Original of our Ideas of Beauty and Virtue*.[8] In this letter he argues that the moral philosophy of his day, whether represented by Hobbes or by Pufendorf and other Christian moralists, represents man as moved to virtuous behavior largely, even exclusively, by considerations of private interest. Hutcheson finds this view misguided and dangerous. Soon thereafter he published, in addition to some letters directed against the rationalist Gilbert Burnet,[9] a series of critical observations on Mandeville's *Fable of the Bees*,[10] a refutation of Hobbes's ex-

---

[7] Others offering *noncognitivist* interpretations of the Hutchesonian moral sense include D. D. Raphael, *The Moral Sense* (London: Oxford University Press, 1947), pp. 6-19; William Frankena, "Hutcheson's Moral Sense Theory," *Journal of the History of Ideas*, 16 (1955): 356-375; Bernard Peach, "Editor's Introduction," *Illustrations on the Moral Sense* (Cambridge, Mass.: Harvard University Press, 1971); and Henning Jensen, *Motivation and the Moral Sense in Francis Hutcheson's Moral Theory* (The Hague: Martinus Nijhoff, 1972). I have discussed the shortcomings of Frankena's emotivist interpretation of the moral sense in "Hutcheson's Moral Sense Theory Reconsidered," *Dialogue*, 13 (1974): 3-23.

[8] Published in *London Journal*, no. 277 (November 14, 1724), pp. 1-2, and no. 278 (November 21, 1724), pp. 1-2. The letter is discussed by A. O. Aldridge, "A Preview of Hutcheson's Ethics," *Modern Language Notes* 61 (1946): 153-161. The *Inquiry* itself was published, according to William R. Scott, in January or February 1725; *Francis Hutcheson. His Life, Teaching and Position in the History of Philosophy* (Cambridge: At the University Press, 1900), p. 31.

[9] See *London Journal*, June 12 and 19, October 9, 1725. Burnet initiated the exchange; his letters appear in the same periodical on April 10, July 31, August 7, November 27, and December 25, 1725. The repeated misdating of these letters (to 1728) has been corrected by Bernard Peach, "The Correspondence between Francis Hutcheson and Gilbert Burnet: The Problem of the Date," *Journal of the History of Philosophy* 8 (1970): 87-91.

[10] "Observations on the Fable of the Bees," *Dublin Journal*, February 4, 12, and 19, 1726.

planation of laughter according to the principle of self-interest,[11] and the first edition of the *Inquiry*. The full, original title of this first major work alone establishes Hutcheson's antiegoistical stance: *An Inquiry into the Original of our Ideas of Beauty and Virtue; in two treatises, in which the Principles of the late Earl of Shaftesbury are explained and defended, against the Author of the Fable of the Bees; and the Ideas of Moral Good and Evil are established, according to the Sentiments of the Ancient Moralists with an Attempt to introduce a Mathematical Calculation in subjects of Morality.*[12]

Already, we can begin to see how unlikely are the various noncognitivist interpretations of Hutcheson. He attacked Hobbes and sought to defend Shaftesbury's principles against Mandeville, the newest moral sceptic. But on any reasonable account, Shaftesbury's principles included opposition to the dangerous and insidious moral scepticism of Hobbes and Locke (whom he thought were moral sceptics because they dogmatically denied the reality of virtue); insistence upon the value of an empirical and introspective study of human nature; the conclusion that man has a particular constitution or nature, one which includes a moral faculty called the "moral sense"; and the belief that the operation of this faculty enables man to be a genuinely moral creature as well as revealing the real and objective nature of virtue. Clearly, it is difficult to see how Hutcheson could defend some of these views while he himself maintained a subjectivist theory of moral judgments. If our moral judgments are merely reports of subjective phenomena (affections, feelings), they would obviously not convey information about, or even make reference to, aspects of an outer, public reality. Yet Shaftesbury had tried to establish that our judgments about virtue and vice have just such an objective

[11] "Thoughts on Laughter," *Dublin Journal*, June 5, 12, and 19, 1725.

[12] (London: J. and J. Knapton, 1725). Whenever possible, I have cited from the *Inquiry* as (incompletely) reprinted in *British Moralists*, ed. L. A. Selby-Bigge, 2 vols. (Oxford: Clarendon Press, 1897; reprint ed., New York: Bobbs-Merrill, 1964). Otherwise, I have cited from the fourth edition, *An Inquiry into the Original of our Ideas of Beauty and Virtue; In Two Treatises. I. Concerning Beauty, Order, Harmony, Design. II. Concerning Moral Good and Evil* (London: D. Midwinter et al., 1738; reprint ed., Farnborough: Gregg International Publishers, 1969). Hereafter cited as *Inquiry*.

character, or that *virtue* and *vice* are terms that refer to irreducible features of reality.

But whatever we may believe about Hutcheson's intentions, it could yet be asked whether he in fact maintains that there is an objective moral reality. Surely he does. He begins his *Inquiry* with the claim that the most important and most rewarding subject of philosophical investigation is human nature itself: "There is no Part of *Philosophy* of more Importance, than a *just Knowledge* of *Human Nature*, and its various Powers and Dispositions." This subject, it is said, has not been properly pursued. There have been inquiries into the understanding and our means of obtaining truth, but little effort has been made to ascertain why it is that truth is sought, why it makes men happy. What is needed is a study of the ends for which truth itself is the means, or more particularly, a study which will result in "distinct Conceptions" of the happiness which is man's end, as well as the means by which it is to be obtained.[13]

This preamble Hutcheson translates into a work whose "principle Design" is to show that "*Human Nature* was not left quite indifferent in the Affair of *Virtue*," and "to prove what we call the *Reality of Virtue*." Noting that man is commonly said to be capable of both sensible and rational pleasures, he discards as trite and incomplete most modern discussions of these. One needs to begin, he insists, by discovering the pleasures which man is capable of receiving, and "what Senses or Powers of Perception" enable him to receive them. He notes that the pleasure or pain which we perceive by our external senses is not subject to our will. Some objects please us, others displease us, and we cannot change this fact. We cannot because "by the very *Frame* of our Nature" some things are made the occasion of pleasure, and others of pain. He then suggests that besides material objects there are other sources of pleasure and pain, and analogously, other senses that are capable of perceiving these sources. At this preliminary stage, two such senses are mentioned, those which are discussed

---

[13] *Inquiry*, pp. ix-x. Hume's remarks of September 17, 1739 (cited above, p. 3) may well be a response to this Preface, noticed by him again in the fourth edition of the *Inquiry* published the year before.

in the two treatises that make up the *Inquiry*: a "Sense of Beauty,"
or the "Power of perceiving the *Beauty* of *Regularity, Order, Harmony*" (discussed in part 1); and that "Determination" to be
pleased with, or approve of those "*Affections, Actions, or Characters* of *rational Agents*, which we call *virtuous*," and which he
calls the "Moral Sense."[14]

Hutcheson's interest in the sense of beauty is decidedly subsidiary, intended only, he says, to pave the way for the proof of
the moral sense which follows. Because he assumes that there is
general agreement among mankind with regard to what is considered beautiful, he believes he can show that there is a natural
sense of beauty more easily than he can show that there is a
natural moral sense. Once we are convinced of the natural sense
of beauty, "it will be no difficult matter to apprehend another
superior *Sense, natural* also to Men, determining them to be pleas'd
with *Actions, Characters, Affections*." What he calls the sense of
beauty is, he says, appropriately termed a sense because of the
close affinity which it bears to the external senses, including not
only the power to perceive beauty, but a disposition to know or
appreciate beauty which is exactly like the disposition to know
or appreciate color that is provided by the sense of sight. The
gratification of the sense of beauty is as natural, as real, and as
satisfying as that of any external sense. And, like the external
senses, it was provided for our advantage, convenience, and pleasure by a wise and benevolent Deity.[15]

In Treatise II Hutcheson reveals what was only hinted at in
his Preface. His primary purpose is not merely a compilation of
the faculties of the mind. Such a compilation may be necessary,
but his ultimate concern is proving that man is a genuinely moral
being who is sometimes motivated by something other than self-interest. Like Shaftesbury, Hutcheson finds the egoism of Hobbes
a real threat to the well-being of mankind. To say, as both thought
Hobbes had said, that every act is undertaken only for the gain
or advantage of the actor was to say that moral distinctions are
meaningless, for it implies that all acts have the same motivation.

[14] *Inquiry*, pp. xi-xv.
[15] *Inquiry*, pp. xvi-xvii.

Further, it was to begin an argument that ends with the claim that what we call "virtue and vice" is in one sense reducible to convention, and in another sense reducible to mere pleasure and pain. Hobbes had said, in effect, that there are no real qualitative differences among actions and characters, only apparent ones, and thus that virtue and vice are not objective and not natural.

In Hutcheson's eyes, as the Herculean first title of the *Inquiry* indicates, these vicious views of Hobbes had found a new spokesman in Bernard de Mandeville, whose *Fable of the Bees* maintained both the fact and the value of egoism. Man, Mandeville seemed to be saying, is motivated by selfish interests alone, and this fact stands as the foundation and blessing of society. Central to Mandeville's work is a verse allegory, "The Grumbling Hive or Knaves Turn'd Honest," which recounts the history of a hive of bees. Thriving and prosperous, but thoroughly dishonest at the outset, the hive came first to hard times, then to utter ruin, and all because Jove, tiring of constant complaints about the dishonesty of others, made everyone honest. With honesty and virtue came unemployment; there were no vices to cater to. With unemployment came disintegration of the "society"; many bees sought work elsewhere. The weakened hive was attacked once, then again; the few inhabitants remaining left. And to avoid all appearance of extravagance, they took residence in a hollow tree.

In subsequent editions Mandeville amplified his views, adding "An Enquiry into the Origin of Moral Virtue" and "A Search into the Nature of Society." In the former he insists that experience of the world shows that all "untaught Animals," including men, "are only solicitous of pleasing themselves, and naturally follow the bent of their own Inclinations, without considering the good or harm that from their being pleased will accrue to others." And those features which appear to be virtues in some men are only the effect of teaching, of the subtle propaganda of dishonest civic leaders. The closer we examine human nature, the more shall we be convinced, he says, that "moral virtues are the political offspring which flattery begot upon pride." In the second of these essays he addresses himself to Shaftesbury directly, noting that this noble philosopher believed that man is naturally good and that he naturally seeks the good of society. What a pity, it is said, that these optimistic and generous views are not true, but they are not. They are "inconsistent with our daily Experience," and they are based upon the illusion that virtue is real. Any successful society is and must be built upon vice. Furthermore, there is no *real* virtue anyway. Morality is no more certain than fashion, and the search for real virtue is a "Wild-Goose-Chace."[16]

Hutcheson, by his inquiry into human nature and moral good and evil, clearly intended to refute these pessimistic and cynical views. The method he chooses to follow is, first of all, observational, and then transcendental. Noting that his opponents had arrived at their dangerous conclusions by subtle reasoning, and that any philosophical endeavor which is not accompanied by a close study of human nature can "have scarce any other Tendency than to lead us into *speculative Knowledge* itself," he urges us to "quit the Disputes of the Learned" and observe man in his common settings.[17] Thus by a method that is both introspective and outward looking—and while urging his readers to turn their attention inward to their own minds and hearts, and to imagine how they might think or feel if they were simple men and not refined philosophers—he tries to establish some brute facts about our moral world and experience. In Treatise II, section 1 (entitled "Of the Moral Sense by which we perceive Virtue and Vice, and approve or disapprove them in others"), this observational approach prevails. That our perceptions of *natural* good, or advantageous objects, differ essentially from our perceptions of *moral* good, is something, he says, of which "every one must convince himself, by reflecting upon the different Manner in which he

[16] Bernard de Mandeville, *The Fable of the Bees: or, Private Vices, Publick Benefits*, ed. F. B. Kaye, 2 vols. (Oxford: Clarendon Press, 1957), 1: 41, 51, 323-331.

[17] *Inquiry*, pp. ix-x; *British Moralists*, 1: 100. In the *Essay* Hutcheson complains that recent philosophers have so "treated our *Desires* or *Affections*" that they have made it seem as though "the most generous, kind and disinterested of them . . . proceed from *Self-Love*, by some subtle Trains of Reasoning, to which honest Hearts are often wholly Strangers." *Essay on the Nature and Conduct of the Passions and Affections. With Illustrations on the Moral Sense*, 3d ed. (London: A. Ward et al., 1742; reprint ed., Gainesville: Scholars' Fascimiles and Reprints, 1969), p. [vi]. Hereafter cited as *Essay*. The first edition of this work appeared in 1728.

finds himself affected when these Objects occur to him." If we will so reflect, he insists, we will see that an inanimate object affects us differently than does a rational agent, or that a man serving us from constraint provokes a reaction that is different from one acting out of love. We may find a fruitful field to be to our advantage, and even beautiful; we may hold it in esteem. But everyone can see that this esteem is not the same sentiment that results from the observation of the generous action of a friend. This second sentiment is love. Two men may perform precisely the same action, resulting in precisely the same advantage to us. But if we see that one man acts from constraint or self-interest, and that the other acts from love toward us, we shall have very different reactions to them. Both examples show that our sentiments are not all based on opinions or feelings of self-interest, and that we are conscious of a difference between perceptions of "moral Excellence" and those of mere "natural Goodness" or advantage. It is also here that Hutcheson shows that the moral perceptions we have are independent of the will, for although we may easily enough bribe an enemy, and thus give him a reason to perform an act, which is to our advantage, we do not find this act virtuous, but traitorous and reprehensible—nor would a payment to us change our opinion. A bribe may be reason enough for an individual to do or say whatever one wishes, but it will not cause him to see evil as good any more than it would cause him to see black as white.[18] In similar fashion Hutcheson attempts to show that men do sometimes act altruistically, and that they do so naturally. Indeed, throughout his early works he can be found pointing to one fact after another, facts which are said to confound the subtle explanations of his opponents.[19]

[18] British Moralists, 1: 72-80.

[19] See, for example, British Moralists, 1: 86, 89-90, 94, 127-134. A similar approach may be found in the three articles on laughter in the Dublin Journal. The Essay Hutcheson considered to be, in effect, a continuation of the Inquiry, and thus little is there said to reinforce the "facts" already pointed out in the earlier work. As he says, "In this Essay on the Passions, the Proofs and Illustrations of this Point, that we have a moral Sense, and a Sense of Honour, by which we discern an immediate Good in Virtue and Honour, not referred to any further Enjoyment, are not much insisted on since they are already laid down in the Inquiry into Moral Good and Evil, in the first and fifth Sections" (Essay, p. ix).

III.   By this appeal to moral facts, then, Hutcheson attempts to establish that there are real and objective differences between various acts, or that some acts are such that they can be judged morally good, while others are morally evil, still others morally neutral. Once this evidence is adduced, he goes on to a transcendental argument, to asking, that is, what the fact of our moral perceptions and moral judgments presupposes.[20] For example, at the beginning of the *Illustrations on the Moral Sense*, Hutcheson notes that some actions are privately useful or hurtful, some publicly useful or hurtful, and others combine these characteristics. Such differences are described as "natural Tendencies" and "natural Differences." Two questions then arise:

"What *Quality* in any Action determines our *Election* of it rather than the contrary?"
"What *Quality* determines our *Approbation* of one Action, rather than of the contrary Action?"

To answer these questions, he says, let us consider what it is that moral good and evil are taken to be, and "what *Senses, Instincts*, or *Affections*, must be necessarily supposed to account for our *Approbation* or Election." The "Epicureans," who include Hobbes, maintain that "all the Desires of the *human Mind . . .* are reducible to *Self-Love*, or *Desire of private Happiness*," and the "*Christian Moralists*," although they introduce other kinds of happiness which may be desired, yet retain the "*Prospect of private*

[20] It may be said that Hutcheson's transcendental argument differs from more recent versions of this argument. Barry Stroud says that "transcendental arguments are supposed to demonstrate the impossibility or illegitimacy of [the] skeptical challenge by proving that certain concepts are necessary for thought or experience" and that "transcendental arguments are supposed to prove that certain particular concepts are necessary for experience or thought; they establish the necessity or indispensability of certain concepts." "Transcendental Arguments," *Journal of Philosophy* 65 (1968): 242, 243. Hutcheson's argument is not intended to meet the sceptical challenge by proving that certain concepts are necessary for thought or experience, but by showing that certain faculties are so necessary. In this, perhaps, Hutcheson resembles Plato more than Strawson, for Plato's argument for the transcendental Forms is not simply an argument to establish the necessity or indispensability of certain concepts; it also seeks to establish the existence of hitherto unnoticed aspects of reality. Hutcheson and Plato use their transcendental arguments for metaphysical as well as epistemological purposes.

Happiness" as the sole motive of election and approbation. But this private interest theory leaves unexplained the facts of our moral experience. It "can never account for the principal Actions of human Life." Friendship, generosity, public spirit, compassion, and so forth, are known to exist. They are facts of our moral life. Given the private interest theory, they could not be facts. Therefore, that theory must be mistaken. On the other hand, if we suppose the contrary opinion, that we are not motivated by self-interest alone, but also have a moral sense which approves and motivates us to useful and kindly actions, we can account for these facts. The two theories, he says, "seem both intelligible, each consistent with itself. The former seems not to represent human Nature as it is; the other seems to do it."[21]

Hutcheson did not, on the basis of this one argument alone, conclude that the moral sense view must be correct. The difficulty is, he continues, that there are a number of moral theories, and some of these seem different from the two discussed. Most especially there is the rationalist view, which, generally speaking, identifies virtue with conformity to reason. To examine this view, "to explain more fully how the *Moral Sense* alledged to be in Mankind, must be pre-supposed even in these [rationalist] Schemes," is the central aim of the *Illustrations*. Thus in the subsequent sections of this treatise we again find Hutcheson noting moral differences and moral facts, showing that the rationalists' theories are also inadequate to account for these facts, and concluding, again, that a moral sense must be posited. He argues that all "justifying Reasons" presuppose a moral sense; that although we correct our moral sense by reason, we cannot by reason obtain any "new Species of Ideas," but, as we do have new moral ideas, there must be a moral sense. He also argues that the view that fitness or unfitness of relations is the basis for morality so much presupposes a moral sense that the theory "is no otherwise

[21] *Essay*, pp. 207-213. Hutcheson also suggests, as had Shaftesbury, that the selfish theory leaves inexplicable the fact of our moral vocabulary, the fact, that is, that we are able to use this vocabulary as though the terms were meaningful. Hume, it may be recalled from chapter 1, also raises this objection to the theory. For Hutcheson's remarks, see *British Moralists*, 1: 159; for Hume's remarks, see pp. 47-48 above.

intelligible, but upon the Supposition of a *moral Sense*": the very notion of moral fitness, fitness to an end, is dependent for its meaning upon the perceptions of the moral sense. Moral fitness is either a simple idea, or it is dependent upon other simple ideas; a survey of the situation shows it to be dependent upon other simple ideas, or that its peculiar *moral* aspect can have been obtained only by a prior *moral* perception attained by a moral sense.[22]

It is clear, then, that Hutcheson found both the rationalist and egoist accounts of our moral experience inadequate, and it is certainly correct to say that he set himself to refute the rationalists. Nevertheless, his dispute with that group of philosophers was a dispute among friends—the friends of virtue—concerning the foundations of morality, with both these parties agreeing that virtue and vice are real and objective features of the world.[23] The enemies (for the rationalists as well) were Hobbes, Locke, Mandeville, and Pufendorf: egoists and conventionalists who were often lumped together as "selfish moralists" and anathematized for their moral scepticism. To suppose, as Kemp Smith does, that Hutcheson was a moral subjectivist is to include him among that group of moral sceptics that he sought to refute, and contravenes fundamental aspects of his work.

IV. Hutcheson's view of the moral sense is considerably more complex than is usually thought, a fact which may account for the noncognitivist interpretations of it. The moral sense as he describes it does have noncognitivist elements, a not entirely surprising fact, given that this faculty is defined, if not discovered, by a transcendental procedure. The moral sceptics had, in Hutcheson's opinion, denied the reality of virtue by maintaining: (1) that all human acts are motivated solely by self-interest or self-love; (2) that although we use the terms *virtue* and *vice* and

---

[22] *Essay*, pp. 214, 229, 240-241, 252-257.

[23] Selby-Bigge notes that the rationalists and sentimentalists were alike in thinking virtue real and natural. "The dispute between them," he adds, "is as to the most effective way of attaining this object. . . ." See *British Moralists*, 1: l-lii.

speak of moral *good* and *evil*, the fact is that such distinctions are morally meaningless, for they serve only to express individual pleasure and pain, or as conventional forms of expressing approbation and disapprobation, or as the arbitrary linguistic tools whereby a few men may control the behavior of others; and hence, (3) that when we say that a particular act is morally good, or that a given person is virtuous, we cannot in fact be making distinctively moral claims, for there are no irreducible moral particulars about which such claims could be made. In short, the moral sceptics seemed to be saying that we have neither the motivation nor the insight to be genuinely moral creatures. In response, Hutcheson seizes upon the notion, conveniently brought to the fore by Shaftesbury, that man has a moral sense. However, the sense he defends is not a simple, unifunctional faculty, but, rather, a faculty of some complexity, precisely the faculty that is needed to account for the apparent moral facts. Since the moral sense is given specific form by a transcendental procedure, and since the moral facts to be accounted for were found to be of different sorts, it is understandable that Hutcheson found the moral sense to be a disposition with both motivating and cognitive functions.

Showing that man has a distinctly moral disposition can be taken as Hutcheson's paramount interest from the very beginning of Treatise II of the *Inquiry*. Had we no moral sense, he says (sec. 1, art. 1) we could never distinguish between the pleasures arising from natural good, or advantage, and those arising from moral good. Without a moral sense, we could never be brought to admire virtue or virtuous qualities in others, where these were not to our advantage. Nor could we make any judgment about the actions that were of no consequence to us. At the close of the following article, this view is stated very elegantly:

> It is true indeed, that the Actions we approve in others, are generally imagin'd to tend to the natural Good of Mankind, or of some Parts of it. From whence this secret Chain between each Person and Mankind? How is my Interest connected with the most distant Parts of it? And yet I must

admire Actions which are beneficial to them, and love the Author [of these]. Whence this Love, Compassion, Indignation and Hatred toward even feign'd Characters, in the most distant Ages, and Nations, according as they appear Kind, Faithful, Compassionate, or of the opposite Dispositions, toward their imaginary Contemporaries? If there is no moral Sense, which makes rational Actions appear Beautiful, or Deform'd; if all Approbation be from the Interest of the Approver, *What's* HECUBA *to us, or we to* HECUBA?[24]

In section 4 of the same work, Hutcheson returns to this subject to tell us that had we no moral sense, we would think no differently of incest than we do of financial ruin, and that "without a moral Sense, we could receive no Prejudice against Actions, under any other View than as naturally disadvantageous to our selves." He then goes on to argue for the "Universality of this moral Sense" and to claim that it is natural, or "antecedent to Instruction." Both features are established, he believes, by "observing the Sentiments of Children," who, without need of any teaching, are "mov'd by . . . moral Representations."[25]

If there are any doubts that we are here being told about a disposition, these are removed when we turn to section 5, which is entitled, in part, "A further Confirmation, that we have practical Dispositions to Virtue implanted in our nature," and wherein we are told: "Had we no Sense of moral Qualitys in Actions, nor any Conceptions of them, except as advantageous or hurtful, we never could have honour'd or lov'd Agents for publick Love, or had any regard to their Actions, further than they affected our selves in particular. We might have form'd the metaphysical Idea of publick Good, but we had never . . . admir'd and lov'd those who were studious of it, without a moral Sense."[26]

That this moral disposition motivates or directs our action is made equally clear. In the first place, it is a sense. For Hutcheson, all our senses are sources of pleasure and pain, and are thus

[24] *British Moralists*, 1: 75.
[25] *British Moralists*, 1: 126-127.
[26] *British Moralists*, 1: 134. See also *Essay*, p. 213.

motivating insofar as our desires and aversions follow from pleasure or pain. As the "AUTHOR of Nature," he says, "has determin'd us to receive, by our external Senses, pleasant or disagreeble Ideas of Objects, according as they are useful or hurtful to our Bodys," so has he "given us a MORAL SENSE, to direct our Actions, and to give us still nobler Pleasures." But, beyond this, he also claims that it is the moral sense which determines us to seek out such publicly advantageous phenomena as "Association, Friendships, Familys, natural Affections, and other human Sentiments," and he says that it is the moral sense which directs our action. Without it, we would never be motivated to participate in society, for there would be nothing which could move us to do so: "Were there no moral Sense, no Happiness in Benevolence, and did we act from no other Principle than Self-Love; sure there is no Pleasure of the external Senses, which we could not enjoy alone, with less trouble and expence than in Society."[27] Even in the *Essay*, where Hutcheson explicitly distinguishes both the "Public Sense" and the "Sense of Honour" from the moral sense, and explicitly states that both of these senses are motivational, the moral sense is given a motivating or exciting role, as is revealed by the critique of the rational moralists that is found there. It is not, he says, "any *reasoning* antecedent to a *moral Sense*, which determines us to *approve* the Study of Publick Good," but the moral sense itself. It is the moral sense which determines us to love the benevolent and "to desire their Happiness," or, again, it is because we have a moral sense that the soul is "naturally determined to . . . the Desire of certain Events when it has an Idea of them, as Brutes are, by their lower Instincts, to their Actions."[28]

That the moral sense has a cognitive function is doubtless the more fundamental point.[29] Fortunately, there is surprisingly strong

[27] *British Moralists*, 1: 83, 97, 147. Cf. *British Moralists*, 1: 133-134.

[28] *Essay*, pp. 5-6, 240, 291-292, 298.

[29] The question is, simply, whether or not the moral sense is a faculty capable of apprehending independently existing, intersubjective features (objectively real features) of the world about us, just as the other, ordinary senses presumably do. This is also the meaning of *cognitive* that is used by Frankena; see n. 7 of this chapter.

support for this claim. In fact, much of what has been said earlier in this chapter serves as evidence to this end. Hutcheson's intentions, we have seen, included the refutation of egoism and attendant moral scepticism; in opposition to those sceptical views he sought to establish the reality of virtue. But if there is no means by which virtue can be known—no faculty capable of apprehending it—then his enterprise must have ended in failure, even in his own eyes. It would not be enough for Hutcheson to establish in some abstract way that virtue and vice are genuine features of reality. To accomplish only this would be to leave the field to the moral sceptics. To refute these sceptics effectively he would also need to show that man is equipped to discover and distinguish these features of reality; if the moral sense were not a cognitive sense its discovery would have been of little use to the warmhearted Hutcheson whose gentle zeal for morals was a legend in its time.

There is even more direct evidence of this interpretation. Hutcheson portrays the moral sense as analogous to the external senses, the paradigm here of cognitive senses, and he explains the process of moral perception in terms which reinforce this analogy. A sense, he declares in the *Inquiry*, is "a Determination of the Mind, to receive any Idea from the Presence of an Object which occurs to us, independent on our Will," and the *moral sense* is "a Determination of our Minds to receive amiable or disagreeable Ideas of Actions, when they occur to Observation. . . ."[30] In the *Essay* he defines a sense as "*every Determination of our Minds to receive Ideas independently on our Will, and to have perceptions of Pleasure and Pain.*" In this work, five kinds of senses are noted, including the "External Senses," which are said to be "universally known," and the moral sense, the sense by which "we perceive *Virtue* or *Vice*, in ourselves, or others."[31] In both works, Hutcheson insists on the close similarity between the

[30] *British Moralists*, 1: 74, 83.

[31] *Essay*, pp. 4-6. The other senses in Hutcheson's list (which is not intended to be exhaustive) are the Internal Sense, or what Addison called the Imagination; the Public Sense, or determination to be pleased at the happiness, uneasy at the misery, of others; and the Sense of Honor, which makes the approbation of our acts by others pleasing to us, their disapprobation displeasing.

external senses and the moral sense. At least six points of likeness are mentioned:

1. Pleasure and pain are produced by the external senses as well as by the moral sense. Hutcheson claims that by the "immediate Powers of Perception internal or external" we have pleasure and pain. This corresponds with the definition of a sense cited, and is confirmed by the passage which immediately precedes that definition: "It is by some Power of Perception, or *Sense*, that we first receive the Ideas of these Objects we are conversant with, or by some *Reasoning* upon these perceived Objects of Sense. By Sensation we not only receive the *Image* or *Representation*, but some feelings of *Pleasure* or *Pain*; nay sometimes the sole Perception is that of Pleasure or Pain, as in Smells, and the Feelings of Hunger or Thirst. . . ."[32]

2. The perceptions of the external senses and of the moral sense are involuntary. The definition of a sense itself establishes this: a determination of the mind to receive ideas independently of the will. But Hutcheson seems to make an even stronger claim, namely, that the senses are also independent of *interest*: "This moral Sense, either of our own Actions, or of those of others, has this in common with our other Senses, that however our Desire of Virtue may be counterballanc'd by Interest, our Sentiment *or* Perception of its Beauty cannot. . . ."[33]

3. Both the external senses and the moral sense are universal principles of the human constitution. No one, Hutcheson says, doubts that all men have the external senses; likewise, the "*moral sense is universal.*" The principal argument against the universality of the moral sense is the variation in moral perception which is observed. However, such variation does not show that the moral sense does not exist; it shows only that it is as liable to mistake as the external senses. Variations in what we perceive as virtue and vice provide no more reason to deny that there is a universal

[32] *Essay*, pp. 2, 241. Hutcheson further suggests that the pleasure (or pain) of our sensible perceptions reveals that there are objects exciting or affecting us: "The Pleasure in our sensible Perceptions of any kind, gives us our first Idea of natural Good, or Happiness; and then all Objects which are apt to excite this Pleasure are call'd immediately Good." *British Moralists*, 1: 70.

[33] *British Moralists*, 1: 78. See also pp. 80-82, and *Essay*, p. 118.

74

moral sense than variations in the perceptions of the external senses provide grounds to suppose that these are not everywhere the same, or that variations in opinion indicate that reason varies from place to place.[34]

4. Like the external senses, the moral sense operates immediately, without inference. Reason, Hutcheson argues, is too slow and full of doubt to decide what is most important to us. Consequently, we have been provided with faculties which operate immediately and instinctively. These include the external senses, which assist in our preservation, and the moral sense, which serves to direct our action: "Notwithstanding the mighty Reason we boast of above other Animals, its Processes are too slow, too full of doubt and hesitation, to serve us in every Exigency, either for our own Preservation, without the external Senses, or to direct our Actions for the Good of the Whole, without this moral Sense."[35]

5. Both the external senses and the moral sense may be mistaken; and may be subsequently corrected by reason. May there not, Hutcheson asks, "be a *right* or *wrong State* of our *Moral Sense*, as there is of our other *Senses*, according as they represent their Objects to be *as they really are*, or represent them otherwise?"[36] However, even though the moral sense may be sometimes confused by "Motives of external Advantage," it is "like our other Senses" in that it "ceases not to operate." It still makes us "uneasy and dissatisfy'd with our selves; even as the Sense of Tasting makes us loath, and dislike the nauseous Potion which we may force our selves, from Interest, to swallow."[37]

In the *Essay*, arguing against the rationalists, Hutcheson goes into more detail:

But must we not own, that we judge of all our *Senses* by

---

[34] *Essay*, p. 280. Compare *British Moralists*, 1: 122-123: "Reason is universally allow'd to Men, notwithstanding all the stupid, ridiculous Opinions receiv'd in many Places . . . bad Conduct is not owing to any Irregularity in the moral Sense, but to a wrong Judgment or Opinion."

[35] *British Moralists*, 1: 156. See also pp. 72, 155; *Essay*, pp. 240-241.

[36] *Essay*, p. 286.

[37] *British Moralists*, 1: 119.

our *Reason*, and often correct their *Reports* of the *Magnitude*, *Figure*, *Colour*, *Taste* of Objects, and pronounce them *right* or *wrong*, as they agree or disagree with *Reason*? This is true. But does it then follow, that *Extension*, *Figure*, *Colour*, *Taste*, are not *sensible Ideas*, but only denote *Reasonableness*, or *Agreement with Reason*? Or that these Qualities are perceivable antecedently to any *Sense*, by our *Power of finding out Truth*? Just so *a compassionate Temper* may rashly imagine the *Correction of a Child*, or the *Execution of a Criminal*, to be cruel and inhuman: but by *reasoning* may discover the *superior Good* arising from them in the whole; and then the same *moral Sense* may determine the Observer to approve them. But we must not hence conclude, that it is any *reasoning* antecedent to a *moral Sense*, which determines us to *approve* the Study of publick Good, any more than we can in the former Case conclude, that we perceive *Extension*, *Figure*, *Colour*, *Taste*, antecedently to a Sense. All these Sensations are often corrected by *Reasoning*, as well as our *Approbations* of Actions as Good or Evil: and yet no body ever placed the *Original Idea* of Extension, Figure, Colour, or Taste, in *Conformity to Reason*.[38]

6. The moral sense, as well as the external senses, is said to apprehend aspects of objective or publicly available reality through perceptions that are presented directly to consciousness. That the

[38] *Essay*, pp. 239-240. Hutcheson does not limit the moral use of reason to correcting mistaken sentiments: "Reasoning or *Intellect* seems to raise no new Species of Ideas, but to discover or discern the *Relations* of those received. Reason shews what Acts are conformable to a *Law*, a *Will* of a Superior; or what Acts tend to Private Good, or to Publick Good: In like manner, Reason discovers contrary Tendencies of contrary Actions. Both Contraries are alike the Object of the Understanding, and may give that sort of Pleasure which arises upon Discovery of Truth. A Demonstration that certain Actions are detrimental to Society is attended with the peculiar *Pleasure of new Knowledge*, as much as a like Demonstration of the Benefit of Virtue. But when we *approve* a kind beneficent Action, let us consider whether this *Feeling*, or *Action*, or *Modification* of the Soul more resembles an Act of *Contemplation*, such as this (when strait Lines intersect each other, the vertical Angles are equal;) or that *Liking* we have to a beautiful Form, an harmonious Composition, a grateful Sound" (*Essay*, pp. 241-242; see also pp. 167-168, 219-223, 236, 284-289, and *British Moralists*, 1: 155). Hume's views on these issues is remarkably similar; see chap. 3 of this book.

moral sense is an apprehending sense is suggested by the language in which its function is described, and by explicit comparisons of the two kinds of senses.[39] For example:

> Esteem . . . Dislike . . . are entirely excited by some moral Qualitys, Good or Evil, apprehended to be in the Objects.
> . . .
> We may observe, that no Action of any other Person was ever approv'd by us, but upon some Apprehension, well or ill grounded, of some really good moral Quality.
>
> The *Apprehension* of morally good Qualities, is the necessary Cause of *Approbation*, by our moral Sense. . . .[40]

V. In contrast to the similarities between the moral sense and the external senses, there is one notable difference. No bodily organ is known to correspond to the moral sense as such organs do, presumably, correspond to the external senses. It is for this reason, of course, that we must say the Hutchesonian moral sense is only analogous to the external senses. However, when we go

[39] Frankena argues ("Hutcheson's Moral Sense Theory") that the presence in Hutcheson of this apparently cognitive terminology is not conclusive, on the grounds that the eighteenth-century use of such terms might well differ from our own. But this argument is itself inconclusive without specific evidence that these terms were then used *only* in a sense different from our own, and is in any case overturned by the account of Hutcheson's theories of perception and moral perception which follows.

[40] *British Moralists*, 1: 85, 118-119; *Essay*, p. 89. See also *British Moralists*, 1: 120; *Essay*, pp. 208-209, 237. In the latter work (pp. 240-241), Hutcheson explicitly compares the external and moral senses, and notes four of the six shared features mentioned: " 'Tis manifest we have in our *Understanding moral Ideas*, or they are Perceptions of the Soul: we reason about them, we compare, we judge; but then we do all the same Acts about *Extension, Figure, Colour, Taste, Sound*, which Perceptions all Men call *Sensations*. All our Ideas, or the materials of our reasoning or judging, are received by some immediate Powers of Perception internal or external, which we may call *Senses*; by these too we have Pleasure and Pain. All Perception is by the Soul, not by the Body, tho' some Impressions on the bodily Organs are the Occasions of some of them; and in others the Soul is determined to other sorts of *Feelings* or *Sensations*, where no bodily Impression is the immediate Occasion. A certain *incorporeal Form*, if one may use that Name, a *Temper* observed, *a Character, an Affection, a State* of a sensitive Being, known or understood, may raise *Liking, Approbation, Sympathy*, as naturally from the very Constitution of the Soul, as any bodily Impression raises external Sensations."

on to sketch out Hutcheson's theory of perception, and then his theory of moral perception, we can see that the analogy is far more than a casual one, and that Hutcheson actually went to some length to explain how the moral sense informs us of moral reality.

Hutcheson's writings on moral philosophy contain very little on perception in general, and that little is remarkably dense. In the *Essay* (sec. 1, art. 1), he states that "Objects, Actions, or Events obtain the Name of *Good*, or *Evil*, according as they are the Causes, or Occasions, mediately, or immediately, of a grateful, or ungrateful *Perception* to some sensitive Nature." If we are to understand the several kinds of good or evil, we must understand the different senses which are natural to us. Generally speaking, it is either by a sense or by reasoning about objects already sensed that we obtain the ideas we have of the objects with which we are conversant. By sensation we receive images or representative ideas, but we also receive certain feelings of pleasure and pain, such as, for example, the pleasures of some smells or the pains of thirst.

The pleasures or pains that are perceived by the senses, he continues, are either simple, which is to say they occur in an isolated manner, independent of other ideas or images, or "not simple," in that they arise only on the occasion of some preceding idea, assemblage of ideas, or comparison of ideas.[41] At this point, we are referred to a lengthy footnote and are told that the "following general Account" of perception "may possibly be useful."

1. Certain "Motions raised in our Bodies are by a *general Law* constituted the Occasion of *Perceptions* in the Mind." Nothing further is said here regarding the causes or sources of these motions, but later discussions indicate that objects independent of the mind are assumed to exist.

2. These perceptions or sensible ideas "never come entirely

---

[41] Hutcheson does not follow Locke and call these "complex ideas," and neither shall I. For a brief discussion of whether or not Hutcheson is a Lockean, see my "Hutcheson on Perception and Moral Perception," *Archiv für Geschichte der Philosophie* 59 (1977), nn. 11 and 17. I conclude that he is less influenced by Locke than most other commentators suggest.

alone" to the mind, but are always accompanied by other perceptions. Thus if "sensible Ideas" is taken to refer to the perceptions that are raised by motions in our bodies, we can then say that sensible ideas are always accompanied by certain "nonsensible" ideas, such as those of duration or number. These latter ideas can be seen to be nonsensible in that they also accompany "*Ideas of Internal Consciousness* or Reflection."

3. Some of our (nonsensible) ideas accompany quite different sensible ideas ("Sensations"), but these nonsensible ideas "are not to be perceived separately" from some sensible idea. Examples of this particular kind of accompanying idea are the ideas of extension, figure, motion, and rest, which can accompany either the sensible ideas of sight (colors), or those of touch (certain feelings), or both. It is proper, then, to call the ideas of extension, figure, motion, and rest "accompanying" or "concomitant" ideas, for they can occur concomitantly with the ideas of sight or touch, but "never without the one or the other."

Hutcheson then summarizes: The purely sensible perceptions of ideas, each of which is perceived by its "proper Sense," are tastes, smells, colors, sounds, cold, heat, and so forth. The "universal Concomitant *Ideas*," which attend all other ideas, are duration and number. The (ordinary) concomitant ideas which "*are reputed Images of something External*," and which accompany only sensible ideas, are extension, figure, motion, and rest.[42]

[42] Italics here added. I have hereafter given the title "representative concomitant ideas" to those concomitant ideas "reputed Images of something external." Hutcheson, in his posthumous *System of Moral Philosophy*, 2 vols. (Glasgow: R. and A. Foulis, 1755), 1: 6, suggests the name "Concomitant ideas of sensation," but this seems likely to lead to confusion with "ideas of sensation," his title for sensible ideas. Of the universal concomitant ideas Hutcheson here remarks that "duration and number are applicable to every perception or action of the mind, whether dependent on bodily organs or not." See also Hutcheson's letter to William Mace, September 6, 1727, published in *European Magazine and London Review*, September 1788, pp. 158-160. This letter is partially reprinted and helpfully discussed by David Berman, "Francis Hutcheson on Berkeley and the Molyneux Problem," *Proceedings of the Royal Irish Academy* 74 (1974): 259-265.

The letter to Mace is made all the more fascinating by the fact that, as Berman notes, it attributes to Mace (a lecturer at Gresham College after 1744) the bundle theory of the self that is later found in Hume, and then offers a rebuttal typical of Scottish philosophers: "As to your notion of our mind as only a system of

In his *Synopsis metaphysicae* Hutcheson offers the same account, but he amplifies his remarks about concomitant ideas.[43] Extension, figure, motion, and rest, he says, are not inappropriately called primary qualities (*"affectiones primarias"*) in view of the fact that we are naturally led to believe these qualities are in things themselves, in just the way that they are perceived, and because the natural philosophers claim that the power of things to produce our ideas of secondary qualities depends on the primary qualities. On the other hand, there is nothing in external things which resembles the ideas of secondary qualities. Nevertheless, the importance of these nonresembling ideas is not to be overlooked, for it is by their agency that we come to our knowledge of the existence and nature of external things.[44] Our sensible

perceptions, I imagine you'll find that every one has an immediate simple perception of *self*; to which all his other perceptions are some way connected, otherwise I cannot conceive how I could be in any way affected with pleasure or pain from any past action, affection, or perception, or have any present uneasiness or concern about any future event or perception; or how there could be any unity of person, or any desire of future happiness or aversion to misery. My past perceptions or future ones are not my present [ones and] would be as distinct [from me] as your perceptions are from mine: that it is otherwise I believe every one is conscious." Hutcheson then continues in a somewhat surprising manner, before returning to the subject of concomitant ideas and their representational role: "As to material *substrata*, I own I am a sceptic; all the phenomena might be as they are, were there nothing but perceptions, for the phenomena are perceptions. And yet, were there external objects, I cannot imagine how we could be better informed of them than we are. I own I cannot see the force of the arguments against external objects, i.e. something like, or proportional, to our concomitant ideas, as I call extension, figure, motion, rest, solidity" (as cited in Berman, pp. 263-264).

[43] *Synopsis metaphysicae, ontologiam et pneumatologiam complectens* (Glasgow: R. and A. Foulis, 1744). This work was first published, without Hutcheson's knowledge, in 1742. The edition cited here was corrected by Hutcheson. It is significant to note that Hutcheson's position in the *Synopsis* seems essentially the same as that found in the *Essay*, despite the sixteen-year interval.

[44] Hutcheson is apparently saying that it is *only* by means of such nonresembling ideas, or affections, that we apprehend external objects. And it is only by means of another set of nonresembling ideas, or affections (feelings of approbation and disapprobation) that we apprehend moral objects or moral reality. He does not, so far as I know, specifically affirm that *all* apprehension is by the agency of the affections, but neither does he mention a specific alternative, nor even suggest that there could be such an alternative. He is satisfied that the perception of moral and physical reality, or knowledge of objective, publicly available features of both physical and moral reality, is dependent on affective states or feelings.

ideas, which are either pleasurable, disagreeable, or indifferent, do not, Hutcheson says, depict either external things or the bodily motions they arouse in us. But without these sensible ideas we would remain completely unaware of all bodies as well as of their location, figure, motion, and magnitude, for our sensations are the signs or marks of those things which could be either helpful or harmful to our bodies. Our disagreeable sensations warn us so that we avoid harmful things, our pleasurable sensations excite us so that we seek those things which may be of use to us.[45]

Hutcheson's general account of perception can be summarized as follows: Certain bodily motions, by a natural law which God himself has established, are regularly the occasion of certain *sensible ideas* in the mind. These sensible ideas are always accompanied by the *universal concomitant ideas* (duration and number), and some of them are accompanied by the *representative concomitant ideas* (extension, figure, and so forth). In this regard one can say that the sensible ideas are the occasion of the concomitant ideas, and that the sensible ideas, while not themselves the images or representations of external and objective reality, are in fact the signs by which external and objective reality is known. In one sense, sensible ideas are mere secondary qualities with only subjective or psychological status, but they are nevertheless the first and absolutely essential part of a process that ends in knowledge of objective reality. Thus, for Hutcheson, knowledge of external and objective reality, of bodies and their attributes, is dependent upon purely affective, nonrepresentative states of mind.

Moral perception is explained in much the same way. First, Hutcheson claims that all the ideas so far discussed (sensible,

---

[45] *Synopsis*, p. 49. The passage in the *Synopsis* is somewhat ambiguous, but the interpretation I have given it is confirmed in the *System of Moral Philosophy*, 1: 5, where Hutcheson writes: "These sensations [of the external senses], as the learned agree, are not pictures or representations of like external qualities in objects, nor of the impression or change made in bodily organs. They are either *signals*, as it were, of new events happening to the body, of which experience and observation will shew us the cause; or *marks*, settled by the Author of Nature, to shew us what things are salutary, innocent, or hurtful; or intimations of things not otherways discernable which may affect our state; tho' these marks or signals bear no more resemblance to the external reality, than the report of a gun, or the flash of the powder, bears to the distress of a ship."

universal concomitant, representative concomitant) can come into the mind independently of "previous Ideas assembled, or compared." This is not true of the ideas of the "Internal Sense" (the Imagination, or Sense of Beauty, in the terminology of the *Essay*), for these ideas always follow and are dependent upon sensible ideas and the concomitant ideas that arise with them. By this, Hutcheson means to say no more than that the Internal Sense is dependent upon the external senses in that the Internal Sense cannot operate until the temporally and logically prior processes of external perception have reached a stage of relative completeness. We cannot see that an item is beautiful until we have seen it; only after our sensible ideas and their concomitants are experienced can the uniformities or resemblances they possess be perceived by the Internal Sense. This same restriction applies, *mutatis mutandis*, to perception by the moral sense.

Second, the "*Affections, Tempers, Sentiments, or Actions*" which we find in ourselves or others, Hutcheson thinks, are the equivalent of the bodily motions that occasion external perception and may thus be considered the occasions of moral perception, or the "*Occasions* of agreeable or disagreeable Perceptions, which we call *Approbation* or *Dislike*."[46] These "Moral Perceptions" are as real and natural and as necessary a part of our experience as any other sensations, and they are quite as unavoidable and unalterable. Thus when we consider what a sense is (every determination of our minds to receive ideas independently of the will, and to have perceptions of pleasure and pain), we see that the common opinion that there are only five senses is quite inadequate; there are "many other *Senses* besides those commonly explained." Again we can turn to the *Synopsis* for amplification.[47] It is from certain pleasant sensations that our notion of good arises, and from unpleasant ones, our notion of evil, while the things which serve to produce these sensations are called useful or harmful, respectively. When certain higher senses function, more important goods and evils are sensed, and we are able from these to understand which things are the basis of a happy life. One of these

[46] I am still explicating the opening section of the *Essay*.
[47] See pp. 52-54.

82

higher senses is here called the sense of honor and morality. This sense is one of the reflective or subsequent senses which perceive those "species" of things which arise on reflection. These species Hutcheson calls "sensations" because they also arise as the result of a fixed law of nature, and not from any desire or volition of our own.

This sense of honor or morality judges everything men do or think to do, and does so in much the manner that a court of justice judges. It discerns what is moral and what is the criterion or standard of the moral. It pronounces the animal pleasures, for example, to be worthless, but it values all things which elevate our natural powers or which show a fixed resolution to the good. That this moral faculty is innate and independent is made certain by the fact that each of us judges deeds, not in terms of the pleasure or utility they afford, but according to whether they were done with danger or loss to the agent, or performed with little or no regard to the agent's own utility, honor, or fame; we give moral praise to the acts of others of which we have heard, even to the extent that we praise the courage and patriotism of an enemy.

We are now, I believe, in a position to explicate Hutcheson's most sustained comment regarding moral perception. In part 2, sec. 4 of the *Essay* he takes up the issue of "the use of *Reason* concerning *Virtue* and *Vice*, upon [the] Supposition that we receive these Ideas by a *Moral Sense.*" It is in the course of this discussion that he asks whether there can be a wrong state of the moral sense, or whether the moral sense can be mistaken. Could not the moral sense disapprove what is virtuous, just as a diseased palate may dislike wholesome food, or vitiated eyesight may misrepresent colors or dimension? If so, does not this prove that we know what is morally good or evil prior to the operation of the moral sense, for only by means of such prior knowledge could we know that the moral sense is wrong?[48]

In answer to this query we are reminded that our sensible ideas are only perceptions in the mind, and not images of similar ex-

---

[48] *Essay*, p. 286. The relevant text is cited at p. 75, above.

ternal qualities; only the "*concomitant Ideas of Sensation*," or *representative concomitant ideas*, are images of the external. Further, we know that our sensible ideas are altered if there is a substantial alteration in our organs of sense, that sometimes these ideas are different "from what arise[s] in us from the same Objects at other times." Similarly, circumstances can cause diversity in our concomitant ideas. In neither case, however, do we take our understanding of objects from the ideas of objects received while our organs are disordered or the circumstances are unusual. Nor does anyone suggest that colors and tastes are *reasonable* ideas or that it is *reason* that first perceives the concomitant ideas. Such suggestions would be absurd.

The situation is said to be precisely the same with respect to what could be appropriately termed *moral objects*. Hutcheson concedes that the tendency of certain human actions (which are themselves first known by the external senses) and the "*Affections in the Agent*" are inferred by reason, but he insists that there is, nonetheless, a function which must be performed by the moral sense: as observers of a given agent we perceive in ourselves approbation or disapprobation "according as the *Affections of the Agent* are apprehended [as] *kind* in their *just Degree*, or *deficient*, or *malicious*." It is not to be supposed that our approbation or disapprobation is an "*Image of any thing external,*" any more than are our sensible ideas. Neither is it to be thought that "calling the *Ideas of Virtue* and *Vice* Perceptions of a *Sense*, upon apprehending the *Actions* and *Affections* of another," diminishes the "*Reality*" of virtue and vice. On the contrary, these ideas arise upon the occasion of what are clearly independently existing actions or affections of an agent, and they serve as signs of the moral nature of these actions or affections. An individual with a well-functioning moral sense (it will be recalled that Hutcheson grants that the moral sense as much as the external senses can be in a disordered state) will, upon the observation of an agent's actions or affections, feel approbation or disapprobation. If approbation is felt, this will be accompanied by the idea of virtue, an idea that represents the moral character of the agent or action under observation. If disapprobation is felt, then it will be the idea of vice that is concomitant and representative. Whether approbation or disapprobation is felt, the observer's feelings or affections will have again served as the signs of objective reality, this time of objective moral reality.[49]

In summary form, Hutcheson might well have said something like this: "Moral perception is essentially analogous to ordinary perception as I understand it. In ordinary perception (physical and anatomical details aside), we have certain feelings or *sensible ideas*—that is, colors, tastes, or what Locke called the ideas of secondary qualities—and along with each of these sensible ideas we also have ideas of duration and number, the *universal concomitant ideas*. And along with some of these sensible ideas we have ideas of extension, figure, and so forth, the *representative concomitant ideas*, or what Locke called ideas of primary qualities. The sensible ideas are not images or representative of things, but signs or marks of them, while the concomitant ideas do represent external reality. When we experience these three kinds of ideas together (for the sensible ideas are only logically prior) we have what we call the idea of an object, or knowledge of an object.

"Moral perception is much the same. It too depends upon nonrepresentative ideas, affections, or feelings which function as the signs of external reality. Of course, there is no moral organ,

---

[49] *Essay*, pp. 287-288. Two further remarks of Hutcheson underscore this interpretation: "*Approbation* is not what we can *voluntarily* bring upon ourselves. When we are contemplating Actions, we do not *chuse* to approve, because *Approbation* is pleasant; . . . *Approbation* is plainly a *Perception* arising without previous *Volition*. . . . The Occasion of it is the *Perception of benevolent Affections* in ourselves, or the discovering the like in others. . ." (*Essay*, p. 248). "The Quality approved by our moral Sense is conceived to reside in the Person approved, and to be a Perfection and Dignity in him. . . . The admired Quality is conceived as the Perfection of the Agent, and such a one as is distinct from the *Pleasure* either in the Agent or the Approver; tho' 'tis a sure Source of Pleasure to the Agent. The Perception of the Approver, tho' attended with Pleasure, *plainly represents something quite distinct from this Pleasure; even as the Perception of external Forms is attended with Pleasure, and yet represents something distinct from this Pleasure.* This may prevent many Cavils upon this Subject." (*Inquiry*, pp. 130-131, italics added in the last sentence but one; the sentences following the ellipses were added by Hutcheson to the fourth edition of the *Inquiry*. They do not appear to have eliminated misunderstandings, as he hoped.)

85

but once we have by ordinary perception perceived certain human actions our moral sense responds with feelings of approbation or disapprobation. Concomitant with these ideas, in addition to duration and number, are the moral concomitants, the ideas of virtue and vice, which *are* representative of external or objective moral reality. When we experience these kinds of ideas together (for again the feelings appear to be only logically prior) we have an idea of moral objects, or moral knowledge."

VI. Hutcheson's is a paradigm response (of a certain kind) to the *crise morale* to which I have drawn attention. His theory is, in effect, an attempt to elaborate a moral epistemology that is consonant with a dualistic metaphysics of a Cartesian sort, and a metaphysics of human nature that is contrary to, and more convincing than, that of the egoists. Hutcheson was, to consider his moral epistemology first, trying to bridge the gulf which the Cartesian ontology had seemed to reveal. That is, once the Cartesians had found reality divided into the disparate elements of mind and extension, there seemed to be an ontological gulf between objects and certain qualities (colors, sounds, tastes, smells) which previously had been thought to be in objects themselves, but which were now understood to be ideas that arise in the mind, and for which there could be no resembling qualities in objects.

Hutcheson's response to this situation is, generally speaking, uncomplicated. He was not only unconvinced, but alarmed, by the moral sceptics. He was not alarmed by the rationalists, but he was unconvinced. Locke's critique of innate ideas, one might guess, persuaded him that a neo-Platonic ethical theory (such as Cudworth's) was untenable, and the theories offered by subsequent rationalists he found deficient—for example, their *a priori* analyses of virtue, their moral epistemology, and, especially, their account (or, as Hutcheson thought, their nonaccount) of our motivation to perform morally good acts. At the same time, Hutcheson was committed, as I have emphasized, to moral realism, and so he tried to formulate a moral theory which is consistent with the view that *virtue* and *vice* are terms with objective reference and which transcend self-interest and private or idiosyncratic psychological reactions. At the same time, he granted that affections of the mind play an important role in coming to know objective moral phenomena. Given the ontology he accepted, Hutcheson could not but grant that moral actions are, *qua* events, simply events in the physical world having, at most, a tendency to certain ends. But the very fact that moral actions are not, as events, different from other events in the physical world provided him with just the solution that the problem of moral knowledge required. If the nature and import of physical reality is known (as seemed the case) only through affective states or subjective reactions (sensible ideas which occasion the various concomitant ideas), then why should not moral reality be known in the same way? In short, Hutcheson accepted Cartesian dualism. Furthermore, he agreed that our moral approbation and disapprobation are, in effect, secondary qualities, or nonrepresentative affections of the mind and only the mind. But he also insisted that it is just such affections that enable us to obtain knowledge of extrapersonal reality. In his opinion, affections of the mind enable us to know physical objects that exist independently of our minds and (generally) ourselves. There is nothing ad hoc, then, about his claim that such affections enable us to know an independently existing moral reality.

VII. It is also important that we give further attention to the providential dimension of Hutcheson's thought. In part, this can be understood as his attempt to reinstate, in somewhat different form, the teleological conception of nature which had been seriously undercut by the new science, and openly challenged by others. The work of the new scientists clearly seemed to indicate, to take only one example, that the scholastic belief in the primacy of rest over motion (for the terrestrial sphere) was untenable. In its place was substituted the principle of inertia which specified that there is no privileged state or natural place for objects. Thus, at least with respect to motion and rest, bodies were said to have no particular nature, to be essentially unstructured and completely

open to external influence. Left to itself, according to this principle, a body would continue to behave in whatever manner its
most recent influence had brought about; it would not, as scholastic physics claimed, seek its "natural place."

Not only was the general thrust of the new science and metaphysics of this sort, it seems fair to say, but Hobbes, among others,
also openly and clearly challenged the older teleological conception of nature, and he extended his nonteleological metaphysics
to include man himself, whom he described as having no natural
or unique *summum bonum* beyond the desire to fulfill desires. "But
for an *utmost* end," he writes in *Human Nature*, "in which the
ancient philosophers have placed *felicity*, and disputed much concerning the way thereto, there is no such thing in this world,
nor way to it, more than to Utopia: for while we live, we have
desires, and desire presupposeth a further end."[50] In *Leviathan* he
is if anything more explicit: "For there is no such thing as perpetual tranquillity of mind, while we live here; because life itself
is but motion, and can never be without desire. . . ."[51] Hobbes,
as I have already suggested, resolutely reverses the scholastic tendency to see nature anthropomorphically (in terms of appetites
and ends), and instead sees man physiocentrically (as object in
motion under the influence of other objects and motions). The
result, given the new physics, is to see man as a being of no
particular nature, essentially unstructured and completely open
to external influence.[52]

Against these nonteleological ways of thought, Hutcheson does
not attempt to reinstate an orthodox Scholastic teleology, or (one
might say) an *intrinsic* teleology based on an Aristotelian analysis
of causes. Rather, he adopts an *extrinsic* teleology, or one which
derives particular (but mutable) natures, relations, and purposes

[50] Chap. 7, par. 6.
[51] Part 1, chap. 6.
[52] For Hobbes to see man as unstructured, having no particular nature, is not
inconsistent with his view that man is self-interested. In fact, what seems to be
meant by saying that Hobbesian man is self-interested is that he has no particular
nature (moral or social) to contravene those forces which affect him, and hence
he can *only* be self-centered, only take account of things as they affect him. On
this understanding, Hobbes's claims are not inconsistent, but tautologous.

from the free activity of a benevolent and omnipotent Deity who
has designed and created man and nature. Thus Hutcheson emphasizes, contra Hobbes, the natural character of our faculties,
and then goes on to claim that the natural is that which is the
result of a wise and benevolent Providence, or is, more simply,
God-given.[53] Again, however, Hutcheson proceeds by comparison with the nonmoral world. He notes, for example, the "Principle of Gravitation, which perhaps extends to all Bodys in the
Universe," and suggests that the "practical dispositions to Virtue
implanted in our nature" are analogous to this "Principle."[54] Our
dispositions, he suggests, are comparable to gravity not only because they are outside our control (adventitious and spontaneous), but also because they arise universally and operate with
the same regularity as gravity does. Hence we have as much reason
to suppose there is a moral nature as that there is a physical one:

> If we call 'that State, those Dispositions and Actions, natural,
> to which we are inclined by some part of our Constitution,
> antecedently to any Volition of our own; or which flow from
> some Principles in our Nature, not brought upon us by our
> own Art, or that of others;' then it may appear, from what
> was said above, that 'a State of Good-will, Humanity, Com-
> passion, mutual Aid, propagating and supporting Offspring, Love
> of a Community or Country, Devotion, or Love and Gratitude
> to some governing Mind, is our natural State,' to which we
> are naturally inclined, and do actually arrive, as universally,
> and with as much uniformity, as we do to a certain Stature
> and Shape.[55]

Hutcheson does indeed hold that there is a distinctive human
nature, and that the universe itself has a nature insofar as it is

---

[53] "Human Nature was not left quite indifferent in the Affair of Virtue, to form
to itself Observations concerning the Advantage or Disadvantage of Actions. . . .
The AUTHOR of Nature has much better furnish'd us for a virtuous Conduct, than
our Moralists seem to imagine. . . ." Inquiry, pp. xiii-xiv. This providential
component in Hutcheson's work is, incidentally, remarked in Kemp Smith, p. 45.
[54] British Moralists, 1: 127, 130.
[55] Essay, p. 201.

organized according to universal nomic principles. However, the teleological content of these natures, the ultimate purpose they are to serve, is yet to be revealed. The things of the universe prove to be beneficial to man, man himself has a benevolent bent, things (nature) and man interact in a systematic fashion that is to our benefit. When we ask how this comes about, we are not referred to intrinsic *telos*, or to formal and final principles, intrinsic to nature and man, and that just are both causes and essences. Instead, we are referred to an extrinsic source, the Deity, from which design, order, and purpose flow. We could say that just as our stature is fixed by nature, so have been our dispositions or senses. But this for Hutcheson is in fact only another way of saying that these matters have been "fixed for us by the AUTHOR of our Nature, subservient to the Interest of the *System*" he has created;[56] it is God who has conceived of and given a purpose to man and nature. This may seem to suggest, Hutcheson grants, that the Creator could have produced a quite different universe, and even have given us, so to speak, a contrary nature and faculties, for such an act would be entirely consistent with his powers. But in fact, he counters, the present creation, the present system or design, is morally necessary, for God himself is predisposed to regularity and benevolence.[57]

Finally, it should be noted that affirming this particular teleological conception of man and nature—affirming, in effect, a benevolent Providence—further buttresses Hutcheson's argument against moral scepticism and gives further confirmation to my

[56] *Essay*, p. 118.

[57] There does not, he says, "appear to be any necessary Connection, antecedent to the Constitution of the AUTHOR of *Nature*, between *regular Forms*, *Actions*, *Theorems*, and that sudden sensible *Pleasure* excited in us upon Observation of them, even when we do not reflect upon the Advantage mention'd in the former Proposition. And possibly, the DEITY could have form'd us so as to have receiv'd no immediate Pleasure from such Object[s], or connected Pleasure to those of a quite contrary Nature. . . . It [is] probable, that the *Pleasure* is not the necessary Result of the *Form* itself, otherwise it would equally affect all Apprehensions in what Species soever; but depends upon a voluntary *Constitution*, adapted to preserve the *Regularity* of the *Universe*, and is probably not the Effect of *Necessity*, but *Choice*, in the SUPREME AGENT, who constituted our Senses" (*Inquiry*, pp. 99-100). See also *British Moralists*, 1: 83, 175 (the latter is cited in the following paragraph).

claim that he was concerned to refute this scepticism. He attempts, of course, to establish that man has a distinct nature, and that this nature includes a moral sense by which virtue and vice are known. But establishing that the moral sense is natural does not necessarily establish that it is reliable (see Descartes's remarks about his natural inclinations). Establishing that it is natural may be to indicate that it is a guide that must be believed, but that it is also one whose authority must be accepted, whose perceptions are not only credible but known to be reliable—that is another matter. Hutcheson settles this matter to his own satisfaction by affirming that nature and man are the products of an all-powerful creator who has designed the present "System" in conformity to his benevolent purposes. It is God's benevolence that guarantees the veracity of our moral perceptions. In fact, Hutcheson argues that the senses we have are morally necessary, given God's nature: from his love of regular forms and his divine goodness comes, for example, our sense of beauty. We have even more reason, he says, "to ascribe the present Constitution of our moral Sense to his goodness. For if the Deity be really benevolent, or delights in the happiness of others, he could not rationally act otherwise, or give us a moral Sense upon another Foundation, without counteracting his own benevolent Intentions."[58] If with Hutcheson we suppose the Deity to be both benevolent and powerful, and the source of our several faculties, we would seem to have grounds for concluding that these faculties are reliable. If "in our own nature" we discern "a universal Mind, watchful for the whole," a mind that has designed our faculties and the world "with a View to a general good End,"[59] or so that they operate in harmony and provide us with the information (moral, physical, aesthetic) that is needed for our well-being, and if one of these faculties tells us that some things are genuinely virtuous, others genuinely vicious, then we have knowledge of virtue. We may on occasion be mistaken about the true nature of a particular act; nonetheless, we can distinguish individual instances of virtue,

[58] *British Moralists*, 1: 125, 175-176.
[59] *Essay*, p. 180.

and, consequently, we can know that it is real. Those who deny that virtue is real or that it can be known are demonstrably wrong.

VIII. Hume, I agree, was influenced by Hutcheson, and in this chapter I have shown what this influence might have been. From his reading of Hutcheson, Hume might have been led to think that man is able to gain moral knowledge by means of feelings or purely affective states which serve as signs of objective moral reality. This, I have shown, is Hutcheson's view. From this same reading Hume might also have been led to suppose that man's moral knowledge is guaranteed, as it were, because it is the product of a natural and instinctive moral sense that is provided for us by a benevolent and well-designing Deity. That, too, is Hutcheson's view. In short, I have shown that Hutcheson was not a subjectivist and noncognitivist in morals, but an objectivist who maintained, in contrast to the moral sceptics, that knowledge of virtue and vice, good and evil, is well within the ken of ordinary human beings, thanks, as noted, to the efforts of the Deity. Further, it is important to have shown this, for Kemp Smith, who rightly understood that Hutcheson influenced Hume, misunderstood the nature of this influence because he falsely supposed that Hutcheson maintained a merely subjectivist theory, and he gave little or no attention to the supernatural elements that were incorporated into Hutcheson's theory. As a consequence, not only Kemp Smith but others influenced by him have been led to seek in Hume, and, alas, claim to find there, exactly corresponding subjectivist features,[60] while at the same time completely

[60] W. H. Walsh, for example, writes: "According to Hutcheson, beauty and goodness are not objective characteristics of things or actions, but qualities that they have when contemplated by an observer; to put it crudely, they are subjective. An attempt to transfer the Hutchesonian account of moral and aesthetic judgements to judgements about matter of fact and existence involves inevitably saying that there is something similarly subjective about truth. That Hume never does this explicitly must be admitted. But that his whole account of the understanding committed him to this conclusion seems to me quite obvious." "Hume's Concept of Truth," in *Reason and Reality*, Royal Institute of Philosophy Lectures (London, 1972), 5: 113. Walsh indicates that his view of Hutcheson is derived from Kemp Smith.

overlooking the vastly different religious perspectives taken by the two philosophers. Hume is like Hutcheson in some respects, but not just like him in any respect. As I show in the following chapters, the differences between the two philosophers are at least as important as the similarities.

« 3 »

Hume's Common-Sense
Moral Theory

> Your Notion of [the] correcting Subtility of Sentiment is
> certainly very just with regard to Morals, which depend
> upon Sentiment; & in Politics & natural Philosophy, what-
> ever Conclusion is contrary to certain Matter of Fact must
> certainly be wrong, and there must some Error lie some-
> where in the Argument, whether we be able to show it or
> not.
>
> David Hume to
> Gilbert Elliot of Minto,
> 1751

I.   There is in the ethical theories of the moral sense philosophers an implicit and unavoidable tension between sentiment
and reason. The characteristic claim of these theories is that it
is sentiment, not reason, that enables us to distinguish virtue
from vice, but this claim is nonetheless an integral part of a
theory, and one that is eminently, unmistakably rational. Thus,
although Hutcheson appeals to the (presumably) natural and un-
adulterated affections of the "honest farmer," his explanation or
justification of this appeal is directed not to the unlearned farmer,
but to the learned philosopher, and (presumably, again) proceeds
according to the accepted canons of argumentation or reasoning.
In fact, Hutcheson seems to be aware of this tension when he
remarks that his *Essay* may seem "too subtile for common Apprehension, and consequently not necessary for the Instruction
of Men in *Morals*, which are the common business of Mankind,"
and then goes on to explain that his inquiry has been made
necessary by the cynical views of previous writers.[1]

---

[1] *Essay*, Preface, pp. iv-v.

However, any tension between sentimentalist moral epistemology and a rational explanation and defense of such a position
is inconsequential in comparison to the tension that is found
within moral sense theories themselves, for there reason and
sentiment are represented as being in more or less continuous
interaction, and despite Hume's disclaimer, conflict. To be sure,
it is by the moral sense that we are said to distinguish virtue from
vice. However, it is reason, according to Hutcheson, that corrects
the moral sense, and has thus, literally, a critical role in moral
evaluation.[2] Similarly, Hume emphasizes the fundamental role of
the nonrational sentiments, and evidences, to an even greater
degree, the profound tension between sentiment and reason that
marks Hutcheson's moral philosophy: the paradigm moral individual in Hume's philosophy is much more sophisticated and
much more rational than Hutcheson's "honest farmer." Hume
consistently argues that moral evaluation requires the prior activity of reason, and Hume's ideal of the morally acute individual
is that of a person who can correct for certain normal and widely
occurring biases, and thus judge matters, if not *sub specie aeter-
nitatis*, then at least at very long range and according to rationally
derived general rules. Hume may even be thought to be suggesting
that all our unreasoned, reflex judgments are biased, and as demanding that our moral judgments be informed by reason, or,
that is, as maintaining that it is only after we attain a reflective,
unbiased attitude that a moral judgment is possible. And it is
well known that he holds that many of the particular virtues—
justice, allegiance, chastity, politeness, for example—are *artificial*
virtues, or, in his words, those that result from "the intervention
of thought or reflexion."[3]

[2] See chap. 2, pp. 75-76.
[3] *Treatise*, p. 484. This contrast between Hume and Hutcheson could easily
be overemphasized. Granted that Hutcheson fears that his moral philosophy will
appear oversubtle, and that he appeals to the views of the "honest farmer," he
nonetheless agrees with Hume that our moral approbations or disapprobations
must be preceded by reflective inquiry and analysis. In fact, Hutcheson's appeal
to the honest farmer begins to appear inconsistent once his views about prior
reflection are noted: he suggests that the plain, common man is the ideal moral
observer-evaluator; a careful look at his theory reveals, however, that moral
evaluations are reflex acts that occur only after a certain amount of ratiocination—
analysis, comparison, inference, prediction—has taken place. Hume, I suggest,

Yet Hume tells us that reason is the slave of the passions, which it must serve and obey, and that this domestic arrangement finds its paradigm expression in his moral theory, from which it is said to have been extended to the balance of his philosophy. Hume's striking expression of the relationship of reason and the passions and Kemp Smith's interpretation of him notwithstanding, there is in his moral philosophy a deep and enduring tension between reason and the passions or sentiments, such that they are profoundly interdependent, if not at times in actual conflict. This interdependence must be explored as a preliminary to the central concerns of this chapter.

II. Hume's views on the relationship of reason and sentiment are first presented in *Treatise* II, 3, 3, "Of the influencing motives of the will." In the opening part of this section, Hume seems anxious to show the limitations of reason, to show that it cannot, in any form, influence the will or cause action. Philosophers, both popular and abstruse, he notes, commonly suggest that reason and passion are in conflict, and that the virtuous course is to follow reason in opposition to the passions. For them, reason is seen as eternal and divine, and the passions inconstant and deceitful. But that this point of view is fallacious will become clear if it can be proven, he says, "*first*, that reason alone can never be a motive to any action of the will; and *secondly*, that it can never oppose passion in the direction of the will." There are, he reminds us, two activities of the understanding: it "judges" by *demonstration* the abstract relations of ideas, or by *probability* the relations of objects learned of through experience.[4] Taken alone,

---

exhibits some of this same inconsistency, although his more elaborate exposition includes an attempt, as will be shown, to reconcile these disparate tendencies.

[4] There is both in this section and throughout the *Treatise* a noticeable ambiguity about Hume's use of *reason*. I am not certain that this ambiguity can be completely eliminated nor even that, once noted, it presents any insurmountable difficulties. In general terms, the ambiguity can be seen to have several sources: Hume's quite normal tendency to use interchangeably names for the whole (understanding) and part (reason); his quite normal tendency to use interchangeably names for a capacity (reason) and the activities of that capacity (reasoning); and his not quite so normal (for a philosopher) tendency to reverse himself and to use *reason* or *reasoning* to refer to capacities or activities that he has previously

Hume says, demonstration is so unlike what is needed to influence the will—to motivate actions, that is—that he doubts that any claim to this effect has or would be made. Our abstract reasoning is, by definition, concerned with ideas; the will, which is to be influenced, is practical, and deals with reality. Our abstract rea-

distinguished from reason. This ambiguity is not particularly significant here because the issue before us is the relationship between sentiment and reason in each of the more traditional senses of reason. Nevertheless, it may be helpful to note the principle senses in which Hume uses the term:

Reason and understanding as synonyms. This is a part-whole/whole-part interchange. In the section of the Treatise just taken up Hume begins by speaking of the alleged "combat of passion and reason," and persists in speaking of reason as a "principle" throughout the entire introductory paragraph. He then, without warning, begins the second paragraph by saying that "the understanding exerts itself after two different ways," goes on to speak of the two activities (kinds of reasoning), and in the fourth paragraph reverts to talk of reason as the faculty that concerns him. Other examples of this usage may be seen at Treatise, pp. 456-457, 463 (where "thought and understanding" are also used as equivalent terms), and 468.

Reason as the achievement of truth or falsehood. On only one occasion, I believe, does Hume explicitly identify reason as such an achievement: "Reason is the discovery of truth or falshood," he says at Treatise, p. 458. In doing so, he clearly distinguishes reason as the faculty or capacity that is concerned with agreement or disagreement of the "relations of ideas," or of "real existence and matter of fact." More often he speaks of reason as though it were one or the other of the two activities (not the achievement) that he normally associates with such an achievement.

Reason as abstract reasoning, demonstrative reasoning, or demonstration. After claiming that the understanding exerts itself in two ways Hume indicates that one of these is judging from demonstration or from a consideration of the abstract relations of things. This I suppose he means to be the equivalent of discovering truth or falsehood by attending to the agreement or disagreement of the relations of ideas (p. 458), or those comparative activities which are said (pp. 69-73) to be the "foundation of science" or "knowledge." In this sense, reason is the faculty of comparing ideas.

Reason as probable reasoning, factual reasoning, or probability. The second manner in which the understanding exerts itself (p. 413) is by judging from "probability" or with regard to "those relations of objects, of which experience only gives us information." This I suppose Hume means to be the equivalent of discovering truth or falsehood by attending to the agreement or disagreement of "real existence and matter of fact" (of, strictly speaking, our ideas and real existence or matter of fact; "original facts and realities" are not themselves "susceptible of any such agreement or disagreement"), or by undertaking those comparative activities that are said (in book I, part 3) to provide the foundation of proofs and probabilities. In this sense, reason is the faculty of inferring matters of fact.

Reason as noninferential present awareness. Hume's considered position appears to preclude any such understanding of reason, although perhaps it precludes only

soning cannot, therefore, influence the will unless it is found (as in mathematics) to direct "our judgments concerning causes and effects." In that case, however, we will have already entered into reasoning of the second kind, that which involves probability and real existences. The only question, then, is whether this second form of reasoning affects the will.

If an object appears to offer us the prospect of pleasure, we

---

such an understanding of *reasoning*. His considered opinion is that reasoning consists "in nothing but a *comparison*, and a discovery of those relations . . . which two or more objects bear to each other. This comparison we may make, either when both the objects are present to the senses, or when neither of them is present, or when only one. When both the objects are present to the senses along with the relation, we call *this* perception rather than reasoning; nor is there in this case any exercise of the thought, or any action, properly speaking, but a mere passive admission of the impressions thro' the organs of sensation" (p. 73). On another occasion, however, Hume speaks as though the *understanding* or *reason* (both terms are used) *could* be expected to provide direct insight or, in effect, to perceive. It should be noted, however, that the passage in question (p. 468) is part of Hume's argument against the rationalists; as such the position it represents may be adopted only for the sake of argument.

Reason as instinct; reason as inference, or as the psychological transition from one perception to another. At the close of book I, part 3, Hume says that "reason is nothing but a wonderful and unintelligible instinct in our souls, which carries us along a certain train of ideas, and endows them with particular qualities, according to their particular situations and relations" (p. 179). Here Hume himself seems to have been carried along by the force of his discovery that our causal inferences are not based on either demonstrative reasoning or the perception of causal relations. If not, his use of *reason* here is still a part of the apparent paradox he poses when he says that our causal inferences are not justified by either reason or experience, and yet that we "infer a cause immediately from its effect; and this inference is not only a true species of reasoning, but the strongest of all others . . ." (p. 97). Here we see that reason means *inference* where *inference* itself is understood to refer to psychological (vs. logical) features of thought, or to the transition from one perception to another.

Reason as a calm, reflective passion. Certain of our passions are *mistakenly* taken to be "determinations of reason, and are suppos'd to proceed from the same faculty, with that, which judges of truth and falshood" (p. 417). It is in this sense that there could be combat between reason (that is, a calm passion, really) and passion. Although Hume first suggests that this use of *reason* is the result of confusion on the part of philosophers, he appears later to sanction the usage by writing: "By *reason* we mean affections of the very same kind with the former [passions, that is]; but such as operate more calmly, and cause no disorder in the temper. . ." (p. 437).

My principle concern is the relationship of sentiment to reason in any of the first five of the senses noted.

will, as a consequence, Hume claims, feel the emotion or passion of desire and attempt to obtain that object. This same emotion will also give us a favorable disposition toward setting in motion that chain of causes and effects which will enable us to obtain the object. We find, then, that there is some part to be played by the reason or understanding, but it is not the leading part. Our desire or impulse arises from the prospect of pleasure, and extends itself, as it were, to the causal relations bearing on the object of that desire. It is the role of reason to point out the causes and effects of the object, but the desire for the object, and the subsequent impulse to set in motion the chain of causes which will result in attainment of the object, arise entirely from the prospect of pleasure, not from reason. As Hume says "The impulse arises not from reason, but is only directed by it." The evidence that is offered to confirm this limitation on reason is the fact that knowledge of objects, causes, and effects—of those connections which are discovered by reason—can be totally indifferent to us. We may know of an object, know perfectly well how to obtain it, and know we are perfectly capable of attaining it. But if this object does not excite us, does not seem to us something which would be pleasurable, these insights of the understanding will go for naught, and we shall not be influenced to take one step toward the attainment of it.

Once it has been concluded that reason alone cannot be the cause of an action, or influence the will to act, it follows as a necessary consequence, Hume says, that reason alone is "incapable of preventing volition, or of disputing the preference with any passion or emotion." Reason could prevent volition only by giving a contrary impulse, but if it can give a contrary impulse, nothing could prevent it from giving an original one; this we have seen it cannot do. So, as reason has no original influence of the sort required, it is clear that it cannot oppose the passions, which do have the efficacy required. If there is a principle which opposes the passions, it cannot be reason, and could be called reason only improperly; hence the fallaciousness of talk about the "combat of passion and of reason" has been shown. It has been granted that reason does affect the operation of the will, but only after a directing impulse of passion; reason serves the will only at the behest of the passions, and then only to direct impulses that have already been given. In this regard, reason is merely a slave of the passions, a lackey whose function is to map a course to the ends set by the passions.

Having stated what he takes to be an "extraordinary" opinion in this attention-getting fashion,[5] Hume suggests that it will not be improper to offer further confirmations of it. A passion, he tells us, is an original existence, not a copy of another thing. It is itself a real thing, an object, in effect, and as such it cannot contradict any truth or conclusion of reason, for such contradictions involve the disagreement of ideas, or copies of real existences. Furthermore, a thing can be contrary to reason only if it has a "reference" or relation to reason, a qualification met only by judgments of the understanding. This means that passions can be contrary to reason or "call'd unreasonable" in only two senses: when they are based on the supposition that given objects exist, while in fact these objects do not exist; or when the impulse of a passion is being followed, although we have chosen means that are insufficient to obtain the end sought. If one of these conditions is met, we can say that the passion is unreasonable, although to speak most correctly, it is the judgment, not the passion, which is unreasonable.[6]

Whatever may be said, the consequences are apparent. A passion is unreasonable only when it is founded on a false judgment, and hence, " 'tis impossible, that reason and passion can ever

[5] The fact that Hume supposes his opinion "extraordinary" undercuts, I should think, Kemp Smith's claim that it was just this opinion that was borrowed from Hutcheson. That is, Hutcheson, the most important moralist in Scotland, and one of the two or three best-known among living moralists in Britain, allegedly bequeathed this view to Hume. Why then does Hume think it extraordinary? In fact, Hutcheson does not say that reason is the slave of the passions, not even hyperbolically.

[6] The judgment is unreasonable because it is false or, that is, because it asserts between ideas or between an idea and an object a relationship which is not in fact the case. Hume's views remind one of Hutcheson's suggestion that "bad conduct is not owing to any Irregularity in the moral Sense, but to a wrong Judgment or Opinion." *British Moralists*, 1: 122.

oppose each other, or dispute for the government of the will and actions. The moment we perceive the falshood of any supposition, or the insufficiency of any means our passions yield to our reason without any opposition."

I may have the desire of a certain object, believing it pleasant. Another person may inform me that the object is quite other than I believe it to be. My desire for the object ceases. In short, although the reason is a lackey if there is a passion or impulse to be served, the passions, too, have their limitations, and yield completely to new insights of reason. Hume's confirmation—or clarification—shows that reason is not opposed by the passions because an appropriate judgment of reason can quite extinguish a passion. Thus, while it is correct to say that reason in his view must do the bidding of the passions, it is equally true that the servitude of reason is limited, and limited by its own insights. Whatever reason finds impossible or inappropriate ceases to be desired and required by its master, the passions.

III.   Both Hume's discussions of the foundation of morals and his overall moral theory confirm this reading of his account of the relationship of reason and sentiment. Thus, while it is true that Hume gives to sentiment the central role in founding morals, it is also true that he gives to reason an essential part in morals. Not even in morals does Hume thoroughly subordinate reason to sentiment in any but the highly restricted sense of subordination outlined in *Treatise* II, 3, 3: If I do not have a desire for an object, reason cannot cause in the will an impulse toward—desire for— that object. And if I do have a desire, reason cannot in any direct sense eliminate that desire by blocking the impulse of the will. But reason can and does modify our desires, it can and does modify our sentiments, and it plays sometimes a crucial role in the formation of our moral sentiments.

It is in the opening sections of book III of the *Treatise* that Hume first outlines his position in morals. In III, 1, 1 ("Moral Distinctions not deriv'd from Reason")[7] he begins by reminding

---

[7] Pp. 455-470.

us that there are present to the mind only impressions or ideas, and then he goes on to suggest that a decision as to which of these enables us to distinguish between virtue or vice will also enable us to settle on the source of our moral distinctions. There are those—he is referring to the rationalists, Clarke, Wollaston, Balguy—who maintain that virtue consists in a conformity to reason involving "eternal fitnesses and unfitnesses of things" and "immutable measures of right and wrong" which impose an obligation. These ethicists agree in their opinion that "morality, like truth, is discern'd merely by ideas, and their juxta-position and comparison." To test their systems, Hume says, we need only discover "whether it be possible, from reason alone, to distinguish betwixt moral good and evil, or whether there must concur some other principles to enable us to make that distinction." In view of the fact that he has titled the following section "Moral distinctions deriv'd from a moral sense," there is no need to wonder about Hume's conclusion, although what he has said in reaching it bears directly on the issues raised here.

We are told first that any attempt to inculcate morality would be quite pointless if mankind had not a prior, natural inclination to be influenced by it; otherwise, a legion of moral teachers and a legion of moral rules would never make us moral or even concern us. "Philosophy," Hume says, "is commonly divided into *speculative* and *practical*; and as morality is always comprehended under the latter division, 'tis supposed to influence our passions and actions, and to go beyond the calm and indolent judgments of the understanding." This view is confirmed by our common experience, which shows that we are "often govern'd" by moral considerations. If we then recall that reason has already been proven to be inert or impotent, we can see that it can have "no influence on our passions and actions," and justly conclude that morality is not founded on reason.[8] We are also reminded that

[8] Hume is adamant on this point: "An active principle can never be founded on an inactive; and if reason be inactive in itself, it must remain so in all its shapes and appearances, whether it exerts itself in natural or moral subjects, whether it considers the powers of external bodies, or the actions of rational beings." And again, "Reason is wholly inactive, and can never be the source of so active a principle as conscience, or a sense of morals." *Treatise*, pp. 457-458.

"reason is the discovery of truth or falshood," and that these are a matter of the agreement or disagreement of "*real* relations of ideas, or . . . *real* existence and matter of fact," from which it appears to follow that reason cannot operate on our passions, volitions, and actions, for these are "original facts and realities, compleat in themselves, and implying no reference to other passions, volitions, and actions." In other words, our passions, volitions, and actions do not agree or disagree relative to one another, hence cannot be true or false, and hence cannot be the object of reason. This argument, Hume claims, has the advantage of showing directly that actions do not become meritorious by conformity to reason, while establishing the same conclusion indirectly, for, as reason cannot contradict or agree with an action, and thus cannot prevent or motivate that action; and, as moral good or evil *do* have that influence, it again follows that reason is not the source of moral good or evil: Moral good or evil are active principles and must have their source in a like, active principle.

Next, repeating substantial parts of the argument found in *Treatise* II, 3, 3, Hume points out that "reason . . . can have an influence on our conduct" in either of two ways. It can excite a passion by informing us that there exists an object proper to the passion, or it can discover a relation of causes and effects which would result in the fulfillment of a given passion. Judgments of this sort can be seen to "accompany our actions" and can in some manner be said to "produce" them. These judgments can also be seen to be frequently mistaken, and it may seem that our actions can be said to be unreasonable. But, while granting that actions in such instances may be termed *unreasonable*, Hume notes that such "false" actions are not necessarily immoral, and they are indeed commonly taken to be mere mistakes of *fact* which are not supposed blameworthy. He then concludes that as an *error* of reason is not alone the source of immorality, neither is reason alone the source.

Hume makes two further points before he concludes this part of his discussion. First, agreement and disagreement do not admit of degrees, which seems to imply that were judgments of truth a source of morality, all crimes would be equal. The theft of an apple would equal the theft of a kingdom, a consequence which so violates our moral experience that Hume does not bother to say that it is absurd. Second, if the rationalist should say that mistakes of *fact* are not culpable, but that mistakes of *right* are, then we must inform him that he has begged the question. A mistake of right is certainly not the source of immorality, for its rightness has obviously been judged by some standard quite independent of the act of reason or judgment. "Thus upon the whole," he concludes, " 'tis impossible, that the distinction betwixt moral good and evil, can be made by reason; since that distinction has an influence upon our actions, of which reason alone is incapable."

The second part of section 1 is taken up with showing that the rationalists' notion of the "eternal immutable fitnesses and unfitnesses of things cannot be defended by sound philosophy." It is also informative of the nature and status of reason. If it is said, Hume argues, that the understanding alone can fix moral boundaries, then it follows that moral character "must lie" in certain demonstrable relations of objects, or it "must be a matter of fact, which is discovered by our reasoning," for comparison of ideas and discovery of facts are the only operations of the understanding. He then proceeds to show that neither of these alternatives can account for our specifically moral experience. If, for example, it is maintained that morality lies in specifiable and demonstrably certain relations, we find that we have no consistent means of limiting our moral categories to animate and rational creatures. There are four demonstrable relations—resemblance, contrariety, degrees in quality, proportions in quantity and number—which are as applicable to the inanimate and irrational as to the rational, to matter as well as mind. If virtue and vice are discovered by demonstrative reason, these "moral qualities, therefore, must be relations." And thus, according to the rationalist, when we cast blame on any action, this must be because our reason has discovered "certain relations, wherein the essence of vice consists." In that case, however, we should find ourselves reacting to the "parricide or ingratitude" of the sapling which

104

eventually overtops its parent in the same *moral* fashion in which we respond to the gross ingratitude of human parricide. The relations are the same; the same "essence of vice" is present. We should count the sapling vicious; we do not. It is clear then that the essence of virtue and vice are not to be found in the demonstrable relations of objects of which we have knowledge.

If the rationalist should reply that there is some other demonstrable relation on which morality is founded, we must ask him to produce an example of that relation. Until he does, we can only point out that this relation, whatever it is, must fulfill two conditions if the difficulties of his system are to be cleared away. First, a relation must be found which can hold between the mind and external objects, but not between perceptions only or external objects only. Our experience shows that moral qualities attach only to certain actions of the mind in relation to external objects. A relation uniquely holding between these terms must be specified, then; otherwise, it will be found to hold between thoughts or inanimate beings, and we would also find our very thoughts or such beings morally culpable, but this latter we do not do.

If finding this unique relation is not difficult enough, the second condition proves impossible to fulfill. Those who claim there is an abstract rational difference between virtue and vice suppose that there are eternal and immutable relations which are regarded in the same way by every rational creature. Furthermore, they suppose that these relations have, necessarily, the same effects on each creature; they are as influential in "directing the will of the deity" as they are in guiding the rational and virtuous among men. But to show that these "measures of right and wrong" are eternal and obligatory on every rational mind, one must show not only the relations on which they are founded, but also the connection which holds between the relation(s) and the will, as well as that this is a necessary connection which will influence a possibly infinite variety of rational minds. It is clear, of course, that connections of cause and effect are not known in this fashion. They are known only through experience. All that we know in this case is that there is a set of beings who seem generally similar, but our knowledge extends no further. Our knowledge of the deity, to take only the most obvious example, comes nowhere near what is required.[9]

In addition, even if one were to grant that moral distinctions could be perceived by reason, it would not follow that they have their source in reason. Why, Hume asks, do we find that incest among humans is criminal, but that "the very same action, and the same relations in animals have not the smallest moral turpitude and deformity?" The rationalist replies by saying that this action is not morally wrong for animals because they are not endowed with "reason sufficient to discover its turpitude," but criminal for man because he is sufficiently endowed with reason. This, Hume says, is to argue in a circle. In order for reason to "perceive this turpitude, the turpitude must exist; and consequently is independent of the decisions of our reason, and is their object more properly than their effect." But this means that any animal with sense, appetite, and will—or any animal, Hume says—must, contrary to all our moral experience or sensibility, "be susceptible of all the same virtues and vices, for which we ascribe praise and blame to human creatures." The only difference between humans and animals is the "superior reason" that enables us to discover vice or virtue and affix blame or praise. Although animals may lack this reason, their appetites, wills, and actions make, nonetheless, relations that conform or fail to conform to those that are said to constitute morality. Animals, we might say, are unfortunate in their lack of reason, for this "may hinder them from perceiving the duties and obligations of morality," but

---

[9] The rationalist appears to come up against the same insurmountable barriers that confront those who look for evidence that the same cause will have always the same effect, or that create the problem of induction. Demonstrative reason can produce no evidence that any given relation is effective in directing the will of all rational creatures; it is especially weak with respect to God's will. Probable reason is informative about experience, but it cannot extend itself beyond experience when it is just such an extension that is needed. Another of Hume's remarks to Hutcheson is apropos: "If Morality were determind by Reason, that is the same to all rational Beings: But nothing but Experience can assure us, that the Sentiments are the same. What Experience have we with regard to superior Beings? How can we ascribe to them any Sentiments at all? They have implanted those Sentiments in us for the Conduct of Life like our bodily Sensations, which they possess not themselves." Letter of March 16, 1740, *Letters*, 1: 40.

these duties would, on the rationalist account, exist, and animals would be culpable.[10]

Hume concludes this portion of his argument by noting that although it has been granted for the sake of argument that reason could perceive moral distinctions, this concession does not make it easier for the rationalist to show that reason is the source of moral distinctions. On the contrary, the moral distinctions that are said to be perceived by reason have an existence independent of reason. The discovery of vice or virtue by reason presupposes, Hume claims, "a separate being in these moral distinctions" or that the distinctions "must antecedently exist, in order to their being perceiv'd." But the rationalist cannot consistently explain how reason can bring this about. We can perhaps imagine how reason could discover moral distinctions, but not how it could be their source. At best, as Hume tersely says, "Reason must find them, and can never produce them."

Hume turns immediately to what he calls the second part of his argument. In this argument, he intends to show the obvious inadequacy of supposing that morality consists "in any *matter of fact*, which can be discover'd by the understanding," or to show that "morality is not an object of reason" even if reason is taken to include what he elsewhere calls perception. The argument, a familiar one, is also in a familiar Humean form, the challenge: There is no difficulty in showing that "vice and virtue are not matters of fact, whose existence we can infer by reason."[11] All

---

[10] Throughout this discussion Hume appears to ascribe to the principle that whatever is (in fact) perceived must exist and must exist independently of the act of perception. In saying that the turpitude must exist if it is to be perceived he appears to reverse, in effect, Berkeley's view that *esse est percipere*, supposing instead that *percipere est esse*. This will help to explain why in the following section I am concerned about Hume's moral ontology. He is at pains to explain how we perceive moral distinctions by means of the moral sentiments. Given this fact and his apparent commitment to the view that whatever is perceived exists, it is more than reasonable to consider the mode of existence of the perceived distinctions.

[11] Hume's use of *infer* here appears to be a harmless slip. He is clearly speaking of noninferential present awareness of the sort described at *Treatise* I, 3, 2, and there termed *perception*. I do take it to be significant, however, that Hume twice stipulates that the matter of fact in question (an instance of vice) is not discoverable by reason or the understanding, thus paving the way for the claim that

one needs to do is examine an action that is agreed to be vicious
(or virtuous). Focus your attention ever so carefully on this action,
Hume says, but you will never in this manner discover

> that matter of fact, or real existence, which you call *vice*.
> In which-ever way you take it, you find only certain passions,
> motives, volitions, and thoughts. There is no other matter
> of fact in the case. The vice entirely escapes you, as long as
> you consider the object. You never can find it, till you turn
> your reflexion into your own breast, and find a sentiment of
> disapprobation, which arises in you, towards this action.
> Here is a matter of fact; but 'tis the object of feeling, not of
> reason.

IV. Given Hume's initial assumptions, it follows that if the
source of moral distinctions is not to be found in ideas and their
relations, the province of reason, then this source must be in our
impressions, and, although Hume does not explicitly say so at
this juncture of his argument, in impressions of reflection. As he
puts it in III, 1, 2, "Decisions concerning moral rectitude and
depravity are evidently perceptions; and as all perceptions are
either impressions or ideas, the exclusion of the one is a convincing argument for the other." It should be noted, however,
that each time that Hume reaches a conclusion which is favorable
to his view that moral distinctions are not derived from or discovered by reason, he restrains himself and reports that it is not
by *reason alone* that we recognize these distinctions. Virtue and

---

there is a matter of fact discoverable in another way. In whichever way we view
the action by reason or the understanding, we "find only certain passions, motives,
volitions and thoughts," he says. He also adds that "there is no other matter of
fact in the case," by which he can only mean that "there is no other matter of
fact *that can be perceived in this manner.*" He clearly thinks there is one other
matter of fact which can be perceived by reflection or by looking "into your own
breast," a matter of fact which is the "object of feeling, not of reason." Initially,
of course, Hume suggests that this matter of fact is merely a sentiment in the
observer. The question raised by the discussion that follows is whether or not
this sentiment is the only fact discovered by the observation or examination of
actions or characters. It is my contention that it is not, or that on the more
complete view of book III of the *Treatise* virtue and vice are claimed to be more
than merely sentiments.

vice, he says in section 2, "are not discoverable merely by reason, or the comparison of ideas," and similar remarks were noted in section 1. Admittedly, doubts could be raised about these remarks. Perhaps they have only rhetorical force. On the other hand, they may result from Hume's concern to indicate that reason, although not the source of moral distinctions, has, nonetheless, an important role to play in morality. The latter is the correct assessment. According to Hume, reason does not make moral experience possible in the same way that sentiment does, but it does, nonetheless, make moral experience possible, for it is reason that enables us to constitute, recognize, and modify our moral feelings.[12]

A not untypical Humean hyperbole has apparently prevented numerous readers from recognizing this fact, as well as a second of equal significance: Hume is not an affective subjectivist in morals. He does not claim that morality is merely sentiment, feeling, approbation, or disapprobation. On the contrary, Hume is a moral realist who believes that virtue and vice have objective status, and a realist for whom both sentiment and reason have significant epistemological roles to play.

[12] In anticipation of many of my own conclusions found below, it may be useful to cite the parallel conclusions of a discussion of Hume's aesthetic principles, namely, those of Peter Jones in his "Cause, Reason, and Objectivity in Hume's Aesthetics" (Re-evaluation, pp. 323-342). For Hume, writes Jones, "reasoned discussion can focus . . . on the putative causes of a man's sentiments, and by altering his perception set off a new causal chain, as a result of which he experiences different sentiments. In this way perceptual judgments may be said to be mediate causes of our sentiments (Treatise, p. 462), in contrast to perceptions themselves, which are immediate causes. Hume regards the discussion of beauty as thoroughly objective; that is, beautiful objects have properties, which may be difficult to perceive or describe, but whose characterisation can be achieved within conventions necessary for communication. Sometimes the conditions for determining such characteristics are complex, and sometimes they are satisfied by, and known to, only a minority in a given community. It should be clear, already, why Hume's main arguments in aesthetics occur in contexts where man is considered as a social being, for only there is reasoning requisite and indeed possible. And we shall soon see, also, why he holds that one can neither make a judgment of beauty without some concept of the object to which beauty is ascribed, nor justify such a judgment without appeal to the type of beauty in question" (p. 324). Hume's tendency to suppose that natural beauty and moral beauty are each illustrative of the other gives added import to the unusual level of agreement which marks the conclusions which Jones and I have reached independently.

The hyperbole that has bedazzled readers and hidden Hume's moral realism is found near the end of *Treatise* III, 1, 1. A review of our moral experience reveals to us, he says, that whenever "you pronounce any action or character to be vicious, you mean nothing, but that from the constitution of your nature you have a feeling or sentiment of blame from the contemplation of it. Vice and virtue, therefore, may be compar'd to sounds, colours, heat and cold, which, according to modern philosophy, are not qualities in objects, but perceptions in the mind. . . . "[13]

One can see that, taken by itself, this remark could lead one to think that "Hume's theory conflicts with ordinary views" or "reverses the view of Common-sense," which is said to be that certain actions or things "would be good and others would be bad whether the contemplation of them did or did not call forth emotions of approval in all or most men *because* they are good and *because* men are so constituted as to feel this kind of emotion towards what they believe to be good. . . . On Hume's contrary view if men did not feel these emotions nothing would *be* good or bad. . . . "[14]

[13] *Treatise*, p. 469. In the letter of March 16, 1740, cited in n. 9, Hume consults Hutcheson on a "Point of Prudence. I have concluded a Reasoning with these two Sentences," he writes, and he then cites with "only two trifling alterations" (according to Greig) the passage beginning "When you pronounce . . ." and ending, ". . . little or no influence on practice." He then goes on: "Is not this laid a little too strong? I desire your Opinion of it, tho I cannot entirely promise to conform myself to it. I wish from my Heart, I coud avoid concluding, that since Morality, according to your Opinion as well as mine, is determin'd merely by Sentiment, it regards only human Nature & human Life." If we are to take Hume's remark literally (his "I have *concluded* a Reasoning") then it would appear that the final sentence of the paragraph in the *Treatise* (cited just below) was a later addition, and very likely one intended to soften what he feared was an overstatement.

[14] C. D. Broad, *Five Types of Ethical Theory* (London: Routledge and Kegan Paul, 1962), pp. x, 85-86. Others who have by this passage been led to offer similarly subjectivistic readings of Hume include Geoffrey Hunter, "Hume on Is and Ought," *Philosophy* 37 (1962): 151-152; Philippa Foot, "Hume on Moral Judgement," in *David Hume: A Symposium* (London: Macmillan, 1966), pp. 70-72; Antony Flew, "Hume," in *A Critical History of Western Philosophy*, ed. D. J. O'Connor (London: Macmillan, 1964), p. 271. For a reading of Hume which runs counter to these see Páll S. Árdal, *Passion and Value in Hume's Treatise* (Edinburgh, Edinburgh University Press, 1966). Árdal suggests that too much emphasis has been placed on this passage, and he argues that, for Hume, " 'virtue' refers to a quality of mind or character that causes, in an observer, a feeling of

However, even what Hume says in the balance of this striking paragraph appears to be inconsistent with any purely subjectivistic interpretation of his position. The final sentences of the paragraph suggest that virtue and vice are not simply the sentiments of approbation or disapprobation that he has just claimed them to be, and even that they are not sentiments at all: "And this discovery in morals, like that other in physics, is to be regarded as a considerable advancement of the speculative sciences; tho', like that too, it has little or no influence on practice. Nothing can be more real, or concern us more, than our own sentiments of pleasure and uneasiness; and if these be favourable to virtue, and unfavourable to vice, no more can be requisite to the regulation of our conduct and behaviour."

To summarize, Hume first says that virtue and vice may be compared to colors and sounds, or aspects of experience that modern philosophy holds to be merely perceptions in the mind. This seems equivalent to suggesting that virtue and vice are identical with, respectively, approbation and disapprobation, that they are merely such sentiments. But he then goes on to say that we have a "sentiment of blame from the contemplation" of vice, and that our sentiments can be "unfavourable to vice." In thus suggesting that disapprobation and vice are separable, Hume implies either that they are not identical, although both could yet be sentiments, or that disapprobation and vice are not only not identical, but also that vice itself is not, strictly speaking a sentiment. Whichever of these alternatives is intended, the second suggestion is not consistent with the first: vice and the sentiment of disapprobation are either identical or they are not. The task before us is to determine Hume's considered view on this important issue. I submit that he holds that vice and disapprobation are not identical and that moral qualities are not merely sentiments but, rather, the objective correlates of sentiments.[15]

---

approval in special circumstances" (p. 208). Árdal also discusses this matter in "Another Look at Hume's Account of Moral Evaluation," *Journal of the History of Philosophy* 15 (1977): 405-422.

[15] No rash conclusions should be drawn from this claim about objective correlates. I do not suggest that virtue and vice are objects in the ordinary sense (physical objects), or that they are transcendently existing qualities of some kind.

At the outset of *Treatise* III, 1, 2 ("Moral distinctions deriv'd from a moral sense"), Hume, satisfied that virtue and vice are not discovered by reason alone, remarks that "it must be," therefore, "by means of some impression or sentiment they [virtue and vice] occasion, that we are able to mark the difference betwixt them." He goes on to note that the impression or sentiment "arising from virtue" is agreeable, while that "proceeding from vice" is disagreeable. He then insists that we do not "infer a character to be virtuous because it pleases: But in feeling that it pleases after such a particular manner, we in effect feel that it is virtuous." Thus in three different ways does Hume suggest that virtue or vice are not by any means identical with the sentiments of approbation and disapprobation, but are in fact sufficiently

---

On the contrary, I suggest that for Hume virtue and vice are publicly available aspects of man's world (specifically, particular modifications or qualities of this world), and that they are aspects which serve as the occasion or cause of specific feelings. These feelings in turn make us aware of these objective correlatives and of their particular moral character. The feelings in question are in an obvious sense private: they are affections of the particular person who feels. In another sense they are not private: the feelings of two or more individuals may be of an identical character, not only because they share the same cause, but also because the operation of sympathy insures this kind of uniformity. I have sketched Hume's view of sympathy and its role in producing common sentiments in "Hume's Common Sense Morality," *Canadian Journal of Philosophy* 5 (1975): 523-543. See also n. 50 of this chapter.

It should also be noted that to say that virtue and vice are analogous to heat and cold, color, sound, and so forth is not necessarily to commit oneself to a complete subjectivism regarding these moral qualities. Granted, the doctrine of secondary qualities has it that objects are not themselves hot or colored, and that sensations of temperature or color are affections or modifications of the observer. But the modern philosophers who maintained the doctrine also supposed that these qualities have objective correlates or that they are caused by qualities that are in the objects. Hume, of course, was doubtful of this view, at least insofar as it was a feature of the broader distinction between primary and secondary qualities and included any ontological commitments about the objective correlates of our perceptions of these qualities. But his position in morals appears to be analogous to that of the modern philosopher who maintained that our perceptions of secondary qualities have objective correlates, or are in fact affective responses to publicly available aspects of the world. Indeed, in this regard Hume is not sceptical, for he argues that specific affective responses (approbation, disapprobation) arising in specific circumstances inform us that certain features of the world exist. Furthermore, they inform us of the moral nature of these features. Later (pp. 133-147), I outline the reasons Hume gives for adopting this nonsceptical moral position.

different from these sentiments to be said to be the occasion or cause of them. It is clear, then, that there is something misleading about the suggestion that vice is just the feeling of blame or disapprobation.

Furthermore, if we follow up Hume's reference to "character," we can see that he believes virtue and vice have a basis in aspects of reality that are quite independent of the mind of the person who pronounces actions or characters to be virtuous or vicious. That is, Hume not only suggests that virtue and vice are qualities of actions which give rise to certain psychological states in those who observe these actions, but he also suggests that these qualities have in turn an ontological foundation in those qualities of mind found in the moral agents whose actions are observed. A few months before the publication of book III of the *Treatise*, Hume wrote to Francis Hutcheson: "Actions are not virtuous nor vicious; but only so far as they are proofs of certain Qualitys or durable Principles in the Mind. This is a Point I shou'd have establish'd more expressly than I have done."[16] The self-criticism may be apt, but Hume did express precisely the same view in the *Treatise*, where he says in at least a half-dozen different ways that *virtuous* and *vicious* are terms that refer to actions insofar as those actions reflect or proceed from the qualities or character of moral agents. "The approbation of moral qualities," he says in III, 3, 1, "proceeds entirely from a moral taste, and from certain sentiments of pleasure and disgust, which arise upon the contemplation and view of particular qualities or characters," while earlier in the same section he claims that "if any *action* be either virtuous or vicious, 'tis only as a sign of some quality or character."[17]

Hume's account of the indirect passions lends further support to the claim that he thought virtue and vice had objective status or had existence independent of the minds of observers. The four indirect passions—pride and humility, esteem and hatred—have always as their objects, he says, a person who possesses enduringly certain qualities which cause us, by means of a double set of

[16] Hume to Hutcheson, September 17, 1739, in *Letters*, 1: 34.
[17] *Treatise*, pp. 581, 575.

relations of impressions and ideas, to feel pride or shame, esteem or hatred. We feel these passions, but we do so only when there exists a specifiable state of affairs of which we are conscious observers. Passions are indeed psychological states, but they are not, so to speak, loose states of mind; they are tied to, or dependent upon, certain states of affairs whose existence is independent of and separate from the passions themselves.

In other words, our passions are found to be dependent upon features of the world we experience, upon, namely, certain enduring qualities of persons. Here, then, is precisely the relationship (between the qualities of persons and my psychological states) that is used to account for our feelings of approbation and disapprobation, or the moral sentiments. In both cases, it is a particular state of affairs, one which involves another person and the perceived qualities of that person, that gives rise to particular feelings.[18]

It is, however, somewhat misleading to speak as I have of "both cases," for Hume partially fuses the two. Those qualities of mind (but not other qualities) that give rise to pride or esteem are precisely the same qualities of mind which we denominate *virtuous*, while, *mutatis mutandis*, the same is true of *vice*. According to Hume,

> since every quality in ourselves or others, which gives pleasure, always causes pride or love; as every one, that produces uneasiness, excites humility or hatred: It follows, that these two particulars are to be consider'd as equivalent, with regard to our mental qualities, *virtue* and the power of producing love or pride, *vice* and the power of producing humility or hatred. In every case, therefore, we must judge of the one by the other; and may pronounce any *quality* of the mind virtuous, which causes love or pride; and any one vicious, which causes hatred or humility.[19]

[18] Hume's discussion of the four indirect passions comprises the larger part of book 2 of the *Treatise*. A detailed summary of his view can be found in Ardal, *Passion and Value*, pp. 17-40, while a helpful account is incorporated into chap. 5 ("The Passions") of Terence Penelhum, *Hume* (London: Macmillan, 1975).

[19] *Treatise*, p. 575. I say "partially fuses" because although it is true that every

Thus, for example, if we feel esteem or love for another because of some quality of his mind, it follows that he has indeed virtuous qualities, for such esteem is a corollary of his virtue. It is only on condition of a certain objective state of affairs (his being virtuous) that the passion of esteem is produced. But if on specific occasions the indirect passions are in this way corollaries of moral qualities; and if the indirect passions are dependent upon and reflect objective states of affairs, as Hume claims they do; then it follows that the virtues corollate with these passions also depend upon and reflect these same objective states of affairs.[20] And hence it also follows that Hume takes *virtue* and *vice* to have reference

quality of mind that gives rise to pride or esteem is denominated virtuous, not everything that gives rise to these indirect passions is so denominated. A beautiful house gives rise to pride in its owner, and esteem of its owner in those who view it, but not even Hume, whose catalog of virtues is classical rather than Christian, would say the owner of the house is *virtuous* because he owns it. "Our country, family, children, relations, riches, houses, gardens, horses, dogs, cloaths; any of these may become a cause either of pride or of humility," he says, after first indicating that these are not, as is obvious, qualities of mind (*Treatise*, p. 279). This feature of his theory is one reason that I maintain (contra Árdal, if I have understood him correctly) that the indirect passions of pride, humility, love and hatred (esteem and disesteem) are no more than signs of virtue and vice in the objects (persons) of these passions and that the moral sentiments are calm, reflective passions, not indirect passions of any form. On Hume's view, one will experience an indirect passion whenever a moral sentiment is experienced, but one may experience an indirect passion without at the same time experiencing a moral sentiment. *Treatise*, p. 473, for example, indicates that the indirect passions and the moral sentiments are distinct. Hume says that virtue and vice "give rise to one of these four [indirect] passions," and that they do so, when presented to us, by producing "a separate sensation [pleasure or uneasiness, or approbation, disapprobation] *related to the sensation of the passion.*" (Italics added.) Árdal appears not to have taken this claim into account when he argues that the moral sentiments are indirect passions, or even that the two are identical. However, if the moral sentiments and the indirect passions are separate sensations it would seem that the former must for Hume be calm, reflective passions. Important to this issue and my understanding of it are Thomas K. Hearn, "Árdal on the Moral Sentiments in Hume's *Treatise*," *Philosophy* 48 (1973): 288-292; and Louis E. Loeb, "Hume's Moral Sentiments and the Structure of the *Treatise*," *Journal of the History of Philosophy* 15 (1977): 395-403.

[20] In "Of the Standard of Taste," Hume remarks that "particular forms or qualities, from the original structure of the internal fabric [of the object], are calculated to please, and others to displease; and if they fail of their effect in any particular instance, it is from some apparent defect or imperfection in the organ" (*Works*, 3: 268, 271).

to items beyond the psychological states of those who utter them. *Virtue* and *vice* also refer to the real qualities of agents and their actions.[21]

[21] Hume's ontology of morals is elusive. He clearly does not believe that virtue and vice are qualities of actions or events per se. Moral qualities entirely escape us so long as we consider the action, he says, and he adds elsewhere that actions are praised only "as signs or indications of certain principles in the mind and temper" (*Treatise*, pp. 468, 477). Consistent with this position he argues that it is virtuous motives or characters that make actions virtuous, hence clearly indicating that the ontological locus of moral qualities is (at least partially) motives or characters. But he denies that *a desire to be virtuous* produces a virtuous act: *"No action can be virtuous, or morally good, unless there be in human nature some motive to produce it, distinct from the sense of its morality"* (*Treatise*, p. 479). Virtuous acts stem not from a desire to be virtuous, but from natural affections, both generous and selfish. The question is, what makes these motives, of such different sorts, *virtuous*—what transforms them from *natural* entities into *moral* entities? Hume's suggestion that this is done by the operation of sympathy merely puts off the ontological question by a further description of the means of transformation; it does not tell us how moral qualities can be genuinely different from the materials out of which they apparently arise, or how they can have a unique ontological status.

A helpful explication of Hume's position, but one that can only be suggested here, might result from recasting his account along the lines of a later, emergenticist position. Emergenticists attempt, generally speaking, to account for certain ontological developments (life, mind, society, for example) in a nonreductivist fashion, or to explain how new features of existence can arise and yet not be mere epiphenomena of the previously existing things which gave rise to them. They attempt to show that there are supervening developments that introduce genuine novelty into the world, or that qualities emerge that are, as T. A. Goudge explains,

"not simply a rearrangement of pre-existing elements, although such rearrangements may be one of [the] determining conditions" of the emergent;

not simply quantitatively, but qualitatively, *unlike* anything that existed before;

not predictable either on the basis of the actual knowledge that existed prior to emergence, or "even on the basis of ideally complete knowledge of the state of the cosmos" prior to the emergence of the characteristic in question (*Encyclopedia of Philosophy*, s.v. "Emergent Evolution").

Of course, virtue and vice are on Hume's account qualities that repeatedly emerge (to retain but perhaps distort the model) from natural or nonmoral states of affairs. But in other ways, his account appears to fit the model, for he suggests that, an appropriate set of conditions being met (two or more human beings, as presently constituted, and with natural affections and intentions, for example), moral qualities will arise that are unique and discontinuous in the sense that they are not merely epiphenomena which can be reductively accounted for by these conditions. In turn, these moral qualities give rise to particular feelings (approbation and disapprobation) which are not only causally related to these qualities

We come to a conclusion with much the same import if we follow Hume's discussion of the peculiar nature of our moral sentiments. Putting in a more positive form his remark that we do not conclude that a character is virtuous because it pleases, he emphasizes that moral pleasure and pain are *"particular* pains

and *themselves unique,* but also, for just that reason, able to function as informative signs of the qualities giving rise to them.

Hume's language gives some credence to this suggestion: "Now virtue and vice," he writes, *"are attended with these circumstances,"* namely, that they both bear a relation to the objects of the four indirect passions, and produce a "separate sensation related to" the sensations of these passions (*Treatise,* p. 473, italics added). Or, more clearly suggestive: "Consequently, we may infer, that the crime of ingratitude is not any particular individual *fact;* but arises from a complication of circumstances, which, being presented to the spectator, excites the *sentiment* of blame, by the particular structure and fabric of his mind" (*Second Enquiry,* pp. 287-288; see also p. 292). And again, "Now, it is evident, that this [moral or aesthetic] sentiment must depend upon the particular fabric or structure of the mind, which enables such particlar forms to operate in such a particular manner, and produces a sympathy or conformity between the mind and its objects. Vary the structure of the mind or inward organs, the sentiment no longer follows, though the form remains the same. The sentiment being different from the object, and arising from its operations upon the organs of the mind, an alteration upon the latter must vary the effect, nor can the same object, presented to a mind totally different, produce the same sentiment" (*Works,* 3: 218). Jones, it seems to me, is wrestling with this same elusive ontology when he writes, "Judgment requires the perception and delineation of the causes of the calm passion, and the causes are objective properties internal to the [aesthetic] work itself, but discernible only from certain viewpoints. A man of taste must have the internal sentiment, or at least *an* internal sentiment, of course, since this is the effect whose cause he seeks; his judgments are *objective triadic relational judgments—* 'triadic' because they depend on the work, the critic, and the viewpoint" (*Reevaluation,* p. 336).

The significance of this speculation would be apparent if one were able to show that it is because Hume lacked any ontological model or conception akin to that of the emergenticists that he misleads his readers by remarks such as that at *Treatise,* p. 469 ("When you pronounce any action or character to be vicious, you mean nothing, but that . . . you have a feeling or sentiment of blame from the contemplation of it"). That is, if one were able to show that, lacking this model, he was left to refer to the emergent qualities (virtue, vice) as "sentiments," or thus to confuse the unique sentiments that arise (he clearly believes) in response to the moral realities that emerge from those "circumstances" or "complications" to which he refers, with the emergent realities themselves. Virtue and vice arise under complex circumstances, according to Hume, but he did not develop the complex ontological terminology to describe this matter accurately and unambiguously.

117

« COMMON-SENSE MORAL THEORY »

or pleasures," so that to "have the sense of virtue, is nothing but to *feel* a satisfaction of a particular kind from the contemplation of a character." There are many different pleasures which arise from different sensations; these can be easily distinguished—for example, a good wine pleases one way, good music another.[22] In the same way, we are quite capable of distinguishing the pleasure which arises from a good action or character from that which arises from inanimate objects. Nor is every sentiment of pleasure which arises from action or character of that peculiar sort which leads to moral approbation, for there are at least three distinguishing features of moral pleasure and pain.

1. Moral pleasure and pain arise only from signs of mental qualities or character, and hence our moral sentiments are always accompanied by one of the four indirect passions that have already been mentioned. As Hume puts it, isolated actions, or those which do not follow from any "durable principles of mind," are "never consider'd in morality."[23] It is only if an action is the offspring of some relatively stable quality of mind (motives are explicitly mentioned) that one of these four passions is produced, and further, only if one of these passions has been produced can we say that we have a moral feeling. Hence it is clear once more that a moral feeling is always the corollary of some enduring quality of the agent's mind, or, alternatively, the quality of the agent's mind is the objective correlate of the moral feeling.

2. It is only characters and actions to which we give a general or disinterested regard that can evoke the kind of sentiment that leads us to say certain actions are morally good or evil. This means, of course, that Hume has built disinterested reaction into his system as a necessary condition of moral evaluation. He is quite willing to grant that we may sometimes confuse a sentiment of interest with a moral sentiment; for example, we may think an enemy is vicious because we have not distinguished between the sentiment resulting from his opposition to us, and that occasioned by his character. But this does not mean we can never distinguish between these sentiments—"a man of temper and

[22] *Treatise*, pp. 471-472.
[23] *Treatise*, p. 575.

118

judgment" can do so—nor does it mean, as the egoists would have us believe, that we take pleasure only in those actions or characters which we conceive to be beneficial to ourselves directly or indirectly.[24] We do, by means of sympathy, take pleasure in the qualities of others which are of no direct or indirect benefit to us; sympathy enables us to go beyond our own interest, to get out of ourselves, as it were, and enables us to feel the only kind of pleasure and pain which has moral significance.

3. As Hume insists later, virtue and vice, and our "judgments" concerning them, are independent of the intensity or degree of pleasure and pain that is felt. Some qualities or characters have a tendency to promote the good of mankind, and for that reason they give us pleasure through the operation of sympathy. This sympathy is said to be variable. The living affect us more than those long dead, for example, and so "it may be thought, that our sentiments of morals must admit of the same variations." However, this is not the case. An ancient Greek does not give us so lively a pleasure as does a close friend, or we may love a servant more than Marcus Brutus, but we do not for that reason think that our friend or servant is more virtuous than those ancients. Rather, we make allowances for time and distance and correct our sentiments insofar as we realize that were Brutus here now he would excite an even livelier sentiment than does the servant. "Such corrections are common with regard to all the senses," says Hume, and they enable us to escape the particularity of present appearances and our present situation, with the consequence that we are able to talk together and to communicate our sentiments to one another. As a result, we discount our

[24] *Treatise*, p. 472. Jones reaches similar conclusions concerning Hume's views in aesthetics. Writing of the essay titled "Of the Standard of Taste," he remarks: "The whole discussion about feeling the *proper* sentiment is designed to establish that only certain sentiments are appropriate to certain objects," and then he goes on to state that Hume is "quite insistent upon the fact that publicly available viewpoints are conditions of objectivity, and publicly ascertainable conventions conditions of discussion and judgment." Earlier he had suggested that "the proper sentiment depends on the proper discernment, and the latter may involve many complex factors" (*Re-evaluation*, pp. 337, 329).

particular location in space and time and we praise and blame as if we had close but impersonal relations with the person judged.[25]

We can say, then, that Hume (in the *Treatise*, at least) is a moral realist in two senses. He holds the view that there are moral distinctions grounded in real existences that are independent of the observer's mind (a metaphysical position). He also holds that these distinctions can be known (an epistemological position). If what we feel is accompanied by one of the indirect passions, produced through our own or others' qualities of mind, and if this feeling is not directed by private interest or the idiosyncrasies of our particular environment, then the character of our feeling serves to reveal the moral character of an objective (publicly available) situation. In fact, Hume is relatively optimistic about moral knowledge. When we succeed in eliminating the purely idiosyncratic elements from our perceptions of actions or characters, thus enabling ourselves to see things without the "perpetual contradictions" that private interest causes, and when others have done the same, then, he says, there is such an interchange of sentiments that we are able to form a "general inalterable standard, by which we may approve or disapprove of characters and manners." It does not follow that we always feel as this standard would suggest, and certainly we do not always act as it suggests. Yet the standard of "general notions" thus created continues to be effective, and it is found to "serve all our purposes in company, in the pulpit, on the theatre, and in the schools."[26]

V.   A second extended discussion of the roles that are taken by

[25] *Treatise*, pp. 580-582. Hume also says, "The case is here the same as in our judgments concerning external bodies. All objects seem to diminish by their distance: But tho' the appearance of objects to our senses be the original standard, by which we judge of them, yet we do not say, that they actually diminish by the distance; but correcting the appearance by reflexion, arrive at a more constant and establish'd judgment concerning them. In like manner, tho' sympathy be much fainter than our concern for ourselves, and a sympathy with persons remote from us much fainter than that with persons near and contiguous; yet we neglect all these differences in our calm judgments concerning the characters of men" (p. 603).

[26] *Treatise*, pp. 602-603.

reason and sentiment in the origin of morality is found in the *Enquiry concerning the Principles of Morals*. The discussion there does not add extensively to what has been said in the *Treatise*, but it serves to clarify and confirm much of what is said in the preceding sections. For that reason, it merits our attention.

Hume opens the second *Enquiry* with some remarks concerning disputes with the disingenuous, and then he goes on to review the two positions taken on the issue of the foundation of morals. There are, he notes, apparently sound arguments on each side, and he summarizes these in an unqualified way that need not be taken as expressing his own position in the debate. Those who support reason argue that the very nature of the moral disputes in which we participate makes clear that moral distinctions are discerned by reason. That is, in these disputes we commonly find references to authorities, analogical reasoning, logical criticism, and inferences and conclusions. But if it is true that there is no disputing of tastes, but there is such rational dispute in morals, morals must be more than a matter of taste. Furthermore, as feeling or sentiment provides no standard of objective reality, while we do make objective judgments in morals, it follows that morals must be a domain of the class which includes physics and geometry, subjects wherein reason (the understanding) discerns distinctions.

In contrast, those who base morals on sentiment argue that reason is unable to draw moral conclusions. The fact that virtue is amiable, vice odious, and that reason cannot deduce such conclusions shows that it cannot be their source. In addition, moral philosophy aims to teach us our duty by depicting the beauty of virtue and the deformity of vice. These pictures in turn create habits of virtue. Surely, it is argued, the operations of reason could never accomplish this end, for reason produces truth, which is indifferent to virtue and satisfies only our speculative curiosity. It is only the feelings that favor virtue, or disfavor vice, or which guarantee that we are not totally indifferent about moral distinctions, and which make morals a practical matter. In brief, the arguments for both views have a certain plausibility, and led Hume to speculate that reason and sentiment will be found to concur in most of the determinations and conclusions of morals, for although it is likely that sentiment pronounces the final sentence regarding the virtue or vice of actions and characters, nonetheless reason, through examination, discovery, and analysis prepares the way for this sentence by providing a proper understanding of the situation in question.[27]

Hume does not go directly about resolving this issue, but waits until his enquiry into the origins of morals has been completed. This enquiry shows that, under appropriate circumstances, a complex interaction of man's universal and comprehensive sentiment of humanity and an individual's usefulness gives rise to the sentiments of praise and blame which mark out moral distinctions. It also shows that personal merit, which is examined in detail in order to reveal this origin, "consists entirely in the usefulness or agreeableness of qualities to the person himself possessed of them, or to others, who have any intercourse with him."[28] If this theory is accepted, Hume says, then we have an answer to the question regarding the extent that moral approval or censure depends on reason or sentiment: As predicted, both are found to have essential roles in these reactions. Reason has an important role if considerations of usefulness are significant, for it is reason that informs us of the "tendency of qualities and actions, and point[s] out their beneficial consequences to society and to their possessor."[29] This in itself may be a difficult task, requiring the creation of laws, debate, and study, but if so, then we see all the more clearly that reasoning is required, and especially so if one is to

[27] *Second Enquiry*, pp. 169-173. At p. 173, Hume, clearly speaking for himself, adds: "it is probable, I say, that this final sentence depends on some internal sense or feeling, which nature has made universal in the whole species. For what else can have an influence of this nature? But in order to pave the way for such a sentiment, and give a proper discernment of its object, it is often necessary, we find, that much reasoning should precede, that nice distinctions be made, just conclusions drawn, distant comparisons formed, complicated relations examined, and general facts fixed and ascertained . . . moral beauty . . . demands the assistance of our intellectual faculties, in order to give it a suitable influence on the human mind."

[28] *Second Enquiry*, p. 278.

[29] *Second Enquiry*, p. 285. The balance of the material discussed and cited in this section is drawn from pp. 285-294, which constitute Appendix I of this work.

achieve the sort of general benefit at which justice aims. But reason alone cannot produce the actual moral approval or censure, for usefulness is merely a "tendency to a certain end." If we remain indifferent to that end, we shall be equally indifferent toward the tendency or means to the end; sentiment is required to motivate us to usefulness. We need, for example, a "feeling for the happiness of mankind" if we are to choose means which promote that end. Reason "instructs us in the several tendencies of actions," but it is the sentiment of humanity that distinguishes those which are beneficial to mankind and motivates us to the end they produce.

It is possible, Hume grants, that this general theory of morals is mistaken. It is nevertheless clear, he insists, that reason cannot be the sole foundation of morals. Five arguments are offered in support of this claim.

1. If one is content to speak generally, the rationalist hypothesis may seem plausible, but if one applies it to particular cases, it is not so much as intelligible. How can reason be said to discover the blame attaching to ingratitude, for example, when all that it detects is goodwill on the part of one man, and ill will on the part of a second? It cannot. Reason deals with matters of fact or relations of ideas. In this case, we cannot by "reason alone" discover a particular fact which is the "crime" of ingratitude, for no such fact is found in the acts or objects.[30] Nor will it do to say that the fact is in the mind of the ungrateful person who feels or is otherwise conscious of it, for then reference is made to a passion or a sentiment which cannot be discovered by reason, but must be felt. If it is said that the crime is not to be found as a fact, but in "certain *moral relations*, discovered by reason," no gain is made, for then we see that the relation of goodwill to ill will is one of mere contrariety. That cannot be the crime, or sufficient justification for calling an action a crime, for the same relation is found when goodwill is returned for ill will. If still another position is taken, namely, that actions are moral insofar

[30] It is here (*Second Enquiry*, pp. 287-288) that Hume says that "we may infer, that the crime of ingratitude is not any particular individual *fact*; but arises from a complication of circumstances, which . . . excites the *sentiment* of blame. . . ."

as they agree or disagree with a rule of right, then we need only ask how this rule is determined, and we shall see the speciousness of the view. For the rationalist must say that the rule is determined by reason, upon consideration of the moral relations of objects and actions, while at the same time maintaining that reason determines moral relations by comparing actions and objects to the rule, an obvious *petitio*.

Mere metaphysics, the rationalists may say of these arguments. Indeed, this is metaphysics, Hume grants, and that alone is enough "to give a strong presumption of falsehood." But metaphysics was introduced by the rationalists, who advanced "an abstruse hypothesis, which can never be made intelligible, nor quadrate with any particular instance or illustration." The objections made return in kind the metaphysics introduced, while at the same time a simpler hypothesis, one based on plain fact and real cases, has been set forth. Anyone who objects that this latter enterprise is also abstruse and metaphysical may conclude that his "turn of mind is not suited to the moral sciences."

2. While it may be true that we must deliberate in morals much as we do in geometry, these deliberations are far from being exactly similar. The mathematician begins with the known or given, and he infers the unknown; in morals we deliberate in order to ascertain all the facts, and only when we are certain that all the facts are known do we "fix any sentence of blame or approbation." This means that the operations of the understanding have been completed before any judgment takes place. Reason considers only relations of ideas and matters of fact. When these considerations are complete, we praise or blame, but not before. From the known circumstances, as presented and considered by the mind, a new impression, an active sentiment of the heart, is felt. When no new relations can follow, no new discoveries (are thought to) remain; when "nothing remains but to feel," then some "sentiment of blame or approbation" arises.

3. A comparison of our reactions to natural beauty may be taken as confirming and clarifying what has just been said. It is true that beauty depends on proportion, relation, and position, features which must be seen and understood, but it does not follow

that the perception of beauty is entirely dependent on the understanding. These relations are first seen, and then an appropriate sentiment is felt. Euclid or any other geometer can explain fully the circle without mentioning its beauty, for this beauty is "only the effect which that figure produces upon the mind."

4. We find between inanimate objects precisely the same relationships that are found between moral agents. A young tree may eventually cause the death of the parent tree, but this arouses no moral reaction—neither a sentiment of disapprobation nor any other censure. If morality consisted entirely in relations, moral reactions would be aroused in such cases.

5. The ultimate ends of human action can never be accounted for by reason, but require appeal to sentiments or affections. "Why do you exercise?" "For my health." "Why do you prefer health?" "Because it is necessary for my profession." "Why do you care about your profession?" "I desire money." "Why?" "It is an instrument of pleasure." Here the questions stop, for an ultimate object has been reached, and a further question, "Why do you desire pleasure?" would be an absurdity. In the same way, virtue is an end, desirable on its own account and giving immediate satisfaction. Thus there must be some sentiment which it arouses, some "internal taste or feeling, or whatever you please to call it, which distinguishes moral good and evil," and which is the ultimate cause of any act which tends to the good, or away from evil.

Thus, says Hume in conclusion, the "distinct boundaries and offices of *reason* and of *taste* are easily ascertained." Reason, although it is no motive to action, discloses truth and falsity, reveals objects as they really stand in nature, directs our impulses to action by showing us how to attain our inclinations, and leads us to discover the unknown from the known; it takes as its standard the immutable nature of things. Taste or sense, on the other hand, is the source of the sentiments of beauty and virtue and their opposites, spreads these internal sentiments onto external objects, motivates us to action as the first impulse of desire and volition, and causes us to feel, from the facts reason lays before us, new sentiments of praise or censure; its standard arises from

the "Supreme Will" from whom we derive that "internal frame
and constitution" with which we have been endowed.[31]

VI.   If we are to take literally Hume's remark that "reason is,
and ought only to be the slave of the passions," then we must
give some thought to the model of slavery he had in mind.
Certainly, it was not the chattel slavery so long practiced in North
America, and which is most familiar to us. Rather, it must have
been the slavery of classical Rome, whereby, we are told, educated
Greeks were required to instruct Roman youths in the arts and
sciences. These Greeks were, no doubt, restricted in their activities and rights, and they were subordinate to their Roman masters. However, given that they educated those very masters and
influenced not only their ideas of what was true and false, but
also their ideas of good and evil, it seems scarcely credible to
claim that their subordination was thorough or complete. Similarly, although Hume says that reason is subordinate to the passions and that it must "serve and obey" these passions, there is
little evidence that the thorough subordination of reason to feeling is the central teaching of his philosophy, and much evidence
to the contrary.

From the review just completed it is clear that for Hume:

1. Reason can affect—change, even extinguish—passions or
   desires.
2. Reason can influence the will indirectly.

---

[31] Hume ends this discussion on a theistic note which manages to ascribe both
reason and sentiment to the Deity, and to capture the important difference of
view which characterizes the rationalists (who emphasize the eternal, immutable
nature of God and truth) and the sentimentalists (who, as did even Hutcheson,
emphasize God's freedom and the contingency of his creation): "The standard of
the one, being founded on the nature of things, is eternal and inflexible, even
by the will of the Supreme Being: the standard of the other, arising from the
internal frame and constitution of animals, is ultimately derived from that Supreme Will, which bestowed on each being its peculiar nature, and arranged the
several classes and orders of existence" (*Second Enquiry*, p. 294). As Hume has
in this way played the one theistic view against the other, perhaps we need not
take too seriously this theism. But since I lack that intuitive grasp of irony so
marked among some of Hume's commentators, I am unable to say with authority
that Hume is here being only ironical.

3. Reason corrects the passions and sentiments.[32]

1. *Reason can affect—even change—our passions and desires.* In saying that reason cannot oppose the passions, Hume seems to have meant that the understanding cannot, in any authoritarian fashion, prevent or modify desires. If I desire D, the understanding cannot affect my desire merely by pronouncing that "D is undesirable," or by pronouncing that "D ought not to be desired," or "You ought not desire D."[33] However, if the understanding is activated by my desire of D, and if it then discovers that no such object exists (D is a unicorn, for example), or that D is in fact dangerous (D is a mushroom for my salad, but likely a toxic one), or D is unattainable (D is the silvery moon brought to my terrace), my desire will be, or at least may be, modified or extinguished as a consequence. What Hume rejects, quite sensibly, is a role for reason akin to the authoritarian stance assumed by the conservative divines he knew so well. The understanding, if it assumes a pulpit-thumping posture, is ineffective, just as ineffective as the clergyman who tells us we must not desire an attractive woman or man whom we do in fact desire. Hume does, however, imply that reason has another kind of role, a role akin to the

[32] These are clearly overlapping claims. Each represents a particular perspective on the alternative to Kemp Smith's naturalistic interpretation I am developing. That is, these claims, if correct, support somewhat repetitiously my contention that Hume conceives of reason as having central and relatively independent functions in both morals and metaphysics. For a more extended analysis of these and related matters, see Rachel Kydd, *Reason and Conduct in Hume's Treatise* (London: Oxford University Press, 1946), chap. 5. Kydd also concludes, to speak generally, that the slavery of reason is severely limited and that the moral sentiments are in significant ways affected by and even dependent upon reason. This welcome propaedeutic to Kemp Smith's interpretation of the role of reason is marred, however, by insufficient attention to book 1 of the *Treatise*, one result of which is the claim that Hume thought that "there is no desire to reason for its own sake" (p. 160). Kydd also supposes that Hume's position requires that the ideal observer be in fact omniscient, a point effectively rebutted by Hearn, "General Rules and Moral Sentiments in Hume's *Treatise*," *Review of Metaphysics* 30 (1976): 57-72; see especially pp. 68-71.

[33] Hume clearly thought that we could by reason alone make such pronouncements. He does not challenge the rationalists on that particular matter. Furthermore, according to his doctrine of philosophical relations, all manner of ideas may be linked together. He maintains, rather, that such pronouncements of reason, made independently of desires or sentiments, are ineffective.

behind-the-scenes activity of the director of a play. The director does not contract for a theater and sell tickets with the notion of haranguing the audience, of ordering them to laugh or cry, feel anger or emotional uplift. Rather, he chooses actors, an interpretation of his play, costumes, a set, props, and lights in order to evoke a certain emotional response. If his choices are skillfully managed he evokes the desired response. Another director, using the same play, may evoke a different response. A third, choosing not to produce a play, produces no response at all.

The role of reason, vis-à-vis the passions, is analogous. By presenting objects (as Hume indicates reason does) in one manner rather than another, as attainable or unattainable, real or unreal, reason in an indirect and nonauthoritarian fashion controls desires. Reason, then, is no abject slave, but, in varying degrees, a clever, instructing slave who, if clever enough, can alter and even reverse the wishes of the master passions.

2. *Reason can influence the will indirectly.* Hume says, it appears, that reason is inert, the will active, and hence that reason does not influence the will. When we look more carefully, we see that he says only that reason does not influence the will directly, or as he puts it, an action may be caused by the reason only "obliquely." Again, Hume seems to be rejecting a conception of reason as an authoritarian guide to action and to be saying that mere pronouncements of reason will never stem an impulse of the will that is brought about by desire. But what the reason can do is influence or modify desires, which in turn determine the impulses of the will. The director of a play may, without explicit, haranguing pronouncements, evoke in his audience a desire to achieve some end (a particular social amelioration, for example), and this desire may in turn provide (accepting Hume's distinction of desire and will) an impulse of the will to act for that end. Just so may the understanding, on Hume's account, indirectly influence our actions.

3. *Reason corrects the passions and sentiments.* Kemp Smith has made much of Hume's debt to Hutcheson, but he seems not to have noticed that Hutcheson argued that the senses in general,

and the moral sense in particular, are corrected by reason. Although he was concerned equally with Hume to reveal the errors of those who maintain that reason is the moral faculty, and that virtue consists in conformity to reason, Hutcheson granted that "we judge of all our Senses by our Reason, and often correct their Reports."[34] He does not exclude the moral sensations or moral sentiments from this correcting process, but points out that just as there are no grounds for supposing extension, figure, color, or taste are merely rational ideas because they are corrected by reason, so there are no grounds for supposing that our moral approbations or feelings are *merely* rational because they are corrected by reason.

Hume explicitly adopts the same position. Speaking of the variability of our moral sentiments because of variations in the proximity of those characters to which we respond, and of the need to make allowances for those variations, he says that "such corrections are common with regard to all the senses."[35] We feel more intensely in response to our servant than we do about Brutus, but we disregard this difference in intensity because "experience" has taught us a "method of correcting our sentiments, or at least, of correcting our language, where the sentiments are more stubborn and inalterable."[36] Since this particular correction (and many others like it) requires a knowledge of the facts of history, as well as of the effects to be expected by being in close proximity to Brutus, it is obvious that it is the understanding or reason which is responsible for the corrections of which Hume speaks.[37]

Similarly, Hume insists that it is only when we consider char-

[34] See chap. 2 of this book, pp. 75-76.
[35] *Treatise*, p. 582. This sentence continues: ". . . and indeed 'twere impossible we cou'd ever make use of language, or communicate our sentiments to one another, did we not correct the momentary appearances of things, and overlook our present situation."
[36] *Treatise*, p. 582. See also n. 25 to this chapter.
[37] As Jones puts it, reasoning or discussion can "bring about a different survey of an object, and thus a different causal sequence, and thus a different sentiment, and thus a different verdict" (*Re-evaluation*, p. 329). It is because Hume represents our moral judgments as resulting from such relatively elaborate procedures that I have suggested that his ideal moral individual is more sophisticated than that of Hutcheson.

acters and actions disinterestedly that we attain moral sentiments, and he indicates that we can achieve such disinterested consideration only by the aid of reason, which enables the man of temper and judgment, or the judicious spectator, to take a general view of matters, one that allows him to distinguish self-interested response from genuinely moral response. It should not be thought that Hume is saying that the feeling which arises upon the view and contemplation of villainy is the same as that which arises when an enemy acts against our interest. The "sentiments are, in themselves, distinct," he says. If we take the opposition of an honorable enemy to be villainous, this is a mistake, but one that can be corrected. If it is corrected, it is because of the operation of the understanding, which enables us to take a less idiosyncratic, more disinterested—more general—view of the situation, through, again, the use of the general rules that the understanding has enabled us to formulate.[38]

Hume repeatedly asserts that it is not by reason alone that we recognize moral distinctions. Taking account of the claims he makes, we discover that he could equally well have said that it is not by sentiment alone that we recognize these distinctions, or that moral sentiments depend upon reason.[39] He argues that reason formulates general rules that serve not only to correct our sentiments, but also enable us to distinguish between sentiments which may seem alike. Thus reason saves us from moral illusions. Presumably, reason plays a similar role in distinguishing sentiments not so nearly alike (utilizing the same general rules), but

[38] *Treatise*, p. 472. Cf. p. 583: "We make allowance for a certain degree of selfishness in men; because we know it to be inseparable from human nature, and inherent in our frame and constitution. By this reflexion we correct those sentiments of blame, which so naturally arise upon any opposition." See also the remarks cited above, nn. 25 and 27. For an important, useful discussion of a number of points that are relevant to my concerns here, see Thomas K. Hearn, "General Rules in Hume's *Treatise*," *Journal of the History of Philosophy* 8 (1970): 405-422; and, especially, "General Rules and the Moral Sentiments in Hume's *Treatise*," previously cited.
[39] Cf. Kydd: "When a desire accords with what is in itself preferable because it is 'founded on a distant view or reflection,' we have a desire which is dependent upon the judgement which results from this reflection" (*Reason and Conduct*, p. 150).

Hume does not emphasize this point. In addition, it is clear that our moral sentiments arise only after the understanding has provided us with a full complement of the facts relevant to the situation. Specific qualities of mind give rise to moral sentiments. That is, if any action is said to be "either virtuous or vicious, 'tis only as a sign of some quality or character."[40] But the understanding or reason is centrally concerned in the discovery of these qualities. They are, as Hume also says, "durable principles of mind," and as such require for their discovery attention to perceptions of sensation, memory, and imagination, and a comparison of various impressions and ideas. Feeling a particular moral sentiment is the subjective correlate which functions as the sign of an objective correlate, some publicly available state of affairs. But the publicly available state of affairs is the cause or occasion of the feeling. Furthermore, according to Hume, it is able to be such a cause or occasion only because the operation of the understanding has made it available to us. Finally, the indirect passions are the effect of the double relation of impressions and ideas that is described at length in book II of the *Treatise*, and could not so much as be experienced without the operation of the understanding. These, however, are necessary concomitants of our moral sentiments and hence, in a restricted sense, indicators that the feeling which accompanies any one of them could be a moral sentiment. At the very least, then, we must consider whether a particular feeling—a putative moral sentiment—is accompanied by an indirect passion, thus setting for ourselves a problem which again must be solved by reason. In short, there are a number of different ways in which our moral sentiments depend on reason.

If this conclusion is at all surprising, it will seem less so if two further points are recalled. First, the theory of moral perception that emerges in Hume's work is in important ways similar to that found in Hutcheson. As has been shown, Hutcheson had argued that all knowledge of things beyond our own states of mind is dependent on *feelings* which serve as signs of these things. Certain

[40] *Treatise*, p. 575. See also pp. 589-590 and 593ff., where the principle of comparison is discussed.

131

bodily motions, he says, are, by a natural law God himself has established, regularly the occasion of certain sensible ideas (color, taste, sound, and so forth) in the mind. These sensible ideas are all accompanied by what Hutcheson calls the "universal concomitant ideas" (duration and number), and some of them are accompanied by "representative concomitant ideas" (extension, figure, and so forth). The sensible ideas are not, Hutcheson grants, representative of external reality, but because they occasion the two kinds of concomitant ideas, which are representative of the external world, it must be said that these nonrepresentative sensible ideas are the signs by which external and objective reality is known. Strictly speaking, sensible ideas are merely modifications of the mind, or affections, but they are, nevertheless, the first and absolutely essential part of a process that ends in knowledge of the external world.

It is not only our knowledge of physical reality, bodies and their attributes, that Hutcheson finds dependent upon purely affective states; so, too, is our knowledge of moral reality. Moral perception, too, is dependent upon nonrepresentative, subjective feelings which function as signs of external reality. There is no separate organ of moral perception, he grants, but once we have by ordinary perception perceived some human action, our moral sense responds with feelings of approbation and disapprobation. It is these feelings that serve as signs, and they do so because they are also accompanied by certain concomitant ideas: duration and number, of course, but also by the moral concomitants that are representative of extramental moral reality. When we experience a certain feeling accompanied by appropriate concomitants (approbation coupled with motive, for example), we form a normative idea (virtue in this case) which has reference to extramental reality—or, in other words, we attain moral knowledge.

Making allowances for differences of terminology and emphasis, Hume's moral epistemology is, I submit, similar to Hutcheson's. Noting this similarity solves no exegetical problems, of course, but it does provide some additional support for the interpretation offered here, and especially so if one believes the claim of Hutcheson's great influence on Hume is essentially correct.

Secondly, it should be remembered that our passions and sentiments are, according to Hume, impressions of reflection, and that they are

> derived in a great measure from our ideas, and that in the following order. An impression first strikes upon the senses, and makes us perceive heat or cold, thirst or hunger, pleasure or pain of some kind or other. Of this impression there is a copy taken by the mind . . . this we call an idea. This idea of pleasure or pain, when it returns upon the soul, produces the new impressions of desire and aversion, hope and fear, which may properly be called impressions of reflexion, because derived from it. . . . the impressions of reflexion, viz. passions, desires, and emotions . . . arise mostly from ideas. . . .[41]

It is entirely consistent, then, to suppose that these impressions, although "original facts and realities" rather than copies,[42] are *causally* dependent upon the impressions and ideas which give rise to them not only for their very existence, but for the particular form they take. Unless I believe (or know) that Dr. Watson exists, and have some minimal beliefs (or knowledge) about Dr. Watson, I cannot have esteem for him. And what I do know about him will determine whether I esteem or despise him, feel approbation or disapprobation for him, count him as good or evil. All of this seems patently obvious when pointed out. Nevertheless, important parts of it have not been obvious to those who have claimed that Hume thought moral judgments reflected only affective states, nor to those who have claimed that Hume thought the understanding was thoroughly subservient to the passions.

VII. We are left, however, with a problem. Hume tells his friend Elliot that he is correct to suppose that his notion of the "correcting Subtility of Sentiment is certainly very just with regard to Morals," but one might now wonder if Hume in fact believed this: As we have just seen, he assigns to reason a substantial role

[41] *Treatise*, pp. 7-8.
[42] *Treatise*, p. 458.

in morals, and this role includes correction of our sentiments. If we are provided "a remedy in the judgment and understanding, for what is irregular and incommodious in the affections,"[43] then it would appear more accurate to speak of the "correcting Subtility of Reason."

However, it is not illogical to suggest that both the sentiments and the understanding have a correcting function, especially when it is seen that the two functions apply at, as it were, different levels. The understanding allows us to eliminate the idiosyncratic or biased from our moral evaluations by bringing our reactions under the influence of general rules and a generalized or ideal perspective. Our sentiments, on the other hand—and this is what Hume is saying to Elliot—are not only the foundation of our moral evaluations, but are also a gauge of moral theories. If we cannot judge all "air-built notions" by our "instinctive feelings," we can at least judge in this manner the claims of moral theorists, and we can reject those that run counter to these feelings. Reason corrects individual sentiments; our sentiments correct moral generalizations.

To be satisfied that this is Hume's position, one needs to recall my earlier discussion of his concern with moral scepticism.[44] There it was noted that Hume agreed with certain earlier moralists in thinking that there were troublesome moral sceptics (those who accepted neither the reality of moral distinctions nor the procedures and methods proper to morality) and sought to refute these sceptics, largely through appeals to sentiment and common sense. It was noted, for example, that Hume allied himself with the friends of virtue as early as 1739, and that his later work, especially the second *Enquiry*, is explicitly hostile to moral sceptics. There, we are told that even the most peevish and determined moral sceptic will be unable to maintain his scepticism in practice (he will pronounce some actions or persons good or evil), and it is also suggested that this kind of sceptic is easier to refute than are his metaphysical colleagues: "Nothing can be more superficial than this paradox [that all moral distinctions are due to

[43] *Treatise*, p. 489.
[44] See chap. 1 of this book, pp. 43-48.

artifice] of the sceptics; and it were well, if, in the abstruser studies of logic and metaphysics, we could as easily obviate the cavils of that sect, as in the practical and more intelligible sciences of politics and morals."[45]

It is against these moral sceptics, but only *moral* sceptics, that Hume invokes the authority of our sentiments. He took what he considered a "natural unforced interpretation of the phenomena of human life," and this convinced him that our sentiments are and ought to be the ultimate standard of truth in moral theory, although the manner in which he expresses this view is not so much what one would expect from a moral sense philosopher as from a common-sense philosopher of a particular kind.[46] That is, Hume's most explicit appeals to ultimate authority are to common sense or our common sentiments, and to the common experiences, instincts, interests, observations, and principles that are said to give rise to these common or universal sentiments.

That Hume maintains that any conflicts between moral theories and our common-sensical views of morality are always to be resolved in favor of the common-sense view cannot be seriously doubted. A moralist who claimed that a particular ruler had no right to his throne because that right cannot be defended by any "receiv'd system of ethics," he says, "wou'd be justly thought to maintain a very extravagant paradox, and to shock the common sense and judgment of mankind."[47] A few pages later, he tells us that there are general principles which are "authoriz'd by common sense, and the practice of all ages," and that one such principle is the right of the people to resist a tyrannical ruler.[48] Correlatively, those who "deny the right of resistance, have renounc'd all pretensions to common sense, and do not merit a serious answer."[49] As a matter of fact, it should be noted, Hume had already given a serious answer to such absurd claims. Pointing

---

[45] *Second Enquiry*, p. 214.
[46] *Second Enquiry*, p. 244. Our sentiments and instinctive beliefs may in fact run counter to other forms of scepticism, but according to Hume, as is shown in chap. 5, these beliefs are not authoritative nor the final arbiters in such cases.
[47] *Treatise*, p. 558.
[48] *Treatise*, p. 563.
[49] *Treatise*, p. 564.

out that the notion of passive obedience is an absurd one, Hume
had maintained that every reader of history favors those who
resisted Nero or Philip the Second, and "nothing but the most
violent perversion of common sense can ever lead us to condemn
them" for so resisting. "The general opinion of mankind has some
authority in all cases; but in this of morals 'tis perfectly infallible."[50] The "vulgar" in all likelihood would not understand the
subtle argument by which resistance to tyranny can be justified.
But that is no matter, for " 'tis certain, that all men have an
implicit notion of it," and because they do have this notion, the
general opinion of men is in this matter said to be infallible.[51]

On another occasion, when his arguments against the contract
theory may seem not entirely convincing, Hume is unconcerned,
for, he says, "I shall have recourse to authority . . . the universal
consent of mankind." He then proceeds to explain why it is that
he is justified in relying on this authority. No one, he says,

> need . . . wonder, that tho' I have all along endeavour'd to
> establish my system on pure reason, and have scarce ever
> cited the judgment even of philosophers or historians on any
> article, I shou'd now appeal to popular authority, and oppose
> the sentiments of the rabble to any philosophical reasoning.

[50] *Treatise*, p. 552. Hume's willingness to rely on the "general opinion of
mankind" in morals may well derive from his belief that human nature itself is
unchangeable (Men "cannot change their natures," he says at *Treatise*, p. 537;
"in all nations and ages . . . human nature remains still the same, in its principles
and operations" *First Enquiry*, p. 83.) and the further belief that our moral
sentiments are "rooted" in this unchangeable nature. If "ever there was any thing,"
he says, "which cou'd be call'd natural in this sense [frequent as opposed to rare],
the sentiments of morality certainly may; since there never was any nation of the
world, nor any single person in any nation, who was utterly depriv'd of them,
and who never, in any instance, shew'd the least approbation or dislike of manners
[of human action or behavior]. These sentiments are so rooted in our constitution
and temper, that without entirely confounding the human mind by disease or
madness, 'tis impossible to extirpate and destroy them" (*Treatise*, p. 474). A
principle of communication ("sympathy" or "fellow feeling") has also, of course,
a central role in bringing about the uniformity of our sentiments, in making them
common sentiments. I have outlined what I take to be Hume's view of this matter
in "Hume's Common Sense Morality," *Canadian Journal of Philosophy* 5 (1975):
523-543; see especially pp. 539-543.
[51] *Treatise*, p. 553.

For it must be observ'd, that the opinions of men, in this case, carry with them a peculiar authority, and are, in a great measure, infallible. The distinction of moral good and evil is founded on the pleasure or pain, which results from the view of any sentiment, or character; and as that pleasure or pain cannot be unknown to the person who feels it, it follows, that there is just so much vice or virtue in any character, as every one places in it, and that 'tis impossible in this particular we can ever be mistaken. . . . Since the question in this case regards not any philosophical origin of an obligation, but a plain matter of fact, 'tis not easily conceiv'd how we can fall into an error.[52]

The "speculative reasonings, which cost so much pains to philosophers," he later adds, are "often form'd by the world naturally, and without reflection," while the "practice of the world" does more to teach us our duty than the most careful philosophy. Thus we find that even when philosophy and common sense agree, the ordinary man is saved a good deal of effort, at no loss of insight or efficacy, which itself is said to be a proof that all men have, implicitly or naturally, certain moral notions.[53]

Elsewhere in the *Treatise* Hume appeals to our "common experience," and he says that it refutes the selfish moralists' accounts of our behavior; to our "common sense of interest," which is said to correct for the partiality of our sentiments; to our "common instinct," and to our "common experience and observation," which are said to be superior to both art and philosophy; and to the "common point of view," from which we survey moral objects in order to obtain like views of them.[54] He also speaks of the "uniformity in the general sentiments of mankind" (a uniformity so obvious that questions of whether there can be right or wrong sentiments in morals are of "small importance") and of the "common principles" of human nature, which account for the universality that characterizes the moral opinions and sentiments of

[52] *Treatise*, pp. 546-547. For a further discussion of this important passage, see pp. 142-147.
[53] *Treatise*, pp. 569, 572.
[54] *Treatise*, pp. 487-495, 591.

men of "all nations, and all ages." And near the end of the *Treatise*, he recommends that moralists follow the lead of "common life and conversation."[55]

Furthermore, such explicit and implicit appeals to common sense are found in Hume's later writings. When in his *Essays* he again took up Locke's theory of the original contract, considering the claim that an absolute monarchy, because it is not founded on an original contract, is no government at all, Hume again tells us that this theory need not be taken seriously since it is too far from common sense to be believed:

> An appeal to general opinion may justly, in the speculative sciences of metaphysics, natural philosophy, or astronomy, be deemed unfair and inconclusive, yet in all questions with regard to morals, as well as criticism, there is really no other standard, by which any controversy can ever be decided. And nothing is a clearer proof, that a theory of this kind is erroneous, than to find, that it leads to paradoxes, repugnant to the common sentiments of mankind, and to the practice and opinion of all nations and all ages. The doctrine, which founds all lawful government on an *original contract*, or consent of the people, is plainly of this kind. . . . What authority any moral reasoning can have, which leads into opinions so wide of the general practice of mankind . . . it is easy to determine.[56]

Section 1 of the *Enquiry concerning Human Understanding*, after revealing that philosophy may be divided between that which is easy and obvious, and that which is difficult and abstruse, gives at least an implicit sanction to a common-sense test of moral theories. A philosopher engaged in subtle reasoning on abstract and abstruse matters can easily make an error, Hume says, which then leads to another, and that to another, and so on. This chain of errors is possible, and even likely, because such a philosopher does not refrain from a conclusion merely because it is unusual or contrary to popular opinion. In contrast, the philosopher who

[55] *Treatise*, pp. 533, 547n, 577, 609.
[56] *Works*, 3: 460.

138

considers only moral issues, who considers man only insofar as he is a creature of action pursuing virtue or vice, or who attempts only to represent in heightened colors "the common sense of mankind," is immediately aware of any error. If "by accident he falls into error, [he] goes no farther; but renewing his appeal to common sense, and the natural sentiments of the mind, returns into the right path, and secures himself from any dangerous illusions."[57]

The *Enquiry concerning the Principles of Morals* begins with the remarks (cited in chapter 1) regarding disingenuous moral disputants who deny the reality of moral distinctions, and it contains Hume's clearest strictures on the moral sceptics. However, because the central sections (2-8) of this work are intended to be an analysis of "what in common life, we call 'personal merit,' " Hume attempts to curtail his reliance on common sense.[58] But he still manages in section 1 to bring to our attention the "quick sensibility" which is "so universal among mankind" and which gives "a philosopher sufficient assurance, that he can never be considerably mistaken" in the task undertaken, for either his own breast or the "very nature of language" will guide him "almost infallibly" to the truth. And once Hume has completed his anal-

---

[57] *First Enquiry*, p. 7. It would be difficult to overestimate the importance of this section to an understanding of Hume's views about philosophy per se, and hence to an understanding of his quite different views about *practical*, as compared to *speculative* philosophy. But it is only in chaps. 5 and 6 that the full import of Hume's discussion becomes clear. Antony Flew has, of course, noted that Hume here offers a justification for pursuing another sort of limited metaphysical inquiry (*Hume's Philosophy of Belief* [London: Routledge & Kegan Paul, 1961], p. 11), which he then discusses briefly. But he does not explore the full range of metaphilosophical views disclosed in this section.

[58] Not, however, with complete success. He begins section 2 with an appeal to universal language, a move which was throughout the eighteenth century a standard part of the common sense repertoire. Terms, he says, which denote estimable social qualities are "known in all languages, and universally express the highest merit. . . ." A few paragraphs later he seems to catch himself, and reminds us that his inquiry is to have "more the speculative, than the practical part of morals" as its concern. It also appears, however, that he lets the damage stand, and uses the fact so established (that there are social virtues) as a basis for his subsequent arguments. And later he again reverts to what "historians and even common sense" tell us as confirmation of his views about perfect equality. *Second Inquiry*, pp. 176-178; 194.

ysis he wastes no time before putting himself on what he thinks is firm and common-sensical ground. It may seem surprising, he says, that an elaborate proof is needed to show "that Personal Merit consists altogether in the possession of mental qualities, *useful* or *agreeable* to the *person himself* or to *others*," for, however much "systems and hypotheses have perverted our natural understanding," the fact is that this elaborate proof demonstrates nothing but the common-sense view of the matter: "In common life these principles are still implicitly maintained," he says, and then he adds that "every quality which is useful or agreeable to ourselves or others is, in common life, allowed to be a part of personal merit."[59] In short, Hume has presented us with an elaborate anatomy of morals, but he is quite satisfied that this be taken for what it is: a detail of morals which will help correct the false anatomies of the sceptical moralists, as well as provide aid for the moral painters. And he is satisfied with this accomplishment because morality itself is something natural which even the perversions of self-love have not destroyed. In common life we continue to make moral distinctions, and they are real and reliable:

> The notion of morals implies some sentiment common to all mankind, which recommends the same object to general approbation, and makes every man, or most men, agree in the same opinion or decision concerning it. It also implies some sentiment, so universal and comprehensive as to extend to all mankind, and render the actions and conduct, even of the persons the most remote, an object of applause or censure, according as they agree or disagree with that rule of right which is established.[60]

It is clear enough that Hume believed that moral theories could be corrected by our common or instinctive sentiments. It is not apparent why he did so or that he did so on good grounds. That is, he suggests that our ordinary, common-sense experience constitutes a practical or pragmatic test of moral theories, and it

[59] *Second Inquiry*, pp. 268-270.
[60] *Second Inquiry*, p. 272.

enables us to reject those that are false. The moment the *moral* theorist departs from the correct account of our moral experience there is an instinctive, definitive intervention which corrects him and returns him to the "right path," provided at least that his mind has not been corrupted by adherence to some oversimplifying philosophical system. In this respect, Hume says, morals has the advantage over abstract and abstruse philosophy, which *is* dependent upon subtle reasoning, presumably because there can be no pragmatic or common-sensical tests of abstract metaphysical claims.

There are, however, difficulties. In the first place, it looks as though Hume's private remark about the "correcting Subtility of Sentiment" is badly phrased, and that he would have been more consistent and perspicacious had he indicated that our moral sentiments can and do correct certain metaphysical subtleties, namely, those that are part of oversubtle moral theories. Our sentiments undercut these theories, bring them down to earth, and offer in their place a plain, unforced interpretation of moral phenomena, a morality of common sense or common sentiment. Hume is telling Elliot that our sentiments provide not merely an essential foundation for moral evaluation, but also that these same feelings provide a standard by which moral theories can be evaluated. But, by our own reckoning, and by Hume's, too, one might think, moral theories include metaphysical elements, and hence Hume is misleading when he casually suggests that morals are distinct and different from metaphysics.

This first problem could be dismissed as merely terminological and unimportant did it not mask a deeper issue. Hume clearly does appeal to common sentiments in evaluating moral theories. We need to understand why, in his opinion, this appeal is justified. But when we do find his justification, it appears *ab initio* to conflict with the objectivist account of moral evaluation that he has been developing, and even afterward to miss the point at issue.

What little Hume says to explain why in morals we can rely on our common sentiments seems to imply acceptance of one form of the moral scepticism—individualistic subjectivism—which he has taken pains to refute. Why do I, he asks, appeal to "popular authority, and oppose the sentiments of the rabble to any philosophical reasoning?" Because, he replies, the distinction of moral good and evil is founded on feelings of pleasure and pain. Further, because such feelings "cannot be unknown to the person who feels" them, it follows that "there is just so much vice or virtue in any character, as every one places in it," and that " 'tis impossible in this particular we can ever be mistaken. . . ."[61] This sounds very much like saying that things are (morally) just what each person feels they are *because* that person feels them to be such and cannot be mistaken about his or her feelings. Or, it sounds like saying in so many words that moral evaluations are reducible to individual feelings, and for that reason are beyond dispute.

Despite appearances, Hume has not by this remark intended to embrace such a reductive subjectivism. He does not mean to say, merely, that we know what we feel about the character of others, and that is all there is to it for *de gustibus non disputandum*. To say that would undercut the very common-sense appeal he is trying to justify, and effectively, too, for he would then be contradicting what he had said earlier. However, if one is willing to accept an amplification of Hume's argument, one can see that this important remark is not only consistent with his appeal to common sentiments, but also that it is, if Hume's other conclusions are accepted, part of an attempt to provide a justification of this appeal.

The argument underlying this justification consists of three premises, only two of which does Hume make sufficiently explicit:

1. Moral distinctions are founded on the pleasure and pain which arise from the morally proper observation of character or motive (a fixed principle of mind).
2. These pleasures and pains (as well as others, of course) must be known to those who feel them.

To these explicit premises Hume should have added a third:

[61] See above, pp. 136-137.

3. When one has a pleasure or pain of the sort specified (arising from the observation of character), one *attributes* virtue or vice to the character observed, and, further, there is an exact correlation between the pleasure or pain felt and the virtue or vice which gives rise to them.[62]

With this premise made explicit, Hume's objectivist conclusion does follow:

4. "There is just so much vice or virtue in any character, as every one places in it," which is to say that as we have direct access to the pleasures and pains produced in ourselves upon the morally proper observation of a character, and as there is an exact correlation between these feelings and the moral qualities of the character giving rise to them, " 'tis impossible in this particular we can ever be mistaken. . . ." If one does in fact notice a *moral* distinction, one cannot be mistaken about it, for the pleasure or pain that give notice of the distinction are, under these conditions, infallible signs of virtue or vice.[63]

I believe this amplification is justified by Hume's text. As has been noted, he is extremely careful to point out that moral evaluation requires not only that we observe fixed principles of mind (character or motive), but also that we observe properly, that is, impartially, as the judicious ideal spectator. From character observed arise approbation or disapprobation, the moral sentiments, but the observation of character is not a casual or haphazard matter. Rather, it requires that our quite normal partiality be

[62] It should be understood that I am defending Hume's views only in the sense that I am attempting to explicate them. Hume *should* have added this premise in order to make his position clearer, consistent, not because it is (in my opinion) sound.

[63] Erroneous judgments of morals can still arise, however. One can say that "Regulus is a vicious man" and be wrong because one has mistaken a nonmoral sentiment (dislike of an enemy) for a moral sentiment. I believe this accords with Hume's position, especially with his obvious concern to specify the conditions in which a moral sentiment is experienced. It also explains why he says that our moral sentiments and moral judgments are infallible. On this theory the difficulty is knowing when in fact a *moral* sentiment has been experienced. In this latter regard we are certainly fallible.

eliminated and that the observed phenomenon be certified a *moral* phenomenon by the presence, in the observer, of the indirect passions, which are the constant corollaries of the moral sentiments. In other words, by speaking of the pleasures and pains arising from the observation of character, Hume makes it clear that he is not here talking about any or all unspecified pleasures and pains, nor even any or all indirect passions. He is not, therefore, lapsing into an affective, individualistic subjectivism that makes final appeal to individual sentiment because, in effect, there is no disputing of tastes. On the contrary, he is referring to specific and specified pleasures and pains, those that have resulted from a proper view and that merit the appellation "moral sentiments."

In addition, Hume explicitly claims in *Treatise* III, 1, 2 that we do not infer that a character is virtuous because it pleases; but because "it pleases after a particular manner, we in effect feel that it is virtuous." It seems just, then, to suppose that this claim is part of the context of the justification he is offering, and equally just to make this context explicit by means of premise 3. To say that we in the manner specified attribute virtue or vice to the character observed is just to iterate the essentials of this earlier claim. Finally, it can be noted that it is this earlier claim which is restated ambiguously in Hume's justification of his appeal (see the passage at *Treatise*, pp. 546-547), where it may seem that attribution of another sort (something akin to projection) is intended: "Just so much virtue or vice . . . as every one places in it" is ambiguous in its immediate context. However, when this clause is taken to be a part of the systematic position that Hume develops, the subjectivistic reading of it can be eliminated, and it can be taken to mean simply that a character is as virtuous as we take it to be because, as there is a reliable means of moral perception, the conditions of which have been fulfilled, what we attribute to the character is entirely consonant with the character itself. That feeling particular pleasures and pains happens to be a necessary aspect of coming to take this character to be as it is makes our morality no more subjective and individualistic for Hume than it did for Hutcheson, whose theories of perception (physical and moral) include a similar use of affective states as signs of objective fact or character.

This explanation, even when complete, may seem, nonetheless, to miss the point. Hume should be telling us why we can rely on our sentiments to correct or refute the moral sceptics. Instead, he tells us that our individual moral evaluations are reliable, apparently forgetting that the question is the broader one he himself has raised: Why is it justifiable for him to appeal to the common sentiments of the rabble in overturning the theories of the speculative moralists?

In Hume's defense, I should like to argue that he has neither missed the point nor failed to answer the question he has raised, although it must be granted that this answer is not so direct as one might like, for it is left implicit in his justification of his appeal to common sentiments. We can, he says, appeal to our moral sentiments in replying to those who claim, for example, that rebellion against a tyrant is *never* justified because our individual moral evaluations are reliable and because these show us that some rebellions have been justified. Thus the moralist who makes such a radical and general claim—rebellion is always morally wrong—is found to be in error. He is found to be factually wrong when others find the actions of some of those who have rebelled against tyrants to be in fact virtuous or justified. Furthermore, this factual error shows that his general claim, his theory, is also false. Hume mirrors Shaftesbury and Hutcheson, who refuted the moral sceptics in just this way. That is, the moral sceptics had said either that there are no real moral distinctions, that our "moral" terms (*virtue*, *vice*, and so forth) are created by artifice alone, and hence have no irreducible moral reference, or that all motivations or characters are the same (selfish). Hence they conclude that all distinctions of character (*virtuous*, *vicious*, and so forth) are only pseudodistinctions. Shaftesbury and Hutcheson refuted these "systems" by demonstrating (so they thought) the "reality of virtue," or by an indirect attack on the systems of the moral sceptics. The attack is indirect in that it does not immediately challenge the sociological or psychological principles underlying these theories. Rather, it is the crucial moral consequence of these theories, namely, the inference that there are no real moral distinctions, that is attacked. Hume also found moral scepticism unsatisfactory, and he uses an approach not unlike his predecessors. Contra the theories of the sceptical, cynical moralists, he posits individual moral facts that are inconsistent with these theories, thus showing they cannot be true, and also providing himself as he interrupts his own argument to inject metaphilosophical remarks, with grounds for the following generalization about philosophical argument: Whenever the *moral* experience of individuals contradicts claims that are part of a moral theory we can appeal to this experience as a refutation of the claims and theories, for such moral experience is not only reliable, it is also "in great measure, infallible." Or, as Hume says in his first *Enquiry*, the philosopher dealing with moral issues per se (not, that is, with moral anatomy) can "appeal to common sense, and the natural sentiments of mankind," for these will keep him on "the right path" and secure him "from any dangerous illusions."

To summarize, Hume seems to say that the signs (the pleasures and pains) are the moral realilty, but this is clearly inconsistent with earlier and more carefully articulated formulations of his theory, and it is clearly inconsistent with his appeal to the authority of our common sentiments. Further examination shows that his remarks, although ambiguous, are consistent with the earlier, clearer formulations of his theory, and that, when they are understood in this way, they do constitute an explanation of his appeal to common opinion. We can rely on common opinion in morality, Hume is saying—we can take it as our authority—because it is in fact common *sentiment*, and these common sentiments are reliable because each moral *sentiment* is a reliable, infallible sign of a fixed principle of mind (for only these give rise to moral sentiments), and our common sentiments are, simply, those infallible moral sentiments that we have in common. Furthermore, since the moral sentiments are pleasures and pains of a particular sort, and everyone is aware of his pleasures and pains, each of us has access to an infallible guide in matters of morality. *That* we feel cannot be missed; *what* we feel is "a plain matter of fact"; hence " 'tis not easily conceiv'd how we can fall into an error in morality," unless, of course, we insist upon maintaining some philosophical theory in the face of contradictory facts. So far as his views on morals and moral theory are concerned, then, the letter to Elliot does summarize, albeit vaguely, Hume's position.

VIII.   I began this chapter by noting the tension between reason and sentiment in moral sense philosophies, and I elaborated on that tension by discussing the role of reason in morals according to Hume. In the course of this discussion I mentioned several times similarities between the views of Francis Hutcheson and those of Hume. Lest I imply there exists between these two philosophers a greater similarity than is in fact the case, a more systematic comparison of them must be offered.

Hume's debt to Hutcheson is genuine, and the similarities between their moral theories are more than superficial. But Hume's moral theory is by no means a carbon copy of Hutcheson's. Both, for example, are concerned—even profoundly concerned—with moral scepticism, and both undertake to reveal the errors of the moral sceptics. Hume, though, is less optimistic about human nature than is Hutcheson, and certainly less so than Shaftesbury, who also shared this concern. Thus, although Hume attempts to show that Hobbes and Mandeville are wrong to claim that all acts are selfishly motivated, and all moral distinctions artificial, he nevertheless agrees with them in part. Hume maintains that man's generosity is severely restricted, so that natural benevolence operates within a quite limited circle, and that some moral distinctions are artificial, at least in the sense that they are dependent upon reflection, or, as he puts it, "are perform'd with a certain design and intention."[64] As a consequence, reason appears to

---

[64] *Treatise*, p. 475. "In his attachment to artificial rules of social conduct Hume was emphasizing the dimension of social life that had been explored by Mandeville. But Hume's artificial rules were not artifices or tricks played by politicians and men of fashion, as Mandeville had claimed; their artificiality derived from their origin in judgment and their role in regulating the natural relations formed by sympathy and the imagination." James Moore, "The Social Background of Hume's Science of Human Nature," *McGill Hume Studies*, p. 40.

have a larger role in morals for Hume than for Hutcheson. For the latter, reason has an important correcting function; for Hume, it has that function plus a more positive or creative function, namely, the development of the artificial virtues, and it also supplies factual information on which the moral sentiments depend. In short, Hume takes on certain concerns and principles that are found in Hutcheson, and these lead him to disagree with Hobbes and Mandeville; at the same time, revealing his typical nonpartisan attitude, he accepts from Hobbes and Mandeville certain insights which, when incorporated into his moral system, set it apart from Hutcheson's.[65]

In addition, Hume's moral epistemology, wherein affective states of mind (feelings of approbation and disapprobation) function as signs whereby objective states of affairs (motives, characters) are known, is not unlike the theories of perception and moral perception found in Hutcheson's work. Again, though, there are important differences: Hume reveals, if nothing else, a greater concern about questions of moral knowledge, and his well-known discussions of the competing claims of reason and sentiment are the foundation of a relatively well-elaborated moral epistemology, quite in contrast to Hutcheson's dense and miserly asides. As a result, we know that Hume saw that standard epistemological concerns (attitude of the observer, distance from the object, nature of the medium, criterion of veracity, and so forth) were also concerns in moral epistemology, and we find in his writings, especially in the *Treatise*, a comprehensive effort to explicate moral knowing. Secondly, although Hume grants to reason a

---

[65] Hume is also capable of turning the arguments of the antisceptics against them in order to show that their views are likewise deficient. Such, it seems to me, he does when he argues that it is mistaken to suppose "that the mere regard to the virtue of the action, may be the first motive, which produc'd the action, and render'd it virtuous," for his argument there seems to parallel the well-known one used by Hutcheson (and Butler) against Hobbes, namely (in rough form), that it is a mistake to suppose that a regard for the pleasure an object gives is the first motive which induces us to seek and obtain that object. Rather, Hutcheson and Butler point out, we desire the object itself (water when thirsty, e.g.), and pleasure arises later, concomitantly, when the desire has been fulfilled. Hume's parallel analysis is found at *Treatise*, pp. 477-479. He also raises the issue with Hutcheson directly. See his letter of September 17, 1739, *Letters*, 1: 34-35.

greater role in morals, he appears, nonetheless, more consistently empirical and less rationalistic than does Hutcheson. The latter, for example, exhibits through his universal and representative concomitant ideas a near affinity, in my opinion, with innate idea theorists. For, taking what he says at face value, it appears that these ideas are present in the mind prior to experience, and they are aroused, brought to consciousness, and applied to objective reality on the occasion of the occurrence of specific sensible ideas. Surely, this is true of the universal concomitant ideas, which are said to accompany all experience, and hence cannot have had their origin in experience. Hume, in contrast, seems determined to eschew that form of innatism (although clearly a nativist regarding the principles or faculties of the mind) and to trace to experience all our ideas, including those of duration, on the one hand, and of virtue and vice, on the other. Indeed, this determination accounts in part for the greater detail of Hume's moral epistemology, for, not being content to tell us that approbation of a certain sort "occasions" the concomitant ideas of morality, he outlines in detail the conditions which must pertain before there can be moral reality, moral feelings, and an epistemic relationship between them, or precisely how it is that moral reality occasions moral approbation.

Thirdly, and perhaps most importantly, Hume's "naturalism" is altogether different from that of Hutcheson. The older moralist was not content to claim merely that we have, naturally, reliable moral faculties, but went beyond this to claim for these a providential design, a *supernatural* origin and purpose, a necessary (as the world is presently constituted) and a necessarily reliable nature. Hume, although not prepared to champion a blind and overriding mechanism, would have none of this, even at the expense of leaving certain ultimate questions unanswered. "I cannot agree," he wrote to Hutcheson, "to your Sense of *Natural*. Tis founded on final Causes; which is a Consideration, that appears to me pretty uncertain & unphilosophical."[66] By this brief

---

[66] Hume to Hutcheson, September 17, 1739, in *Letters*, 1: 33.

remark and all it implies, Hume reveals himself a philosopher
who is significantly different from Hutcheson and his fellow Scots.

IX. In this chapter I have argued that Hume adopts a common-
sense moral theory, or that in opposition to the moral sceptics
he regards certain common sentiments as providing a sound foundation for morality. As providing, indeed, rationalists notwithstanding, the only sound foundation of morality. Hume's is not
a common-sense morality in what is probably the typical manner;
he does not rely on naïve appeals to the opinions of ordinary
men and claim that what they cannot help believing must be
true, although we have seen that Hume does make use of something very like the *consensus gentium* argument. Rather, Hume
goes beyond the typical and naïve appeal to common sense,
arguing instead that we are all capable of experiencing and iso-
lating those common sentiments that enable us to distinguish
virtue from vice or right from wrong. He does not suppose that
the "honest farmer" will, without taking thought, be able to make
entirely adequate moral assessments, but if he does take thought,
he will be able to do so because there arise in him sentiments,
natural sentiments shared by all humans, that enable him to
distinguish moral differences.

If there is resistance to calling such a theory a "common-sense"
theory I would be willing to consider other titles. But I would
nonetheless maintain that this chapter has established these important points:

1. Hume believes that we have moral knowledge. We need
not, on his view, succumb to the moral sceptics, for our natural
abilities or faculties (reason and sense together) enable us to
distinguish different forms of moral reality.

2. Hume argues that our *moral* sentiments serve as signs of
moral fact, and as standards by which moral theories can be
judged.

3. Hume's moral theory is one in which reason, even reason
as traditionally understood, is assigned a highly significant sup-

porting role.[67] It has, according to Hume, at least these roles: (*a*) finding out the facts of the situation to be assessed morally; (*b*) enabling us to distinguish *moral* approbations and disapprobations from our other sentiments; (*c*) insuring that our moral assessments are clear of distortions due to self-interest, bias, or proximity; and (*d*) developing the artificial virtues.

4. Hume adopts a religious stance very different from that of Hutcheson, and as a consequence, he never suggests that our moral insights are divinely guaranteed. As we consider other aspects of Hume's philosophy—his logic and metaphysics, to use his terms—this difference will be seen to be of even greater significance than it has appeared here.

[67] Hume's occasional hyperboles pale beside those of some of his commentators. Stroud writes that Hume's arguments "show that reason, as traditionally understood, has no role in human life." *Hume*, p. 14. Equally disappointing is Stroud's decision to reject the suggestion that Hume holds something like "an 'ideal observer' theory of the meaning of moral judgments" because this would require a revision of his interpretation of the role of reason in Hume's moral theory. However, given Stroud's allegiance to the "masterly work" of Kemp Smith, perhaps such disappointment should be directed to its ultimate source and not to Stroud (See *Hume*, pp. 191-192, 265).

« **4** »

The Providential Naturalism
of Turnbull and Kames

I often imagine to myself, that I perceive within me a certain
instinctive feeling, which shoves away at once all subtle
refinements, and tells me with authority, that these air-
built notions are inconsistent with life and experience, and,
by consequence cannot be true or solid. From this I am led
to think, that the speculative principles of our nature ought
to go hand in hand with the practical ones. . . . This notion
first occurred to me at London, in conversation with a man
of some depth of thinking; and talking of it since to your
friend H. Home, he seems to entertain some notions nearly
of the same kind, and to have pushed them much farther.
Gilbert Elliot of Minto
to David Hume,
1751

PART 1

I. Certain of Hume's views, particularly ethical views, owe much
to the ideas of Shaftesbury and Hutcheson. But there were within
the moral sense school strains of thought which Hume was never
to accept or develop, and as a result, one of the most useful
perspectives on Hume's philosophy is that provided by contrasting
it with the views of those who remained truer to the Hutchesonian
vision of philosophy. Among these are George Turnbull and
Henry Home, Lord Kames. Turnbull (1698-1749) was a Regent
at Marischal College, Aberdeen, from 1721 to 1727, and is chiefly
remembered, when he is remembered, as the teacher of Thomas
Reid, on whom he had "a greater influence than all other masters

152

and writers put together."[1] Kames (1696-1782) was Hume's kinsman and early patron (or would-be patron) and is one writer
whose influence on Reid rivals or surpasses that of Turnbull.[2]
Together, these two authors represent the extension of the Hutchesonian philosophy in a manner consistent with it—and with
results very different from anything found in David Hume. The
full extent of Hume's differences will be seen only in chapter 5.
Nonetheless, it will become clear here why Hume maintained
that reason, even speculative reason, has a legitimate, necessary,
and preeminent part to play in some kinds of philosophy, and
hence rejected the Elliot-Kames thesis that sentiment is the standard of all philosophy.

II.   George Turnbull, as the teacher who introduced Reid to
modern philosophy, represents an important link in the chain of
development that reaches from Shaftesbury to Reid and beyond.
But it is as the author of the *Principles of Moral Philosophy*, a work
that appeared in the same year as book 3 of Hume's *Treatise*, that
Turnbull is of interest here.[3] For the *Principles* is not only an

[1] James McCosh in *The Scottish Philosophy, Biographical, Expository, Critical from
Hutcheson to Hamilton* (New York: Carter, 1875), pp. 95, 106; cited hereafter as
Scottish Philosophy.

[2] For the relationship between Hume and Kames, see Mossner, *The Life of
David Hume*, pp. 54-64, et passim; and I. S. Ross, *Lord Kames and the Scotland
of His Day* (Oxford: Oxford University Press, 1972), pp. 75-87, et passim. For
Kames's influence on Reid, see below, pp. 189-190.

[3] *The Principles of Moral Philosophy* (hereafter *Principles*) encompasses two volumes: I: *An Enquiry into the Wise and Good Government of the Moral World, in
which the Continuance of Good Administration, and of Due Care about Virtue, for
ever, is inferred from Present Order in All Things, in that Part chiefly where Virtue is
concerned*; II: *Christian Philosophy: Or the Christian Doctrine concerning God, Providence, Virtue, and a Future State, proved to be agreeable to True Philosophy, and to
be attended with a Truly Philosophical Evidence* (London: J. Noon, 1740). Turnbull's
other writings include *A Philosophical Enquiry Concerning the Connexion between
the Doctrines and Miracles of Jesus Christ . . .* 2d ed. (London: R. Willock, 1732);
*Christianity neither False nor Useless, tho' not as Old as the Creation: or, An Essay
to Prove the Usefulness, Truth and Excellency of the Christian Religion . . .* (London:
R. Willock, 1732); *A Treatise on Ancient Painting* (London, 1740; reprint ed.,
München: W. Fink, 1971); *A Discourse upon the Nature and Origin of Moral and
Civil Laws* appended to an annotated translation of Heineccius, *Elementa juris
naturae et gentium* 2 vols., 2d ed. (London: George Keith, 1763), and *Observations
upon Liberal Education* (London: A. Millar, 1740). Curiously, Hume's *Treatise*

attempt to deal systematically with the moral issues arising at the
time, but it is also an ideal foil to Hume's less conventional but
contemporary work.

In the Epistle Dedicatory of the *Principles*, Turnbull announces
that his aim is to "account for MORAL, as the great *Newton* has
taught us to explain NATURAL Appearances," and thus show that
man is not only now governed by a "perfectly wise and good
administration," but also that this same good order will prevail
to eternity. To this end, he says in the preface, it will be necessary
to overcome the shameful ignorance concerning the human mind,
and the open contempt for inquiries into it—which are sneered
at as "metaphysical"—because it is only by "strictly examining
the structure and fabrick of the mind, the frame and connexion
of all its powers and affections, and the manner of their operation"
that we can come to understand our ends or the functioning of
our "moral part." Notwithstanding this (allegedly) prevailing ignorance about the mind, Turnbull cheerfully acknowledges several modern authors who have been of great assistance to his
inquiry. The most important of these are, he indicates, Hutcheson, Shaftesbury, and Butler, although John Clarke and Berkeley
are also mentioned.[4]

In still another preliminary discussion, the Introduction to part
1 of the *Principles*, Turnbull compares moral philosophy to natural
philosophy, and sets forth the rules or principles by which both
types are to be undertaken. According to him, if we understand
"what natural philosophy is, or how it proceeds in its enquiries,"
we will have no difficulty understanding what moral philosophy
is, and how it must proceed, for both kinds of inquiry are factual,

was once attributed to Turnbull, probably because of the publisher's advertise-
ments (for the *Treatise* and Turnbull's other works) at the end of vol. 2 of some
copies of the *Principles*. See Johan Anton Trinius, *Freydenker Lexicon* (Leipzig
and Bernberg, 1759; reprint ed., Torino, 1960), p. 456.

[4] *Principles*, 1: [iv-xv]. Turnbull here also mentions Pope, saying that he "hath
shown us, that the seemingly most abstruse matters in philosophy, may be rendered
. . . exceeding pleasing and agreeable." The *Essay on Man* is cited throughout
both volumes, including the title page of vol. 1, where is found: "And if *Natural
Philosophy*, in all its Parts, by pursuing this Method, shall at length be perfected,
the Bounds of *Moral Philosophy* will also be enlarged" (Newton's *Optics*, book 3),
and "Account for Moral, as for Nat'ral Things" (*Essay on Man*, Ep. 1).

and "all enquiries into fact, reality, or any part of nature must be set about, and carried on in the same way." Thus, after defining natural philosophy as an "enquiry into the sensible world: that is into the general laws, according to which its appearances are produced; and into the beauty, order, and good which these general laws produce," he attempts to articulate the principles presupposed by and governing such an enterprise. These principles are:

1. The sensible world is governed by general, or uniform and constant, laws.
2. Those laws or principles which are "observed to prevail and operate uniformly" are justly denominated "general" laws.
3. Any general law which tends to produce a prevalence of "good, beauty, and perfection in the whole" is a good law. [5]

The first of these principles amounts to a necessary presupposition, a presupposition of the constancy and uniformity of nature that is absolutely necessary if there is to be science at all. As Turnbull puts it, "Science presupposes a certain determinate object; or fixed ascertainable relations. . . . Nature, in order to be understood by us, must always speak the same language to us. . . ." In contrast, principles 2 and 3 appear to be procedural. That is, they are attempts to give order to natural philosophy by indicating when one is to consider a principle *general*, and a general principle *good*. When this terminology is stripped away, however, it seems clear that Turnbull is introducing prescriptive principles which have an important metaphysical role to play. The second, one finds, is understood in such a way that analogical reasoning is validated: "Wherever we find analogy, or similarity of effects, there we find the same law prevailing." And the third principle clearly serves as a means of importing teleological presuppositions. In explication of it, Turnbull says in effect that the merit of a principle is determined by its contribution as a final

[5] *Principles*, 1: 1-6.

cause to the good of the whole: "a good general law" is one that is "conducive to the greatest good, beauty, and perfection" of the system of which it is a part. Furthermore, "all the effects of general laws which are good with respect to a whole, are good absolutely considered, or referred to that whole."[6]

This account of the principles of natural philosophy is followed by the claim that although they are often distinguished from one another, natural philosophy and moral philosophy have a direct link: as soon as the former leads us to conclusions concerning the order and purpose of the world, or explains phenomena in terms of "good general laws," it has in reality taken on a moral dimension. Indeed, any inquiry that does not reach this moral dimension "hardly deserves the name of philosophy" as this applies to the work of Socrates, Plato, Bacon, Boyle, Newton, and "the other best moral or natural philosophers." It might seem, then, that no separate description of moral philosophy is necessary. Generally speaking, such a conclusion is correct, for moral philosophy is said to presuppose and proceed upon the principles that have just been outlined, and Turnbull comes quickly to the conclusion that moral phenomena are just as subject to scientific inquiry as are physical phenomena. He also concludes that, if we are to establish moral philosophy on a par with "knowledge of the material world, as it now stands," then "we must enquire into moral phenomena, in the same manner as we do into physical ones. . . ."[7]

Turnbull's preliminary remarks are important, for they direct us to the proper interpretation of the long, rambling, and repetitive work that follows. They are central because they reveal Turnbull's concern to establish that the science of human nature is essentially analogous to natural science. To see what is most noteworthy about this concern, a comparison may be helpful: Hume's *Treatise*, which is subtitled "an Attempt to introduce the experimental Method of Reasoning into Moral Subjects," calls for the development of a science of man which is to be the foundation of all other sciences. However, aside from advising

[6] *Principles*, 1: 2, 5-7.
[7] *Principles*, 1: 9-12.

us that no science can go beyond experience, and hence that the science of human nature must be content to "glean up" experiments "from a cautious observation of human life," Hume has relatively little to say about the connection of this science with the several others.[8]

Turnbull is also committed to the development of a moral science, and he indicates that it is in the end the basis of all sciences. In contrast to Hume, he makes an effort to characterize science in general, and thereby makes available an ideal of science that moral philosophers should strive to attain, and by which their achievements are to be judged. Turnbull, one can say, agreed with Hume that we should account for moral matters in the same way that we account for natural things, but he was more comprehensive in his effort to spell out what this would mean, and how it was to be done.

On further reflection, one can see that between Hume and Turnbull there is a difference of emphasis as well as of comprehensiveness, and that it is the difference of emphasis which is most important. Hume does indeed attempt to introduce into moral philosophy the experimental method, and he does this presumably because of the successes accruing to natural philosophy since its (relatively) recent adoption of this method. But— to understate what is well known—Hume is nothing if not cautious about these successes: for all their impressiveness it is far from certain that they take us beyond experience, and in the end we seem to be left, he says, with the "impossibility of explaining ultimate principles." Turnbull is not at all cautious. Writing on the eve of Hume's influence in Britain, Turnbull does not see the methods and results of experimental natural science as mere models to be emulated for possible good effect, but as *established* knowledge or truth which serves as a standard or exemplar of all

---

[8] Certainly, though, Hume's work is fundamentally affected by his desire to establish a science of human nature, and the notion of a moral science is central to the *Treatise*. I have discussed Hume's science of man in "History and Philosophy in Hume's Thought" in *David Hume: Philosophical Historian*, ed. D. F. Norton and R. H. Popkin (Indianapolis: Bobbs-Merrill, 1965). A helpful discussion of Hume and the natural science of his time is "Hume's Newtonian Program," chap. 3 of N. Capaldi, *David Hume: The Newtonian Philosopher* (Boston: Twayne, 1975).

knowledge, and proof that truth and certainty are attainable by human means. When he asserts that moral philosophy must proceed by the same principles which govern the natural philosophy of a Boyle or Newton, there is none of Hume's reserve. It is not because—for all its defects—this is the best method available to us. Turnbull has no ear for such doubts, for the method has proven itself: "In a word," he says, "it has been proved, that our mundan system in all its parts is governed by excellent general laws." We know this, he suggests, because by the "discoveries made in natural philosophy, we know, that no sooner are facts collected, and laid together in proper order, than the true theory of the phenomenon in question presents itself."[9] Turnbull has taken fully to heart the familiar expression of his favorite poet,

> Nature, and Nature's laws, lay hid in night:
> God said, "Let Newton be!" and all was light.

and his epistemological optimism is unbounded.[10]

The new natural philosophy has found a means to certainty, a means, Turnbull insists, which must be supposed to work equally well in moral philosophy. His *Principles* can be understood best as a lengthy spelling out of the "analogy" between our enlightened understanding of the material world, and an even more important, but still darkened, understanding of the moral world. The analogy is elaborate and often vague or opaque because it is interlarded with elements of optimistic theodicy, Lockean or Berkeleyan epistemology, moral sense ethical views, and a miscellany of unidentifiable items, as well as the expected aspects of the argument from design. But once it is seen that the "excellent general laws" of Newtonian natural science are an Archimedean point by which all else may be moved, the welter of ingredients ceases to baffle.

If the existence of a true and certain natural philosophy is the

---

[9] *Principles*, 1: 59, 63.
[10] "And yet after all," says Turnbull, "with respect to mankind, the acquirement of natural knowledge may be said to be a very easy purchase" (*Principles*, 2: 78).

first "premise" in Turnbull's analogical argument,[11] then the second is the fact that we are by Nature well fitted for knowledge of the material world. But whereas the first premise was so evident that it could be taken for granted, the second premise requires Turnbull to "consider a little the faculties and dispositions with which we are provided and furnished for making progress in knowledge." When he makes this survey, Turnbull finds that we are impressively well adapted for knowledge of the external world. Nature has provided certain "assistances" that enable us to increase our knowledge. There are, for example, elements of prerational knowledge "which it is necessary for us to have in our infant state," while other things which must be known for survival and general well-being—natural connections, proper perspectives, the relationship of objects seen to objects touched, facility in language—are learned very easily. In addition, pain and uneasy sensations serve to warn or guide us; we have a tendency to be satisfied with the kind of probable or analogical evidence which often is all that is available to us; there are hints from the behavior of animals; and the connections of nature herself "lie open to our view."[12]

Added to these assistances is a set of "natural furniture for knowledge." Turnbull finds that man has a natural appetite for knowledge, that knowledge is agreeable to him, and thus it is sought by him. He finds that we take a natural delight in the activity which is the source of knowledge and general laws, namely, the comparison of ideas for agreement and disagreement, resemblance and difference. He also finds that we have a natural curiosity for new objects or new experiences and thus expand our knowledge, although this tendency is wisely balanced by another natural tendency to form habits, which keep our endeavors from

[11] Here I am using *analogy* in the rather loose manner in which it is used by Turnbull, who can speak of "presumptions founded upon analogy or likeness" (*Principles*, 1: 41), and also suggest that the "great part of science consist[s] in the knowledge of analogies and oppositions among objects" (*Principles*, 1: 101), as well as offer (as will be shown) what can be called, speaking more strictly, analogical arguments.

[12] *Principles*, 1: 38-44.

becoming too superficial.[13] Nor is this all. There are also several "faculties or powers, by which we are fitted for knowledge," and although he here seems to lose the thread of his survey, Turnbull surely means to refer to the imagination, which serves as a source of the powers of memory and invention, and assists in depicting sensible objects; the senses; and the understanding, a faculty of both intuitive and deliberative powers. In short, there is the fact of successful natural science, and a battery of natural assistances, dispositions, and faculties that have enabled man to gain the knowledge this science represents. It is no surprise, then, to find Turnbull concluding that we are well adapted for knowledge— that we are fitted to know the world about us, just as the world is designed in such a way that we can know it.[14]

It is obvious that Turnbull is relatively unconcerned by any sceptical doubts that may have been raised about our knowledge of the physical world; epistemological scepticism is not for him an issue. However, he was concerned about moral scepticism, that "other scepticism," as he calls it, "about internal experience," and part of his concern is to determine whether this internal scepticism "be not equally ridiculous" with the scepticism—external or epistemological—that Newton had so conclusively refuted.[15] Obviously, he believed that this is so, and the elaborate analogy which he developed is intended to show just how ridiculous and unfounded this moral scepticism is.

Such a concern with internal or moral scepticism was no doubt predictable. Turnbull acknowledges his philosophical debts to Shaftesbury, Hutcheson, and Butler, each of whom gave priority to the refutation of the moral scepticism they imputed to Hobbes, Locke, or, later, to Mandeville. Turnbull was well aware, for example, that Shaftesbury had attacked Hobbes for attempting to explain all human behavior on the principle of self-love, thus

---

[13] *Principles*, 1: 44-52. Further furniture or instincts of this sort are mentioned from time to time. The "human mind," Turnbull says, "is a very complicated structure . . . composed not of one, but of many principles. . . ." *Discourse upon the Nature and Origin of Moral and Civil Laws*, in Heineccius, *Elementa juris naturae et gentium.*
[14] *Principles*, 1: 54-62.
[15] *Principles*, 2: 71.

apparently denying the reality of virtue, and that he had been even more upset with Locke for reducing morality to a matter of fashion or custom. Nor had Turnbull missed the reason for Shaftesbury's concern with these absurd views (their potential to beguile and mislead), or the method he had chosen (an observational inquiry into man and his nature) in order to refute them, and he quite approved of the outcome. Shaftesbury, he writes, has refuted the "gloomy pernicious doctrine of Hobbes," and he has shown us how to deal with other philosophers of that kind.[16]

In addition, Turnbull has his own comments to make on the methods and claims of the sceptical moralists. Those, he says, who would "ascribe all that is social in our nature to art, custom, and super-added habit" clearly "shock all common sense." He explicitly terms "scepticks" those philosophers who have unjust notions of human dignity, who zealously propagate "doctrines tending to discourage virtue," and who "throw a most gloomy damp upon all truly noble and generous ambition." In contrast, he seeks, he says, to place "beyond all doubt" the "reality of public affections in our nature, the immediate object of which is the good of others, and of a moral sense by which we are necessarily determined to approve such affections." And as he later says, he seeks to show the essential reality of virtue and vice, and to give a "full refutation" of those who claim these are merely arbitrary or conventional.[17]

The absurd questions, verbal labyrinths, and metaphysical janglings which mark the productions of the moral sceptics are to Turnbull an indication that these philosophers have gone off the proper track. Truth, he insists, is simple, and there is a plain and evident way to it. That is the way of simple fact and observation, and not any other. Indeed, echoing his moral sense predecessors, Turnbull attributes the absurdity and falsity of moral scepticism entirely to a fondness for airy speculation and subtle generalization which has infected so many philosophers, even some who may have been well-meaning. Foremost among those who have erred in this fashion are those who would explain all acts by the mo-

[16] *Principles*, 1: 300, 358.
[17] *Principles*, 1: 196-197, 430, 123; 2: 216.

tivation of self-love: "We see what sad shifts they are reduced to, who would explain away into certain selfish subtle reflexions, all that has the appearance of social, kindly and generous in our frame; and the perplexity and subtlety of such philosophy is the same argument against it, which is reckoned a very good one against complicated, perplexing hypotheses in natural philosophy, compared with more simple ones."[18]

Turnbull does not merely assert the absurdity of such moral scepticism, but he also undertakes to establish the contrary moral facts. This is consistent with his desire to account for morality in a scientific way, and with his claim that the *Principles* constitutes "an enquiry into the frame and connexion of those various powers, appetites and affections, which, by . . . joint-operation, constitute the soul and its temper, or disposition, . . ." and which, if successful, will reduce at least "the more remarkable appearances in the human system to excellent general laws." That is, to laws which vindicate human nature and the ways of God to man by showing that the mind of man is as ordered a part of nature as any other, and hence that there is no reason to doubt that Providence has aptly fitted us for the successful pursuit of virtue. In brief, Turnbull finds that man is equipped with a natural and reliable moral sense, and he suggests that this is not a difficult fact to establish: "I am apt to think, that every one shall immediately perceive, that he has a moral sense inherent in him, and really inseparable from him." Each of us can see upon the least reflection that we have a natural disposition to approve or disapprove actions and affections. But if there are actions which we cannot avoid assessing, then it is clear that we are necessarily determined by nature to assess, or, in other words, it is clear that we have a specific determination by nature, a moral sense: "If we experience approbation and disapprobation, then must we have an approving and disapproving faculty; a determination to approve and disapprove. . . ."[19]

[18] *Principles*, 1: 105, 109; 2: [viii], 79; *Methodical System*, 1: 167.
[19] *Principles*, 1: ii, iv, 111-112. Turnbull adds, "And there must likewise be objects to excite our approbation, and objects to move our disapprobation. So that the remaining question is, what these objects are." Thus does the discovery of the moral sense also prove the reality of virtue—at least as soon as these objects are identified as virtue and vice.

Other proofs of the existence of this moral sense reveal at the same time significant details about it. It is only by a moral sense, it is argued, that we could have for any event or action a concern other than mere self-interest; if our nature contains no such sense, then Hobbes and others are right, and "virtue is really but an empty name; that is, the fitness or approveableness of affections, actions and characters in themselves, is an idle dream that hath no foundation." Nothing but a moral sense could teach us the difference between mere life, an uninterrupted succession of sensual pleasures, and genuine living, "between life itself, and the causes of living which are worthy of man." Again we can easily convince ourselves that there is such a sense. As it is a question which depends for its answer upon inward experience, we have only to ask ourselves whether we do not find a vast and total difference between doing something because it is good, or out of love and affection, and doing it simply to gain some pleasure or external advantage. And, of course, no heart, unless it be one that is completely villainous, fails to find such a difference. No matter how cunning, how prudent, how sagaciously favoring self-interest an act may be, it does not move us to approval as does the simplest act of integrity. That is, we simply cannot approve baseness no matter how advantageous it may seem, nor disapprove regard for virtue even when it is seemingly disadvantageous.[20]

III.   It is clear that much of what Turnbull has to say about the moral sense is an echo of his predecessors. At the same time, he adds significantly, if not always perspicuously, to their views. For example, far more often than Shaftesbury or Hutcheson, Turnbull makes explicit appeal to "common sense" as some kind of standard of religious and moral truth. In the first of his theological writings, the *Philosophical Enquiry Concerning the Connexion between the Doctrines and Miracles of Jesus Christ*, a defense of Christianity against those who have been said to impugn its doctrines, he states unequivocally that "common sense is certainly sufficient to teach those who think of the matter with tolerable seriousness and attention, all the duties and offices of human life; all our

---

[20] *Principles*, 1: 134-136.

obligations to God; and our fellow-creatures, all that is morally fit and binding."[21] He then goes on to say that there was no need (in theory, at least) for the miracles of Christ to prove what common sense so clearly shows, and indeed, no work of any sort can prove something to be morally fit which "common sense and reason proves to be the reverse." Thus he concludes, "Works of the most extraordinary nature can be of no further use, with regard to precepts and lessons of morality, except to beget attention, and to make the spectators and hearers reflect seriously upon that moral fitness, which common sense clearly points out to every thinking person."[22]

Later in the same work, the same attitude is evinced. If, it is said, there are doctrines preached which "are not consistent with our natural notions of God and virtue; or if the conduct of the preacher is not suitable to the claim of a divine mission," we have good reason to suppose there is no such mission: "The cheat is manifest. Common sense may easily see through the mask, and discern the imposture."[23] Less significant, perhaps, because more casual, are the remarks from a later work, where we are told that we ought to "behave as common sense and reason tells" us to, and where Turnbull discusses the relationship between divine intervention and what "common sense and reason tells us we ought to do."[24] In addition to the remark about shocking common sense, there is in the *Principles* a suggestion that morality is founded on common sense: On behalf "of the clearness and certainty of rational morality" we can say that it has a sure foundation; it is "easily deducible from obvious principles of reason and common sense."[25]

Turnbull also adds to the moral sense appeal to common language. Typical of Shaftesbury and Hutcheson is an argument purporting to show that the authenticity of moral categories is

[21] P. 5; hereafter cited as *Philosophical Enquiry*.

[22] *Philosophical Enquiry*, pp. 5-6.

[23] *Philosophical Enquiry*, p. 47; see also p. 31.

[24] *Christianity neither False nor Useless tho' not as Old as the Creation: or An Essay to prove the Usefulness, Truth, and Excellency of the Christian Religion . . .* pp. 9, 14.

[25] *Principles*, 1: 430-431; see also 1: 188, 317.

revealed by our ordinary ways of speaking. Hobbes or others claim that all acts are selfishly motivated, but if this were in fact the case, there would be no reason for us to have a vocabulary which permits the characterizations of *selfish* and *unselfish*. Neither of the two relative terms would be required, and, consequently, neither would have become a part of our language. Conversely, such moral relatives as *good* and *evil*, *virtue* and *vice* are part of every language, hence their source must be in genuine moral differences. Turnbull's view seems very similar. In his discussion of the freedom of the will, he maintains that those "ways of speaking" which suggest that we have freedom are universal, and that to say, as a necessitarian in effect does, that all such ways of speaking are meaningless, is to assert an absurdity that is no less ridiculous than the claim that we never understand the conversation of another. Everyone understands what it means to have freedom of choice and power to act—except a few "philosophers, who seeking the knowledge of human nature, not from experience, but from I know not what subtle theories of their own invention, depart from common language, and therefore are not understood by others, and sadly perplex and involve themselves." And since "common language is built upon fact, or universal feeling," we should simply speak and understand as does this comprehensive everyone, dismiss the perplexing sophistries of the philosophers, and accept as fact that which is implied by ordinary language. "Language," he says later in the *Principles*, "not being invented by philosophers, but contrived to express common sentiments, or what everyone perceives, we may be morally sure, that where universally all languages make a distinction, there is really in nature a difference."[26]

However, although his appeals to common sense and to common language seem to come finally to the same thing, Turnbull does not rest his theory on the foundation they provide, for that is not the ultimate basis of philosophical authority. In fact, Turnbull clearly believes that common sense and common language can be appealed to because they are themselves founded on two

[26] *Principles*, 1: 15-16, 118. Strict adherence to common language is also suggested as a remedy for philosophical perplexity (*Philosophical Enquiry*, p. 37).

other features of the moral creation: the fact that there is a human nature, meaning, most importantly, that certain dispositions and faculties of mind are common to all men; and the fact that these dispositions and faculties have been furnished for us by a wise Providence, and thus may be trusted as reliable guides.

The continual references which Turnbull makes to the "frame" or "constitution" of man are themselves enough to demonstrate his belief in a universal human nature. But he also offers more detailed comment, and even what appears to be intended as a proof of this difficult point. Idiosyncrasies of perception are, he grants, apparent in every individual; however, these are to be expected, given our idiosyncratic points of view and experience. Furthermore, these differences are only superficial. Man is universally one species with one nature, and the members of the species share experience that is essentially the same. The "organizations" of men are so alike, he says, "that they may be justly said to be specifically the same; our sensations conveyed from without, must likewise be so alike, that they too may be said to be specifically the same." In addition, man's nature and the relations of things relative to him and his actions are fixed in an invariable relationship, one which constitutes a natural law to man and which serves to limit or fix the effects of his behavior, and which is no more subject to his will than are the natural laws of mechanics.[27] Even if we look in the least likely places, at the "most hardened, callous wretch," or the least literate and intelligent of men, we shall find the moral sense operative and accurate. "No man can put himself to the proper trial by examination without feeling he has a moral sense," his argument begins, and it leads to the conclusion that nature has given all men a moral sense which "directs us to an enquiry the most assistant to virtuous temper, and of the most pleasing kind; and which at the same time directs us in every case, if we will but consult it, to our duty . . . independently of all computations with respect to

[27] *Principles*, 1: 33, 135-139. Consider also: "In the same sense that it is necessary for man to act consonantly to the properties of air and water, in order to gain certain purposes, such as raising water, etc., in the same sense are the connexions relative to our affections, laws or rules to us. . ." (*Discourse*, p. 300).

private good, or interest. This sense is therefore justly said to be engraven on our hearts, innate, original, and universal."[28]

Turnbull is equally direct about the second of these two beliefs, that our dispositions and faculties are reliable. He maintains, for example, that "truth and simplicity are in all instances so inseparable" that we always prefer the simpler hypothesis to any others, and this because "we are naturally framed so to do." Further, natural philosophy always confirms the simpler hypothesis, and thus we are shown "that our determination by nature to embrace the most simple hypotheses, is by no means a deceit." Our *natural disposition* is to prefer and approve the simplest hypothesis; our experience shows that these are indeed the true hypotheses; our natural disposition is thus shown to be reliable. This, continues Turnbull, "is a very strong argument of the care of nature about us," as well as evidence of the veracity of the author of our nature. To have given us an "instinct or determination" which deceives would have been falsehood, while to give one that does not is veracity. Since there can be little doubt about the veracity of many of these instincts (they have, after all, enabled us to obtain an authentic body of knowledge in natural philosophy), Turnbull believes it is safe to conclude that "all our determinations [are] right guides, or guides which do not deceive, or lead astray," and that they do not because the "Author of our frame" has carefully and properly designed them for us, for our needs and our interaction with the world.[29]

Finally, there is Turnbull's analogical proof of the reality of virtue, which is significantly different from anything found in the earlier moral sense writers. Hutcheson had, to be sure, insisted in detail upon the likeness of the moral sense to the external senses, and he had first concerned himself with the sense of beauty because he thought its presence was relatively easy to demonstrate, and that once demonstrated, the way would be prepared for arguments in support of the claim that man has a moral sense and that virtue is real. But the analogical argument in Turnbull

[28] *Discourse*, pp. 251-252.
[29] *Principles*, 2: 164-165.

167

is at once more central, more explicit, and more epistemologically oriented than anything in Hutcheson or the other sentimentalists.

This analogical argument consists of three known factors in the form of principles or propositions which have been discussed:

1. There is an established body of natural philosophy, that is, a body of authentic, reliable, and useful knowledge concerning the material world.
2. Man's natural furniture of the mind includes dispositions and faculties which make knowledge of the material world possible.
3. Man's natural furniture of the mind includes dispositions and faculties which are essentially similar to those which make knowledge of the material world possible, but whose orientation is toward the moral world.

From these propositions Turnbull claims to deduce a fourth:

4. There can be, and is, an established body of moral philosophy, that is, a body of authentic, reliable, and useful knowledge concerning the moral world.

In short, Turnbull concludes that just as we have been given by Providence mental equipment which suits us for knowledge and control of the material world, so have we been given by Providence mental equipment for knowledge and control of the moral world. "*Order*," he says, "*is kept in man* as well as *in nature.*" We see what we can do and how we do it in *natural* philosophy. We need only do the same—for we have the analogous faculties— and we will establish an equally valid *moral* science. We have natural powers, which have natural objects, and which produce natural knowledge. We have moral powers; our experience of the domain of natural philosophy demands that we conclude that all the "powers given to man, are so placed, that they have their proper materials, occasions, means and objects for their exercise and gratification."[30] Morality is far from being the arbitrary fiction that Hobbes and Mandeville claim. It is, rather, as fixed and as

[30] *Principles*, 1: 396-398.

real as Newtonian mechanics. Or at least it will be as soon as our faculties for moral knowledge are used in the same manner that our faculties for natural knowledge have already been used. Then, it might be said, we shall see that virtue is as real as celestial dynamics, and vice as real as the laws of falling bodies.

IV. It is clear, then, that Turnbull joined the moral sense school in the attack on ethical scepticism, and in an effort to identify man's moral faculty and to authenticate its workings and objects. To accomplish these identical ends, Turnbull obviously borrowed heavily from the earlier members of the school. His work, like theirs, is marked by an inductive-introspective approach that places a premium on "ordinary" moral experience and language, as against metaphysical speculation and philosophical subtlety; a tendency to resolve certain philosophical difficulties through the elaboration of a faculty psychology; an *a priori* commitment (empiricist claims notwithstanding) to the view that human nature is uniform and unchanging; and an unswerving confidence in man and nature and in their providential foundation. In most respects, then, Turnbull is too derivative to be of great interest. However, in the clarity of his explanation of the reliability of our senses, and in his willingness to take for granted what epistemological sceptics doubt, he is of interest. When it comes to justifying his appeals to common sense, common language, and common experience, Turnbull is clearer than his predecessors. If one approaches his writings with this query, "Why does Turnbull think we can rely on our common sense beliefs and why does he believe that we can trust our mental faculties to the extent that they are taken to be fully reliable and authoritative?" one does not fail to find an explicit reply. We can rely on common sense, he plainly says, because it is a manifestation of common (universally shared) faculties of mind that are guaranteed reliable by the wise and providential design of nature.

Speaking of a certain argument regarding the moral sense, Turnbull says, for example, that "this reasoning is not above the reach of any one; it is what every person who thinks at all, is naturally led to by the turn and disposition of the human mind."

It is not that beliefs and ideas themselves are innate, for Turnbull does not believe that there are innate ideas or innate knowledge. Rather, there is a capacity for finding true wisdom, a natural sense of knowledge, and, of course, the moral sense.[31] It is these that are innate and universal, and it is because of them that certain propositions are universally accepted and self-evident: every man can discover them or will recognize them if they are pointed out to him. Similarly, it is because such common senses or dispositions underlie all operations of the mind that our common language is a reliable philosophical guide. Because mankind shares these senses, each man speaks, *philosophically*, alike; each expresses common experiences and beliefs in one "general voice of mankind."[32]

Furthermore, these faculties are said to be universally good faculties. Man has been "excellently provided by nature for very great acquisitions in knowledge, power, virtue and merit," assuming only that he uses his natural abilities as they themselves direct. Or, again, we have by the "Author" of our nature been "excellently equipped and furnished for attaining to a very considerable degree of moral perfection, or of knowledge and virtue by due culture of our natural endowments." When to this is added that there is no more ultimate explanation for these faculties and powers than to say that they were "so framed by nature," or that the Author of our nature "hath so constituted us, and so appointed things," it becomes clear that Turnbull's belief in universal and providentially placed faculties and powers underlies his appeal to common sense and common language. It is, as he says, the ultimate principle of explanation.[33]

V. An appropriate short title for Turnbull's position might well be "Teleological Realism." His is not a perceptual realism in the sense that we are said to perceive objects directly as a naïve realist claims, but an epistemology which insists that what we come to believe as a result of the operation of our natural faculties

[31] *Principles*, 1: 137-139, 205; 2: 241.
[32] *Discourse*, p. 272.
[33] *Principles*, 1: 133-134, 221, 227.

is in fact true. Whatever may be the precise mechanism of the several kinds of human perception, the result is veridical belief, knowledge of things as they really are. We have the faculties to perceive real things. Nature is adjusted to us so that we may so perceive, and hence we know that those things which we seem to see and feel and know are in fact seen and felt and known because we also know that we have been made in a reliable fashion. Teleological Realism is the view that from the instinctive nature of our perceptions, and our instinctive belief in them, we can infer that the objects or qualities believed in are in fact real, and that we can make this inference because we are well designed by a benevolent Nature or Deity. Or, alternatively, Teleological Realism is a form of *naturalism* which claims that those things that our God-given faculties cause us necessarily to believe are by this very necessity guaranteed to exist. It is, in short, what I have earlier called "Providential Naturalism."

It is the (relative) clarity with which Turnbull enunciates this form of naturalism, I suggest, that constitutes his most important philosophical contribution. The view that those things which our God-given faculties necessarily cause us to believe in are by this very necessity guaranteed to exist is, to be sure, implicit in the earlier philosophers who influenced Turnbull. However, he makes this view explicit in a way they do not. Further, it seems safe to assume that it was he who first brought this position to the attention of his more famous and more talented student, Thomas Reid. This latter fact is important for there are grounds for claiming that the most fundamental point of difference between Reid and Hume is to be found in the tendency of Reid to adopt this supernaturalistic, teleological perspective, while Hume, of course, rejects all such supernatural guarantees of our faculties and beliefs. Reid, along with his teacher, insists that every man has an implicit, unavoidable "natural belief" in his senses. Not even sceptics, who have maintained that the senses are fallacious, have been able to avoid this trust: In "all the history of philosophy, we never read of any sceptic that ever stepped into fire or water because he did not believe his senses, or that shewed in the

conduct of his life less trust in his senses than other men have."[34]
Reid also agrees with Turnbull that the mind has a distinct constitution or nature, which includes innate instincts, faculties, and
powers of several sorts, and, even more importantly, is well adapted
to its purposes. At the outset of his *Inquiry into the Human Mind*,
he announces that the "fabric of the human mind is curious and
wonderful, as well as that of the human body. *The faculties of the
one are with no less wisdom adapted to their several ends than the
organs of the other*."[35] And, as did Turnbull, he considers our
instincts, faculties, and powers to be the "natural furniture" of
the mind; his "first principles," which are "the immediate dictates
of our natural faculties," include a belief in the propositions that
"*those things do really exist which we distinctly perceive by our senses,
and are what we perceive them to be*," and that "*the natural faculties,
by which we distinguish truth from error, are not fallacious*."[36] And
finally, it is not just that these principles are dictated by our
natural faculties; the faculties are themselves guaranteed by God.
It is indeed natural for me to believe that there is an external
object of a specifiable quality causing the sensations I now have,
and it is natural because it is due to an original principle of human

[34] *The Works of Thomas Reid*, 1: 259 (hereafter cited as *Works of Reid*).

[35] *Works of Reid*, 1: 97. Not even in morals does Hume make this claim. His
view is more nearly that, because morality is an entirely human affair, moral
knowledge has been adapted to man. That is, as morality is a human affair, one
that grows out of human nature and human experience, it is, not surprisingly,
suited to human needs and capacities. There is no transcendental moral dimension
(known or of concern to us). Hence we need no supernatural or transcendental
guarantee of our moral perceptions.

[36] *Works of Reid*, 1: 441-447; 2: 591. In the later location Reid adds, "Thus
we shall find that all moral reasonings rest upon one or more first principles of
morals, whose truth is immediately perceived without reasoning, by all men come
to years of understanding. . . . As we rely upon the clear and distinct testimony
of our eyes, concerning the colours and figures of bodies about us, we have the
same reason *to rely with security* upon the clear and unbiassed testimony of our
conscience. . . ." Reid goes on to say that we "cannot indeed prove that those
faculties are not fallacious, unless God should give us new faculties to sit in
judgment upon the old." But this is a meaningless concession, given that he has
already asserted that our faculties, moral as well as natural, immediately perceive
the truth and can be relied upon with security. In these circumstances, what
further proof would be desired?

nature, while the guarantee of such beliefs lies in the fact that they are based on principles or powers which are the "gift of Heaven."[37] It is the Supreme Being who has given us the powers and faculties which He saw would be necessary for our survival and progress, and who has implanted in us principles that lead us to think and act in a way suited to the rest of His creation.[38] It is because the laws of our nature are established by the will of the Supreme Being that we can trust them implicitly. Since it is God himself who has established a connection of belief between our sensations and the external world, then we surely know as fully as man could ever know that there is an external world, and that it is not unlike what we believe it to be. Whether or not Reid was fully committed to this particular realism,[39] Hume was not—despite the fact that, irony of ironies, the authorship of the *Treatise* was once attributed to Turnbull.

[37] *Works of Reid*, 1: 105-106, 425.

[38] *Works of Reid*, 1: 423. McCosh published a paper by Reid entitled "Of Constitution." In it Reid says, "As soon as this truth is understood that two and two make four, I immediately assent to it, because God has given me the faculty of discerning immediately its truth. . ." (*Scottish Philosophy*, p. 475). Reid also notes, somewhat less optimistically, that we may as well trust our natural faculties, for if we are deceived by them, "we are deceived by Him that made us, and there is no remedy" (*Works of Reid*, p. 130). It seems clear, however, that Reid thinks that our faculties are reliable, and that his optimism does not really waver.

[39] I have said only that Reid shows a tendency to adopt Turnbull's realism because an alternative interpretation, one that denies that God serves as a ground of Reid's refutation of scepticism, is possible. See, for example, Paul Vernier, "Thomas Reid on the Foundations of Knowledge and his Answer to Skepticism," in *Thomas Reid*, ed. S. F. Barker and T. L. Beauchamp (Philadelphia: Philosophical Monographs, 1976), pp. 14-24. Vernier interprets Reid as "an epistemologist . . . who directly challenges the Cartesian doctrine that knowledge must have foundations immune to all possible doubt." Vernier is almost certainly correct to say that Reid rejected any "extrinsic justification" of beliefs such as an appeal to God's nondeceptiveness would provide, at least so long as *extrinsic* is understood as the kind of appeal to God that is found in Descartes. This appeal Reid does explicitly reject, but not without going on to say that the reliability of our faculties must be admitted as a first principle if any other truths are to be admitted, as they are admitted, of course, by Reid. Sometimes Reid seems to be saying that we need not search out the foundations of our knowledge (so far is Vernier correct) because these foundations come from Nature or Heaven or God. Reid's position may be considerably less crude than Turnbull's, but it is far more akin to his than to Hume's.

PART 2

I. Henry Home (Lord Kames after 1752) did not publish his *Essays on the Principles of Morality and Natural Religion* until 1751,[40] but this is no reason to exclude him or this work from a discussion of the context in which Hume's philosophy developed. Kames had been, or had tried to be, a patron to his younger kinsman and, as both men were intensely interested in philosophy—both are said to have participated in the discussions of the Rankenian Club—there can be little doubt that they discussed philosophy before the composition of the *Treatise*. That they did so after 1739-1740 is beyond doubt, for not only did Hume present Kames with a corrected copy of the *Treatise*, but we have the testimony of Boswell (who abandoned a biography of Kames in favor of Johnson's), who reports that Kames finally, one spring morning when there was nothing more important to do, read the *Treatise* and made some observations on it. When next the two men met, Kames greeted Hume: "Well, David, I'll tell you news. I understand your book quite well." And then, according to Boswell, "he shewed him his Objections, and David, who was not very ready to yield, acknowledged he was right in every one of them."[41]

Unfortunately, we cannot be sure that the objections to Hume that Kames published in March 1751 are those that allegedly silenced Hume earlier. If they are, it seems unlikely that Hume was silenced, although he may well have remained silent, for he approved of the manner in which Kames had responded to the *Treatise*. "Have you seen our Friend Harrys Essays?" he wrote to Michael Ramsay. "They are well wrote; and are an unusual instance of an obliging method of answering a Book. Philosophers must judge of the question; but the Clergy have already decided

[40] Published anonymously by Kincaid and Donaldson, Edinburgh, in March 1751, according to an advertisement in the *Scot's Magazine* (see Ross, *Lord Kames and the Scotland of His Day*, p. 98). Hereafter cited as *Essays*. A second edition of the work, also anonymous, appeared in 1758, and a third, with Kames's signature, in 1779. The second edition has been reprinted (Hildesheim and New York: Olm Verlag, 1976), and because of its ready availability, it is cited here, with significant variants from the first edition noted.

[41] James Boswell, *Private Papers . . . from Malahide Castle*, ed. G. Scott and F. A. Pottle, 18 vols. (New York: privately printed, 1928-1934), 15: 273-274.

it, & say he is as bad as me. Nay some affirm him to be worse, as much as a treacherous friend is worse than an open Enemy."[42] But, whether silenced or not, it is clear that Hume took Kames to be answering the *Treatise*, not in agreement with it; and this, too, will be seen to show that those who claim there is no essential difference between Hume and his Scottish critics—who interpret Hume and Reid, for example, as two peas in the same naturalistic pod—are quite mistaken.

II. Kames's *Essays* is in two parts, with the first devoted to morality, the second to epistemological and metaphysical issues. In the former, Kames reveals himself to be a disciple of Shaftesbury, Hutcheson, and Butler, for he adopts the moral sense position in regard to the moral sceptics, and gives high praise to Butler's recognition that our moral faculties are authoritative. Some moralists—Locke is the one most often mentioned—acknowledge no motive to action except self-love, a very defective representation of human nature, Kames says, and one so far from the truth that it could be ignored were it not that errors in morality "seldom fail to have a bad tendency." Like his predecessors, Kames traces this error to the inability of Locke and others to restrain their speculative tendencies in favor of "the slow and more painful method of facts and experiments; a method that has been applied to natural philosophy with great effect."[43] Following this method also leads Kames to the conclusion that there is a clearly discernible human nature, which "manifests itself in a

[42] Hume to Michael Ramsay, June 22, 1751, in *Letters*, 1: 162. Kames was thought as bad or worse than Hume because of his suggestion that although man's actions are determined, they are accompanied by a delusive sense of freedom. Kames retracted this view in the second edition of the *Essays*, and offered still another opinion in the third and final edition. For an account of Kames's changing views on freedom, and the possible influence on them of Jonathan Edwards, see Paul Ramsay, "Introduction," *Remarks on the Essays on the Principles of Morality and Natural Religion . . . by the Reverend Mr. Jonathan Edwards. . . .* in *The Works of Jonathan Edwards*, 5 vols. (New Haven: Yale University Press, 1957-1977), 1: 443-452.

[43] *Essays*, pp. 23-24. In contrast, the "accurate Locke" and "several ingenious writers" are said to have followed the preferred method in the "science of logics" (p. 23).

certain uniformity of conduct," and which is constituted of specific "principles" (faculties, instincts, and powers). Included among these is the faculty known as the moral sense, whose operation causes there to arise in us simple, undefinable feelings of right or wrong whenever we observe with attention human action or character, or by which we perceive the morality or immorality of actions. Contrary to Hutcheson, Kames does not claim that the moral sense is a motivating principle, but he does see it as the authoritative guide to action, such that whenever a moral object is presented to us, we have, "without the intervention of any sort of reflection," a particular feeling: we feel that a certain character or action is good (or evil), and that we are obliged to approve the character or perform the act. Thus in Kames, the moral sense is very much like what Butler termed "conscience," and is, as Kames (not Butler) says, "the voice of God within us."[44]

III.   Kames's views in morals are almost entirely derivative, but in speculative (epistemological and metaphysical) matters, he appears to make a genuinely original contribution, for he transforms the moral sense attack on moral scepticism into the common-sense attack on epistemological scepticism. Other disciples of Shaftesbury and Hutcheson (Turnbull, for example) had utilized their arguments, but had not broadened the focus of this approach to include a refutation of other forms of scepticism. Kames, in the second part of the *Essay* does refocus the moral sense position in just this way, and, building on the stock-in-trade of the moral sense school—the appeal to man's well-designed faculties and feelings—lays out in systematic fashion the foundations of the Scottish common-sense attack on the sceptical views of Berkeley and Hume.

In part 2 of the *Essays*, Kames says in his prefatory "advertisement," that he has attempted to throw "new light upon the principles of human knowledge" by following a plan which supports "the authority of our senses, external and internal," and

---

[44] *Essays*, pp. 26-45.

which reveals that "our reasonings on some of the most important subjects, rest ultimately upon sense and feeling."[45] Berkeley, a "bold genius," had undermined the foundation of the authority that was generally accorded the senses by "denying the reality of external objects." If, as Berkeley implies, our senses deceive us in a matter as important as this, what possible authority can they have in other matters? asks Kames. Will we not soon find ourselves doubting, as Hume had, of things in our minds, "of the reality of our ideas and perceptions"? No doubt we shall, and then we shall go on to the ultimate doubt, again as did Hume, "doubt of our own existence." The progression of these doubts is, given an initial doubt about the reality of external objects, natural, for each of the questionable beliefs—in the reality of objects, of ideas and perceptions, and of ourselves—rests on the same foundation: the evidence of our senses.[46]

The first step in Kames's redemptive plan is a reconsideration of belief, a notion "so familiar, as to have escaped the inquiry of all philosophers, except the author of the treatise of human nature."

Kames agrees with Hume that belief is a certain manner of perceiving, and not a distinct perception or activity of the mind. Nor is it a concomitant of all perceptions. However, he finds unsatisfactory Hume's positive view, namely, that belief is a matter of the force and vivacity of some perceptions. Belief, Kames

[45] Essays, p. [iii].
[46] Essays, p. 195. Kames's summary bears repeating in its entirety: "When the authority of our senses is thus founded on the necessity of our nature, and confirmed by constant experience, it cannot but appear strange, that it should come into the thought of any man to call it in question. But the influence of novelty is great; and when a man of a bold genius, in spite of common sense, will strike out new paths to himself, it is not easy to foresee, how far his airy metaphysical notions may carry him. A late author, who gives us a treatise concerning the principles of human knowledge, by denying the reality of external objects, strikes at the root of the authority of our senses, and thereby paves the way to the most inveterate scepticism. For what reliance can we have upon our senses, if they deceive us in a point so material? If we can be prevailed upon to doubt of the reality of external objects, the next step will be, to doubt of what passes in our own minds, of the reality of our ideas and perceptions; for we have not a stronger consciousness, nor a clearer conviction of the one, than of the other. And the last step will be, to doubt of our own existence; . . ."

insists, is not simply a lively manner of conceiving an idea, for the ideas produced by poetry and painting are often forceful and lively, while those produced by history or testimony are not. Yet poetry and painting seldom produce belief, while history and testimony often do. Obviously, then, force and vivacity are not concomitants of all beliefs. Nor are they, equally obviously, the essence or the equivalent of belief, as Hume claims. The real truth, Kames counters, is that belief, although it may well be a modification of the mind, or a "certain peculiar manner of perceiving objects, and conceiving propositions," has no essential relation to force and vivacity. Rather, belief is a simple feeling or unanalyzable modification of mind that cannot be described, only felt.[47]

More important, however, is the source or cause of belief, and this can be determined: It is our senses themselves or, more accurately, the authority of our senses. We believe what we have seen or heard (and what others say they have seen or heard) because we are made in such a way that we cannot, with rare exception, do otherwise. We are so constituted by nature, Kames says, that our senses have an irresistible authority which commands belief in their reports. "There is nothing," he says, "to which all mankind are more necessarily determined, than to put confidence in their senses. We entertain no doubt of their authority, because we are so constituted, that it is not in our power to doubt."[48]

Of course, one may grant that the senses rule with absolute authority, yet question the reliability of that authority. Just so, Kames gives the impression there are very serious grounds for questioning the reports of the senses. He begins the most important essay of his book, that which is titled "Of the Authority of our Senses," by noting that things may often enough "appear to us different from what they truly are," or, in other words, that our senses may deceive us. This comes about either because of some temporary adversity (distance, disturbance of the sense organ, grossness of the medium) or because "there is a deception

---

[47] *Essays*, pp. 181-185. Some of Kames's "arguments" are merely counterassertions (to Hume and Berkeley) and hence are as superficial as they appear here.
[48] *Essays*, pp. 194-195.

established by the laws of nature; as in the case of secondary qualities. . . ." Despite these seemingly crucial shortcomings, he insists that we both *should* and *do* retain confidence in the beliefs our senses give us: "These exceptions notwithstanding, the testimony of our senses still remains a sufficient ground of confidence and trust."[49] Why? Because any irregularly fallacious perceptions give us warning of their fallaciousness—they are confused or obscure, rather than distinct and lively, and hence in "no way invalidate the authority of the senses." Neither are the established and systematic deceptions of more significance. In certain ways the senses regularly deceive us, but Nature has at the same time provided us with the means to discover deceptions, and to make corrections: "In the foregoing instance of secondary qualities," for example, "philosophy easily corrects the false appearances, and teacheth us, that they are to be considered as impressions made upon the mind, and not as qualities of objects."[50]

Furthermore, and more importantly, Kames finds the deceptions of Nature no ground for sceptical alarm. On the contrary, when "any sense presents to our view an appearance that may be called deceitful, we plainly discover some useful purpose intended. The deceit is not the effect of an imperfect or arbitrary constitution; but wisely contrived, to give us such notice of things as may best suit the purposes of life. From this very consideration, we are the more confirmed in the veracity of nature."[51] The appearance of secondary qualities, an impression of warmth or of color, for example, greatly enhances and facilitates our existence; all such deceptions have a similar effect, and hence all ought to be seen for what they are—merely "rational exceptions" to Nature's veracity—that is, as further proof that the commands of our senses are the best and truest guide of thought and conduct.[52]

[49] *Essays*, p. 193.
[50] *Essays*, pp. 193-194.
[51] *Essays*, p. 194.
[52] Kames's diffidence regarding these systematic deceptions is obviously explained by this linking of them to an overall design for our well-being. Because he has already shown, to his own satisfaction at least, that man's nature is perfectly suited to his environment, he believes that he need only show that these deceptions do in fact contribute to man's overall well-being, for this is sufficient to

Kames concludes, then, that our senses have, both de facto and de jure, full authority in the matter of belief, and that this authority is well placed, for it always directs us to our own good. Thinking that he had established these important antisceptical points, Kames might well have been satisfied had he not feared the effects of scepticism. If it were not for the dangerous tendencies of the views of Berkeley and Hume, no effort would be necessary, he says, echoing earlier moral sense philosophers, to establish the reality of the external world or to refute any metaphysical paradox of the philosophers. Such paradoxes are better refuted by common sense than by elaborate reasoning. However, as they could have a damaging influence by leading others to doubt in perversion of nature,[53] a careful examination of the views of Berkeley and Hume is in order.

IV. The "fundamental proposition" of Berkeley's philosophy, Kames argues, is the claim that "we can perceive nothing but our own ideas or perceptions." But this proposition, which does indeed seem fundamental to Berkeley and the entire "way of ideas," fails to withstand Kames's examination. He begins by noting that the claim is ambiguous. If we take *perception* in its proper sense,[54] as signifying every object we perceive, there can be no objection to the proposition, for it is nothing but a tautology

---

prove their trustworthiness, which is not the same as absolute truthfulness. His point apparently is: Yes, we are deceived by secondary qualities, but were we not our pleasures would *necessarily* be reduced, our safety *necessarily* diminished. Therefore, it is clear that the guidance of our senses ought to be accepted, as in fact it is.

[53] Kames makes clear which damaging influence is of most concern to him. If Berkeley's argument does not lead to "universal scepticism," it does at least "favour . . . Atheism. If I can only be conscious of what passes in my own mind, and if I cannot trust my senses when they give me notice of external and independent existences; it follows, that I am the only being in the world; at least, that I can have no evidence from my senses, of any other being, body or spirit. This is certainly an unwary concession; because it deprives us of our chief or only means for attaining knowledge of the Deity" (*Essays*, p. 196).

[54] In the first edition of the *Essays*, Kames often uses *impression* where he writes *perception* in the second. Also, the latter occasionally substitutes *feeling* for *idea*. Cf. pp. 243-247 and 279 of the first edition, to pp. 197-200 and 222 of the second. This change may result in greater clarity or precision, but it does not alter Kames's fundamental position.

telling us that we perceive only what we perceive. However, if we understand the proposition in the sense in which Berkeley intended it, if, that is, we take it to mean that we can perceive nothing but "what exists in our own minds," the matter is quite different. First, no evidence whatsoever is offered in its support: Berkeley has simply taken it for granted, expecting us to do likewise. But a proposition of this import, Kames maintains, one which has the effect of "annihilating the whole universe," Berkeley's mind excepted, must be supported by clear and convincing evidence if we are not to reject it summarily. Nor can it be said that the proposition is self-evident. Berkeley himself seems to agree that it is contrary to the opinion that prevails among mankind, and Kames reinforces this view by insisting that it is an opinion "contradictory to common sense" and the direct contrary of evident fact: We are "conscious of many things which are not present to the mind; that is, which are not, like perceptions and ideas, within the mind." Thirdly, although we may not find it easy to explain just how it is that we perceive external objects, we gain nothing from Berkeley's theory; it is just as difficult to explain how we perceive "our own ideas, or the impressions made upon us," as it is to explain perception of external objects.[55] And finally, this "bold doctrine" sets limits on the power of the author of nature, for Berkeley is left to argue that "a faculty in man to perceive external objects, would be a contradiction, and consequently a privilege not in the power of the Deity to bestow on him." However, this contradiction has not been proven, says Kames, and as it has not, the existence of such a faculty is possible. Given that it is possible, "we have the very highest evidence of

[55] *Essays*, pp. 207-210. These arguments are all repeated by Reid, who acknowledges his debt to Kames. This perhaps explains why Reid emphasizes "*my philosophy*" when he writes to James Gregory, "The merit of what you are pleased to call *my philosophy*, lies, I think, chiefly, in having called in question the common theory of ideas, or images of things in the mind, being the only objects of thought" (*Works of Reid*, 1: 88). Reid does present, however, other and more profound arguments against the theory of ideas. See D. F. Norton, "Reid's Abstract of the *Inquiry into the Human Mind*," in *Thomas Reid*, pp. 125-132; and S. M. Weldon, "Thomas Reid's Theory of Vision" (Ph.D. diss., McGill University, 1978), esp. chap. 3.

its reality that our nature is capable of, not less than the testimony of our senses."[56]

In contrast to Berkeley, Kames argues that by both sight and touch we have an immediate (intuitive, noninferential) perception[57] "of things as having an independent and continued or permanent existence." If we look at an object, a tree, for example, we perceive color, figure, extension, and sometimes motion. When these perceptions are considered more carefully, we discover that they are not perceived as isolated entities bearing no relation one to the other, but as related or connected together. We can obviously look from one place to another, seeing color here, motion there, extension in a third place, but these perceptions are altogether different from the "impression made by a tree, where the extension, motion, and other qualities, are introduced into the mind as intimately united and connected." If we go on to ask how these perceptions are related, everyone will recognize that they are qualities of some substance and that "they are perceived as inhering in or belonging to some *substance* or *thing*, of which they are *qualities*. . . . Thus it is that the perception of *substance*, as well as of *qualities*, is derived from sight." Furthermore, just as the qualities are *perceived* to inhere in the substance, so, too, the substance and its qualities, the tree, "are perceived as altogether independent of us, as really existing, and as having a permanent existence."[58] In fact, the only puzzle is that philosophers who show no hesitation in speaking of qualities should question the existence of substance. To call something a quality is to imply that it is a quality of something. For example, to speak of *figure* necessarily presupposes that there is *something* figured: "A quality is not intelligible, unless upon the supposition of some other thing, of which it is the quality," nor can we even conceive of the qualities that are perceived by sight and touch separate from the things in which they inhere. "It is not in our power to

[56] *Essays*, pp. 208-209.
[57] On the immediacy, or noninferential character, of our perceptual or "intuitive" knowledge, see *Essays*, p. 268n.
[58] *Essays*, pp. 198-199. The sense of touch is said to give similar impressions, but hearing and smelling "do not suggest any impression of independency, or permanent existence."

separate, even in imagination, colour, figure, motion, and extension, from body and substance," Kames says, and concludes that it thus "comes out, that *substance* makes a part, not only of every perception of sight and touch, but of every conception we can form of colour, figure, extension, and motion."[59]

It is not difficult to explain, Kames continues, how it is that an external object can make an impression on us in such a way as to result in a "direct perception" of the object itself. First, it is granted that some impressions make us conscious only of themselves, not of external objects, and furthermore, that all the impressions of two senses, smelling and hearing, are of this sort. If, for example, we experience a particular sweet fragrance, we "feel" a smell and no more. It is only by additional experience obtained through sight or touch that we learn that a particular fragrance is always to be found when a particular body, a rose, may be seen or touched.[60] On the other hand, by taste and touch we are "conscious not only of an impression made at the organ, but also of a body which makes the impression." There is nothing to learn and nothing to infer; we have a direct perception of the objects sensed. Touch alone, says Kames, that "least intricate of our feelings," gives proof enough to overthrow Berkeley's entire philosophy: "We have, from that sense, the fullest and clearest perception of external existences that can be conceived, subject to no doubt, ambiguity, nor even cavil."[61]

The most problematic sense of all is sight. The puzzling feature is action at a distance. Kames agrees that a body that is distant from the mind cannot itself act on the mind, and hence that there is need of some medium or "intermediate means" to complete an act of vision. The fact that an image of the object seen

[59] *Essays*, pp. 200-201.

[60] Kames grants that sounds and smells are also taken to be qualities, and yet do not, on his account, presuppose substance. This he explains by saying that sounds and smells come to be called qualities only derivatively. After the quality-substance distinction has been made, we by habit apply the term *quality* to sounds and smells because they more resemble qualities than substances. That this is no real solution to the problem raised does not occur to Kames, but that is scarcely surprising, given his failure to distinguish between generic and individual senses of substance (*Essays*, pp. 200-201).

[61] *Essays*, pp. 210-212.

is found on the retina suggests that it may be somehow "painted" on the eye, a supposition that is no more difficult to understand than the supposition that the image on the retina is itself transferred to the mind. If this suggestion is correct, then sight is somewhat like touch: both depend upon an impression made at the organ. But sight also differs from touch and all other senses in that this impression at the organ is not felt. Nature has "carefully concealed this impression from us, in order to remove all ambiguity, and to give us a distinct perception of the object itself, and of that only." In this way, all confusion as to the location of the object is eliminated—we take the object to be at a distance because we feel it only, not it and the impression on the eye.[62]

Speaking generally, then, Kames's theory of perception varies according to the sense involved. In smelling and hearing there is an impression or feeling at the organ affected, but none of an external object. In seeing there is no feeling at the organ, no first impression, as he calls it, but there is a second impression, a feeling of the object of vision, which is to say, a feeling of the real, independent, and continuing existence of that which is seen. Tasting and touching, the remaining senses, include both first and second impressions, so that they, along with seeing, give us directly evidence of a real, external world. If we then take what Kames has said about the human constitution to be correct, we can now see that our evidence of the external world is first-rate. It is the evidence of a reliable constitution which has been shown to bespeak an external world from every perspective, and with no contrary evidence. Our belief in the external world is the result of the natural workings of our senses. Unlike our belief that secondary qualities are external, this belief stands every test and survives every criticism. There is no need to correct our natural belief in real objects, and no possibility of doing so. In the words of the concluding paragraph of this essay:

[62] *Essays*, pp. 212-215. Kames grants that some aspects of visual perception surpass our understanding, but in this regard they are no different from "the operation of magnetism, electricity, and a thousand other natural appearances; and our ignorance of the cause, ought not to make us suspect deceit in the one case, more than in the other."

Whether our perception of the reality of external objects correspond to the truth of things, or whether it be a mere illusion, is a question, which, from the nature of the thing, cannot admit of a strict demonstration. One thing is certain, that supposing the reality of external objects, we can form no conception of their being displayed to us in a more lively and convincing manner, than in fact is done. Why call a thing in doubt, of which we have as good evidence as human nature is capable of receiving? But we cannot call it in doubt, otherways than in speculation, and even then but for a moment. We have a thorough conviction of the reality of external objects; it rises to the highest certainty of belief; and we act, in consequence of it, with the greatest security of not being deceived. Nor are we in fact deceived. When we put the matter to a trial, every experiment answers to our perceptions, and confirms us more and more in our belief.[63]

V.   With the authority of the senses and the existence of external objects so handily established, Kames turns his attention to Hume's sceptical doubts about personal identity, necessary connection and our knowledge of the future, and our knowledge of the existence and nature of the Deity.

Kames agrees with Hume that had we only the perceptions of the external senses, we "never could have any consciousness of *self*," and would be in a perpetual reverie of ideas unconnected to ourselves, and with no notion of personal identity. However, man is not in Kames's view constituted with external senses only, but has also internal senses, including one that gives him "an original perception or consciousness of himself, and of his existence."[64] It is surprising, too, that Hume did not detect this perception, for it is of the "liveliest kind," as befits an impression necessary for self-preservation. And, had Hume detected this impression, his puzzles regarding personal identity would have been at an end, for it is this immediate, intuitive, and unana-

---

[63] *Essays*, pp. 215-216.

[64] *Essays*, p. 189. This sense is inactive at times, Kames notes; as when we are asleep or when we are lulled by relaxing phenomena or books.

lyzable "consciousness of self, carried through all the different
stages of life, and all the variety of action, which is the foundation
of *personal identity*. It is by means of this perception, that I consider
myself to be the same person, in all varieties of fortune, and in
every change of life."[65]

Kames's main purpose in the essay titled "Of the *Idea* of *Self*,
and of *Personal Identity*," he says, is to point out that our knowledge of our selves and of our continuousness is not obtained by
reasoning or argument, but is an immediate and intuitive perception. Similarly, knowledge of causal connections and of future
events cannot be obtained by reasoning, nor by the external
senses, but is the result of the same kind of direct perception.
Once again Kames accepts Hume's critical arguments,[66] but once
again he maintains that Hume has missed the fact that there are
internal senses and internal perceptions that give one knowledge
not only of the connections between one's will and actions, but
also of the connections between entirely external objects. Consequently, Hume's conclusions on this matter appear prima facie
mistaken, for man everywhere displays a more than adequate
insight into cause and effect. The macrocosm testifies that man
has genuine knowledge of causality and particular causal relations;
if he did not, he could not conduct himself in the efficient manner
that he does; he could not live in such harmony with his complex
surroundings, or prepare for the future. But, Kames concludes,
as man does act coherently and plan sensibly, his knowledge of
causal relations cannot be so limited as Hume has claimed,[67] and

[65] *Essays*, pp. 190-191.

[66] "Our idea of power is not derived, either from reason or experience. . ."
(*Essays*, pp. 221-222).

[67] Kames suggests (pp. 225-232) that Hume is inconsistent in his sceptical
attack on the idea of power or causal efficacy, for he does in fact have and use
an idea of power, as when he speaks in the *Philosophical Essays* (now *An Enquiry
Concerning Human Understanding*) of the power of bread to nourish, of "a power
in one object, by which it infallibly produces the other, and operates with the
greatest certainty, and strongest necessity" (cited from *Essays*, pp. 231-232). This
shows, Kames goes on, how difficult it is to stifle "natural perceptions and sentiments," and he then in a note cites Horace: "Naturam expellas furca, tamen
usque recurret." Concerning this motto, Turnbull, Kames, and Hume, see below,
p. 191.

186

he takes this conclusion as support of the claim that our knowledge of causal relations is a matter of direct and immediate perception. When we see one body come in contact with a second,
which then alters its condition, the "power" which binds one to
the other is, he says, "perceived as a quality in the acting body."
Furthermore, the same sense makes it "self-evident" that nothing
could come into existence without a cause, while another internal
sense discovers to us the uniformity of nature, and hence gives
us knowledge of future events.[68]

Last, but most importantly for Kames, this internal sense enables us to perceive, along with the "perception we have of any
object as an effect . . . a cause proportioned to the effect." This
is most important to him because as he had earlier written, "The
main purpose [of the *Essays*] is, to show, that our senses, external
and internal, are the true sources from whence the knowledge of
the Deity is derived to us." Kames entertains no doubts about
having achieved this end, given his self-proclaimed discovery of
the remarkable battery of inner senses that had escaped the more
sceptical—or less careful—Hume. After all, if the perception of
an object includes insight into the cause of the object, then any
object that appears to us as brought about for some end will
necessarily include knowledge of its designer. We are "necessarily
determined, by a principle in our nature, to attribute such effects
[as show design] to some intelligent and designing cause." It may
be in our power to conceive that such an effect is the result of
blind fate or chance, but it is not in our power to believe such
an account: "Every object which appears beautiful, as fitted to a

---

[68] *Essays*, pp. 227, 234. Regarding our knowledge of the uniformity of nature,
Kames writes: "And this subject will afford, it is hoped, a fresh instance of the
admirable correspondence which is discovered betwixt the nature of man and his
external circumstances. What is already made out, will lead us directly to our
point. If our conviction of the uniformity of nature be not founded upon reason
nor experience, it can have no other foundation but sense. The fact truly is, that
we are so constituted, as, by a necessary determination of nature, to transfer our
past experience to futurity, and to have a direct perception of the constancy and
uniformity of nature. Our knowledge here is intuitive, and is more firm and solid
than any conclusion from reasoning can be. This perception must belong to an
internal sense, because it evidently hath no relation to any of our external senses"
(*Essays*, pp. 239-240).

187

good end or purpose, is the effect of a designing and benevolent cause. We are so constituted, that we cannot entertain a doubt of this, if we would." If, then, as Kames says, the world itself is perceived as the effect of some invisible and designing cause, the dictates of our nature lead us immediately to the conclusion that there is a supreme First Cause, while the beauty and order of the effect lead us to recognize the intelligence, power, and benevolence of this First Cause. In short, our inner senses lead us intuitively to certain belief in the Deity as necessary cause of the universe, and our nature itself prevents us from giving the least credence to Hume's sceptical attack on the argument from design.[69] As he looks back to enjoy the discoveries he has made, Kames summarizes his position:

> The Deity . . . hath not left us to collect his existence from abstract or perplexed arguments, but makes us perceive intuitively that he exists. When external objects are presented to our view, some are immediately distinguished to be effects, not by any process or deduction of reasoning, but merely by sight, which gives us the perception of cause and effect. Just in the same manner, this whole world is seen or discovered to be an effect produced by some invisible designing cause. The evidence of this perception cannot be rejected, without introducing universal scepticism; without overthrowing all that is built upon perceptions, which, in many capital instances, govern our judgments and actions; and without obliging us to doubt of those things, of which no man ever doubted. . . . From effects so great and so good as those we

[69] *Essays*, pp. 197, 234-235, 269. It would be surprising, Kames says, if we had to learn of the Deity by abstract reasoning or argumentation, given that so many other important matters (our duty, the existence of external objects, for example) are simply perceived. However, Kames does not suppose there is an internal sense designed to give us information on every important topic. In "this grand apparatus of instinctive faculties, by which the secrets of nature are disclosed to us, one faculty seems to be with-held; though in appearance the most useful of all. . . ." This is a faculty to determine what things are harmful, what beneficial. This faculty has been withheld, he thinks, because it is possible to learn by experience what it could disclose, and hence it is unnecessary. Instincts or inner senses are given, he concludes, only when "experience cannot aid us" (pp. 243-244).

see through the universe, we necessarily infer the cause to be both great and good. Mixed or imperfect qualities cannot belong to him.[70]

VI. Kames and Turnbull are alike, I have suggested, in extending Hutcheson's moral epistemology into the speculative or metaphysical domain. However, of the many points of similarity between them, I wish to focus on only two of a more general sort. First, Kames also exercised an important (one scruples to say "profound") influence on Thomas Reid. Turnbull was Reid's teacher, but Reid's philosophical views developed slowly (his *Inquiry* first appeared when he was in his mid-fifties). In the critical period immediately following his first university appointment (1751), Reid read Kames's *Essays* and sometime in the next decade met his fellow antisceptic and began a friendship that was both intimate and long. No philosophical conclusions follow from such facts, of course, but Reid included in his own *Essays on the Intellectual Powers* two comments which reveal a high regard for Kames, and hence suggest that his own work may be usefully viewed as influenced by him:

> It would be ingratitude to a man whose memory I most highly respect, not to mention my obligations to the late Lord Kames, for the concern he was pleased to take in this Work. Having seen a small part of it, he urged me to carry it on; took account of my progress from time to time; revised it more than once, as far as it was carried, before his death; and gave me his observations on it, both with respect to the matter and the expression. On some points we differed in opinion, and debated them keenly, both in conversation and by many letters, without any abatement of his affection, or of his zeal for the work's being carried on and published. . . .[71]

A very respectable writer has given a good example of

[70] *Essays*, pp. 304-305. Kames's solution to the problem of evil, here hinted at and elsewhere (*Essays*, pp. 279-297) discussed in more detail, is entirely conventional.
[71] *Works of Reid*, 1: 215.

[precisely defining terms] by explaining, in an Appendix to his "Elements of Criticism," the terms he has occasion to use. In that Appendix, most of the words are explained on which I have been making observations; and the explication I have given, I think, agrees, for the most part, with his.[72]

Second, Kames, too, is clearly a Providential Naturalist.[73] Nearly every philosophical issue that occurs to him he settles by an appeal to one or another of man's senses which, he claims, give us direct or intuitive knowledge overturning whatever doubts metaphysicians or sceptics have tried to raise. Included in this intuitive grasp of reality is knowledge of the existence of God, and of his intelligent and benevolent design in creating the world that we occupy, and of which we are a part. But if not only nature, but also man's nature is the effect of this intelligent and benevolent design, then there can be, as Kames repeatedly says, no doubt about the reliability of those faculties which are a part of our nature, or those beliefs that arise naturally from them. "The senses which are appropriated to the discovery of truth, unerringly answer their end," he concisely puts it, and the ultimate explanation of this remarkable fact is nearly as concise: "A very slight view of human nature, is sufficient to convince us, that we were not dropt here by accident. This earth is fitted for man, and man is fitted for inhabiting this earth."[74]

Kames, then, is a complete naturalist. He holds that all our crucial beliefs arise naturally and irresistibly. As this shows these beliefs derive from the Author of Nature, we can conclude that

[72] *Works of Reid*, 1: 230. For more on the philosophical exchanges between Reid and Kames, see especially Reid's letters to Kames in *Works of Reid*, 1, and "Unpublished Letters of Thomas Reid to Lord Kames, 1762-1782," ed. I. S. Ross, *Texas Studies in Literature and Language* 7 (1965): 17-65. The point of mentioning the purely historical connection between Reid and Kames is to draw attention once again to Reid's tendency to follow in the direction of his moral-sense predecessors, and, most particularly, to incorporate an appeal to final causes into his philosophy. See n. 39 to this chapter.

[73] As he seems fully and uncompromisingly to recognize: "The application of the argument from final causes, to prove the existence of a Deity, and the force of our conclusion from beautiful and orderly effects to a designing cause" leads to conclusions that are natural and obvious (*Essays*, pp. 267-268; see also p. 306).

[74] *Essays*, pp. 158-159, 243.

they are entirely trustworthy, true. Those who have insisted that
Hume is a naturalist would have done well not only to note this
form of naturalism, but also Hume's own strictures on this ambiguous and overused term. For, if Turnbull, Kames, and Hume
are in agreement with Horace that although nature be expelled
by a pitchfork, she will nonetheless soon return upon us,[75] Hume's
view of what is to be made of this fact—of what, that is, we are
to say about the validity of these natural beliefs—is far from that
of the Providential Naturalists. Hume read on in Horace and was
insistent, no matter how often he was brought back to the safe
shores of natural belief, on setting off again upon doubt's boundless sea:[76] "Methinks I am like a man, who having struck on many
shoals, and having narrowly escap'd ship-wreck in passing a small
frith, has yet the temerity to put out to sea in the same leaky
weather-beaten vessel, and even carries his ambition so far as to
think of compassing the globe under these disadvantageous circumstances. . . ."[77]

[75] "Naturam expellas furca, tamen usque recurret" (*Epistles*, 1: vi, 1).
[76] "Cras ingens iterabimus aequor" (Odes, 1: vii, 32).
[77] *Treatise*, pp. 263-264. Granted, Hume does go on to say that the weakness
of his faculties "reduces me almost to despair, and makes me resolve to perish on
the barren rock, on which I am at present, rather than venture myself upon that
boundless ocean, which runs out into immensity." But these, he says, "are the
sentiments of my spleen and indolence. . . . I feel an ambition to arise in me of
contributing to the instruction of mankind. . . . Since therefore 'tis almost
impossible for the mind of man to rest, like those of beasts, in that narrow circle
of objects, which are the subject of daily conversation and action, we ought only
to deliberate concerning the choice of our guide, and ought to prefer that which
is safest and most agreeable. And in this respect I make bold to recommend
philosophy. . ." (pp. 264, 270-271).

« 5 »

Hume's Scepticism
Regarding Natural Beliefs

> But in Metaphysics or Theology, I cannot see how either
> of these plain & obvious Standards of Truth can have place.
> Nothing there can correct bad Reasoning but good Rea-
> soning: and Sophistry must be oppos'd by Syllogism.
> David Hume to
> Gilbert Elliot of Minto,
> 1751

PART 1

I.   It is well known that David Hume's philosophical views were
actively criticized by a number of his Scottish contemporaries:
first by Henry Home, Lord Kames, and later by Thomas Reid,
James Beattie, and others, all generally known as Scottish common-sense philosophers, or as Scottish realists. Why, it is asked,
did Hume not reply to these philosophers?[1]

The earliest answer to this question, I believe, is that given
by James Boswell and implied by the Scots themselves: Hume did
not answer because he could not answer, because he himself had
been answered. In Boswell's account, Kames read the *Treatise*
and made his objections known to Hume, who had no reply,
except to acknowledge that Kames was entirely correct.[2] If all of

[1] See, for example, Mossner, *Life of Hume*, pp. 297-299, and *Kemp Smith*, pp.
3-8.

[2] See chap. 4, pp. 174-175. Kames's copy of Hume's *Treatise* is located in the
Hoose Library of Philosophy, University of Southern California. For a list of
Hume's more important corrections found in this copy, see Wallace Nethery,
"Hume's Manuscript Corrections in a Copy of A *Treatise of Human Nature*,"
Papers of the Bibliographic Society of America 57 (1963): 446-447.

Hume's Scottish critics were as astute as Kames is alleged to have been, then it seems likely that Hume did not reply because he had nothing to say—nothing, that is, except a difficult-to-make acknowledgment of error. But in that case we shall have to wonder why it was that Hume went on writing and publishing essentially the same errors. For it was after this conversation with Kames that he published (and revised and republished many times) his *Enquiries*, a number of essays, and both the *Natural History of Religion* and the posthumous *Dialogues on Natural Religion*. Thus we can scarcely take Boswell's suggestion seriously.

Another answer, nearly as old and of considerable authority, is that of Hume himself. Very early in life, he tells us in his brief autobiography, he vowed never to enter into any dispute. Much that we know of Hume's life confirms that he was in fact of a nondisputatious character. Two points must be noticed, however: Hume's vow, as with so many resolutions, was not always kept, as the recently discovered *Letter from a Gentleman* seems to indicate. And even if he did not want to enter into a public dispute, Hume was willing to discuss philosophical issues with his friends and did so regularly in the large body of his correspondence that has been preserved. Hume may on principle have refused to write a reply to Kames, Reid, or Beattie, but that would not preclude his having and expressing disagreement with them. Privately, in fact, Hume did express his contempt for Beattie, and is reported to have angrily denounced the *Essay on Truth* as "a horrible large lie in octavo."[3] Despite his anger, he in this case kept his resolve never to answer opponents directly. The most he would do was to compose a brief "advertisement," which was thereafter to be included in all editions of his *Essays and Treatises* and in which he calls the *Treatise* the unsatisfactory product of his immature thought. This advertisement, wrote Hume to Strahan, his printer, "is a compleat Answer to Dr. Reid and to that bigotted silly Fellow, Beattie." In some sense, Hume may be correct; the advertisement may be the "compleat Answer" he took it to be. Nevertheless, his account of his silence is scarcely more satisfying

[3] Mossner, *Life of Hume*, p. 581.

than is Boswell's.[4] Neither account touches philosophical issues
nor adds to our understanding of the philosophical differences
between Hume and his Scottish critics, assuming that there were
such differences.

A third account of Hume's silence is of some philosophical
interest, for it asserts that there were no significant differences
between him and the Scots. In part, this answer is the converse
of Boswell's; that is, Hume was silent not because he was proved
wrong, but because he was in essential agreement with his Scottish critics and there was nothing he needed to say.[5] Thus Norman
Kemp Smith has argued that Hume had no reason to reply to
Reid or even to Beattie, for Hume could see from his perusal of
their work that there were no essential differences between him
and them. With the common-sense beliefs maintained by Reid
and Beattie, says Smith, Hume "had no quarrel; he was no less
ready than Reid or Beattie to agree that a philosophy stands self-
condemned if it forbids us to indulge in them. Any attempt to
displace them either by other beliefs or by a sheerly sceptical
refusal to entertain any beliefs whatsoever is, Hume has insisted,
bound to be self-defeating. If the choice be only between them

[4] Hume to William Strahan, October 26, 1775, in Letters, 2: 299-302. The
advertisement first appeared in 1777. Mossner says of it that "Complete answer,
certainly, it is not. As a matter of fact, it is no answer at all, but the petulant
retort of an aging man, tired of controversy and sick in body" (p. 582). Those
of us who insist on taking the Treatise as Hume's preeminent philosophical work
are indebted to James Noxon's perceptive discussion of this Advertisement. Noxon
points out that the Advertisement is far from a repudiation of the philosophical
positions taken in the Treatise. See Hume's Philosophical Development (Oxford:
Oxford University Press, 1973), pp. 154-155. Noxon's suggestion that the most
important difference between the Treatise and the Enquiries is the vastly reduced
concern with psychology that is found in the latter is, I think, deserving of more
attention.

[5] I have previously suggested that Kant had something of this sort in mind
when he said that the Scottish philosophers were forever missing Hume's point
and forever proving what he never doubted, and "that Hume might fairly have
laid as much claim to common sense as Beattie and, in addition, to a critical
reason (such as the latter did not possess). . . ." (See my "Hume and His Scottish
Critics," McGill Hume Studies, p. 311.) However, David Stove led me to question
this suggestion. Stove argues (letter of January 10, 1980) that Kant was speaking
of Hume as a person and outside philosophy, not suggesting philosophical agreement between him and his Scottish critics.

and a philosophy which denies them, it is common sense that must be held to."[6]

Richard Popkin has offered much the same interpretation. He credits Reid with noting that both Berkeley and Hume had shown that "the basic principles of modern philosophy led systematically to total scepticism" about our ability to know. According to Popkin, Reid's response to this development is not to ignore or scoff at the arguments of Berkeley and Hume, but "to reconsider the assumptions on which modern philosophy is based. When the conclusions of philosophy run counter to common sense, there must be something wrong with philosophy. . . . Reid offered his common-sense realism as a way of avoiding Hume's skepticism by employing as basic principles the beliefs we are psychologically unable to doubt." To this account of Reid, Popkin appends the agreement thesis found in Kemp Smith: "Hume was unimpressed by Reid's argument. Reid, he believed, had seen the problem but actually offered only Hume's solution. . . ."[7]

This account, although it is philosophically interesting, is nevertheless unsatisfactory for the simple reason that it is mistaken. Hume's philosophy is not essentially like Reid's, as Kemp Smith suggests. Nor is Reid's essentially like Hume's, as Popkin appears to suggest.

Hume's philosophy is different from that of Kames, Reid, and Beattie in fundamental ways; his opinions (not just his words, as Thomas Brown suggested) are antithetical to theirs. If we look

[6] *Kemp Smith*, p. 8. Kemp Smith also suggests (pp. 5-11) that Hume recognized this essential agreement, and reveals this fact in his letter to Reid of February 25, 1763. Although Hume's letter may bear this interpretation, it is far from being direct evidence in favor of the view Kemp Smith adopts.

[7] *The Encyclopedia of Philosophy*, s.v. "Skepticism." Popkin also cites the well-known remark of Thomas Brown (1778-1820) in which Brown claims that Hume and Reid differ in words or emphasis, but not in opinion: "Reid bawled out, We must believe in an outward world; but added in a whisper, We can give no reason for our belief. Hume cries out, We can give no reason for such a notion; and whispers, I own we cannot get rid of it." (Cited by Sir James Mackintosh, to whom the remark was made, in his *On the Rise and Progress of Ethical Philosophy*, s.v. "Thomas Brown." This work was first published in 1830 as a part of the eighth edition of the *Encyclopædia Britannica*.) Brown's comment contains an element of truth, but, as will be seen, it glosses over important differences between Hume and Reid.

again at Hume's Scottish critics we will see that this is so, and then how it is that Hume has replied to them.

II. The Scottish common-sense philosophers were centrally concerned to refute scepticism. This is not to say that there is nothing in their philosophy that can be appreciated independently of this concern, but it does seem clear that they were to a great extent motivated by a common desire to refute the influential and allegedly dangerous views of the sceptics. In this, as in much else, the common-sense philosophers follow closely the lead of the earlier moral sense philosophers. Shaftesbury, Hutcheson, and Turnbull had been alarmed by the moral scepticism of Hobbes and Mandeville, and had sought to counter that scepticism by establishing the reality of virtue and the veracity of our moral faculties. Turnbull, it will be recalled from chapter 4, professes a concern over "scepticism about internal experience" or about those "scepticks" who "shock all common sense" by ascribing all of our social behavior to "art, custom, and superadded habit" and who otherwise zealously propagate "doctrines tending to discourage virtue" and "throw a most gloomy damp upon all truly noble and generous ambition."[8] Similarly, Kames expressed the fear that the "metaphysical paradoxes" of Berkeley and Hume would have an unfortunate influence, leading others to the same or even more dangerous perversions of nature.[9]

Reid, Beattie, and the other common-sense philosophers were equally alarmed by the epistemological and metaphysical scepticism which they thought implicit in Locke, partially explicit in Berkeley, and fully explicit—and openly celebrated—in Hume. This scepticism was thought to be equally dangerous, and equally in need of refutation. As Reid says, the sceptics are dangerous because their views are contrary not only to the Christian faith, but also to both natural and moral philosophy and the prudence and virtue of the ordinary man. If scepticism reigned, he insists, all "piety, patriotism, friendship, parental affection, and private

[8] *Principles*, 1: 12-13.
[9] See above, pp. 177-189.

196

virtue, would appear as ridiculous as knight-errantry."[10] It is true, of course, that much of what the sceptics claim is patently absurd, but they strike at the very heart of truth and virtue by denigrating human capacity until man not only appears a mere Yahoo, but feels debased as well. The sceptical philosopher, he says,

> sees human nature in an odd, unamiable, and mortifying light. He considers himself, and the rest of his species, as born under a necessity of believing ten thousand absurdities and contradictions, and endowed with such a pittance of reason as is just sufficient to make this unhappy discovery: and this is all the fruit of his profound speculations. Such notions of human nature tend to slacken every nerve of the soul, to put every noble purpose and sentiment out of countenance, and spread a melancholy gloom over the whole face of things.[11]

Beattie, who was not to be outdone in this regard, remarks that

> every doctrine is dangerous that tends to discredit the evidence of our senses, external or internal, and to subvert the original instinctive principles of human belief. In this respect the most unnatural and incomprehensible absurdities, such as the doctrine of the non-existence of matter, and of perceptions without a percipient, are far from being harmless; as they seem to lead, and actually have led, to universal scepticism; and set an example of a method of reasoning sufficient to overturn all truth, and pervert every human faculty. . . . When a sceptic attacks one principle of common sense, he does in effect attack all; for if we are made distrustful of the veracity of instinctive conviction in one instance, we must, or at least we may, become equally distrustful in every other. A little scepticism introduced into science will soon assimilate the whole to its own nature; the fatal fermentation, once begun, spreads wider and wider

[10] *Works of Reid*, 1: 95.
[11] *Works of Reid*, 1: 102, 127.

every moment, till all the mass be transformed into rotten-
ness and poison.[12]

Epistemological scepticism, it was thus agreed, is also a lively
and dangerous influence that must be refuted. To achieve this
end, one must first consider the nature of philosophy itself and
the manner in which it ought to be pursued. As Reid most systematically puts it, philosophers must follow the directions given
to them by Bacon, and the example set by Newton. True philosophy is compared to the good tree that bears good fruit, while
false and counterfeit philosophy, which includes scepticism, bears
no fruit or evil fruit. In general, such false philosophy is said to
be the result of a tendency to substitute hypothesis and speculation for factual inquiry. A more particular form of this misguided
speculative tendency is analogical reasoning, or the tendency to
explain one part of the world in terms that have been drawn from
the explanation of other aspects of the world. The view, for
example, that we do not perceive external objects directly, but
through the medium of ideas (the view Reid calls the "hypothesis
of ideas" and in which he found the source of Hume's sceptical
conclusions), Reid takes to be the result of such a speculative,
analogical tendency. Modern philosophers, he says, have "taken
over what transpires in the movement of bodies, and too rashly
applied it to the thought of the soul." The more judicious philosopher, one who prizes accuracy, refuses altogether to hypoth-
esize concerning that which he does not know, and when faced
with phenomena that are difficult to comprehend he will admit
ignorance rather than allow himself to be drawn into the distinctions and subtleties of speculation.[13]

[12] James Beattie, An *Essay on the Nature and Immutability of Truth, in Opposition
to Sophistry and Scepticism*, 4th ed. (London: E. and C. Dilly, 1773), pp. 477-
478 (hereafter cited as *Immutability of Truth*). Elsewhere (p. 19), Beattie says that
Hume's philosophy "hath done great harm." See also pp. 17-18. For another
common-sense response to scepticism, see James Oswald, An *Appeal to Common
Sense in Behalf of Religion*, 2 vols. (Edinburgh: Kincaid and Bell, 1766-1772),
passim.

[13] The *Philosophical Orations . . . Delivered at the Graduation Ceremonies in King's
College, Aberdeen, 1753, 1756, 1759, 1762*, ed. W. R. Humphries (Aberdeen:
Aberdeen University Press, 1937), pp. 20-21, 36. The translations used here
were supplied by the late Guy Désautels.

The true philosopher, however, need not be antiintellectual. Speculation is rejected, but we can nonetheless follow the inductive, observational method recommended by Bacon and proven beyond all doubt by Newton. We must, Reid says, put "hypotheses aside" and seek knowledge of "principles from observation and experience alone." The true philosopher will not speculate, will not construct theories; the true philosopher will, following Bacon's advice, observe the particulars of experience and, if he is able, derive from these the general and descriptive laws to which they conform. From the particulars, he says, that "are first known in the nature of things, by means of the senses, experience, testimony and other modes" it is "the task and work of the philosopher . . . to ascend legitimately to laws of nature and general axioms, . . ."[14] or to "trace out the laws of nature, by induction from the phenomena of nature, is all that true philosophy aims at, and all that it can ever reach."[15]

When the Scottish philosophers put aside speculation and devoted themselves in what they were satisfied was a factual, scientific fashion to the subject which most concerned them, human nature or the human mind, they made, so it seemed, surprising progress. We know that Hutcheson, Turnbull, and Kames claimed to discover that the human mind has a specifiable constitution or nature, that it has innately a set of faculties, powers, or instincts that enable us to know the world around us. Reid and Beattie are in accord. Indeed, Reid was so impressed with the design of the human mind that he began his *Inquiry into the Human Mind on the Principles of Common Sense* by announcing, as I have noted, that the "fabric of the human mind is curious and wonderful" as is that of the human body. "The faculties of the one are with no less wisdom adapted to their several ends than the organs of the other."[16] It is no surprise, then, that Reid is unable to accept Locke's view that the mind passively receives the imprint of the world. On the contrary, Reid describes the mind in terms that remind one of a well-equipped factory: he speaks of the "natural furniture," of the "tools and engines," and the "powers" of the

[14] *Orations*, pp. 16, 39.
[15] *Works of Reid*, 1: 157.
[16] *Works of Reid*, 1: 97.

mind, for example, and specifically defines *faculties* as those "pow-ers of the mind which are original and natural, and which make a part of the constitution of the mind."[17] Taken together, Reid's discoveries, as much as those of Turnbull and Kames, lead to the conclusion that we know and understand the world in which we live, for our faculties and powers give us reliable information about the world.

III.   Taking what has so far been said of Scottish common-sense philosophy in a very general sense, it is possible to see some interesting similarities between the views of these philosophers and those of Hume. The *Treatise of Human Nature*, after all, is "an Attempt to introduce the experimental Method of Reasoning into MORAL SUBJECTS," and in the Introduction to it Hume argues that it is time to dispense with speculation in favor of the methods lately developed and proven in natural philosophy. Furthermore, the propensities and instincts Hume postulates are not entirely unlike those made so much of by the common-sense philosophers. Hume, too, finds that the mind is made up of certain natural powers and that these function to make our belief in certain important matters—the existence of the external world or nec-essary connection, for example—more or less automatic and (in many circumstances) unavoidable. There is, though, a crucial

[17] *Works of Reid*, 1: 208, 218, 221. Beattie, though never much given to understatement, seems no more extreme on this point than his predecessors. Speaking of the "internal senses" and the "moral feelings" they produce, he says, "I cannot prove . . . that they are conformable to any intrinsic and eternal relations of things; but I know that my constitution necessarily determines me to believe them just and genuine, even as it determines me to believe that I myself exist, and that things are as my external senses represent them. . . . We cannot disbelieve the evidence of internal sense, without offering violence to our nature." He illustrates his position by the following: " 'I ought to be grateful for a favor received. Why? Because my conscience tells me so. How do you know that you ought to do that of which your conscience enjoins the performance? I can give no further reason for it; but I *feel* that such is my duty.' Here the investigation must stop; or, if carried a little further, it must return to this point: 'I know that I ought to do what my conscience enjoins, because God is the author of my constitution. . . . Why do you obey the will of God? Because it is my duty. How do you know that? Because my conscience tells me so,' &c." (*Immutability of Truth*, pp. 70-74). Very similar remarks are made about the external senses; see pp. 60-90.

difference between Hume and his Scottish critics. However often
Hume may say that we have certain natural propensities to believe
this or that, he does not go so far as to say that what we must
naturally *believe* must be *true*. Hume does not conflate *psychological*
certainty with certain knowledge or unavoidable *doxa* with *epi-
steme*. Nor does he suggest that the latter necessarily follows the
former. Yet his Scottish critics seem to conflate repeatedly and
characteristically these two kinds of certainty, to insist that what
we cannot avoid *believing* must be reliable or true.[18] The deter-

[18] More precisely, the common-sense philosophers conflate psychological certainty and certain knowledge insofar as they suppose that the terms *unavoidable
beliefs* and *known to be true* have the same extension. That they do not suppose
the terms have the same meaning is clear from the discussion which follows.
There it is shown that these philosophers maintain that our unavoidable beliefs
are guaranteed by God or Nature, and it is this that makes them certain, or
certainly true.

Hume does not suppose that the necessity of believing in particular entities
(independently existing objects, for example) constitutes a proof that there must
be such entities. Those who say that his views are essentially like those of his
Scottish critics fail to note this feature of his thought. Conversely, Hume does
not suppose that because we cannot justify our belief in particular entities (independently existing objects, to keep the same example), it is known that there
are no such entities. Those who think that Hume's philosophy was essentially
negative or that he *denied* that there are objects, causes, or an essential self fail
to note this feature of his thought. The two errors are very much alike in ascribing
to Hume an anthropocentrism which he consistently attempted to avoid. Hume
is intensely interested in what humankind believes and in what its members can
or cannot prove to be the case. But he does not suppose that reality must be of
a certain form because a belief that it is so cannot be shaken off, nor does he
suppose that there is no reality of a particular sort because the evidence that is
available to us falls necessarily short of proving the existence of this particular
kind of thing. Hume's logic (*Treatise*, book 1 and the first *Enquiry*) includes a
great deal of psychology, but he has not, on the whole, conflated logic (theory
of proof) and psychology (theory of belief and doubt).

Hume's March 1751, letter to Gilbert Elliot is relevant to this point. He writes:
"I cou'd wish that Cleanthes' Argument [the argument from design in the *Dialogues*] coud be so analys'd, as to be render'd quite formal & regular. The Propensity
of the Mind towards it, unless that Propensity were as strong & universal as that
to believe in our Senses & Experience, will still, I am afraid, be esteem'd a
suspicious Foundation. Tis here I wish for your Assistance. We must endeavour
to prove that this Propensity is somewhat different from our Inclination to find
our own Figures in the Clouds, our Face in the Moon, our Passions & Sentiments
even in inanimate Matter. Such an Inclination may, & ought to be controul'd,
& can never be a legitimate Ground of Assent" (*Letters*, 1: 155). In other words,
although we can in theory distinguish between a mere "Inclination" and what is

minations of our nature, says Turnbull, are by no means deceitful; *all* of them are "right guides, or guides which do not deceive, or lead astray," and hence what we *must* believe can be taken as necessarily true.[19] We cannot doubt our senses, says Kames, but must necessarily repose our confidence in them; if we can trust our natural faculties, says Reid, and he is sure we can, there can be no question about the objective existence of matter. "We are," says Beattie, "convinced [for example] by a proof, because our constitution is such, that we must be convinced by it." Whether our belief in such cases is consistent with the real nature of things is, he adds, "a question which no person of a sound mind can have any scruple to answer, with the fullest assurance, in the affirmative."[20]

It is not difficult to discover why the Scots are so doubly certain, and hence essentially different from Hume. Hume tells us that our natural propensities lead us to specifiable beliefs, but he remains diffident about those beliefs; he does not insist upon their truth or reliability, although they may be the best we have, and more effective than the productions of philosophy. The common-sense philosophers, on the other hand, insist that what we naturally believe is true, and must be accepted as true—that it should not and need not be so much as questioned. And they say this because they are convinced that our natural faculties are God-given, are a part of the overall design of a Providential Nature,

---

more significant, a "Propensity," in any given case we must prove that what seems like a propensity is not merely an inclination, for inclinations provide no ground for assent. But if we must test *apparent* propensities before they can become the ground of assent, then it is not our propensities themselves that provide the ultimate criterion of the legitimacy of assent—what we cannot help believing may be ill-grounded, and what is ill-grounded may be false despite the necessity of our belief. The strongest and most universal propensity provides a ground of assent, or affective certainty, but not a ground for epistemic certainty. Hume's position constitutes at least an implicit criticism of the Cartesian view that indubitability is the criterion of truth. For further contrasts between Hume and Descartes on belief, see part 2, sec. V of this chapter, and secs. III (pt. 3) and IV of chap. 6.

[19] *Principles*, 2: 164-165.
[20] For Kames's remarks to this effect, see chap. 4 of this book, pp. 176-179, 185. In addition, see *Works of Reid*, 1: 289, and *Immutability of Truth*, pp. 61-62.

and can be trusted implicitly. They believe that what we naturally believe is in fact supernaturally guaranteed.

Even leaving aside biographical considerations (Reid was a clergyman, for example), it is not difficult to see why the realists' thought took this religious turn. Dangerous scepticism was loose in the land, and any foothold it might gain would in time poison the whole of society. For them, it was not enough to say (as Hume, who was not alarmed by scepticism, had said) that there are natural faculties and natural beliefs. The nature of the enemy required that one know, not merely believe. But how are we to guarantee that we know that which the sceptic doubts? By looking to the source of those faculties which lead us to believe. Our perception of external objects, Reid tells us, is the result of the operation of one of the original and natural powers of the mind, a part of its constitution. Hence it is by our nature that we are led to believe in external objects. So, replies the sceptic, it may very well be, Dr. Reid, that our natural faculties lead us universally to a belief in an external material world, but it remains to be asked whether this belief is accurate. How does the fact that I am naturally led to this belief help to prove anything at all about the world? The answer returned, in its simplest form, is that our natural faculties are the "gift of Heaven." Our natural faculties tell us that those things really do exist which we distinctly perceive by our senses, and are what we perceive them to be, while the reliability of these faculties themselves is guaranteed by the Creator. The Supreme Being gave us those powers that are necessary for survival and progress, and those faculties that enable us to think and behave in a manner suited to the world in which he has placed us. The faculties that constitute our nature were established by God himself, and hence they may be trusted implicitly. God himself causes us to believe in the external world, and so we know that there is such a world, and that it conforms to our belief in it.[21] Beattie summarizes the position aptly when he says:

---

[21] *Works of Reid*, 1: 425; 445. See also 1: 152, 167, 198, 438, 468, for example. Reid is careful to point out that he does not consider God a guarantor of beliefs in the same way that Descartes did: "The existence of a material world, and of

Certain it is, our constitution is so framed, that we must believe to be true, and conformable to universal nature, that which is intimated to us by the original suggestions of our own understanding. If these are fallacious, it is the Deity who makes them so; and therefore we can never rectify, or even detect, the fallacy. But we cannot even suppose them fallacious, without violating our nature; nor, if we acknowledge a God, without the most absúrd and most audacious impiety; for in this supposition it is implied, that we suppose the Deity a deceiver. Nor can we, consistently with such a supposition, acknowledge any distinction between truth and falsehood, or believe that one inch is less than ten thousand miles, or even that we ourselves exist.[22]

Interestingly, Kames's views seem significantly different from his fellow realists, for he readily admits not only that our senses deceive us, but that they do so systematically. Nevertheless, this exception merely underscores his trust in God's providential design of the mind. Our senses, Kames says, may be deceitful for one of two reasons: either because of some temporary adversity—distance, disturbance of the sense organ, irregularity in the sensory medium—or because there is a deception established by the laws of nature, as in the case of secondary qualities.[23] He still insists, however, that we should and do retain full confidence in the evidence and authority of the senses. Any random fallacious perceptions give us warning of their fallaciousness (by being confused or obscure, for example), and hence these erroneous perceptions in "no way invalidate" the senses. Nor do the systematic decep-

---

what we perceive by our senses, is not self-evident, according to [modern] philosophy. Des Cartes founded it upon this argument, that God, who hath given us our senses, and all our faculties, is no deceiver, and therefore they are not fallacious. I endeavoured to shew that, if it be not admitted as a first principle, that our faculties are not fallacious, nothing else can be admitted; and that it is impossible to prove this by argument, unless God should give us new faculties to sit in judgment upon the old" (p. 464). For a comparison of Reid and Descartes on this point, see L. Marcil-Lacoste, "Dieu, garant de veracité, ou Reid critique de Descartes," *Dialogue* 14 (1975): 5-17.

[22] *Immutability of Truth*, p. 62.
[23] *Essays*, pp. 193-194.

tions present any great problem. The senses deceive us, but not only do we find that Nature provides us with the means to correct these false appearances, but we also discover that the so-called deceptions are by no means the result of any imperfection of design. On the contrary, they are "wisely contrived, to give us such notice of things as may best suit the purposes of life. From this very consideration, we are the more confirmed in the veracity of nature."[24]

IV. Hume, of course, is quite unwilling to rest his philosophical hopes or conclusions on the Deity, providential design, final causes, or any appeals thereto. In his early correspondence with Hutcheson, for example, he is critical of the older moralist on precisely this point: "I cannot agree to your Sense of *Natural*. Tis founded on final Causes; which is a Consideration, that appears to me pretty uncertain & unphilosophical. For pray, what is the End of Man? Is he created for Happiness or for Virtue? For this Life or for the next? For himself or for his Maker? Your Definition of *Natural* depends upon solving these Questions, which are end-less, & *quite wide of my Purpose.*"[25]

Similarly, in the *Enquiry concerning Human Understanding*, Hume flatly rejects the occasionalist account of causal relations, scorn-fully terming it *quasi deus ex machina*. The occasionalists explain all creatures and creaturely activity by reference to God's agency. For Hume, this supernatural element is quite unconvincing, for it rests on claims that are not only beyond our experience, but apparently beyond the very reach of our faculties—which is to say that sound philosophy, for Hume, is not based on religious appeals.[26]

Hume also explicitly rejects any attempt to give a divine guar-antee to our faculties. Men are, he grants, led by a "blind and powerful instinct of nature" to "repose faith" in their senses, and

[24] *Essays*, p. 194.
[25] Hume to Hutcheson, September 17, 1739, in *Letters*, 1: 33 (final italics added).
[26] *First Enquiry*, p. 69. The phrase *quasi deus ex machina* occurs in the first and second editions of this work; in subsequent editions Hume substituted the Greek equivalent.

to believe that external objects correspond to our perceptions. However, this "universal and primary opinion of all men is soon destroyed by the slightest philosophy," for this teaches us otherwise. Philosophy makes us doubt that objects are entirely, or even partially, like our perceptions of them, and thus we are "necessitated by reasoning" to depart from our natural beliefs. Then, complication following complication, the teachings of philosophy come in for scrutiny, and we find ourselves unable by any chain of reasoning to prove, as our philosophical system teaches, that perceptions are caused by resembling objects. At this point we can "no longer plead the infallible and irresistible instinct of nature," for philosophical reasoning has shown that instinct to be deficient; nor can we, he says, have recourse to the Supreme Being as guarantor of our beliefs, for that appeal is both inconsistent and question-begging:

> To have recourse to the veracity of the supreme Being, in order to prove the veracity of our senses, is surely making a very unexpected circuit. If his veracity were at all concerned in this matter, our senses would be entirely infallible; because it is not possible that he can ever deceive. Not to mention, that, if the external world be once called in question, we shall be at a loss to find arguments, by which we may prove the existence of that Being or any of his attributes.[27]

Finally, Hume's philosophy contained from the very beginning the basis for the critical treatment of the argument from design which the posthumous *Dialogues concerning Natural Religion* were intended to reinforce. The *Treatise*, written in the middle 1730s, pronounces clearly Hume's view that our knowledge of causes and effects is dependent on experience, as is, indeed, our belief in causal connections. It is these conclusions about causal rela-

---

[27] *First Enquiry*, pp. 151-153. Hume does speak of "a kind of pre-established harmony between the course of nature and the succession of our ideas" (*First Enquiry*, p. 54), and not, I think, entirely ironically. But nothing he says suggests that he agrees with the theistically oriented teleology of his Scottish contemporaries, or of Leibniz, for that matter. What he may mean is helpfully discussed in J. P. Monteiro, "Hume, Induction, and Natural Selection," *McGill Hume Studies*, pp. 291-308.

tions that enable Hume to undercut so effectively the argument from design. On the other hand, the theistic foundation of the Scottish realists' position depends on acceptance of precisely this argument, and, indeed, one variation of the argument is obvious in their work. The mind, they find, is well designed; therefore, they add, it must be the work of a wise and benevolent Creator. Furthermore, since it is the work of such providential design, the mind and the various faculties of mind must be reliable, which means that our faculties do not deceive us. In briefest form, design of mind discovers Providence, Providence vouches for mind. One need not rehearse Hume's strictures on the argument from design to realize that he could not accept this microcosmic version of it. There are no better grounds for arguing that there is a wise and benevolent Providence who is responsible for and who guarantees the so-called design of the microcosm than there are for arguing that there is a wise and benevolent Providence who is responsible for the so-called design of the macrocosm. Given his remarks to Hutcheson, and other comments he makes regarding the possibility of discovering the ultimate springs and principles of the mind, it seems clear that Hume realized this fact early in life, and he remained aware of it throughout his philosophical career. [28]

It also seems likely, given the evidence just outlined, that

[28] Hume's remark in the Appendix (*Treatise*, p. 633), namely, "The order of the universe proves an omnipotent mind," does not, in my opinion, amount to clear counterevidence to my claim that the fundamentals of his criticism of the argument from design are present in his work from the beginning. The remark in question is made in the context of a discussion about the source of the idea of power or necessary connection. Hume denies that this idea is derived from any discovery made by observation of the exercise of the will, for the will is revealed to be merely another cause whose connection with its effect is just as undiscoverable as the connection between physical causes and effects. We "shou'd in vain hope to attain," he concludes, "an idea of force by consulting our own minds." The footnote then tells us that the "same imperfection attends our ideas of the Deity," or, that is, that these ideas are not derived from introspection, but from experience of the world—it is *the order of the universe*, not introspection, that gives evidence of an omnipotent mind. It is the source of the idea that is Hume's concern here. On other occasions he takes up the quality of such proofs, and he shows these to be less perfect than their proponents think. Furthermore, his claims about these deficiencies rest on precisely those disclosures about our causal reasoning that are first made in the *Treatise*.

Hume was aware that he had answered his Scottish contemporaries, was aware that from the very beginning his philosophy constituted just such an answer, and that subsequent works, especially section 11 ("Of a particular providence and of a future state") of the first *Enquiry*, made this answer even clearer. We can see, then, that the correct answer to the question "Why did Hume not reply to his Scottish critics?" is that the question is misconceived and that he did answer them. And we can see that Kemp Smith's explanation, that Hume did not reply because he had no quarrel with the philosophical positions of Reid or Beattie, is seriously mistaken. Hume and Reid differed in substance as well as words, for Hume rejected that supernaturally founded or motivated reliance on natural belief—that curious supernatural naturalism—which characterizes the works of Reid and the other Scots.

PART 2

I.   I have shown, although by "a very unexpected circuit," that Hume refused to abandon philosophy to providentially guaranteed natural belief. It must also be shown that he refused to abandon all speculative philosophy to even a nonprovidential naturalism wherein reason is, as alleged by Kemp Smith, subordinated to feeling. However, before turning to this centrally important matter, some further clarification of Hume's use of "reason" is in order. To this end, I suggest first that Hume, despite his occasional references to the *faculty* of reason, does not think of reason as any kind of occult faculty. Rather, this manner of speaking is intended only to draw attention to certain generally similar human capabilities.[29] In this general sense, Hume apparently thought of reason as a faculty by which ideas or impressions and ideas are

[29] Compare Hume's discussion of the will in *Treatise*, II, 3, 1: By "*will*, I mean nothing but *the internal impression we feel and are conscious of, when we knowingly give rise to any new motion of our body, or new perception of our mind.*" As Hume does not entirely avoid the use of *faculty*, he may well have intended his scathing remarks at *Treatise*, p. 224 to serve as criticism of himself as well as others.

united or separated. "All men have ever allow'd reasoning," he says, "to be merely an operation of our thoughts or ideas." Certainly, this approximate characterization of reason is broad enough to include all the relevant senses of *reason* that were specified in chapter 3.[30] It excludes only reason as noninferential present awareness and reason as a calm, reflective passion, the two uses Hume himself saw as extended or as, strictly speaking, improper.

However, if reason and reasoning have generally to do with the uniting and separating of ideas, we must recognize a further Humean distinction between what might be termed *reflexive* reasoning on the one hand, and *reflective* reasoning on the other. Our inferences from causes to effects are, on Hume's analysis, examples of reflexive reasoning. They are, as he says, immediate and instinctive, or as we might say, involuntary or unwilled. In contrast, reflective reasoning is characterized by deliberation or voluntary, willful activity, or as Hume says, by an "effort of thought." In comparison to the automatic or natural character of reflexive reasoning, reflective reasoning is "forc'd and unnatural."

This reflective reasoning Hume further characterizes as being capable of abstract, abstruse, accurate, balancing, critical, just, or refined analysis, argument, comparison, examination, reflection, scrutiny, or speculation. And, although reflective reasoning is unnatural insofar as it requires an effort, it is entirely natural insofar as it is the product of specifiable aspects of human nature. In the remainder of this chapter I show that Hume not only believed that humans are capable of such reflective reasoning, but also, contra those holding the subordination thesis, that he believed that this form of reasoning is both valuable and effective

[30] Hume's remark is found at *Treatise*, p. 625. My earlier discussion of some of the ambiguities of Hume's use of *reason* is found above, pp. 96-98. Saying that reason is a faculty by which ideas or ideas and impressions are united or separated does not preclude the possibility that the memory or the imagination, for example, are supposed by Hume to be capable of fulfilling a similar function in both similar and different ways. In that event, reason would be distinguished from these faculties by other characteristics.

even to the point that it is able to correct and overturn our natural propensities or sentiments.[31]

If we turn now to an examination of Hume's views about the uses of reason in what he in his letter to Elliot calls metaphysics, and his views about the value of these uses of reason, we will see that he finds our natural beliefs sometimes deficient, and that he not only welcomes analysis and criticism of them as a possibly effective, fruitful enterprise, but even encourages modest speculation. Hume's reply to Elliot—the "Standard of Truth" in metaphysics and theology can only be reason or reasoning—is no casual remark, but the manifestation of a view that permeates and shapes his philosophy.

According to Hume, there is a very cogent reason for accepting one criterion in morals, but demanding another in metaphysics: there are two different kinds of philosophy, a kind which relies on sentiment and a kind which relies on reason. Morals or ethics is of the first sort, metaphysics of the second. The opening lines of the first *Enquiry* suggest such a distinction: "Moral philosophy, or the science of human nature, may be treated after two different manners; each of which has its peculiar merit, and may contribute to the entertainment, instruction, and reformation of mankind." The one considers man as born largely for action, and as influenced in these actions by "taste and sentiment"; man pursues this object and avoids that "according to the value which these objects seem to possess, and according to the light in which they present themselves." Thus the philosophers who concern themselves with these matters treat their subject in an "easy and obvious manner. . . . They select the most striking observations and instances

---

[31] A reminder of the subordination thesis is perhaps also in order here. A recent and unequivocal version of it is Stroud's claim that "in Hume's hands the denigration of the role of reason and the corresponding elevation of feeling and sentiment is generalized into a total theory of man. Even in the apparently most intellectual or cognitive spheres of human life, even in our empirical judgments about the world and in the process of pure ratiocination itself, feeling is shown to be the dominant force." To which is added the remark cited in the Introduction, namely, that Hume's negative arguments "show that reason, as traditionally understood, has no role in human life" *Hume*, pp. 10-11, 14.

from common life; place opposite characters in a proper contrast; and alluring us into the paths of virtue by the views of glory and happiness, direct our steps in these paths by the soundest precepts and most illustrious examples. They make us *feel* the difference between vice and virtue; they excite and regulate our sentiments; . . ."[32]

The other manner of doing moral philosophy considers man as a reasonable, rather than an active, being, and seeks to form his understanding, not his morals. The philosophers who are engaged in this pursuit regard human nature as a "subject of speculation," and they examine that nature in order to discover the principles by which the understanding is regulated or the sentiments excited. Those devoted to this arduous undertaking consider it a scandal that philosophy has not yet determined the foundation of morals, of reasoning, or of criticism. They attempt, then, to fill this void, and "proceeding from particular instances to general principles, they still push on their enquiries to principles more general," until they discover at last the "original principles, by which, in every science, all human curiosity must be bounded. Though their speculations seem abstract, and even unintelligible to common readers, they aim at the approbation of the learned and the wise; and think themselves sufficiently compensated for the labour of their whole lives, if they can discover some hidden truths, which may contribute to the instruction of posterity."[33]

Hume supports such speculative inquiries despite what appear to him to be two indisputable facts about them. It is more than likely that a philosopher's abstruse studies will result in paradox or sheer nonsense. And no matter how reasonable and cogent metaphysical conclusions may be, belief in them may be over-

[32] *First Enquiry*, pp. 5-6. It should be understood that *moral philosophy* has for Hume a much wider extension than does *morals*. The former comprehends those philosophical topics that are not a part of *natural* philosophy (Hume mentions morals, criticism, politics, and logic, where logic includes metaphysics and what we call epistemology) while *morals* is more or less equivalent to our *ethics*.

[33] *First Enquiry*, p. 6.

turned by contrary natural beliefs or natural sentiments.[34] Sometimes this metaphysics is ineffectual and even entirely halted by
these beliefs or sentiments. Nature "can stop our progress, even
in the midst of our most profound reflections, and keep us from
running on with all the consequences of any philosophical opinion."[35]

All too often, metaphysics is rash, dogmatical, containing
"nothing but sophistry and illusion," and fit only for the flames,
while reason itself, he candidly grants, "is so uncertain a guide
that it will always be exposed to doubt and controversy."[36]

In fact, in one splenetic moment Hume remarks, "Very refin'd
reflections have little or no influence upon us." But this opinion
he retracts almost at once, and in the interim has already gone
on to remark that "we do not, and cannot establish it for a rule,

[34] In the early stages of the *Treatise* (I, 3, 7), Hume suggests that belief "must
lie in the *manner*, in which we conceive" an idea, and he defines belief as "A
LIVELY IDEA RELATED TO OR ASSOCIATED WITH A PRESENT IMPRESSION" (pp. 95-96). By
the time he composed the Appendix he was dissatisfied with this ac-
count/definition, and modified it by emphasizing the affective character of the
perception (idea or impression) in question. "We may, therefore, conclude," he
says, "that belief consists merely in a certain feeling or sentiment" and "There
is nothing but the feeling, or sentiment, to distinguish" the objects "presented
by the wildest imagination" from "the most establish'd truths founded on history
and experience" (p. 624). He also here notes the similarity of this sentiment or
feeling to other impressions, including the passions.

There is ample basis, then, for some imprecision in a discussion of the relation
of reason to sentiment or feeling, especially as Hume also used *common sentiments*
to refer to common beliefs. However, the debate on this issue has stayed generally
within intelligible bounds by being posed in terms of the roles and effectiveness,
respectively, of reason and *natural* belief, or, to elucidate *natural belief*, of reason
and those beliefs, feelings, or sentiments which are the product of natural propensities or inclinations. Those holding the subordination thesis maintain that
for Hume reason is entirely ineffectual against, and dominated by, such natural
beliefs or sentiments, and even that this is the view that he most warmly embraced
and made the central teaching of his philosophy. I have not thought to challenge
the claims that belief for Hume is a feeling or sentiment, or that he supposed
that there are natural beliefs in the sense specified. I have accepted these views
as adequately grounded in Hume's text. The subordination thesis is mistaken not
because of what it says about natural belief per se, but because of what it says
about reason and its relation to natural belief.

[35] *Treatise*, p. 214; see also p. 193.
[36] *First Enquiry*, p. 165; *Works*, 3: 466.

that [these reflections] ought not to have any influence; . . ."[37]
In fact, Hume often discounts entirely the fact that our philosophical conclusions are overturned by resurging natural beliefs.
According to him, that nature does not allow us to give credence
to such a conclusion (whether sceptical or dogmatical) does not
imply that the conclusion is false, or that it has been refuted.
Hume does not conflate credibility and truth, or incredibility and
falsehood. Even abstruse and complex conclusions may be true:
a philosopher's reasonings on his subject may indeed be "abstract,
and of difficult comprehension," but this "affords no presumption
of their falsehood. On the contrary, it seems impossible, that
what has hitherto escaped so many wise and profound philosophers can be very obvious and easy." To denigrate all abstruse
philosophy, to insist that we remain satisfied with what is easy
and obvious, or naturally thought, "may justly be deemed more
rash, precipitate, and dogmatical, than even the boldest and most
affirmative philosophy, that has ever attempted to impose its
crude dictates and principles on mankind."[38]

If making refined judgments—the equivalent of doing abstruse
philosophy—is "not so *useful* as common sense," it nonetheless
has value.[39] At the very least, as Hume not only says, but demonstrates, there is a need to "cultivate true metaphysics with
some care, in order to destroy the false and adulterate. . . .
Accurate and just reasoning is the only catholic remedy . . . able
to subvert that abstruse philosophy and metaphysical jargon, which,
being mixed up with popular superstition . . . [has] the air of
science and wisdom."[40] But in Hume's view, such a "true metaphysics" has other, more positive merits; there are objectives

---

[37] *Treatise*, p. 268.
[38] *First Enquiry*, pp. 15-16.
[39] *Second Enquiry*, p. 241.
[40] *First Enquiry*, pp. 12-13. Árdal suggests that a philosopher engaged in such
philosophical activities would by Hume be called "reasonable" in the sense of
having the virtue of reasonableness. Although this is a rather different claim from
any I am making, I believe Árdal's argument is persuasive and that his conclusion
supports my analysis. See "Some Implications of the Virtue of Reasonableness in
Hume's *Treatise*," *Re-evaluation*, pp. 103-104.

and achievements of significant value to man which can be obtained only by inquiries founded on reason, by a true but nonetheless *rational* metaphysics, and Hume explicitly defends such inquiries from the chilling effects of common opinion and common sentiment.

II. For one thing, Hume says, to establish a "general maxim, that no refin'd or elaborate reasoning" is ever to be pursued is to close man off from his natural curiosity about the underlying causes of all that goes on around him, and to insist upon what is almost an impossibility, namely, that he be content to consider only that "narrow circle of objects, which are the subject of daily conversation and action." It is to ask that man give up entirely something that is also a part of his nature, for he is a reasonable being as well as an active and sociable one. Certainly, it was Hume who found that reason is "incapable of dispelling" those clouds of doubt which it arouses by its refined reflections, and that "nature herself suffices to that purpose" by causing one's attention to be focused elsewhere. "I dine," reads the famous passage, "I play a game of back-gammon, I converse, and am merry with my friends; and when after three or four hours' amusement, I wou'd return to these speculations, they appear so cold, and strain'd, and ridiculous, that I cannot find in my heart to enter into them any farther."[41] But these sentiments of "spleen and indolence" are themselves pushed aside, and the mind, "collected within itself" again, is "naturally *inclin'd*" to continue these disturbing researches. At such times, he reports,

> I cannot forbear having a curiosity to be acquainted with the principles of moral good and evil, the nature and foundation of government, and the cause of those several passions and inclinations, which actuate and govern me. I am uneasy to think I approve of one object, and disapprove of another; call one thing beautiful, and another deform'd; decide concerning truth and falshood, reason and folly, without know-

[41] *Treatise*, pp. 268-271.

ing upon what principles I proceed. I am concern'd for the condition of the learned world, which lies under such a deplorable ignorance in all these particulars.[42]

Such sentiments, he goes on to say, "spring up naturally in my present disposition," and should there be an attempt "to banish them, by attaching myself to any other business or diversion, I *feel* I shou'd be a loser in point of pleasure; and this is the origin of my philosophy." The pleasures of the mind are as natural as those of action and society, and hence there can be no sound argument to the effect that nature compels us to give up completely all metaphysical interests or that nature eliminates the need or possibility of metaphysics.[43]

Further, Hume argues, we cannot depend upon sentiment to decide the refined issues of philosophy, for just at the moment that such an issue is to be decided, our sentiments become disturbed and ineffectual. Hume describes this situation in a general way in the Introduction to the *Treatise*, where he notes that moral philosophy is handicapped in its experimental approach because "reflection and premeditation would so disturb the operation of my natural principles" that it is impossible to reach any just conclusions from the phenomena considered. Later in the *Treatise* he reveals that there are even within moral philosophy differences of this sort, and that some matters absolutely demand a rational settlement. An argument "which wou'd have been esteem'd convincing in a reasoning concerning history or politics, has little or no influence in these abstruser subjects, even tho' it be perfectly comprehended; and that because there is requir'd a study and an effort of thought, in order to its being comprehended: And this

---

[42] *Treatise*, pp. 270-271.
[43] *Treatise*, p. 271. Hume also counterattacks by noting (p. 268) that the argument against "refin'd or elaborate reasoning" is itself built upon reasoning "which will be allow'd to be sufficiently refin'd and metaphysical," and hence is self-contradictory. Speculative activities are natural and pleasurable; the proposed general prohibition against speculation is itself dependent on such activities. On two counts, then, speculation or metaphysics is defended.

effort of thought disturbs the operation of our sentiments, on which the belief depends."[44]

But if Hume believes that sentiment is unable to decide certain abstruse issues because reasoning disturbs the sentiments, he also believes that reliance on our natural impulses would totally eliminate certain abstruse studies, the outcome of which may be both significant and beneficial. In Hume's view, belief in the objective existence and permanence of the external world is natural and, if we take him literally, quite unavoidable: " 'tis in vain to ask," he says, "*Whether there be body or not?* That is a point, which we must take for granted in all our reasonings." If this is so, then there is no real question about the existence of body, there is no possibility of pursuing in any significant fashion one traditional metaphysical issue. "Without any reasoning, or even almost before the use of reason," we are led to believe that there is an objective, external universe.[45] And so it would be with all metaphysical issues were sentiment or natural belief made the standard by which all metaphysical inquiry is to be judged. There would be no problems, nothing to reason about; no metaphysics would be possible. But in that case there would be no abstract and abstruse reasonings to improve our sentiments and natural beliefs, as Hume claims there are. If all our abstruse reasonings are subjected to the test of natural beliefs, such beliefs could never be made more accurate by these reasonings. The criticism of a natural belief implicit in any reasoning would, just to the extent that it

[44] *Treatise*, p. 185. Nature, Hume says elsewhere, trusts reason with certain "operations," or leaves to it certain legitimate "offices." See *Second Enquiry*, pp. 202, 294.

[45] *Treatise*, p. 187; *First Enquiry*, p. 151. Hume surely realized that there is at least one sense in which this issue *can* be raised, for Berkeley had done so. His point is, perhaps, that we cannot *effectively* question the existence of body, cannot disbelieve in such a way that our behavior is permanently affected. He says as much in the *First Enquiry*, p. 155 and again at p. 160 when speaking of the Pyrrhonian. Here is a case in which Hume might well cite Horace on the strength of nature along with his contemporaries. See n. 75, chap. 4 of this book. A Humean paraphrase of "naturam expellas furca, tamen usque recurret," is found at *Works*, 4: 391: "That if you chace away nature, tho' with ever so great indignity, she will always return upon you."

conflicts with that belief, be rejected as vain or unsound and untenable.

That Hume believed a philosophy subservient to reason leads to views that are more accurate than our natural beliefs is apparent. Reason may lack the endurance of some of these beliefs, but it can nonetheless discover in them errors and confusions, and on occasion actually correct—change—what is instinctively accepted. Much as "nature provides a remedy in the judgment and understanding, for what is irregular and incommodious in the affections," so does she provide a remedy for our inaccurate beliefs. There is, for example, the "notable" and "natural" illusion that the tastes of an olive and a fig lie on different spatial coordinates, just as the olive and the fig do. Philosophers, although they may at times share this illusion, are able not only to resist it, but also to account for it, and offer what appears to be a more accurate view.[46] Or, following nature only, we believe that the very images presented by the senses are the external objects themselves; philosophers may be more accurate when they claim that we are presented with representations only, not with the objects themselves.[47]

In the "operation of reasoning," there seems "always a real, though often an unknown standard, in the nature of things," Hume says. He goes on to insist that neither truth nor falsehood vary with the opinions of mankind. How widespread a belief might be—how natural in the sense of *common*—is in this regard irrelevant: "Though all [the] human race should for ever conclude, that the sun moves, and the earth remains at rest, the sun stirs not an inch from his place for all these reasonings; and such conclusions are eternally false and erroneous."[48] It is an instinct, Hume adds elsewhere, which has led us to believe that the future will resemble the past, but this instinct, like others, "may be fallacious and deceitful."[49] And the imagination, another of our instinctive faculties, is not only "inconstant and fallacious," but

---

[46] *Treatise*, pp. 489, 236-237.
[47] *First Enquiry*, pp. 151-152.
[48] *Works*, 3: 217-218.
[49] *First Enquiry*, p. 159.

also leads by natural and necessary steps to conclusions that are contrary to one another.[50] All in all, our natural beliefs or inclinations are not particularly reliable. The implication is that any means by which we might correct them is to be retained and utilized, and that the best means at our disposal is a metaphysics whose truth is to be determined by reason, not by sentiment or conformity to natural beliefs.[51]

In addition, Hume thought that many principles of nature are hidden from view, and for this reason also he wished to encourage a critical, yet speculative, philosophy. The errors of our natural attitude are not mere blunders, but are, rather, systematic short-comings due to the depth and complexity of phenomena. In natural philosophy, he points out, many hypotheses, "contrary to first appearances," have been found on "more accurate scrutiny, solid and satisfactory. Instances of this kind are so frequent that . . . if there be more than one way in which any phenomenon may be produced . . . there is a general presumption for its arising from the causes which are the least obvious and familiar."[52] And if moral philosophy seems different, so that the simplest and most obvious hypothesis is most likely correct, it is nonetheless the case that "irregular and extraordinary appearances" are frequently discovered here as well, and hence that confused common opinions regarding moral philosophy also benefit from critical scrutiny.[53] The ordinary man tends to accept the first appearance of things, and more often than not, he is wise to do so. Sometimes, however, as when he supposes uncertain events have uncertain or chance causes, the ordinary man is simply mistaken, no matter how compelling or prevalent such opinions may be. One merit

[50] *Treatise*, p. 265.
[51] Reason can determine, for example, the conformity of our ideas to matters of fact or the consistency of our arguments and in this way establish the "true metaphysics" of which Hume speaks.
[52] *Second Enquiry*, pp. 298-299.
[53] *Works*, 3: 374. Especially does the study of human nature benefit from such scrutiny: "There are many *positive* advantages, which result from an accurate scrutiny into the powers and faculties of human nature" (*First Inquiry*, p. 13; italics added). These include the "delineation of the distinct parts and powers of the mind," and, it can at least be hoped, the discovery "in some degree, [of] the secret springs and principles, by which the human mind is actuated in its operations" (pp. 13-14).

of the abstruse philosopher lies in his commitment to the opinion that in almost "every part of nature, there is contained a vast variety of springs and principles, which are hid, by reason of their minuteness or remoteness."[54] So believing, this philosopher seeks these principles and gives us as a result a more accurate and a more general explanation of the phenomena we experience.

Finally, Hume is convinced that this abstruse, reflective activity which he recommends has practical and beneficial results. Contrary to those who suppose that reason is entirely subservient to natural impulses, Hume suggests that reflective philosophical activity produces significant change. Serious attention to "the sciences and liberal arts softens and humanizes the temper," he says. Then he adds that the "effects of education" indicate that "the mind is not altogether stubborn and inflexible."[55] He does suggest that opinions that are not based on logic and reasoning cannot be altered by direct application of these tools, but he also suggests that philosophy, working indirectly and insensibly, can modify both opinion and character.[56] Those who are "susceptible of argument and reasoning," he says, are able to see both pro and contra of an issue, but it is left to the "philosopher alone, who is of neither party, to put all the circumstances in the scale, and assign to each of them its proper poise and influence," thus allowing others to accede to the proper conclusion. "Here then," he says, "is the chief triumph of art and philosophy: It insensibly refines the temper, and it points out to us those dispositions which we should endeavour to attain, by a constant *bent* of mind, and by repeated *habit*." Beyond this, it may have little influence, he adds, but the criticism has to do with method, not substance; "exhortations and consolations" are of little value when compared to a philosophy that works in an "indirect manner" and by "secret, insensible influence," but this does not demean the influence of the latter.[57]

More significant, I suggest, is Hume's concession that much of

[54] *First Enquiry*, pp. 86-87.
[55] *Works*, 3: 223.
[56] *Second Enquiry*, p. 169.
[57] *Works*, 3: 474-475; "I will venture to affirm, that, perhaps, the chief benefit, which results from philosophy, arises in an indirect manner, and proceeds more from its secret, insensible influence, than from its immediate application" (*Works*, 3: 222-224).

what is called philosophy serves only to strengthen the inclinations we already have, and to lead us with ever greater resolution to affirm those views which have already, because of prejudice or the natural propensity of our minds, too much influence. Philosophy seeks to make us wiser; some of it appears to make us only more self-indulgent and indolent, more arrogant, more credulous. When it does so, it is no philosophy at all in Hume's view, and worse than none at all. A genuine philosophy, however, manages to avoid this undesirable effect. By a determined effort it strives to avoid partiality, and by the use of whatever faculties are available, to break down prejudice. The philosopher, then, is one who avoids precipitous judgments whenever and however possible. The only "sentiments" he accepts as relevant to his deliberations are "hesitation, and reserve, and suspense," or, perhaps, "derision against the ignorant multitude, who are always clamorous and dogmatical, even in the nicest questions. . . ."[58]

It was because of this essentially humanistic bent in his philosophy that Hume found even the extreme and excessive antecedent scepticism of Descartes a valuable counter to prejudice, and precipitate judgment,[59] although it is clear that Hume's own preference was for a scepticism more nearly like the Academic scepticism of Carneades and Cicero. These Academic sceptics also counsel doubt and suspense of judgment, rather than rash conclusion and prejudice confined within the too narrow bounds of natural belief. At the same time, though, he is quick to criticize those speculations that carry us entirely beyond the bounds of experience.[60] Few students of philosophy have failed to hear that Hume condemned to the flames the vacuous volumes of "divinity or school metaphysics." What has not been properly noticed is Hume's additional concern to "cultivate the true metaphysics"

[58] First Enquiry, pp. 40-41; Works, 3: 475.
[59] First Enquiry, pp. 149-150. "This species of scepticism, when more moderate, may be understood in a very reasonable sense, and is a necessary preparative to the study of philosophy, by preserving a proper impartiality in our judgments, and weaning our mind from all those prejudices, which we may have imbibed from education or rash opinion" (p. 150). Hume's attitudes toward this and other forms of scepticism are discussed in chap. 6.
[60] First Enquiry, pp. 40-42, 161ff.

in order to derive the pleasures and benefits thereof. Just as Hume sees the need for a mitigated scepticism which can shake our dogmatic certainty, so does he encourage a rational, analytic metaphysics as a means of obtaining a better understanding of the world and man.

III.   A number of objections may be lodged against the claims I have made in the previous section. Here I shall try to anticipate these objections, while in Section IV I offer what I believe to be adequate replies to them.

Those who have defended the subordination thesis as capturing what is central to Hume's philosophy may first of all argue that the exposition found above is too one-sided, and that Hume's views of the force of our natural instincts and propensities have been systematically understated. Despite what I have shown him to say, they may argue, Hume does thoroughly subordinate reason to instinct and feeling. He did, after all, think—with this I would certainly agree—that the human frame includes instincts or principles which enable us to exist in the natural world. These instincts produce in us the feelings, sentiments, or beliefs such existence requires. Our belief in the external world, in the continuing and independent existence of bodies, for example, is not dependent on philosophical inquiry. This Hume claims, echoing Hutcheson, is too important a matter to be trusted to speculation, and it has not been left to our choice; we do not need to reason and philosophize about it, and only a few have opportunity to do so.[61] "It seems evident," he says elsewhere, "that men are carried, by a natural instinct or prepossession, to repose faith in their senses; and that, without any reasoning, or even almost before the use of reason, we always suppose an external universe, which depends not on our perception, but would exist, though

[61] *Treatise*, p. 187. "Thus the sceptic still continues to reason and believe . . . and by the same rule he must assent to the principle concerning the existence of body, tho' he cannot pretend by any arguments of philosophy to maintain its veracity. Nature has not left this to his choice, and has doubtless esteem'd it an affair of too great importance to be trusted to our uncertain reasonings and speculations."

221

we and every sensible creature were absent or annihilated."[62] Further, "*total* scepticism," if that is taken to mean a comprehensive suspension of belief about certain matters that are not fully demonstrable, is simply not possible: "Nature, by an absolute and uncontroulable necessity has determin'd us to judge as well as to breathe and feel. . . . Whoever has taken the pains to refute the cavils of this *total* scepticism, has really disputed without an antagonist, and endeavour'd by arguments to establish a faculty, which nature has antecedently implanted in the mind, and render'd unavoidable."[63]

Even less inclusive sceptical positions are subject to the same limitation according to Hume. It takes but little philosophical analysis to destroy our belief in certain commonly held opinions, he says, and thus to cast them in doubt. Sooner or later, though, the force of this sceptical reasoning is also "overcome by nature," and however cogent sceptical doubts may appear to the philosopher isolated in his study, nature will happily dispel them. The tendency of philosophy is to "render us entirely *Pyrrhonian*," reports the *Abstract*, and it would do so "were not nature too strong for it."[64] And in the first *Enquiry* we are told that, while the principles of Pyrrhonism "may flourish and triumph in the schools; where it is, indeed, difficult, if not impossible, to refute them. But as soon as they leave the shade, and by the presence of the real objects, which actuate our passions and sentiments, are put in opposition to the more powerful principles of our nature, they vanish like smoke, and leave the most determined sceptic in the same condition as other mortals."[65]

It will also be noted that the effect of natural principles is equally fundamental to some of Hume's most characteristic views, his analysis of necessary connection, for example. We have no rational grounds for believing that any event will precede or follow any other event: "*There is nothing in any object, consider'd in itself,*

---

[62] *First Enquiry*, p. 151.
[63] *Treatise*, p. 183.
[64] *Abstract*, p. 657 (of the *Treatise*, Nidditch-Selby-Bigge edition).
[65] *First Enquiry*, p. 159.

which can afford us a reason for drawing a conclusion beyond it."[66]
Nor does the repeated experience of objects believed to be causally
related reveal or produce any new qualities in them. Although
we never receive from objects themselves an *impression* of necessary connection or causal relation of any sort, we do have an
idea of necessary connection. We do not experience a causal
relation by means of impressions of sensation; but by repeated
experience of conjunction, contiguity, and succession, we come
to have an impression of reflection, a feeling of the sort that,
when (loosely) copied, produces the idea of necessary connection.
Hume rejects the suggestion that we obtain this idea by analogy
with powers in our own mind, and he stresses the role of repe-
tition, which gives rise to an expectation that is itself felt, and
from which the idea of necessary connection arises to be applied,
automatically, to objects themselves: "The mind has a great propensity to spread itself on external objects, and to conjoin with
them any internal impressions, which they occasion, and which
always make their appearance at the same time that these objects
discover themselves to the senses. . . . the same propensity is the
reason, why we suppose necessity and power to lie in the objects
we consider, not in our mind, that considers them; . . ."[67]

Here then is no outright denial of necessary connection, but
an account of our *idea* of it, and our belief in it, an account that
shows the idea and belief to be products of the instincts and
faculties which nature has given us. And it is clearly Hume's view
that these faculties and instincts are not only a part of a common
human nature, and common to mankind, but also that they arise
quite independently of the activities of reason. These considerations, taken together, certainly reveal that reason cannot but
be, in Hume's view, thoroughly subordinate to feeling and instinct.

Further, Hume's complete subordination of reason to feeling

[66] *Treatise*, p. 139. Cf. *First Enquiry*, pp. 46-47: "All these operations [those
resulting in 'belief of matter of fact'] are a species of natural instincts, which no
reasoning or process of the thought and understanding is able to either produce
or prevent."
[67] *Treatise*, p. 167.

may be said to be revealed by the responses he makes to particular issues that arise in his work. There is, for example, an argument that begins in *Treatise*, I, 4, 1: "In every judgment, which we can form concerning probability, as well as concerning knowledge, we ought always to correct the first judgment, deriv'd from the nature of the object, by another judgment, deriv'd from the nature of the understanding."[68]

This is a claim of perfect generality; it encompasses all subject matters about which judgments are made. Nor is it restricted to any particular kind of reasoning; it includes both probable and demonstrative judgments, as is made clear by Hume's earlier remark that "in all demonstrative sciences the rules are certain and infallible; but when we apply them, our fallible and uncertain faculties are very apt to depart from them, and fall into error. We must, therefore, in every reasoning form a new judgment, as a check or controul on our first judgment or belief; . . ."[69]

But, of course, this new judgment is equally subject to error, and stands equally in need of a correcting judgment:

Having thus found in every probability, beside the original uncertainty inherent in the subject, a new uncertainty deriv'd from the weakness of that faculty, which judges, and having adjusted these two together, we are oblig'd by our reason to add a new doubt deriv'd from the possibility of error in the estimation we make of the truth and fidelity of our faculties. This is a doubt, which immediately occurs to us, and of which, if we wou'd closely pursue our reason, we cannot avoid giving a decision. But this decision, tho' it shou'd be favourable to our preceeding judgment, being [also] founded only on probability, must weaken still further our first evidence, and must itself be weaken'd by a fourth doubt of the same kind, and so on *in infinitum*; till at last there remain nothing of the original probability, however great we may suppose it to have been. . . .[70]

[68] *Treatise*, pp. 181-182. I am indebted to Prof. Robert Fogelin for the formulation of this particular objection.
[69] *Treatise*, p. 180.
[70] *Treatise*, p. 182.

Hume clearly intends here to present a problem for which there is no rational solution. He has sketched what he takes to be a valid argument showing that any assigned degree of probability can be reduced to zero. If our beliefs were to be determined on entirely rational grounds, there would in fact be no beliefs: "If belief, therefore, were a simple act of the thought, without any peculiar manner of conception, or the addition of a force and vivacity, it must infallibly destroy itself, and in every case terminate in a total suspense of judgment." We are left, therefore, to wonder how it is, after all, "we retain a degree of belief, which is sufficient for our purpose, either in philosophy or common life." The answer is that these considerations are "forc'd and unnatural," and that their influence diminishes as they increase in number. The conclusion of zero probability can be reached, at best, with difficulty, and if it is, it has little influence and gains little credence. Belief, on the other hand, is a "lively conception," and while it "can never be entire, where it is not founded on something natural and easy," the fact is that belief in this and other cases is not dependent upon argument.[71]

Further, once the mind tires from its unnatural activities, is belief affected by them. This latter claim is put forward in the conclusion of book 1 of the *Treatise*. There, having noticed that "nothing is more dangerous to reason than the flights of the imagination, and nothing has been the occasion of more mistakes among philosophers," Hume then asks whether it might not be wise to "reject all the trivial suggestions of the fancy, and adhere to the understanding" alone. This, too, he responds, if steadily executed, would be dangerous and attended "with the most fatal consequences. . . . For I have already shewn, that the understanding, when it acts alone, and according to its most general principles, entirely subverts itself, and leaves not the lowest degree of evidence in any proposition, either in philosophy or common life."

The understanding—reason—acting alone would subvert the principles of both philosophy and common life, and leave us with

[71] *Treatise*, pp. 184-186.

a total scepticism. How can we avoid this result? "We save our-selves from this total scepticism only by means of that singular and seemingly trivial property of the fancy, by which we enter with difficulty into remote views of things, and are not able to accompany them with so sensible an impression, as we do those, which are more easy and natural."[72] To survive, in effect, we must forego the sceptical conclusions of the understanding, and allow ourselves to be led—or misled—by the imagination, an unreliable faculty but one, fortunately it would seem, that can lead us to beliefs that are adequate at least for common life. Is this not what is meant by the thorough subordination of reason to instinct and feeling? Say what one might about the value of reason, about its correcting influence, about the pleasures of phi-losophy, it cannot, fortunately for us, hold its own against the superior power of mere instincts. These and these alone, Hume seems to think, control our beliefs, and determine our actions.

Finally, in favor of the subordination thesis, it could also be pointed out that Hume does on at least one occasion suggest that reason itself is an instinct, from which it would appear to follow that even our rational insights and conclusions are instinctive. Men are not, he says, surprised by the operation of their own reason, although they very much admire the instincts of animals, which they find difficult to explain. But, to "consider the matter aright, reason is nothing but a wonderful and unintelligible in-stinct in our souls, which . . . arises from past observation and experience."[73] At first glance, this assertion alone may appear sufficient to defeat my arguments. If Hume says that reason itself is an instinct, then surely it must be said that for Hume all beliefs are instinctive, or natural in the sense Kemp Smith has claimed. And if that were the case, then natural beliefs would indeed reign supreme and undisputed in the minds of men. However, just how this would constitute the claimed subordination of reason—rea-son itself being an instinct—would constitute a problem, and the subordination thesis would be trivially true.

[72] *Treatise*, pp. 267-268.
[73] *Treatise*, p. 179.

IV.   These possible objections to my view, based as they are on Humean texts, must be considered. I begin with the suggestion that reason itself is an instinct, and hence that the conclusions of reason are instinctive, and that those conclusions of reason that are believed are instinctive beliefs. It should first be said that this suggestion, if taken to be a correct representation of Hume's view, would appear to make a mockery of the subordination thesis. To say that Hume thoroughly subordinated an instinct (reason, in this case) to feeling and instinct is at least very curious, and if not in the end tautologous, then probably only an infelicitous way of saying that reason for Hume is just another instinct and, as such, is reflexive and beyond our control. No matter how curious or infelicitous the claim may be, it is very like some of Kemp Smith's claims, and so it must be examined on its merits.[74]

There can be no doubt about what Hume says: if we consider the matter correctly we will see that reason is an instinct. However, if we attend to the context in which he makes this remark, and also keep in mind the several different senses in which he has used the term *reason*, it will be clear that he is not maintaining the thesis that reason in general is one instinct among others. As a consequence, it will also be seen that Hume may indeed believe that reason in some form(s) is reflective (rather than reflexive, as I presume Hume's instincts to be). And if that is the case, then it is at least possible that I am correct when I claim that Hume thinks that reason can and does correct instinctive beliefs or sentiments.

The remark in question is made in the final paragraph of book I, part 3 of the *Treatise*, "Of Knowledge and Probability." In the opening section Hume considers *knowledge* and the intuitive or demonstrative operations of the understanding, or *reason* in one restricted sense of that term.[75] Beginning with section 2, and continuing through the final section (15), Hume is working within

---

[74] See citations 1 and 5, p. 18. Kemp Smith restricts his claim by saying that it is in "matters of fact and existence" that reason is blind and instinctive. My discussion shows that this restricted claim is as mistaken as an unrestricted one would be.

[75] *Treatise*, pp. 69-73.

the broad framework of "probability," and is concerned with those operations of the mind that underlie and give rise to belief or the felt necessity of our causal inferences, or what Hume calls "probable reasoning" and might well have called "causal reasoning."[76] As the thrust of Hume's analysis is directed toward showing that our causal inferences are neither intuitive, nor demonstrable, nor based on perceptions of causal connections or rational inference from past experience,[77] it is not entirely surprising that he finds these inferences instinctive, especially since it is an explanation of the *necessity* of these inferences that provides the puzzle which motivates the greater portion of part 3.[78] If there is a necessity to explain and it is neither a logical nor a perceived necessity, then it must in Hume's system be a felt necessity, and hence is likely the product of some natural propensity or instinct.

Given, then, that from the outset of part 3 Hume's concern is to reveal the operations in which the mind must engage if

[76] Hume speaks of "probable reasoning" at *Treatise*, p. 103. As he says (p. 73) that only the relation of *causation* enables us to reason about (infer) objects beyond those "immediately present to the senses," and as it is exactly this inference he is seeking to understand, I suggest that the term *causal reasoning* is more apt than Hume's *probable reasoning*. By extension, then, we could speak of *causal belief*, or that belief which is the result of causal reasoning, and which is another of Hume's primary interests in part 3.

[77] Hume's official position excludes "perception" from the category of "knowledge" or science and certainty, and hence he appears to differ from Locke, who spoke of "sensitive knowledge." However, Hume goes on to say (*Treatise*, pp. 73-74) that only the relation of causation involves probable reasoning (inference resulting in *belief* in objects not present, but represented by ideas), and thus the official difference with Locke is mitigated. There are two categories, "knowledge" and "probability." Perception is not to be placed in the latter, and hence must be placed in the former. Or, alternatively, Hume might have added a third category suitable for perception.

[78] Near the end of sec. 2 Hume says, "Shall we then rest contented with these two relations of contiguity and succession, as affording a compleat idea of causation? By no means. An object may be contiguous and prior to another, without being consider'd as its cause. There is a NECESSARY CONNEXION to be taken into consideration; and that relation is of much greater importance, than any of the other two above-mention'd" (p. 77). He then goes on to suggest that the solving of the puzzle this necessary connection presents will involve an indirect approach. Carrying out this approach constitutes the remainder of part 3. A detailed commentary on this part, one that follows Hume's argument in the order he presents it, is needed, but obviously not to be expected here.

particular beliefs are to be held about absent causes or effects, or, that is, given that his concern is with a certain kind of "reasonings," it is understandable that he should refer to these operations by the term *reason*.[79] However, using *reason* to refer to an instinctive operation of the mind is only one of the several Humean uses of this term, as my previous discussion has shown. Generically considered, Hume takes reasoning to be an activity by which perceptions are united or separated. But there are a number of different forms that this activity can take: comparison, analysis, composition, inference, and so forth. The inference of a cause from its effect or an effect from its cause is, he says, a "true species of reasoning," and it may be even, because there is no interposing third term involved in such inferences, one of the strongest forms of this activity.[80] Nevertheless, it does not follow that because this species of reasoning is essentially and necessarily instinctive, all others are like it. When Hume tells us that nature can interrupt our most profound reflections,[81] or that "just reasoning ought still, perhaps, to retain its force, however subtle,"[82] that there "is an inconvenience which attends all abstruse reasoning," especially if the reasoning includes a "long chain" of propositions,[83] or even that "reason is, and ought only to be the slave of the passions,"[84] he clearly is not referring to the same species of reason as when he says that reason is a wonderful

---

[79] The use of "reasonings" to refer generally to such activities of thought as discussion and argument may now be obsolete, but the OED lists eighteenth- and nineteenth-century examples of this usage. (For example: "Several people accompanied him, and he had great reasonings with them." "The reasonings in the Essay are confused, contradictory, and often childish.") Hume's "probable reasoning" and his most general characterization of reason ("merely an operation of our thoughts or ideas") suggest this older meaning. In a similar vein J. A. Passmore has suggested that when Hume in the *Enquiry* (p. 110) speaks of "Our reasonings concerning matters of fact," this should be read "in the spirit of Pyrrhonian scepticism, as '*what we are pleased to call* our reasonings.' " "Hume and the Ethics of Belief," in *David Hume: Bicentenary Papers*, ed. G. P. Morice (Austin: University of Texas Press, 1977), p. 87.

[80] *Treatise*, pp. 96-97.
[81] See above, p. 215.
[82] *Treatise*, p. 135.
[83] *Treatise*, p. 455.
[84] *Treatise*, p. 415.

instinct. Nor is there any ground for supposing that these other species of reason are instincts of nature arising from past experience. At least some of the time Hume is referring to species of reason that are, in contrast to this instinctive determination of nature, relatively immune from natural forces, and hence able to analyze and compound with some degree of freedom, or at least at the direction of the will. According to Hume, I apparently cannot will myself to believe that snow will fall from a cloudless summer sky over Montreal, or that I can walk on water, but I can bring together ideas or conceptions in such a way that these events are conceivable. More importantly, Copernicus, for example, was able to separate the conceptions of motion and the sun and those of rest and the earth, and then to recombine these in the now familiar arrangements. When Hume asserts that "even upon the arbitrary union of two ideas in the fancy, *we may think proper to compare them*,"[85] he is in effect asserting this relative freedom of reason, or better, perhaps, attesting our freedom to reflect. It is obvious, then, that at least some of Hume's references to reason are references to a noninstinctive reason that can function as a relatively independent analytical force, able to challenge or oppose even instinctive beliefs. On these occasions Hume is referring to that critical reason which can tell us that, no matter how compelling may be the belief that the sun will rise tomorrow, this event may not occur, or to that faculty which permits us to separate the ideas of tomorrow and sunrise, and to suppose that what the former represents may in fact occur without the accompaniment of what the latter represents, instinctive inferences or beliefs notwithstanding. Hume also supposed that this kind of analysis could have an effect upon such beliefs, causing them to become weaker or even to be extinguished—as, for example, the belief that there will be, literally, a sunrise tomorrow has been widely extinguished.

It would be a mistake to suppose that for Hume any form of reason is completely unrelated to nature or human nature. Nonetheless, he does not suppose that all forms of reason are forms of

[85] *Treatise*, p. 13. Italics added.

instinct. On the contrary, he thinks that nature has provided "a remedy in the judgment and understanding, for what is irregular and incommodious" in our sentiments of belief as well as in our affections. "Does nature," he asks rhetorically, "whose instincts in men are all simple, embrace such complicated and artificial objects, and create a rational creature, without trusting anything to the operation of his reason!"[86] Indeed, she does not. Nature reserves for reason an often indirect but yet effective and highly significant critical role in the shaping of our beliefs and attitudes.[87]

The other objections raised in defense of the subordination thesis constitute a series of subsidiary claims to the effect that Hume does show that instinct and feeling are stronger than reason, either because they can overturn the effects of reason, or because they can accomplish things that reason cannot accomplish. The successful defense of my own thesis does not require that I show these claims are wrong in all respects. I am not claiming that Hume is a full-fledged rationalist, but, rather, that he is not a full-fledged naturalist, where a naturalist is taken to be a philosopher who has made reason "thoroughly subordinate . . . to instinct and feeling." All that I need to show is that even if they are correct as stated, these subsidiary claims do not constitute adequate grounds for saying that Hume is such a naturalist or that he accepted the subordination thesis. Certainly, Hume gives to sentiment and instinct a far greater role than does, say, a rationalist such as Descartes. But to say that a philosopher has thoroughly subordinated reason to instinct and feeling is to say

---

[86] *Treatise*, p. 489; *Second Enquiry*, pp. 201-202. This question is preceded by the following: "But farther, though it seems a very simple proposition to say, that nature, by an instinctive sentiment, distinguishes property, yet in reality we shall find, that there are required for that purpose ten thousand different instincts, and these employed about objects of the greatest intricacy and nicest discernment. For when a definition of *property* is required, that relation is found to resolve itself into any possession acquired by occupation, by industry, by prescription, by inheritance, by contract, &c. Can we think that nature, by an original instinct, instructs us in all these methods of acquistion?"

[87] Those who believe that this conclusion was completely obvious from the start no doubt share my amazement at the suggestion that on Hume's view, a man "believes whatever nature leads him to believe, no more, no less," or that Hume's arguments "show that reason, as traditionally understood, has no role in human life."

that for him, reason is in all cases and at all times subordinate
to instinct or feeling, all appearances to the contrary notwithstanding, and that he has told us that we in all cases and at all
times must accept our natural and instinctive beliefs rather than
any conclusions resulting from the use of (reflective) reason. To
say that reason is thoroughly subordinate to sentiment is to say
that where reason and sentiment conflict, reason must be dismissed or give way, and sentiment followed. To claim that this
is Hume's view or the implication of his work is misleading and
mistaken.

It is misleading because it directs our attention away from
Hume's view (already mentioned) that the operation of the mind
is such that the flow of sentiments is sometimes stopped, and we
are not only able, but required, to rely solely on reason: "As the
emotions of the soul prevent any subtle reasoning and reflection,
so these latter actions of the mind are equally prejudicial to the
former." Hume does, of course, believe that nature will in time
break the force of such arguments, so that sentiment again prevails.[88] But this does not prevent further reflection, which again
stops the flow of sentiment, so that reason again prevails; as he
also says, "sceptical doubt, both with respect to reason and the
senses, is a malady, which can never be radically cur'd, but must
return upon us every moment, however we may chace it away,
and sometimes may seem entirely free from it."[89] What we find,
then, are two generally contrary principles, reason and sentiment,
which gain ascendance alternately. In such circumstances, to say
that reason is "thoroughly subordinate" to instinct and feeling is
simply unacceptable.

Or, consider Hume's recapitulation of his important section,
"Of scepticism with regard to the senses." In our natural and
unphilosophical state, he says, we do not distinguish between the
perceptions of the senses and their objects, but take these perceptions to be their objects, even their only objects. Despite the

[88] *Treatise*, pp. 186-187.
[89] *Treatise*, p. 218. The struggle between reason and sentiment seems not unlike
that between dogmatic and sceptical reason, as described in the *Treatise*, pp. 186-
187.

232

fact that our perceptions are notoriously noncontinuous and seemingly dependent on the mind, the imagination leaves us, in our unphilosophical state, with a belief in the continued and independent existence of these perceptions. By "the natural propensity of the imagination," he says, we are led "to ascribe a continu'd existence to those sensible objects or perceptions, which we find to resemble each other in their interrupted appearance; yet a very little reflection and philosophy is sufficient to make us perceive the fallacy of that opinion."[90] Now, if reason is thoroughly subordinate to sentiment, we should find that the effects of the "little reflection and philosophy" are insignificant, a mere passing aberration, and that we all return to our original belief in the continued existence of our perceptions. But this is not the case. Many individuals, says Hume (the more philosophical to be sure) accept the theory of double existences (objects *and* perceptions), and suppose the former to be continuous and independent, the latter to be interrupted and dependent. He grants, of course, that this philosophical theory depends on the vulgar one for its credit and influence on the imagination, but he also says that the theory is dependent on reason, for it is the latter which furnishes us with the distinction between object and perception which we actually come to believe, and which he insists is a distinction that cannot be gained from experience or sentiment. Thus, while he says that nature has such force that we "stop short," unable "to reject the notion of an independent and continu'd existence," this does not mean that nature forces us to retain our first, unphilosophical belief. The conclusions of reason also attain a force and vivacity, and hence there is between reason and instinct a struggle. To bring peace in this dispute, "a new hypothesis," that of double existence, is proposed. This hypothesis pleases the reason insofar as it permits us to admit that our perceptions are interrupted and not identical, and it pleases the fancy by permitting it to apply the notion of continued existence to something, namely, objects. The new hypothesis is the monstrous, but nonetheless relatively satisfying, offspring of contrary

[90] *Treatise*, p. 210.

principles "which are both at once embrac'd by the mind, and which are unable mutually to destroy each other." In short, the contradictory claims of reason and the imagination are reconciled by the creation of a new fiction that is conformable to both. Dissatisfied with the conclusions of reason alone and the sentiments of the imagination alone, we propose a third and intermediate account, an account which arises from an "intermediate situation of the mind." Or as Hume puts it,

> Nature is obstinate, and will not quit the field, however strongly attack'd by reason; and at the same time reason is so clear in the point, that there is no possibility of disguising her. Not being able to reconcile these two enemies, we endeavour to set ourselves at ease as much as possible, by successively granting to each whatever it demands, and by feigning a double existence, where each may find something, that has all the conditions it desires.[91]

Given, then, that Hume here demonstrates his conviction that reason and instinct (the "natural propensity of the imagination") so oppose one another that the views of both are significantly modified, and a third position results, the absurdity of maintaining the subordination thesis is again demonstrated. I shall add only that a less optimistic version of this argument is found in the first *Enquiry*, where Hume begins by noting "that men are carried, by a natural instinct or prepossession, to repose faith in their senses; and that . . . when men follow this blind and powerful instinct of nature, they always suppose the very images, presented by the senses, to be the external objects. . . ." The "slightest philosophy," he repeats, soon destroys this "universal and primary opinion of all men," and we "are necessitated by reasoning to contradict or depart from the primary instincts of nature, and embrace a new system. . . ." Immediately, however, "philosophy finds herself extremely embarrassed" for lack of a means of justifying her conclusions from the objections of the sceptics: "She can no longer plead the infallible and irresistible instinct of nature: for

[91] *Treatise*, pp. 211-215.

that led us to a quite different system, which is acknowledged fallible and even erroneous. And to justify this pretended philosophical system, by a chain of clear and convincing argument, or even any appearance of argument, exceeds the power of all human capacity." Our primary instincts are acknowledged erroneous; the findings of reason are "contrary to natural instinct" and fail to satisfy reason itself. Instead of claiming that the new hypothesis satisfies both our instincts and our reason, Hume here suggests that it satisfies neither, and hence "the profounder and more philosophical sceptics will always triumph."[92] Thus Hume has once again represented reason as a principle that is on a par with instinct, able to oppose it as an equal force, and able as a result to modify our instinctive beliefs. In both its speculative and sceptical forms, reason sometimes stands to instinctive belief as an effective critical force.

It is true, then, that natural instincts or natural beliefs are given a central role by Hume. We have also seen that he says that our beliefs in "body" and in necessary connection are the result of instincts or feelings. It is true that our escape from "total scepticism" depends upon a trivial suggestion of the fancy. But it does not follow from these facts that reason—reflective reason, consciously chosen analysis, conscientiously undertaken critical examination—is without function and effect, or that the interludes of reason are entirely insignificant when compared to the interludes of backgammon. I have shown that Hume refused to adopt the providentially grounded naturalism of his contemporaries. It is also clear that he did not ascribe to the reason-subordinating naturalism that has been attributed to him by Kemp Smith and others. Hume adopted, if you will, a mitigated naturalism as the complement of his mitigated scepticism.

V. Hume believed, in contrast again with Descartes, that both ordinary men and philosophers must, in the overwhelming majority of practical situations, accept and rely on natural beliefs. But two features of his position must be given their due. First,

---

[92] *First Enquiry*, pp. 151-155.

Hume is not entirely different from Descartes on the matter of the reliability of our natural impulses. Hume, too, distrusted our natural beliefs and instincts, and he refused to place in them complete confidence. Had he not had this element of distrust, he would never have suggested that these instinctive beliefs can be corrected and refined, and never have himself attempted to correct and refine them. Secondly, Hume's account of belief is significantly different from that of Descartes. Hume does not suppose that belief is the result of an act of will. Rather, he sees belief as analogous to the passions: causally explicable, but not subject to direct control. According to Hume, we believe certain propositions or things because we are caused to believe, not because we decide to do so.[93] Consequently, there is a good possibility that reflective reason will reach conclusions that are contrary to some beliefs. But there is also the further possibility that these conclusions of reason will become part of the particular complex of causes that determines particular beliefs, just as reason, as we saw in chapter 3, provides materials which become a part of the complex of causes that determines our passions or moral sentiments. Hume says that belief does not depend on the will, but on causes and principles "of which we are not masters" and even that belief is among those "operations" of the mind that "are a species of natural instincts, which no reasoning or process of the thought and understanding is able either to produce or prevent."[94] However, he does not thereby commit himself to the view that our beliefs are entirely out of our control. The causes and principles which we do not master are the immediate or proximate causes of belief. But these in turn may be influenced by more remote causes over which we do have a measure of control. I cannot but believe there is a typewriter in this room, although I cannot at present see it. If I were to take the typewriter elsewhere, I would presumably alter this belief. Hume does say

[93] Hume is clear on this point: "We may, therefore, conclude, that belief consists merely in a certain feeling or sentiment; in something, that depends not on the will, but must arise from certain determinate causes and principles, of which we are not masters" (*Treatise*, p. 624).
[94] *First Enquiry*, pp. 46-47.

that when we are convinced of a "matter of fact, we do nothing but conceive it, along with a certain feeling, different from what attends the mere *reveries* of the imagination." This indeed could be taken to suggest that we are entirely passive in the matter of belief if he did not continue: "And when we express our incredulity concerning any fact, we mean, *that the arguments for the fact produce not that feeling.* "[95] The activities of reflective reasoning are analogous, this indicates, to my removal of the typewriter from this room. They serve as mediate causes of belief, and are of sufficient strength or importance to alter the character or strength of those sentiments of belief that have resulted from our instincts or natural propensities.[96]

One can say, then, that for Hume belief is natural, and that it is necessarily so. But it is natural in the sense that it is the result of causal factors, including reason, that give rise to belief without the necessity or possibility of merely willing it. Belief is natural in contrast to arbitrary (in the sense of voluntary). In this respect Kemp Smith was quite right to compare Hume to Hutcheson, for each of them is happy enough to find that our beliefs do not depend directly upon reason, for that is a faculty too limited and too slow to provide much of the guidance we

[95] *Treatise*, p. 624.

[96] Passmore ("Hume and the Ethics of Belief," pp. 86-91) suggests that Hume "does not consistently think of belief as an automatic reaction, over which we have in no sense any control." In support of this claim he adduces a number of cases in which Hume appears to be reflective with some effect, or to recommend reflection, and he concludes by saying that Hume adopts an ethics of belief that involves telling us that we *ought* to be prepared to set aside certain beliefs—those arising from what Hume calls "education," for example. It is certainly clear that Hume makes such recommendations. On my account Hume need not be taken to have thought that belief is entirely beyond our control even though it is automatic, for on my account it is always possible to bring reflection to bear on the process that results in belief, and thus to alter the sentiment that automatically arises as an end product.

For a valuable parallel discussion of the issue raised here, see Fred Wilson, "Hume's Theory of Mental Activity," *McGill Hume Studies*, pp. 101-120. Wilson examines the suggestion, traced to Samuel Coleridge and Brand Blanshard, that Hume's associationism prevents him from giving due weight to the *active* (in my terms, the *reflective*) aspects of mind. He argues that this suggestion is mistaken, and that Hume "holds, in a way compatible with his associationism, that mind, guided by the ideal of truth, can actively correct its causal judgments" (p. 107).

need. But this feature of Hume's position does not preclude his offering critical objections to what is believed naturally or instinctively. We have already seen that he does raise such objections. We can now also say that it is not inconsistent for him to have done so. Hume's theory of belief shows our beliefs to be natural, to be the result of very powerful factors whose force cannot be abated by the direct exercise of the will alone. But Hume does not suppose that these factors, however powerful, guarantee the accuracy of the resulting beliefs. Furthermore, he goes out of his way to show how reflective reason, sometimes in the form of his own philosophy, can become a factor in the shaping of beliefs that are more refined and more accurate than those held by the unphilosophical natural man. Finally, on Hume's view of belief, belief and some important forms of scepticism are compatible. The forms of scepticism and the form of Hume's scepticism are the subjects of chapter 6.

« 6 »

Traditional Scepticisms and
Hume's Scepticism

> This begets a very natural question; What is meant by a
> sceptic? And how far it is possible to push these philo-
> sophical principles of doubt and uncertainty?
>
> David Hume,
> *Enquiry concerning Human Understanding*

> If in order to answer the Doubts started, new Principles of
> Philosophy must be laid; are not these Doubts themselves
> very useful? Are they not preferable to blind, & ignorant
> Assent? I hope I can answer my own Doubts: But if I coud
> not, is it to be wonder'd at?
>
> David Hume to
> Gilbert Elliot of Minto,
> March 1751

I.   Much of the difficulty in getting clear about Hume's scepticism can be traced to a failure to give sufficient attention to the
complexities of the sceptical tradition or to the varieties of philosophical doubt which Hume knew and utilized. By his Scottish
contemporaries all scepticism was treated alike, and all was thought
dangerous for its tendency to undermine everything of value.
Even so cool and competent a philosopher as Thomas Reid could
not resist discussing Hume and Hobbes in, as it were, the same
breath, and concluding that both were guilty of making man
appear a mere Yahoo—incompetent, unpleasant, despicable—
and of making a mockery of piety, patriotism, affection, and
virtue, while the warmer protest of James Beattie has been duly
noted. If more recent philosophers have displayed less alarm over

239

scepticism, many, nonetheless, display a like ignorance of its breadth and complexity. Descartes, who was at most a sceptic *malgré lui*, is commonly taken to be the paradigm sceptic, and important contemporary philosophers have "refuted" scepticism with arguments that were philosophically exhausted before the beginning of the Christian era.[1] If it is easy to *caricature* the sceptic—the man who never rows because he cannot tell if the oar is straight or bent, or who develops bedsores because he cannot tell if he is awake or dreaming, or who would starve the plain man, telling him he does not know he has food in his mouth when he has food in his mouth—it is difficult to *characterize* him. Indeed, there may be no single characterization that is both detailed enough to be informative and sufficiently general to apply to all those who have considered themselves sceptics, although it does seem safe to say that sceptics have not only rowed, arisen, or eaten, but that they have displayed little or no interest in dissuading others from a forthright engagement in such activities.[2]

Furthermore, although no simplistic characterization of the sceptic is informative, it is possible, and necessary for the purposes of my overall argument, to give adequate accounts of several forms of scepticism and of some characteristic forms of sceptical activity. Once this has been accomplished (in Sections II-IV of this chapter), it becomes relatively easy to show that Hume engages in these sceptical activities, and even that they constitute the most characteristic features of his work in what he called metaphysics or speculative philosophy. This in turn serves as evidence in support of the two-part thesis of this book, namely, the claim

[1] One still finds scepticism "refuted" by the claim that the practice of the sceptic contradicts his assertions, or that advocating scepticism is "a piece of dogmatism inconsistent with scepticism itself." Indeed, despite the fact that these criticisms are effectively *countered* in the surviving writings of the Greek sceptics, it has recently been suggested that they constitute Hume's "own very special refutation" of scepticism. See Capaldi, *David Hume*, p. 202. In contrast, see Cicero, *Academica*, 2: xxxiv.

[2] Even Descartes recommended a provisional code of behavior that shows he had no intent to interrupt such practical activities: "So in order that . . . I might not omit to carry on my life as happily as I could, I formed for myself a code of morals for the time being. . . ." *Discourse on Method, The Philosophical Works of Descartes*, ed. and trans. E. Haldane and G.R.T. Ross, 2 vols (New York: Dover, 1955), 1: 95.

that Hume's philosophy developed in response to two distinguishable kinds of scepticism, epistemological and moral, and that his response to these distinct scepticisms, his metaphysics and his moral theory, respectively, differed significantly in method and substance. In the final section of the chapter, I show that Hume was not only aware of these differences, but also that he attempted to explain and defend the distinction he had accepted. That he made this attempt confirms, of course, the claim I have made about the divided character of his philosophy.

II.   The first lesson we must learn is that there are varieties of scepticism, a fact which Hume may well have learned, surprisingly perhaps, from Shaftesbury, who provided the paradigm eighteenth-century view of moral scepticism, as well as the paradigm reaction against this form of scepticism. But, unlike the vast majority of eighteenth-century philosophers, Shaftesbury clearly distinguished between moral scepticism and epistemological scepticism, and far from suggesting that the latter resembles the former as a cause for alarm, actually goes on to encourage and espouse it.

Perhaps because of his intimate association with the famous French sceptic Pierre Bayle, Shaftesbury reveals a remarkably clear understanding of the spirit and value of epistemological scepticism. He saw, first of all, no threat to religion or morals in Bayle's Pyrrhonism, and he concluded that one might well be a complete epistemological sceptic without having the least effect upon religious belief or practice, something that Bayle had by personal example made clear to him. He says of Bayle that "whatever he might be in speculation, he was in practice one of the best of Christians, and almost the only man I ever knew who, professing philosophy, lived truly as a *philosopher*; with that innocence, virtue, temperance, humility, and contempt of the world and interest which might be called exemplary."[3] The fact is,

[3] Letter of February 2, 1708, to Mr. Darby, *Life and Letters*, pp. 385-386. For further details concerning the relationship of the two philosophers, see Léo Pierre Courtines, *Bayle's Relation with England and the English* (New York: Columbia University Press, 1938), pp. 123-135, and C. Louise Thyssen-Schoute, "La diffusion européenne des idées de Bayle," in *Pierre Bayle, le philosophe de Rotterdam*, ed. Paul Dibon (Paris: Elsevier, 1959) pp. 172-176.

Shaftesbury explains, that religion and morals are not endangered by Pyrrhonism for the simple reason that correct belief and behavior do not depend upon erudition or speculation: "A man might have been not only a sceptic in all the controverted points of the academies or schools of learning, but even a perfect stranger to all [debates] of this kind; and yet complete in his religion, faith, and worship."[4] But if one can be a perfect moral and religious man without benefit of either education or philosophical speculation, then it must be, he claims, that one can criticize and attack all philosophical speculation without any effect on the beliefs and practices of oneself or of anyone else. There is no essential tie between belief or behavior and speculation, hence no attack on speculation can undermine religion or morals even though it may undermine the speculation.

Furthermore, despite the distaste with which it is almost universally received, epistemological scepticism has a generally salutary effect, according to Shaftesbury. In his *Moralists*, for example, he has Philocles outline the "academic philosophy" or, a "certain way of questioning and doubting." This philosophy must appear unpleasant, Philocles admits, to an age in which philosophical alchemy prevails, and in which "every sect has a recipe" that (allegedly) empowers its members to account for all natural phenomena. Men now, he says, "love to take party instantly"; they cannot bear being kept in suspense, and thus "of all philosophy . . . how absolutely the most disagreeable must that appear which goes upon no established hypothesis, nor presents us with any flattering scheme, talks only of probabilities, suspense of judgment, inquiry, search, and caution not to be imposed on or deceived." Nonetheless, there is much in this sceptical mode which ought to be adopted by all philosophers. It is the "way of

---

[4] *Characteristics*, 2: 203. See also *Life and Letters*, p. 269. Shaftesbury indicates that the debates he has in mind are those concerned with metaphysics and natural philosophy. Hume expresses essentially the same view in his letter to Elliot written March 10, 1751: "What Danger can ever come from ingenious Reasoning & Enquiry? The worst speculative Sceptic ever I knew, was a much better Man than the best superstitious Devotee & Bigot." *Letters*, 1: 154. Concerning Bayle, Shaftesbury adds: "What injury such a one could do the world by such a search of truth with so much moderation, distinterestedness, integrity, and innocency of life I know not; but what good he did I in particular know and feel, and must never cease to speak and own." *Life and Letters*, p. 374.

dialogue, and patience of debate and reasoning," a means by which our ideas are proved, a proper check on enthusiasm. Indeed, if that philosophy which examines things in this manner were found injurious to mankind or religion and, accordingly, "banished from the world . . . nothing but darkness and ignorance" could be foreseen, for "the world, and in particular the learned world, [is] much beholden to such proving spirits as these [sceptics]."[5]

Shaftesbury also reveals his understanding and approval of epistemological scepticism in another way. Because of his view that our beliefs ought to be made to stand the test of ridicule, some of his critics thought that he, too, was a sceptic and branded him as one. In reply he grants that this charge is more or less true if the term *sceptic* is properly understood. Speaking of himself in the third person, he says that "he is as little a sceptic (according to the vulgar sense of that word) as he is Epicurean or atheist." But why, in any case, he wonders, has such a disturbance been raised about "the simple name of sceptic," which, after all, in its original and ordinary sense means only "that state or frame of mind in which every one remains on every subject of which he is not certain." He who is certain or presumes to say that he knows is a dogmatist; all others are sceptics. One is either a sceptic or a dogmatist; if he has not absolute certainty, and admits it, then he is a sceptic. To illustrate this point he argues that whoever is not conscious of revelation, or has not "certain knowledge of any miracle or sign, can be no more than sceptic in the case; and the best Christian in the world, who being destitute of the means of certainty depends only on history and tradition for his belief in these particulars, is at best but a sceptic Christian." In short, Shaftesbury suggests that, properly understood, *sceptic* is the term for a much larger group of individuals than is usually thought, and that so long as it is with this larger group that he is being identified, he is perfectly content to be called a sceptic.[6]

[5] *Characteristics*, 2: 7-9; *Life and Letters*, p. 374.
[6] *Characteristics*, 2: 200-201. Among sceptics Shaftesbury here includes the individual who says he "believes for certain," for this phrase, he argues, can mean either that one "is assured of what he believes," which is absurdly redundant, or that one "believes strongly, but is not sure," which is the essence of the Pyrrhonists' position.

III. Shaftesbury, whom we know to have been an important influence on Hume,[7] distinguishes those two scepticisms to which Hume made such different responses. Furthermore, for epistemological scepticism Shaftesbury evinces regard and much sympathy, while for moral scepticism he shows no regard at all, and great antipathy. Taking this clue from Shaftesbury we can ourselves distinguish several kinds of scepticism, including at least one kind that has its *locus classicus* in a philosopher (Descartes) who did not identify himself with, or wish to be identified with, the sceptics or scepticism. Just how many forms of scepticism there are I would not like to say, but Hume in the *Treatise* and *Enquiries* refers to at least five kinds: ethical or moral scepticism, religious scepticism,[8] antecedent or Cartesian scepticism, Pyrrhonism, and Academic scepticism. My discussion here is confined to these five forms of scepticism.

1. *Ethical or Moral Scepticism.* Moral or ethical scepticism was characterized in chapter 1 as an essentially assertive position, one wherein the objectivity of moral distinctions is denied as a consequence of investigation into human motivation, belief, and action. Insofar as Hobbes argues that all human actions have the same motivation, namely, self-love, he has been called a moral sceptic, for this view is incompatible with a less cynical conception of man's motivations. His position is also incompatible with the views of those who claim that we can in fact distinguish actions that were altruistically motivated from those motivated by self-interest alone. Actions following from altruistic motives would be morally good actions (on a nonconsequentialist theory, at least), while those following from self-interest alone would, at

---

[7] In the *Treatise*, p. xvii, Shaftesbury is listed among the philosophers whose work Hume admires.

[8] Hume seems not actually to use the terms *religious scepticism* or *religious sceptic* in either the *Treatise* or the *Enquiries*, but his discussion of the argument from design in "Of a Particular Providence and of a Future State" begins with this remark, "I was lately engaged in conversation with a friend who loves sceptical paradoxes," while in the final section of the same *Enquiry* he says, "The *Sceptic* is another enemy of religion. . . ." The first enemy mentioned is the *Atheist*. The terms *sceptic, philosophical sceptic,* and *scepticism* are also found in the *Dialogues concerning Natural Religion*. On the whole, it seems safe to say that Hume was aware of religious scepticism even if he does not use precisely this term.

least sometimes, fail to be morally good. The nonsceptic in morals claims to be able to recognize these differences; the moral sceptic denies that there is any such difference, and, by obvious consequence, that it can be known.

Similarly, a philosopher who claims that investigation into the opinions of different individuals, groups, or cultures reveals that there is significant disagreement regarding what is said to be good, what evil—and then goes on to claim that this shows that good and evil are not objective, knowable features of the world—this philosopher is also a moral sceptic. The optimistic (presumably) common-sense view that there not only is a difference between good and evil, but that we can also recognize this difference and know which acts are in fact good, which evil, is once again put in doubt or denied by this philosopher. Also morally sceptical are the claims that *right* and *wrong* gain meaning only as they reflect positive law (are pronouncements of the monarch or God) or that their meaning is entirely dependent upon indoctrination (education offered by self-seeking instructors), for by these claims, belief that good and evil, right and wrong refer to objective, independent, immutable, and naturally knowable entities or qualities is again challenged. Marcus Singer's remark continues to be an apt summary. There are, as he says, many varieties of moral scepticism, but these "agree in maintaining, in one way or another, that there can be no such thing as a good reason for a moral judgment, that there are no valid moral arguments, that morality has no rational basis, and that the difference between right and wrong is merely a matter of taste, opinion, or convention."[9]

[9] M. G. Singer, *Generalization in Ethics*, 2d ed. (New York: Atheneum, 1971), pp. 7-8. References to moral or ethical scepticism are less common than references to epistemological or religious scepticism (each of which may simply be called "scepticism"), but others who use these terms can be cited. See, for example, L. A. Selby-Bigge's "Introduction" to his *British Moralists*, 2 vols. (New York: Bobbs-Merrill, 1964), 1: xxxiv-xxxix, or R. F. Holland and Jonathan Harrison, "Moral Scepticism," Symposium of the Aristotelian Society. *Supplementary Volume 41* (London: Aristotelian Society, 1967), 185-214. Harrison notes (p. 200) that "moral Scepticism is not something which has been invented by a committee of the Mind Association and Aristotelian Society; it has a long and respectable—if this is a word which can properly be applied to moral scepticism—history."

As was shown in chapter 1, Hume was well aware of this form of scepticism, and was opposed to it. He suggests that those who deny the reality of moral distinctions are probably disingenuous, but should it be that they are entirely serious, they are probably misled by one or another pet theory, and clearly they have departed from common sense. However, the depth of Hume's opposition to this form of scepticism can be seen only when we go beyond these retorts to consider his lengthy positive account— as I have done in chapter 3—of moral knowledge and moral reality. Then we see that Hume attempted to provide us with a theory of morals that was suited to the post-Galilean and post-Hobbesian world in which he lived: with an objectivist account of moral distinctions, but one that avoids the characteristic ontological commitments of Scholastic and Cartesian alike.

2. *Religious Scepticism.* This form of scepticism is akin to ethical scepticism in that both are defined, albeit imprecisely, by the subject matter addressed, rather than by any particular method or discipline. In the most general terms, religious scepticism takes the form of unbelief about religious claims, creeds, or practices, although it is clear that *unbelief* in this case refers to dogmatic disbelief and contrary positive beliefs, as well as to unbelief in a more literal sense. The atheist, the deist, and the (believing) critic of established religion, no less than the agnostic, have traditionally been called "sceptics" despite the quite different frame of mind of each. In fact, the atheist, whom we suppose to be as assertive as the believer, has perhaps the better claim to be thought the exemplar of religious scepticism, especially if one recalls that in previous centuries *atheist* was by no means the precise term philosophers and lexicographers have since made it.

In the seventeenth and eighteenth centuries, for example, atheist hunting was a popular literary sport, and long lists of notorious atheists were drawn up, and their intellectual crimes detailed. Whether there were any atheists in the modern sense of the term is unclear, but Aristotle, Democritus, Epicurus, Porphyry, Lucretius, Pomponazzi, Ficino, Erasmus, Luther, Calvin, Alexander VI, Clement VII, Rabelais, Campanella, Cardano, Montaigne, Bruno, Grotius, Charron, Herbert of Cherbury, Descartes, Hobbes,

Spinoza, Blount, Browne, Collins, Toland, Berkeley, Middleton, Hume, and Reid, not to mention the Chinese, Hindus, and Jews, were all called atheists because they represented, variously, such diverse views as Artistotelianism, materialism, Protestantism, Catholicism, fideism, (philosophical) scepticism, rationalism, deism, indifferentism (toleration), Cartesianism, and immaterialism; or because, though avowing the existence of God, they suggested, variously, that the church or the clergy were corrupt, that the direction of the world by Providence is imperfect, or nonexistent, that the age of miracles has ceased, that the evidence for miracles is imperfect, that the soul is not immortal; or because they argued too mildly in favor of theism or the truth of the atheist-hunter's particular faith; or because, simply, they behaved in a profligate manner. [10] In short, any variation from the orthodoxy of a given author, or even from the intensity with which his views were held, was as likely as not to be styled *atheism*. This use of the term survives largely intact in our own *village atheist*—scoffer, unbeliever, agnostic, critic, profligate, deist, freethinker, infidel, whatever. Certainly we can and do use these terms to mark real differences, but the fact is that *religious sceptic* (or *sceptic* in a context of discussions of religion) is used with equal indeterminateness. It tells us only that, from the perspective of someone's orthodoxy, another person is unorthodox, suspect, and, perhaps, dangerous, and *religious scepticism*, unless otherwise noted, seems usually to denote nothing more than such perceived unorthodoxies.

Hume, despite an unconvincing protest on his own part, and some equally unconvincing scholarly theorizing, was clearly a religious sceptic, and not merely in some trivial, insignificant sense. In his undated letter to Hugh Blair regarding George Campbell's *Dissertation on Miracles* Hume says, "I could wish your friend had not denominated me an infidel writer, on account of ten or

[10] For a lively account of atheist hunting, see D. C. Allen, *Doubt's Boundless Sea* (Baltimore: Johns Hopkins Press, 1964). Allen points out that there were practical atheists as well as speculative ones. The former were intemperate, roguish, careless of salvation, but not considered dangerous. The latter, although often completely decorous, challenged one or another orthodoxy, and were thought to be very dangerous indeed.

twelve pages which seem to him to have that tendency: while I have wrote so many volumes on history, literature, politics, trade, morals, which, in that particular at least, are entirely inoffensive. Is a man to be called a drunkard, because he has been seen fuddled once in his lifetime?"[11] For Hume to suggest that the essay on miracles alone was, of all his writings, offensive to Christians such as Campbell is surely disingenuous. Not only had he produced other offensive writings, but he knew that he had—one need only mention the *Five Dissertations*, a work that was withdrawn after printing in order to suppress the essays titled "Of Suicide" and "Of the Immortality of the Soul," and thus to avoid a threatened lawsuit and much furor.[12] Equally likely to give the impression that Hume was an infidel (that is, not a Christian believer) are such writings as the *Natural History of Religion*, "Of Superstition" and "Of Enthusiasm," those parts of the *Enquiries* wherein religion is said to have corrupted true philosophy,[13] and even passages in *The History of England*. Granted, one cannot confidently claim that Hume was an atheist in the modern sense (that he was convinced there is no God), but he openly and consciously undertook to show that belief in the existence of God, as understood by the religions known to him, could not be justified.[14] He was an equally open and scathing critic of organized

[11] *Letters*, 1: 351. Greig suggests this letter was written sometime in 1761, or just prior, that is, to the publication of Campbell's *Dissertation*. An effective rebuttal of those who appear to think Hume was not a religious sceptic is "Hume's Critique of Religion," by J.C.A. Gaskin (*Journal of the History of Philosophy* 14 [1976]: 301-311). However, James Noxon's reply to this article ("In Defence of 'Hume's Agnosticism,'" ibid., pp. 469-473) should not be overlooked.

[12] For an account of these events, see *Works*, 3: 62-72 ("History of the Editions" by T. H. Grose), and Mossner's *Life of Hume*, pp. 319-335.

[13] I give a more detailed analysis of the religious scepticism of the *Enquiry concerning Human Understanding* in sec. IV of this chapter.

[14] R. J. Butler in his "Natural Belief and the Enigma of Hume," *Archiv für Geschichte der Philosophie* 42 (1960): 73-100, argues that Hume considered belief in God a "natural belief" (one not dependent on argument or evidence, but universal and unavoidable) and hence justified. However, this is to use *justification* in an exceptionally loose sense, especially as Hume seems to be of the opinion that one characteristic of such beliefs is their *lack of justification*: neither a priori nor a posteriori reasoning justifies our holding these beliefs. Rather they are instinctive, and, in addition, they are found from time to time to be fallacious. We can give an account of these beliefs that shows that holding them is, for

religion, entirely satisfied to trace the origin of religion to natural
causes, or, that is, to reduce the allegedly supernatural to the
natural.[15]

3. *Cartesian scepticism.* To some it may appear a mistake to
take a philosopher of Descartes's assertive, even dogmatic, character as a model of a form of scepticism. However, for many
philosophers Descartes seems to present the paradigm of scepticism. Nor are his views more assertively couched than those of
the ethical sceptics. It will not do to take Descartes's First Meditation doubts as characteristic of all scepticism, but they do
exemplify a particular form of scepticism, as Hume himself pointed
out.

At one time in his life, Descartes was apparently very uneasy
about the state of learning in general and about the reliability of

---

most of us, most of the time, unavoidable, and hence not intellectually reprehensible despite the fact that the beliefs are, strictly speaking, irrational: These
beliefs arise from certain propensities or principles of human nature. In some
extended sense of the term, then, one could say that such beliefs are "justified,"
but, as these same beliefs may be not only erroneous, but also known to be so,
and as this is a feature of Hume's position that separates him from his more
comfortably naturalistic contemporaries, it seems more sensible not to adopt this
extended usage. See chap. 5, pp. 216-220, 231-238. Gaskin, in his "God, Hume,
and Natural Belief," *Philosophy* 49 (1974): 281-294, challenges Butler's claim on
more restricted grounds. Natural beliefs may be what Butler says they are, and
said to be justified. However, Gaskin shows that belief in the existence of God
fails to qualify as a natural belief for Hume because, according to his investigations
it is neither universal nor unavoidable, nor a precondition of human action. In
support of this conclusion he cites Hume's *Natural History of Religion*: "The belief
of invisible, intelligent power has been very generally diffused over the human
race, in all places and in all ages; but it has neither perhaps been so universal as
to admit of no exception, nor has it been, in any degree, uniform in the ideas,
which it has suggested. Some nations have been discovered, who entertained no
sentiments of Religion, if travellers and historians may be credited; . . . It would
appear, therefore, that this preconception springs not from an original instinct
or primary impression of nature. . ." (Ibid., pp. 288-299; see *Works*, 4: 309).

[15] This attitude is succinctly revealed in the remarks prefacing the account of
Joan of Arc found in *The History of England*: "It is the business of history to
distinguish between the *miraculous* and the *marvellous*; to reject the first in all
narrations merely profane and human; to doubt the second; and when obliged
by unquestionable testimony, as in the present case, to admit of something
extraordinary, to receive as little of it as is consistent with the known facts and
circumstances." The account which follows (chap. 20 of the *History*) gives no
credit to any claims of supernatural events or interventions.

his own beliefs, and hence he cast about for a means of eliminating the uncertainty he found so disturbing. What he finally settled upon, according to both the *Discourse* and the *Meditations*, was the now famous method of doubt: consider any belief, any claim whatsoever; are there any conceivable conditions under which this belief or claim could prove to be false? If not, the belief may be taken as true, but if there is any conceivable circumstance in which the belief might arise, and yet prove erroneous, then the belief must be discarded, disbelieved, taken as false. "I shall proceed," says Descartes, "by setting aside all that in which the least doubt could be supposed to exist, just as if I had discovered that it was absolutely false; . . ."[16] In this manner Descartes approaches his beliefs in the existence and nature of physical objects, other minds, the apparently self-evident truths of mathematics, and even the existence of God, and he finds in each case some reason(s) to think these beliefs could be false, and thus, by an act of will, he disbelieves them, counts them as false.[17]

Descartes compares this method with the actions of a person who, concerned lest an entire barrel of apples should spoil because of one or two rotten ones, removes all the apples from the barrel, inspects each in turn, and replaces only those that are sound.[18]

[16] *Meditations on First Philosophy, Works of Descartes,* 1: 149. In the *Discourse on Method* Descartes says: "I thought that it was necessary for me to take an apparently opposite course, and to reject as absolutely false everything as to which I could imagine the least ground of doubt. . . ." *Works of Descartes,* 1: 101.

[17] He describes what he has done by saying that "in the second Meditation, mind, which making use of the liberty which pertains to it, takes for granted that all those things of whose existence it has the least doubt, are non-existent." Later in the *Meditations* he says, "I suppose, then, that all the things that I see are false; I persuade myself that nothing has ever existed of all that my fallacious memory represents to me," and he describes himself as having "set aside as false all that I had formerly held to be absolutely true, for the sole reason that I remarked that it might in some measure be doubted." *Works of Descartes,* 1: 140, 149, 176.

[18] This comparison is to be found in Descartes's reply to the seventh set of Objections, where he says: "Here I shall make use of a very homely example for the purpose of explaining to [my critic] the rationale of my procedure, in order that in future he may not misunderstand it or dare to pretend that he does not understand it. Supposing he had a basket of apples and, fearing that some of them were rotten, wanted to take those out lest they might make the rest go wrong, how could he do that? Would he not first turn the whole of the apples

In fact, his procedure is more radical than this comparison suggests. Descartes is more akin to a person who, inspecting the apples from the barrel, discards not merely those that are spoiled, but those that may possibly spoil. In addition, he generalizes his procedure (to return from apples to beliefs) so that he does not have to consider every belief individually: he applies his method of doubt (more properly called a method of negation, it has been suggested) to the very faculties that produce belief.[19] Do we, or could we, relying on our senses, ever make an error and arrive at a false belief? "Yes," is the answer of the First Meditation, and thus we must not, according to the procedure outlined there, accept any claim that has a source in the senses. Do we, or could we, relying on our reason, ever make an error and arrive at a false belief? "Yes," is again the answer, and claims resting on the foundation of reason are also discarded. It is as though the apple inspector, having noted that some colored apples and some round apples spoil, decided to discard all apples that are colored or round to save the bother of inspecting each one individually.

For Descartes, then, doubting takes the form of rejecting as false any belief or claim that is not perfectly incorrigible. This suggests, of course, that he takes doubt and belief to be incompatible, and this suggestion is confirmed by the account of error found in the Fourth Meditation. Descartes grants that many persons hold false beliefs (he realizes, for example, that a great many people believe that apples are colored, when, in fact, color per se is not a quality of apples), but he exonerates God from the charge of deceiving mankind. God is not responsible for such

out of the basket and look them over one by one, and then having selected those which he saw not to be rotten, place them again in the basket and leave out the others? It is therefore just in the same way that those who have never rightly philosophized have in their mind a variety of opinions some of which they justly fear not to be true, seeing that it was in their earliest years that they began to amass those beliefs. They then try to separate the false from the true lest the presence of the former should produce a general uncertainty about all. *Now there is no better way of doing this than to reject all at once together as uncertain or false,* and then having inspected each singly and in order, to reinstate only those which they know to be true and indubitable." *Works of Descartes,* 2: 282; italics added.

[19] See Henri Gouhier's important article, "Doute méthodique ou négation méthodique?" *Les études philosophiques* 9 (1954): 135-162.

erroneous beliefs, for he has given us judgment by which we can control the will, the faculty immediately responsible for our beliefs. Error arises just when our will outruns the judgment and leads us to believe before indubitability has been established. Clearly the implication of this is that we both can and should avoid believing anything which can be doubted, or in other words, that we both can and should avoid believing anything that could be false or that we do not yet know to be true. The further implication is that, on Descartes's view of doubt and belief, it is not possible that a philosopher (a sceptic) could at one and the same time doubt a proposition P, *and* claim that he cannot avoid believing P, for on the Cartesian view to say that one *doubts* P is just to say that one *disbelieves* P, that one not only doubts the truth of P, but having suspended belief that P is true, at the same time takes P to be false. In short, on Descartes's model, one can be said to doubt a particular claim or opinion only so long as one withholds belief (by an act of will) in it. In contrast, when the understanding has a clear and distinct idea of a particular matter (fact, proposition), one has then justification for ceasing to withhold assent and beginning to believe regarding this particular matter. As Descartes thinks that individuals may exercise complete control over any belief that is not founded on knowledge itself, he can argue that belief should be permitted by an individual only when he or she has knowledge: "But if I abstain from giving my judgment on any thing when I do not perceive it with sufficient clearness and distinctness, it is plain that I act rightly and am not deceived." To believe on any other grounds is to permit one's relatively powerful will to overrun the weaker understanding, and to lay oneself open to the possibility of error, and is itself blameworthy. Even if I happen by chance (without knowledge, that is) to "judge according to truth . . . I do not escape the blame of misusing my freedom; for the light of nature teaches us that the knowledge of the understanding should always precede the determination of the will."[20]

---

[20] *Works of Descartes*, 1: 176. Descartes adds (p. 178), "For as often as I so restrain my will within the limits of my knowledge that it forms no judgment except on matters which are clearly and distinctly represented to it by the un-

There appear to be two relevant consequences of this position. First, once one has knowledge of a particular matter, there is no longer any need to continue to doubt. If the precondition of responsible belief has been met there can be no further grounds for withholding assent or negating, nor even any grounds for less radical forms of doubt. As belief is justified only when knowledge is perfect, one need not feel constrained when it is perfect to believe with any kind of reservation. No hesitation, no limited doubt, or partial scepticism are called for. Secondly, once one has knowledge of a particular matter, doubt about that matter becomes impossible. That which is known, according to Descartes, is indubitable, a point that may be rephrased by saying that, on his view, one who has knowledge regarding a particular issue cannot remain a sceptic on that issue. The sceptic is just that person who claims not to have this knowledge, while the knowledge itself, once obtained, apparently compels belief, and hence not even by an act of will could one be sceptical.[21] From Cartesian scepticism, then, we find belief excluded; unlike those whose scepticism takes some other forms, the Cartesian sceptic may not, *qua* sceptic, have a belief in P while at the same time doubting P. Hence those who have taken Cartesian scepticism as the paradigm of scepticism have not only relied on a model that was developed with the express purpose of surpassing or

derstanding, I can never be deceived; for every clear and distinct conception is without doubt something, and hence cannot derive its origin from what is nought, but must of necessity have God as its author . . . consequently we must conclude that such a conception . . . is true."

[21] Descartes says in Meditation III, p. 160 that there is a difference between a natural impulse or spontaneous inclination which "impels" him to believe something, and the "natural light which makes [him] recognize that it is true." These "two things are very different," he says, "for I cannot doubt that which the natural light causes me to believe to be true. . . ." Descartes seems to me to be committed to the view that we are compelled to believe every truth presented by the understanding; certainly he says we are compelled to believe some items (those the natural light forces us to believe), and he adds: "I possess no other faculty [besides the natural light] whereby to distinguish truth from falsehood, which can teach me that what this light shows me to be true is not really true . . ." (pp. 160-161). His view would appear to be, then, that we are free to withhold assent from that which is either false or not known to be true, but not from what is known to be true. This may help to explain why he assimilates that which is not known to be true to that which is false.

refuting scepticism, but they have also generalized from an idiosyncratic exemplar.

Hume explicitly criticizes what he calls the "antecedent" scepticism of Descartes, or, that is, that form of scepticism which
"recommends an universal doubt, not only of all our former opinions and principles, but also of our very faculties; . . ." To overcome this particular sceptical beginning would require, he says,
that we show by a deduction from some first principle that our
faculties cannot be subject to error, an impossible task, for there
is no such first principle, and even if there were we could not go
beyond it except by using the very faculties that have been (sup-
posedly) called in question. "The Cartesian doubt," he concludes,
"were it ever possible to be attained by any human creature (as
it plainly is not) would be entirely incurable; and no reasoning
could ever bring us to a state of assurance and conviction upon
any subject."[22]

One can also argue that Hume's account of belief constitutes
a further implicit and more significant criticism of Descartes's
sceptical program. Certainly, the two philosophers have directly
contrary views on this topic. Descartes suggests that when knowledge (clear and distinct ideas) is lacking, belief is entirely within
the control of the will, and hence that what is justifiably believed
must be true. In contrast, the will has no direct role in Hume's
account of the manner in which belief arises and gains force.[23]
Hume is quite content that we should believe on grounds other
than the possession of indubitable knowledge; indeed, in his view,
we have no alternative to such unjustified (as Descartes would
surely say) beliefs, and some such beliefs he even describes as
unavoidable. Further, Hume never supposes that what is believed,
for whatever reasons or causes, must be true. For Hume, even
the best-accounted for natural belief could be mistaken, even
though there may be little likelihood of discovering and confirming such an error. For Descartes, to have no doubts is (in certain
circumstances) to *know*, but for Hume, to have no doubts is (in

[22] *First Enquiry*, pp. 149-150.
[23] Hume's view of the will is discussed in chap. 5, pp. 235-238.

any circumstances) simply to have no doubts.[24] From Hume's perspective, then, Descartes fails to provide a viable form of doubt. He also fails to provide an accurate account of how doubt arises and is overcome by belief, and of the significance of this belief. For Hume, doubt, but not belief, is at least sometimes a consciously chosen act, and the raising of doubts, not the provision of assurance, is the philosopher's important and genuine contribution.[25] I return to this point presently.

4. *Pyrrhonian Scepticism.* Of what appear to be two forms of ancient scepticism, Pyrrhonian and Academic, more seems to be known about the former, and that largely through the writings of Sextus Empiricus. Sextus flourished during the first half of the third century A.D., late enough to be able to summarize the classical Pyrrhonian position while yet a member of the school.

[24] It is more than merely interesting to note that Descartes says that he can prevent the return of his philosophical doubts only by paying strict attention to the principles and proofs that have enabled him to overcome these doubts initially. It is only by concentration that he can maintain assurance and keep down doubts, for when he relaxes his attention, he says, he falls anew into doubt. But Hume finds the situation quite the reverse. When he pays careful attention to philosophical argument, when he concentrates on philosophical issues, then does he begin to doubt. When he relaxes, when he joins his friends in that now famous game of backgammon, then his doubts dissipate, and assurance returns until his next round of philosophical concentration. These divergent accounts reflect the divergent views of the role of the will that are taken by Descartes and Hume, but whether they follow from or inform those views is a question I do not pretend to answer.

[25] That doubt in some forms may be for Hume an act of the will, or more accurately, perhaps, a willfully chosen act of the understanding, is further confirmed by his concession that, properly modified, Cartesian scepticism is valuable: "It must, however, be confessed, that this species of scepticism, when more moderate, may be understood in a very reasonable sense, and is a necessary preparative to the study of philosophy, by preserving a proper impartiality in our judgements, and weaning our mind from all those prejudices, which we may have imbibed from education or rash opinion. To begin with clear and self-evident principles, to advance by timorous and sure steps, to review frequently our conclusions, and examine accurately all their consequences; though by these means we shall make both a slow and a short progress in our systems; are the only methods, by which we can ever hope to reach truth, and attain a proper stability and certainty in our determinations" (*First Inquiry*, p. 150). The effectiveness and significance of such acts of the understanding have been discussed in chaps. 3 (Sect. VI) and 5 (Part II, Sects. II and IV), and there is further discussion in sec. III of this chapter.

In fact, Sextus' allegiance to Pyrrhonism has itself contributed to the misapprehension of scepticism, for it led him to suggest that only the Pyrrhonians were true sceptics. According to him, the Academics hold that truth cannot be apprehended, while the Pyrrhonians claim only that truth does not seem to have been discovered, and continue seeking it. However inaccurate this description of the Academics may be, Sextus does manage to offer it and to make other assertions without undermining his own claim to be a sceptic. He takes his task to be that of presenting "an outline of the Sceptic [Pyrrhonian] discipline," and at the outset declares that "we do not make any positive assertion that anything we shall say is wholly as we affirm it to be. We merely report accurately on each thing as our impressions of it are at the moment."[26] This remark alone reveals two central features of the Pyrrhonian "discipline":[27] a willingness to give a forthright report of how a thing appears to the reporting individual (the Academics say that truth cannot be discovered, for example), preceded or followed by the proviso that what may appear to be an unqualified assertion is intended only as a report of the speaker's experience or reaction. (That is, it looks to me now as though the Academics say that truth cannot be known.) Still another feature of the Pyrrhonian approach is revealed in Sextus' division of philosophers into three groups: those who say the truth has been found (Aristotle, Epicurus, the Stoics—the Dogmatists); those who say it cannot be found (the Academics—negative dogmatists, we might call them); and those who, finding truth not yet discovered, continue to seek it. "The Sceptics," he says, "go on searching,"

[26] *Scepticism, Man and God: Selections from the Major Writings of Sextus Empiricus*, ed. Philip P. Hallie, trans. Sanford G. Etheridge (Middletown, Conn.: Wesleyan University Press, 1964), p. 31. I have whenever possible cited from this more readable translation of Sextus. However, I shall also provide references to the Loeb Classical Library edition of Sextus Empiricus, vol. 1, *Outlines of Pyrrhonism*, or vol. 2, *Against the Logicians*, trans. R. G. Bury (London: William Heineman; Cambridge, Mass.: Harvard University Press, 1933).

[27] The Pyrrhonians' choice of the term *discipline* reflects not only their wish to provide a practical guide, a way of life, but also their concern to emphasize *method* rather than doctrine, a way of doing philosophy rather than a substantive philosophical position or system.

thus indicating a willingness to grant that truth, or a given truth, may be found.[28]

Before he has finished the third page of his *Outlines of Pyrrhonism*, Sextus has mentioned two further features that, together with the three mentioned, comprise the core of Pyrrhonism as he sees it. Scepticism, he says, is "an ability to place in antithesis, in any manner whatever, appearances and judgements, and thus—because of the equality of force in the objects and arguments opposed—to come first of all to a suspension of judgement and then to mental tranquility." Sextus suggests the metaphor of the balance as an appropriate illustration of Pyrrhonian activity: into each pan go appearances and judgments pro and contra until there is seen to be no significant preponderance of evidence for or against the competing claims of the philosophers. Just as the equally weighted pans of a scale balance, so at this point is suspense of judgment attained, and, concomitantly, mental tranquility regarding such "matters of opinion" is also attained.[29]

According to Sextus, then, the Pyrrhonian sceptic,

A. does not deny appearances;
B. makes no unqualified assertions;
C. opposes appearances and judgments, pro and contra, so that, on "matters of opinion," suspension of judgment results;
D. aims to attain the mental tranquility which follows the suspension of judgment regarding matters of opinion, while yet following a practical criterion in the regulation of activities.
E. ceases not to inquire, to search for truth not yet found.

Each of these aspects of the Pyrrhonian discipline merits further elaboration.

A. The Pyrrhonian sceptic does not deny appearances. *Appearances*, Sextus says, is a term referring to the objects of sense perception, as contrasted to the objects of thought.[30] In his sub-

[28] *Scepticism, Man and God*, p. 31 (*Outlines*, I.4).
[29] *Scepticism, Man and God*, pp. 32-34 (*Outlines*, I.5-10).
[30] *Scepticism, Man and God*, p. 33 (*Outlines*, I.9).

sequent discussion of signs, Sextus accepts the distinction between things now *evident* ("the fact that it is day"); things temporarily nonevident ("as the city of Athens now is to me"); things
naturally nonevident (the "intelligible pores" of the skin, which
are not visible to the naked eye); and things absolutely nonevident ("that the stars are even in number"). No informing signs,
he says, are needed for things evident; none are available for the
absolutely nonevident; the *temporarily* nonevident may be apprehended by "recollective signs"; and some claim that the *naturally*
nonevident may be known by "indicative signs." Within this
framework, to say that the Pyrrhonian does not deny appearances
is to say that he accepts the evident as it appears. If the Pyrrhonian
is eating honey, and the honey tastes sweet to him, he would
say, "This honey appears sweet to me now." He would not doubt
or recommend doubt of this firsthand experience. Further, Sextus
is even willing to grant that there are recollective signs, or signs
(smoke, for example) that remind us of a thing (fire) that has,
in our experience, been associated with the sign, but which is
not now perceived: "Our arguments are not directed against every
sign, but (signs being of two kinds, as we said) only against the
indicative type . . ." because this type seems to be "a fabrication
of the dogmatists." *Indicative* signs, it is claimed, are those that
signify their objects, not through association in experience, "but
by virtue of [their] nature and constitution, just as bodily move-
ments are [said to be] signs of the soul." To *recollective* signs the
Pyrrhonian gives his "undogmatic assent," inferring, as does the
world at large, fire from smoke; *indicative* signs he opposes as
"private fabrications."[31] This is all stated succinctly in book 1,
chapter 10 of the *Outlines*:

> Those who say that the Sceptics deny appearances seem
> to me to be ignorant of what we say. As we said above, we
> do not deny those things which, in accordance with the
> passivity of our sense-impressions, lead us involuntarily to
> give our assent to them; and these are the appearances. And
> when we inquire whether an object is such as it appears, we

[31] *Scepticism, Man and God*, pp. 100-102 (*Outlines*, II.97-103).

grant the fact of its appearance. Our inquiry is thus not directed at the appearance itself. Rather, it is a question of what is predicated of it, and this is a different thing from investigating the fact of the appearance itself. For example, honey appears to us to have a sweetening quality. This much we concede, because it affects us with a sensation of sweetness. The question, however, is whether it is sweet in an absolute sense. Hence not the appearance is questioned, but that which is predicated of the appearance.[32]

B. The Pyrrhonian makes no unqualified assertions. The sceptic, says Sextus, does not dogmatize. But, he adds, neither do we understand this notion as those do who take it to mean both approval or acceptance and assertion. The Pyrrhonian, as already noted, "assents to feelings" that arise from appearances; when feeling warm, for example, he would not say, "I believe I am cold," or even "I wonder if I am feeling warm." However, being dogmatic may be understood to have a narrower meaning, namely, "the assent given to one of the non-evident things which form the object of scientific research," or the "acceptance of a thing in so far as the acceptance seems to be confirmed by a line of reasoning or by some proof. . . ." According to Sextus, it is these kinds of dogmatism that the Pyrrhonian avoids: "Concerning non-evident things the Pyrrhonian philosopher holds no opinion," but yields "assent only to such propositions as move us emotionally or drive us under compulsion to do so."[33]

That the Pyrrhonian seeks to make no dogmatic assertions about the real nature of things can be seen from the restricted manner in which appearances and recollective signs are accepted. They are accepted for what they are, and not as something else, or as signs (indicative signs) of something else, and if there appear to be conflicts (honey does not taste sweet to someone), these conflicts are not explained away by insisting that the honey *really* is sweet and that those who do not find it so have made an error.

[32] *Scepticism, Man and God*, p. 38 (*Outlines*, I.19-20).
[33] *Scepticism, Man and God*, pp. 36, 70, 81 (*Outlines*, I.16-17; I.147; I.192-193).

Rather, the relativity of our senses is granted, even celebrated, and the claim that nature made the senses commensurate with their objects is challenged as further dogmatic fabrication, although even claims of this sort are not dogmatically dismissed or denied: "One must also remember that, as for dogmatic assertions about the non-evident, we neither affirm nor deny them," says Sextus, and he is careful to indicate that the methods and conclusions of the Pyrrhonian himself are equally subject to doubt, and are not insisted upon dogmatically: the sceptic "does not even dogmatize when he is uttering the Sceptic formulae in regard to non-evident things . . . in the enunciation of these formulae he is saying what appears to him and is reporting his own feeling, without indulging in opinion or making positive statements about the reality of things outside himself."[34]

C. The Pyrrhonian sceptic opposes appearances and judgments, pro and contra, so that suspension of judgment results in matters of opinion. The "Sceptic formulae" just mentioned are such utterances as "No more," "I determine nothing," and "I suspend judgment," each of which expresses the attitude that arises in the sceptic following the use of the pro and contra mode of balancing arguments. They are, in effect, expressions of a suspension of judgment regarding things that are nonevident.

As a general rule, Sextus reports, such suspension of judgment is attained by setting appearances or judgments in opposition. When it is noted that the same tower appears round when seen from a distance, square when close at hand, appearances are opposed to appearances. When some assert that the order of celestial bodies proves there is divine providence, this is balanced by the contrary claim that the fact that the good often fare ill while the evil prosper proves there is no divine providence; thus judgment opposes judgment. When Anaxagoras argues that snow is black, because it is frozen water, and water is black, the Pyrrhonian may oppose this judgment by noting that to him, snow appears white. In short, whenever appearances or judgments are put forward dogmatically, the Pyrrhonian examines or tests the

---

[34] *Scepticism, Man and God*, pp. 38, 81, 36-37 (*Outlines*, I.19-20; I.193; I.14).

claims made by pointing out contrary appearances or posing contrary judgments, especially the contrary judgments of others. If he is able to bring forward contrary considerations of sufficient weight or quality, he shows that the dogmatic contraries are equally likely (or unlikely), that one is "no more" likely than the other, that, so far as their claims are concerned, "nothing can be determined," and hence he "suspends judgment" on the matter at issue.[35]

To facilitate this testing (opposing) activity, the sceptics prepared brief catalogs of argument forms (*tropes*, modes) that were designed to show the relativity of appearances, judgments, and opinions, or the inadequacy of arguments themselves (as leading to infinite regress or circularity or as relying on unjustified assumptions) or deficiencies in the arguments of particular philosophers (such as the etiologists). Sextus recognizes that these argument forms are by no means the exclusive property of the Pyrrhonians, and that, in fact, they are widely used by such dogmatic philosophers as the Heracleiteans, the Epicureans, or the Platonists and members of the New Academy. Although these philosophers may often "start from a common preconception of mankind," just as the Pyrrhonians do, and although they may often resemble the Pyrrhonians in their opposition of appearances and judgments, the use of these arguments to further various dogmatic aims and establish nonevident conclusions should not be mistaken for a sceptical Pyrrhonian use.[36]

In addition, Sextus suggests that he and his Pyrrhonian colleagues have a tendency to direct their sceptical challenges to the most basic elements of the dogmatists' theories—to the *phantasiai kataleptikai* or cataleptic impressions of the Stoics, for example—for if it can be shown that these basic elements are contrary to appearances, inconsistent, or lacking foundation, then it will be clear that we need not accept as true more grandiose and disturbing consequences built upon them. On other occasions, the approach is varied, and the first principles of one or

[35] *Scepticism, Man and God*, pp. 81-87 (*Outlines*, I.192-209).
[36] *Scepticism, Man and God*, pp. 87-94 (*Outlines*, I.210-230). The ten *tropes* or modes are discussed on pp. 44-72 (*Outlines*, I.36-163).

another system are granted, but only in order to show that these lead to absurd conclusions, and hence need not be accepted as true. In neither case, it is claimed, does the Pyrrhonian put forward substantive claims of his own. Rather, he limits himself (parasitically, some would say) to a critical attack on the claims of others. If the attack is effective, it will reveal that there is no adequate basis on which to choose between competing dogmas, or that, as the Pyrrhonian view is often put, there is no established criterion by which we can judge dogmatic assertions, or no standard by which to determine what is only apparently real from what is in fact real.[37]

D. The Pyrrhonian sceptic aims to attain the mental tranquility which follows from suspension of judgment regarding matters of opinion. According to Sextus, the sceptic initially sought mental tranquility through the making of sound judgments about the truth or falsity of competing appearances and claims. Presumably, uncertainty regarding what is real or true, and what is unreal or false, had created anxiety that the (future) sceptic wished to eliminate by resolving the uncertainty. However, he discovered that the contrary alternatives available to him could each be supported and criticized by persuasive arguments, or that each alternative resolution was equally compelling. Faced with this fact, he despaired of making a decision regarding the issues in question, and so withheld judgment. But no sooner had he suspended judgment than "there followed, by chance, mental tranquility in matters of opinion." The experience of the (original) Pyrrhonian was similar to that of Apelles, an artist who sought to represent the foam on a well-heated horse, but could not get it right. Despairing of his attempt, he threw his sponge at the painting, and this, as it struck, produced there precisely the image he had been striving to create.[38] The initial discovery of the Pyrrhonians was equally accidental, although subsequently the technique of suspending judgment and attaining mental tranquility was brought under control.

[37] *Scepticism, Man and God*, pp. 152-153, 160-161, 167 (*Against the Logicians*, I.369-374; I.405-407; I.426-429).
[38] *Scepticism, Man and God*, pp. 41-42 (*Outlines*, I.25-30).

Sextus emphasizes, however, that mental tranquility can be attained only in matters of opinion. There are other matters that unavoidably disturb even the Pyrrhonian. He is sometimes, for example, cold or hot or hungry or thirsty just as others are. But he differs from the nonsceptic in that he does not overlay these unavoidable disturbances with unwarranted claims about them. He does not add that pain is evil, or that his suffering is a punishment from the gods, or further metaphysical prattle of this sort. It should also be noted that, despite certain (apocryphal?) stories about Pyrrho himself, the founder of this particular school of sceptics, Sextus and the Pyrrhonians are not by their scepticism hindered from acting, nor do they believe themselves less than consistent in this regard. In his chapter titled "The Criterion of Scepticism," Sextus distinguishes between a criterion as "the standard one takes for belief in reality or non-reality," and a criterion as "the standard of action the observance of which regulates our actions in life." The latter the Pyrrhonians have, Sextus says, and it is appearance, or sense presentation, which is "dependent upon feeling and involuntary affection and hence not subject to question." Given, then, that a life of complete inactivity is not possible, the Pyrrhonian lives undogmatically giving "due regard to appearances" in the form of the "guidance of nature, the compulsion of the feelings, the tradition of laws and customs, and the instruction of the arts." Nature guides us by sensation and thought, feelings compel us to action (eating, drinking, and so forth), laws and customs enable us *in everyday life* [to] accept piety as good and impiety as evil," and instruction in the arts gives us the skills needed for our specialized activities.[39] This is not to say that the Pyrrhonian claims his particular thoughts, feelings, or life-styles are ultimately superior or even ultimately correct. Ultimates are the sort of thing on which he has suspended judgment. It is "sufficient, I think," says Sextus, "to pass one's life empirically and undogmatically in accordance with the commonly accepted observances and preconceptions, suspending judgment about statements grounded on dogmatic subtlety and

[39] *Scepticism, Man and God*, pp. 39-40 (*Outlines*, I.21-24).

furthest removed from the business of life."[40] If this seems an indolent, uncritical approach to life, it should be remembered that to the Pyrrhonians it was the dogmatists, conceited, vain of their own cleverness, and certain of their own conclusions, who created unnecessary anxiety and disturbance, and who represent an aggressive intolerance of the errors of others as they assert and champion the truths they have discovered. The Pyrrhonian aims to eliminate aggressive and intolerant systems, to undercut them so that every individual can follow the guidance that is natural to him. "The Sceptic wishes," says Sextus, "from considerations of humanity, to do all he can with the arguments at his disposal to cure the self-conceit and rashness of the dogmatists."[41] It is only toward those who are still uncorrupted by metaphysics and missions that the Pyrrhonist is uncritical.

E. The Pyrrhonian sceptic ceases not to inquire or to search for truth not yet found. Although Sextus claims that the Pyrrhonian does not deny the possibility that truth regarding the nonevident may be found, and does not abandon the search for truth, it is not clear that this aspect of Pyrrhonism is consistent with the aim to attain mental tranquility in matters of opinion—the search for truth being, I take it, intrinsically disturbing. Certainly, the two principles could be made to be consistent by taking the second to mean that while the sceptic abandons the search for truth in matters of opinion, he does not abandon it in the affairs of life, where mental disturbance is recognized to be unavoidable. In that case, however, the earlier attempt at a tripartite division of philosophers (dogmatists, negative dogmatists, and Pyrrhonians) collapses, with the Pyrrhonians becoming, in regard to matters of opinion or the nonevident, indistinguishable from the negative dogmatists, or Academics, an outcome Sextus would scarcely have embraced. Alternatively, one can conceive of an interpretation of the notion of mental tranquility which is consistent with a continued inquiry after truth—a calm, disinterested inquiry, for example—but then it is not clear how this could be the same mental tranquility that results from suspension of judg-

[40] *Scepticism, Man and God*, p. 110 (*Outlines*, II.246).
[41] *Scepticism, Man and God*, p. 128 (*Outlines*, III. 280-281).

ment, or, that is, follows the pro and contra balancing of argument and evidence. Prima facie, it makes little sense to speak of aiming for the mental tranquility that follows suspension of judgment, and a continuing inquiry into just those matters on which judgment is suspended. Alternatively, if the continuing search referred to is the search that resulted in the Pyrrhonian discipline, then it is false to say that the Pyrrhonian goes on searching, for that search seems to have ended. The method that results in tranquility has been found. For all his tentativeness and the elaborateness of the self-canceling formulae ("No more," for example) and devices (the cathartic that itself is purged, for example), Sextus may well be describing what is, for those who follow it to the goal of mental tranquility, a terminal philosophical position.[42]

However, even assuming that the Pyrrhonian discipline contains within it this contradiction, and that the attainment of mental tranquility has as a consequence a cessation of mental movement not unlike that of dogmatism itself, it is clear, nonetheless, that the Pyrrhonian does not assertively deny the existence of hidden reality or unseen causes, nor does he demand the suspension of belief or the curtailment of action. He grants that belief and action are unavoidable and leaves open (as not yet decided and probably not decidable) questions regarding reality beyond appearances. He does, however, challenge the assertions of those who claim to have discovered and comprehended that reality, testing each of these for observational accuracy and completeness or competence of argument. And because no such claims have as yet met the challenge of these tests, the Pyrrhonian joins

---

[42] Bayle is interestingly ambiguous on this very point. Pyrrho, he says, considered arguments pro and contra, and then suspended judgment and "reduced all his conclusions to a *non liquet, let the matter be further enquired into*. Hence it is that he sought truth as long as he lived, but he so contrived the matter, as never to grant he had found it." *The Dictionary Historical and Critical*, 5 vols., 2d English ed. (London, 1734-1738), Article "Pyrrho," 4: 653. Selections from this important article may be found in *Historical and Critical Dictionary*, ed. and trans. R. H. Popkin (Indianapolis: Bobbs-Merrill, 1965), pp. 194-209. Montaigne, less often concerned about inconsistencies, says merely that the Pyrrhonians "use their reason to inquire and debate, but not to conclude and choose." *Complete Essays of Montaigne*, trans. D. M. Frame, 3 vols. (Garden City, N.Y.: Doubleday, 1960), 2: 190.

the world at large, and lives undogmatically according to appearances and the fourfold guidance of nature, feeling, tradition, and the arts.

It is difficult to reconcile this account of Pyrrhonism with Hume's views on the topic. For Hume, Pyrrhonism is synonymous with what would be excessive, were it not untenable, doubt. His remark in the *Abstract*, "Philosophy wou'd render us entirely *Pyrrhonian*, were not nature too strong for it,"[43] is followed in the first *Enquiry* by a discussion of "consequent scepticism," or that wherein "men are supposed to have discovered, either the absolute fallaciousness of their mental faculties, or their unfitness to reach any fixed determination in all those curious subjects of speculation, about which they are commonly employed. Even our very senses are brought into dispute, by a certain species of philosophers; and the maxims of common life are subjected to the same doubt as the most profound principles or conclusions of metaphysics and theology."[44]

That by this description Hume is referring to the Pyrrhonists seems to be indicated by the remark, a few pages further on, that "as in common life, we reason every moment concerning fact and existence, and cannot possibly subsist, without continually employing this species of argument, any popular objections, derived from thence, must be insufficient to destroy that evidence. The great subverter of *Pyrrhonism* or the excessive principles of scepticism is action, and employment, and the occupations of common life."[45]

One cannot say with certainty how Hume came to this distorted

<hr/>

[43] *An Abstract of . . . A Treatise of Human Nature*, in *Treatise*, p. 657.
[44] P. 150.
[45] Pp. 158-159. Hume's remarks in the *Treatise* (p. 183) about "*total* scepticism" or about that "fantastic sect" who maintain that everything is uncertain seem best to fit his conception of the Pyrrhonists as revealed elsewhere. That the remarks are a part of his discussion of belief confirms that he has this form of scepticism in mind. A similar conclusion has been reached by John Immerwahr in his helpful article, "A Skeptic's Progress: Hume's Preference for the First *Enquiry*," *McGill Hume Studies*, pp. 228-229. Popkin in his "David Hume: His Pyrrhonism and His Critique of Pyrrhonism," in *Hume*, ed. V. C. Chappell (New York: Doubleday. 1966), pp. 53-98, assumes that Hume is speaking of the Pyrrhonians, but does not distinguish other types of scepticism.

view of Pyrrhonism, but two explanatory factors can be mentioned. First, Hume, along with a fair number of other philosophers both before and after him, seems to have given considerable credit to the view of Pyrrho found in Diogenes Laertius. According to this account, Pyrrho doubted to such an extent that he did not turn aside in the face of rushing chariots, mad dogs, or imminent precipices (he was allegedly saved from these perils by his followers), and that he was indifferent about everything. Even Bayle, who supposes many of the stories about Pyrrho to be the fabrications of his opponents, notes the "surprising" indifference of Pyrrho:

> Anaxarchus being fallen into a ditch, was seen by Pyrrho, but received no help from him. Pyrrho went his way, without vouchsafing to reach his hand to him. He was justly blamed for it, for he should have helped in such a case, a man unknown to him, but much more his professor. The master knew more than the disciple about that point, for Anaxarchus did not so much as complain of Pyrrho, and approved not that he should be censured; but besides, he praised him for his indifferency, and for loving nothing. Could any one do a thing more surprising under the discipline of the monks of la Trape? . . . [Another time, Pyrrho] was in great danger of suffering shipwrack. He was the only one that was not afraid of the storm; and when he saw every body struck with fear and sorrow, he desired them with a great sedateness of mind, to look upon a hog that was there, and eat as he used to do: Such ought to be, said he, the insensibility of a wise man.[46]

[46] *Dictionary*, Article "Pyrrho," Rem. E. In contrast, Montaigne says that the Pyrrhonians, "lend and accommodate themselves to natural inclinations, to the impulsion and constraint of passions, to the constitutions of laws and customs, and to the tradition of the arts. . . . They let their common actions be guided by those things, without any taking sides or judgment. Which is why I cannot very well reconcile with this principle what they say of Pyrrho. They portray him as stupid and immobile, adopting a wild and unsociable way of life, waiting for carts to hit him, risking himself on precipices, refusing to conform to the laws. That is outdoing his doctrine. He did not want to make himself a stump or a stone; he wanted to make himself a living, thinking, reasoning man, enjoying

Secondly, the Pyrrhonians are quite correctly represented as either suspending judgment, or recommending that judgment be suspended, and hence Hume's opinion has *some* foundation. As he no doubt read in Bayle, Pyrrho "found in all things reasons to affirm and to deny; and therefore he suspended his assent after he had well examined the arguments *pro* and *con*. . . . Though he is not the inventer of that method of philosophizing, yet it goes by his name: the art of disputing about every thing, without doing any thing else but suspending one's judgment, is called *Pyrrhonism* (or Scepticism): this is its most common name."[47]

Sextus would no doubt explain this teaching by saying that while Pyrrho accepted the compulsion of nature (*belief* in "appearances"), he did not make judgments or assertions of a philosophical or metaphysical sort. That is, he did not assent to or make assertions about things nonevident. Hume could perhaps have understood this teaching in such a way as to accommodate it to his own views, but he did not do so.[48] Assuming that Hume's

all natural pleasures and comforts, employing and using all his bodily and spiritual faculties in regular and upright fashion. The fantastic, imaginary, false privileges that man has arrogated to himself, of regimenting, arranging, and fixing truth, he honestly renounced and gave up" (*Complete Essays*, 2: 190-191).

[47] *Dictionary*, Article "Pyrrho."

[48] Had Hume realized that the Pyrrhonians neither, in their terms, doubt appearances nor recommend a total suspension of belief, he would no doubt have evinced more sympathy toward them. Nevertheless, he would still have parted company from them on the matter of assenting to or asserting propositions having to do with the nonevident. Hume saw, as the Pyrrhonians apparently did not, that every causal inference involves a belief about the nonevident, and yet that these are as much a part of everyday life as purely sensory appearances. We cannot, he says, "any more forbear viewing certain objects in a stronger and fuller light, upon account of their customary connexion with a present impression, than we can hinder ourselves from thinking as long as we are awake, or seeing the surrounding bodies, when we turn our eyes towards them in broad sunshine" (*Treatise*, p. 183). In short, we cannot restrict belief to appearances, but must also believe in the nonevident, or in, that is, objects (causes or effects) that are merely represented by an idea related to a present impression; indeed, such belief is the central topic of book I, part 3 of the *Treatise*.

Furthermore, Hume defends his own philosophical "speculations" or "elaborate philosophical researches" on the grounds that the "true sceptic will be diffident of his philosophical doubts, as well as of his philosophical convictions," and that it is "more truly sceptical" to engage in these speculations than it is, having doubts about them, "totally to reject" them. To this he adds that having undertaken such activities, it will be understood that he has sometimes yielded "to

position regarding the manner in which we come to believe has been correctly represented, then we can explain this rejection by the fact that he supposed (incorrectly) the Pyrrhonians comprehended all forms of belief under the heading of assent, assertion, or judgment, and that they thought all beliefs could be suspended. In contrast, Hume maintains that belief and judgment cannot be suspended at will, and that we neither can nor should avoid all beliefs or judgments regarding even nonevident things. Hume does think that we can alter what we assent to or believe, and even cause ourselves to assent pro and contra alternatively, but he does not think that these are matters within the immediate or direct control of the will, or that by an act of will we can achieve suspension of belief. As was seen in chapter 5, Hume says that "belief consists merely in a certain feeling or sentiment; in something that depends not on the will."[49] Consequently, the Pyrrhonians are in his eyes a "fantastic sect" not only because of what they tell us to disbelieve—that given effects have given causes, for example—but also because they tell us that we ought to disbelieve when in fact belief is not an activity that we can suspend or engage in at will. We can no more disbelieve at will than we can love or hate at will or fly at will, and philosophers who exhort us to suspend belief are as absurd as those politicians who concocted the notion of passive obedience.

5. *Academic Scepticism.* For information regarding the Aca-

---

that propensity, which inclines us to be positive and certain in *particular points*, according to the light, in which we survey them in any *particular instant*. . . . On such an occasion we are apt not only to forget our scepticism, but even our modesty too; and make use of such terms as these, *'tis evident, 'tis certain, 'tis undeniable*; . . . I may have fallen into this fault . . . but I here enter a *caveat* . . . that such expressions were extorted from me by the present view of the object, and imply no dogmatical spirit, nor conceited idea of my own judgment, which are sentiments that I am sensible can become no body, and a sceptic still less than any other" (*Treatise*, pp. 273-274). Although this last remark may remind one of the explanation Sextus gives of what sound like Pyrrhonian assertions, there is an important difference: Hume is clearly speaking of philosophical assertions, or assertions about what the Pyrrhonians considered nonevident.

[49] *Treatise*, p. 624. This, I suggest, is what Hume meant when, in the midst of his discussion of the Pyrrhonians, he says that belief is not a "simple act of the thought," but "some sensation or peculiar manner of conception" (*Treatise*, p. 184).

demic sceptics one must generally rely either on Sextus, who says that the Academics are not sceptics, but negative dogmatists, or on Hume's favorite among the ancient philosophers, Cicero, whose writings on this topic are only partially extant. Given these alternatives, Cicero, although perhaps more difficult to synthesize, is the preferred source because he is sympathetic, while Sextus is hostile. Fortunately, however, Charlotte Stough and others who have reconstructed the position of the Academics have attended to both sources, and my account benefits from this earlier work.[50]

Academic scepticism appears to have been largely the creation of Carneades, and to have consisted in both critical and constructive elements. Insofar as they were concerned with the Stoic theory of knowledge, the Academics were, according to Stough, entirely sceptical "in the modern sense of the term, [that is], destructive in intent, and negative in conclusion." The primary focus of this critical attack is the Stoic doctrine of cataleptic impressions. The Stoics claimed that certain of our sense impressions both force our assent and serve as a criterion of truth, and this because they are in fact perfect replicas of the objects which originate them. These they called cataleptic impressions (*kataleptikai phantasiai*). These impressions, the Stoics maintained, include intrinsically a "special mark of certainty" and can generate propositions that are "immediately evident and certain, requiring no supporting evidence beyond the unquestionable experience of the subject himself. . . . In addition to defining the conditions of truth, [such an impression] authorizes a claim to knowledge. And . . . this means it insures that the conditions of truth are satisfied."[51]

[50] Charlotte Stough, *Greek Scepticism: A Study in Epistemology* (Berkeley and Los Angeles: University of California Press, 1969). Two earlier studies of Greek scepticism that are useful are Eduard Zeller, *Stoics, Epicureans, and Sceptics*, trans. O. J. Reichel (London: Longmans, Green, 1880); and Mary Mills Patrick, *The Greek Sceptics* (New York: Columbia University Press, 1929).

[51] Stough, pp. 35-40. Lucullus, spokesman for the Stoics in Cicero's *Academica* 2: xi, speaks of a "presentation" that "may appear to me so true that it could not appear to me in the same way if it were false." (*De natura deorum/Academica*, trans. H. Rackham [Loeb Classical Library: Cambridge, Mass. and London, 1961]; all citations of *Academica* are from this translation.) Interestingly, the Stoics

In challenging this claim to have attained not only objective certainty, but also a workable criterion of truth, Carneades accepted (for the sake of the argument) the perceptual model of the Stoics, namely, the view that our sense organs are affected by objects within their range, and that by means of the resulting affections of the subject (by means of impressions) perception takes place. He criticized, however, the claim that some impressions inform us not only about themselves, but also inform us veridically, and in such a way that they guarantee their own accuracy about the objects from which they originate. Both Stoic and Sceptic could see that not all impressions are cataleptic (veridical and self-guaranteeing); it was agreed that there are perceptual errors, inexact replicas, or false impressions and that only those impressions that copy exactly reveal and guarantee truth.[52] It was also agreed that false impressions are not cataleptic, and that if any two impressions are indistinguishable in character, it is impossible for one to be cataleptic and the other not. The substantive challenge of the Academics came when they proposed that for every true impression it is possible that there is a false impression that is indistinguishable from it, and, therefore, that there are no cataleptic impressions. In support of this counterclaim, the sceptics pointed out that we often assent to impressions that are every bit as compelling as the allegedly cataleptic ones, only to discover that we have been victimized by dream, hallucination, illusion, or the limitations of our sensory faculties and powers, and that the impressions in question were in fact false. Compelling, convincing they were. True they were not. Yet, the sceptics went on, there is no qualitative difference betwen these false impressions and those the Stoics call cataleptic, and one simply cannot detect which are the true messengers, and which

---

appear to have adopted a view of the mind not unlike that of Hume's Scottish opponents. Lucullus says, for example, "Since therefore the mind of man is supremely well adapted for the knowledge of things and for consistency of life, it embraces information very readily. . ." (2: x).

[52] Stough (p. 42) cites Carneades as suggesting that impressions are like messengers, some good, some bad. The latter misrepresent the objects that "dispatch" them.

the false. It follows then, of course, that the Stoics do not have a criterion of truth as they claim to have.[53]

In reply, the Stoics pointed out that the Academics' criticism goes beyond the evidence they adduce. The fact that we do make perceptual errors does not make all experience dubious, nor does the existence of false impressions impugn the claim that there are cataleptic impressions. Indeed, the bizarre perceptual experiences which the sceptics cite are irrelevant, for they are simply examples of noncataleptic impressions from which assent should be withheld. Dreaming is, after all, recognized as such on waking, and so, too, are the other nonveridical states recognized for what they are. The sceptics' position generally, it was said, "rests on the mistaken view that a few isolated errors of perception can call into question the veracity of all experience."[54]

The Stoics, however, says Stough, missed the point of the Academics' criticism. True, abnormal perceptual experience per se does not impugn all sense experience, and to think that it does is to count as evidence only that experience which confirms the occurrence of error, while rejecting the rest, overlooking that the false impressions must be selected from among the other, presumably correct impressions. But the attack of the sceptics was not a generalized attack on sense perception, but a criticism of the attempt to make cataleptic impressions stand as the criterion of truth. The cataleptic impression is said by the Stoics to be both true, an exact replica, and of such a nature that it must be true, must originate from the object it replicates. The Academic objection is that such allegedly cataleptic impressions constitute an inadequate criterion of truth because these impressions are not experienced as different in kind from others. Granted, cataleptic impressions have a force and clarity that compels assent, but so also do impressions that are later found to be false.[55] The experience of dreams, hallucinations, and so forth does not show that

[53] Stough, pp. 42-44.
[54] Stough, pp. 45-46.
[55] Saying that impressions are *found to be false* needs to be understood as saying no more than that they are *taken to be false* because they come in conflict with other impressions that are *taken to be true*. To us these impressions appear to be, as it were, contrary.

272

all experience is dubious, but it does show that not all clear and forceful impressions are true. Further, it is irrelevant to argue that some clear and forceful impressions are later said to be false impressions, and not to have been cataleptic after all. "What we are asking," says Cicero, "is what these things looked like at the time when they were seen."[56] In short, the sceptics challenged the Stoics to show that any impression once taken to be a cataleptic impression never will be taken to be otherwise. The Stoics were unable to meet this challenge.

From considerations of this sort, the Academics drew two conclusions:

A. Cataleptic impressions do not present an adequate criterion by which to distinguish truth from error so that disagreements of fact can be settled. Certainly, an individual receiving a clear impression that forces assent and compels a judgment may as a consequence make a correct judgment. But he will not know that he has made a correct judgment on the basis of the impression per se. If we restrict ourselves to impressions only, we are in a situation like that of a marksman shooting at an unseen target in the dark: the target may in fact be hit, but this cannot (then) be ascertained.

B. No impression can establish its own truth. To be true, the impression must exactly replicate the object from which it originates. But to establish its own truth, it must present both itself and the object replicated, and that it cannot do. The Academics argue that we "cannot be certain that an impression is an exact copy of its object, since it is impossible to compare impressions with the objects they are alleged to resemble. In fact, that is exactly the point of the contention that true impressions are not intrinsically distinguishable from false ones. The cataleptic impression provides no way out of this difficulty. . . . The result is that if we do perceive objects, we cannot be sure when we do (accurately) and when not."[57] Again, the metaphor of shooting in the dark is apt, and it can be seen that the very notion of knowing the truth must be abandoned if the Stoic criterion of

[56] *Academica*, 2: 88, cited by Stough, pp. 48-49.
[57] Stough, p. 49.

truth is insisted upon. By that criterion, knowledge of truth cannot be attained.

However, Carneades and the Academics did not recommend
the abandonment of the notion of truth or of the notion of
knowing the truth. They saw that the failure of any impression
to guarantee its own truth does not imply that all impressions are
dubious; it may mean only that new criteria of truth, criteria of
a significantly different sort, are required. This is precisely what
Carneades attempted to supply, although he does not expect his
criteria to disclose which judgments are absolutely certain. Rather,
they are to indicate which judgments are justifiable even though
our claims are never immune from the possibility of error.

Carneades accepted the distinction between the uncertain, the
nonevident, and the absolutely certain, and he argued that not
only are a great many things neither nonevident nor absolutely
certain, but that within the class of uncertainties we find some
perceptual statements that merit our acceptance more than others.
According to Carneades, our impressions are part of a two-way
relationship: they are linked to the object from which they presumably originate, and to the percipient (subject) to which they
appear. An impression (or the perceptual statement which is a
consequence of it) is true if and only if it conforms to the orig-
inating object (or results in perceptual statements conforming to
the object). Otherwise, it is false. Thus in the first relationship,
that between object and impression, the *conditions* of truth are
found, and, depending upon the impression, they are either met
or not met. On the other hand, an impression (or perceptual
statement) may be said to be true if it relates to the subject in a
specific way. In this second relationship, that between impression
and subject, the criteria of truth are found, and, again depending
upon the impression, they are met or not met by degrees. In this
manner the notion of absolute truth (that is, perfect conformity
of impression to object) is retained, as are the notions of probable
knowledge, or likelihood, and justified assertion. Only the claim
to certain knowledge (that is, knowledge of the perfect conformity
of impressions to their objects) is discarded, for such knowledge

is impossible given that it is only through their impressions that objects are known.

According to Stough, then, Carneades maintained that "any perceptual statement regardless of its justification, may be false." But this did not prevent him from working out a canon of justification. He granted, for example, that some of our impressions are, prima facie, credible, while others are doubtful, and that even among the prima facie credible, some are clearer and more compelling than others. As a first criterion of truth he suggested this stronger form of credibility, and to this he added consistency, or a demand for a "concurrence of impressions," as a second criterion. An impression may on first experience seem entirely credible, but it may be linked with others of a dubious sort; if so, our perceptual statements should be restrained accordingly. Thirdly, impressions should be consciously and conscientiously tested. The conditions in which an object is perceived should be considered, or if the impressions are in the form of testimony, the reliability of the witness must be considered.[58] Furthermore, Carneades suggests that these criteria should be applied in a manner appropriate to the circumstances. An essentially unimportant matter—is my apple wormy?—does not merit the diligence and time that a more momentous issue merits and even requires. In fact, according to Stough, Carneades probably thought that his criteria were

recommended by the virtue of actual use. . . . They are not technical but are intended to be employed in ordinary life. The point of the criteria seems to be not to provide a systematic doctrine of truth but to sketch an informal method

[58] Stough, pp. 60-63. Zeller suggests that Carneades distinguished between the (a) probable, (b) the probable and undisputed, and (c) the probable and undisputed and tested. The first or lowest probability is produced by a "notion" which gives an impression of truth; the second is produced when such an impression is confirmed by the agreement of all the notions related to the initial notion; the third and highest probability is produced when investigation of all these notions corroborates all of them. The three levels are illustrated by the account of the man who saw a coiled object which he took to be a snake (a single notion), but then reconsidered when the object remained motionless (disconfirmation by comparison), and finally concluded that the object was a rope after poking it with his cane. See Scepticism, Man and God, pp. 94-95 (Outlines, I.227-229).

actually employed for deciding whether a given assertion or belief should be regarded as true . . . within the context of a whole network of beliefs already accepted as true. . . . If this interpretation is correct, then by discerning and advocating a criterion of truth that is already in use, Carneades, like the Pyrrhonists, is recommending adherence to the practices and conventions of ordinary life.[59]

Implicit in this recommendation are two further suggestions. First, absolute certainty (or Stoic "perception") is not required for conduct. The genuinely wise man (the Academic sceptic, not the Stoic sage) does not dogmatically pronounce, according to Cicero, but he does not for that reason make any pretense of being "a statue carved out of stone or hewn out of timber." On the contrary, he recognizes that "he has a body and a mind, a mobile intellect and mobile senses, so that many things *seem* to him to be true, although nevertheless they do not seem to him to possess that distinct and peculiar mark leading to perception," or perfect knowledge. The sceptic manages to function quite adequately without even the illusion of perfect knowledge; his beliefs and his criteria of actual use are sufficient for practice.[60]

Secondly, there is here at least a very broad hint about the limits of human knowledge vis-à-vis reality itself. Not only is our mind, on the evidence available, not perfectly well adapted, and hence subject to unnoticed error, but there appear also to be some matters that are by the very nature of things quite beyond our faculties even at their best. The real nature of the entities giving rise to our sensations is an example of such a nonevident matter. Consequently, inquiry into these matters can be discontinued without loss, probably with gain.

Finally, Carneades grants that many of our judgments and actions may in effect be, with all appropriateness, automatic, or, as he puts it, our judgments and actions "are regulated by the standard of the general rule."[61] This is not to say that the jus-

---

[59] Pp. 63-64.

[60] *Academica*, 2: xxxi; italics added.

[61] As cited by Sextus (*Adversos Mathematicos*, 7: 175), and translated by Stough, p. 58.

tification of beliefs and assertions is a simple matter; the criteria applied in any case will on analysis prove complex. But the simplicity and similarity of many of our experiences eliminates the need for the conscious application of all the criteria in all their complexity. In the overwhelming majority of cases it is enough that the impression received is clear and credible. This simple, compelling experience will never justify a claim to "know for certain" that a given perceptual statement is true; justifying belief that it is true is not the same as gaining certain knowledge. Carneades and the Academics may wish to give sanction to ordinary experience as such, but they are adamantly against those who pretentiously translate this experience into "absolute truths" in order to found and form dogmatic metaphysical systems.

Hume, we noted earlier, was relatively warm in his praise of Academic scepticism. He found its proposals regarding doubt and suspense of judgment useful counters to rash conclusions and prejudice. The Academics, he writes,

> always talk of doubt and suspense of judgement, of danger in hasty determinations, of confining to very narrow bounds the enquiries of the understanding, and of renouncing all speculations which lie not within the limits of common life and practice. Nothing, therefore, can be more contrary than such a philosophy to the supine indolence of the mind, its rash arrogance, its lofty pretensions, and its superstitious credulity. Every passion is mortified by it, except the love of truth; and that passion never is, nor can be, carried to too high a degree.[62]

[62] *First Enquiry*, pp. 40-41. Hume's explanation of the unpopularity of such philosophy echoes Shaftesbury's explanation which was cited earlier in this chapter: "It is surprising, therefore, that this philosophy, which, in almost every instance, must be harmless and innocent, should be the subject of so much groundless reproach and obloquy. But, perhaps, the very circumstance which renders it so innocent is what chiefly exposes it to the public hatred and resentment. By flattering no irregular passion, it gains few partizans: By opposing so many vices and follies, it raises to itself abundance of enemies, who stigmatize it as libertine, profane, and irreligious" (p. 41). Hume also discusses "a more *mitigated* scepticism or *academical* philosophy" in section 12, part 3 of this work, and there twice suggests that it may be in part influenced by Pyrrhonism.

Further, Hume's own constructive but undogmatic probabilism bears some resemblance to the theory proposed by Carneades, or at least one might consider the extent to which Hume's knowledge, proofs, and probabilities correspond to the three levels of probability which Zeller and others have attributed to the earlier philosopher.[63] Hume also sounds rather like the Academics when he suggests that the wise man proportions his belief to the evidence, for Hume leaves one to wonder whether he thought there were any wise men (those, for example, who *can* proportion belief to evidence), while the Academics were forthrightly attempting to show that the wise man (The Stoic sage, that is) had no such perfect control over his assents. Finally, Hume is generally in accord with the Academics' suggestions that we limit our inquiries to those concerning matters within the scope of our faculties and experience, and, given his response to the Pyrrhonists, he seems curiously open to the Academic call for suspension of judgment. Perhaps because of his extensive reading in Cicero, Hume saw that these sceptics, when they spoke of suspension of judgment, meant not suspension of belief, but suspension of dogmatic assertion. Whatever the reason, Hume in his earlier *Enquiry* is able to express in classical terms what he had put more idiosyncratically in the *Treatise*, namely, that finding oneself compelled to believe something tells one nothing definitive about the truth of that thing.[64] In short, if one were forced to put Hume's scepticism

[63] It seems to me an overstatement to say that the *Treatise* argument allegedly showing that there are only "judgments of probability . . . is exactly the position held by Academic scepticism" (Immerwahr, "A Skeptic's Progress," p. 228). Hume's probabilism is perhaps closer to that of Gassendi and the early members of the Royal Society than to that of Carneades, though doubtless Gassendi was also influenced by the Academics. Helpful in this regard is Henry G. Van Leeuwen, *The Problem of Certainty in English Thought, 1630-1690*, International Archives of the History of Ideas, vol. 3 (The Hague: Martinus Nijhoff, 1963).

[64] I have by no means exhausted the interesting comparisons to be made between Hume and the Academics. Zeller, e.g., suggests that Carneades' refutation of the Stoic version of the argument from design has come down to us through Cicero and Hume. Whether one accepts this suggestion completely or not, one could wish that *De natura deorum* and *Academica* (at least) were read by more than the occasional Hume scholar. For a valuable recent article on Hume and Cicero, see Christine Battersby, "The *Dialogues* as Original Imitation: Cicero and the Nature of Hume's Skepticism," *McGill Hume Studies*, pp. 239-252.

in some historical mold, that of Academic scepticism would provide the nearest fit. But, however much we have learned about
Hume by comparing his views with those of the Academics, or
comparing and contrasting them with those of other sceptics,
there is yet more to be learned about his scepticism, for some
aspects ·of it are not to be found in the earlier sceptics.

IV.   I have argued that for Hume belief is a natural consequence
rather than the consequence of an act of the will. I have also
suggested that on Hume's view, one can find oneself under natural
compulsion to believe something while yet able to ask if that
something is true. He also thinks that, in some cases at least, we
are able to act contrary to our beliefs. This in turn suggests that
in Hume's opinion one can at the same time believe and doubt
about the same thing. To summarize, Hume holds that belief is
not an act of will, but that doubt may be such an act. For Hume,
belief is a natural consequence of "determinate causes and principles" that are outside our direct control, but at least one form
of doubt is an intellectual activity that one can willfully undertake. Furthermore, having once doubted in this way one may
find that one has indirectly influenced one's belief, just as by the
use of reason one may indirectly influence one's passions. Just
how this can be must be clarified.

If the foregoing review of the leading forms of scepticism has
revealed anything, it is that there are few significant features that
can be said to be common to these several forms. Indeed, even
the seemingly trivial claim that all sceptics doubt would be misleading if *doubt* were understood in any univocal sense, for sceptical doubt is nearly as variable as scepticism itself. It must be said,
however, that this is a further fact that philosophers concerned
with scepticism have tended, with unfortunate consequences, to
overlook. There is, for example, a widespread tendency to suppose
that *doubt* as a term refers to a particular state of mind or particular
disposition, each characterized in its own way by uncertainty, an
uncertainty on which sceptical doubts are said to be dependent,
and of which sceptical arguments and hesitant behavior are predictable consequences. This account of doubt is often implicit in

purported refutations of scepticism, such as when a philosopher tells us that it is not in the power of the sceptic to doubt certain beliefs or propositions, and hence, whatever the sceptic may say he is doing, he is not in fact *doubting* these beliefs or propositions. He may recommend that these beliefs be doubted, and he may sincerely try to do so, but, as he cannot bring himself to be uncertain about them, or cannot attain that particular frame of mind called "being in doubt," he fails actually to doubt.[65]

This same account of doubt is also avowed explicitly. C. S. Peirce, for example, insists that Descartes's methodic doubt is "not real doubt" at all because it shows none of the mental activity that characterizes doubt. "Let us not," he says, "pretend to doubt in philosophy what we do not doubt in our hearts." Elsewhere, he adds that "doubt is an uneasy and dissatisfied state from which we struggle to free ourselves and pass into a state of belief, while the latter is a calm and satisfactory state which we do not wish to avoid, or to change to a belief in anything else," and "all doubt is a state of hesitancy about an imagined state of things. . . ."[66] G. E. Moore, although less clearly, also identifies doubt

[65] It is also sometimes supposed that the fact that the would-be sceptic cannot maintain his puzzlement (he avoids the onrushing chariot willy-nilly) is good evidence that he cannot really doubt. As nature (always) overcomes the doubt, it is not real doubt. Reid retorts Hume's doubts in this fashion, for example. See *Works of Reid*, 1: 259. See also John Wisdom, *Philosophy and Psychoanalysis* (Oxford: Blackwell's, 1957), p. 170.

[66] *The Collected Papers of Charles Sanders Peirce*, ed. C. Hartshorne, P. Weiss, and A. W. Burks, 8 vols. (Cambridge, Mass.: Harvard University Press, 1931-1958), 1: 156; 509. This view Peirce later modified by drawing back from the unqualified identification of doubt with a state of mind to a more dispositionally oriented account, or one in which a true doubt is said to be one which causes the usual working of the mind to come to a stop. "Doubt is a state of mind marked by a feeling of uneasiness; but we cannot, from a logical, least of all from a pragmaticist point of view, regard the doubt as consisting in the feeling. A man in doubt is usually trying to imagine how he shall, or should, act when or if he finds himself to have an end in view, and two different and inconsistent lines of action offer themselves. His action is in imagination (or perhaps really) brought to a stop. . . . His pent up activity finds vent in a feeling, which becomes the more prominent from his attention being no longer absorbed in action. A true doubt is accordingly a doubt which really interferes with the smooth working of the belief-habit." Granted, then, that doubt is not merely a feeling or state of mind on this later view, a particular state of mind is nonetheless said to be a necessary part of the doubting process, and a particular feeling (assuming states

with a particular feeling when he writes: "A man who denies that
we ever know for certain things of a certain sort, obviously need
not feel any doubt about that which he asserts . . . and in fact
many who have made this sort of denial seem to have *felt no doubt
at all* that they were right. . . . There is, therefore, a sort of
scepticism which is compatible with a complete absence of doubt
on any subject whatever."[67]

Of course, a philosopher who thinks mentalistic accounts are
misleading will avoid claiming that doubt is a state of mind. But
in that case it may be suggested that doubt or "real" doubt is
characterized by behavior of a particular and identifiable sort.
The individual who doubts will be hesitant or vacillating, or will
act quite differently from the manner in which he would act if
he were not affected by doubt, while the *philosophical* sceptic
reveals his lack of real doubt when he fails to exhibit these be-
havioral characteristics. In this case, doubt is identified with or
seen as necessarily concomitant with a specific disposition, a
hesitating disposition. According to John Wisdom, Wittgenstein
was inclined to question whether a person giving "none of the
normal signs of doubt" was actually doubting or in doubt. "What
Wittgenstein had in mind I think," writes Wisdom, "was that
the Sceptic gives none of the *contextual* signs of doubt. He is still
just as considerate of Smith's feelings although he says with an
air of doubt that he doubts their existence."[68]

That there is a serious error here is clear, given the preceding
historical review. The atheist doubts the existence of God with

---

of mind and feelings to be different things) a likely if not necessary consequence
of the same process (5: 373, n. 1).
[67] *Philosophical Papers* (London: Allen and Unwin, 1959), pp. 198-199. Moore
grants that one can be sceptical without feeling doubt, but implicitly denies that
one can doubt without *feeling* doubt, or more generally, being in a state of doubt.
[68] *Other Minds* (Oxford: Blackwell's, 1956), p. 9. Wisdom also writes, "I say,
'Does the Sceptic, the philosophical sceptic really doubt about the minds of
others?' But I *don't* say the philosophic sceptic gives all the normal signs of
doubting. On the contrary, what I say is, 'He looks and feels *at the moment* as if
he is doubting but the feeling will not in the usual way be accompanied by any
hesitancy in preparations for the future or surprise or relief as it unrolls.' " In
other words, it only looks like doubt, but will prove not to be real doubt because
there will be no accompanying hesitating disposition.

all the calm satisfaction of the theist who believes in that existence. The agnostic may, knowing not whether God exists or not,
doubt with complete peace of mind and total indifference the
claims of both theist and atheist. The humanistic critic may cast
doubt on organized religion without being or feeling puzzled or
hesitant. Similarly, the ethical sceptic doubts the altruist's optimistic claims about man's motivations, or the ethical absolutist's
claims to have access to universal moral principles. The ethical
sceptic is convinced that man is entirely self-interested, or that
ethical relativism is indubitable. Descartes can systematically doubt
his beliefs, and in doing so pass directly from belief and affirmation
to disbelief and negation—"I believe X," he says, "but it could
be false. Therefore, I shall take it to be false." No hesitation, no
uncertainty, no indecision before branching paths; only a simple
reversal: if X is not certain, then it is taken to be false. The
Pyrrhonian sips his honeyed tea, looks his Stoic opponent in the
eye, and tells him that he doubts that there are cataleptic impressions and, if there are, that they can by any reliable means be
distinguished from ordinary, corrigible impressions. His opponent
replies, is rebutted with further doubts, and the discussion of the
reliability of sense perception continues. All the while, the sceptic, an old hand at such debates, remains undisturbed, without
desire or impetus to substitute a philosophical belief for the tran-
quil acceptance of appearances that he has attained. Elsewhere,
an Academic sceptic, engaged in a similar debate, doubts the
dogmatic metaphysical claims of his opponent, and suggests instead a modest probabilism as a less disturbing, more valuable
guide.

Some of these doubting individuals could also, in different
circumstances, combine these doubts with being in doubt, for
doubting is sometimes accompanied by a particular state of mind
or a particular disposition—that frame of mind characterized by
uncertainty or uneasiness, or that disposition to hesitate or appear
puzzled. Indeed, the etymology of *doubt* (which links it to *duo*,
"two," through *dubare*, "to vacillate") suggests vacillation and
being of two minds. But, to begin with a purely grammatical
point, *doubt* is not only a noun used to refer to a state of mind

or being, and an intransitive verb, but also a transitive verb. We can say of Smith that he is "in doubt," thus describing his state of mind or disposition, and we can say of ourselves, "I am in doubt," or "I am doubtful," meaning thereby, "I am uncertain," or "I am of two minds," and thus intend to describe our own states or dispositions. However, these uses of *doubt* are supplemented by others of no less importance. I can also say, "I doubt that God exists," or "I doubt that there are any incorrigible perceptions," and thereby, quite independently of any particular state or disposition, perform a particular function or *act* in a certain way. That is, doubt itself not only is a particular state or disposition characterized by saying that one is "in doubt," uncertain, hesitant, puzzled, vacillating or of two minds, but also is an activity—an activity that can be engaged in quite independently of the state or disposition that has just been characterized.[69]

Recognizing this simple fact—that doubt may be either an activity or a disposition, and that the activity does not depend upon one and only one disposition—enables us to see what the several forms of scepticism have in common. One does not become a sceptic by virtue of being in doubt or obtaining a unique disposition or state of mind. Rather, the sceptic is characterized by a certain kind of activity, an activity that one may engage in without feeling uneasy or being disposed to hesitate. The sceptic can be taken as saying, in a variety of circumstances and regarding

[69] The somewhat old-fashioned verb *scruple* suggests itself as a likely synonym for *doubt* used in this way, and was certainly so used by Hume and his contemporaries. The *Oxford English Dictionary* gives as the second meaning of *scruple* (verb, transitive) the following: "To doubt, question, hesitate to believe (a fact, allegation, etc.); to question the truth, goodness, or genuineness of." Seventeenth- and eighteenth-century examples of this use are cited. The general similarity of my suggestion to the more recent views of Austin and others will not be missed (on *doubt* in particular, see *How to Do Things with Words*, pp. 88, 161), but it is not my intention to enter into or contribute to the "speech acts" controversy. I am satisfied simply to point out that there are different uses of *doubt*, that one of these is equivalent to *question* in a sentence such as "Come now, I question that," and incidentally, that such uses are what Austin would have called performative ones. Consequently, I conclude that the demand that doubting always be accompanied by a particular mental or dispositional correlative is misguided.

283

a wide range of entities, beliefs, or propositions, "I doubt that X," or "I doubt P." But, if uttering these sentences is not necessarily to manifest an uneasy state of mind or a hesitating disposition, it is, nonetheless, in a great many circumstances, to doubt; it is to raise questions, to scruple, to cast (X or P) in doubt.[70] In these cases, once the sentence "I doubt that X" has been uttered, no question can arise about the reality of the doubt.[71]

Further, one who wishes to engage in this doubting activity does not need to use precisely the forms of utterance cited. In fact, one need not use *doubt* in any of its forms, nor even be fully aware that one is engaged in the act of doubting. The atheist who, simply retorting the believer, says, "But God does not exist," is doubting (questioning, challenging) just as much as the perhaps more philosophical atheist who responds to the same believer, "I doubt that God exists." Likewise, when the classical sceptic suggests to the Stoic that he lacks a criterion by which to distinguish infallibly true presentations from false, he has doubted just as much, and perhaps more effectively, as has the philosopher who more directly and explicitly raises doubts about the ultimate claims of Stoic ethics. The expression of quiet criticism is also the expression of doubt; indeed, for several of the historical forms of scepticism, criticism is the paradigm not only of the doubting activity of which I am speaking, but also of doubt in general.[72]

[70] If it is insisted that each of our acts follows necessarily from some disposition, then clearly acts of doubt will follow from some disposition. But these might be dispositions to question or scruple, or dispositions to caution, as well as hesitating dispositions. The doubting activity or doubt that arises in conjunction with either scrupling dispositions or cautioning dispositions is here styled "active doubt." The doubt associated with hesitation and unease can in contrast be appropriately called "affective doubt."

[71] This in no way prevents one from asking whether the doubt evidenced is well founded, shows good judgment, is trivially or profoundly motivated, and so forth. That when speaking loosely we evaluate things by saying they are not *real* ("He's not a real contender," when in fact he is scheduled to fight the title match) should not be allowed to mislead us about doubting.

[72] The Pyrrhonians, for example, had no desire to produce or increase affective doubt, but sought rather to bring about mental tranquility through the use of arguments pro and contra. The only form of doubt that was important to their discipline was active doubt, for they hoped that this could be carried out on a foundation of unconcern or peace of mind. Affective doubt or an uneasy state of mind would destroy the very tranquility the Pyrrhonians sought, and hence

Finally, I propose that we can make an imperfect but usable division of doubting activity into that sort which arises from the disposition to scruple and that which arises from the disposition to be cautious. The former can be roughly characterized as *challenging behavior*, the latter as *cautionary behavior*.

As challenging behavior, doubting is perhaps most clearly represented in the familiar examples of the ethical and religious sceptics. The ethical sceptic openly challenges the opinions of the altruists or absolutists by attempting to show that these views are unfounded, or that egoism or relativism are true (and hence their contraries false), or both. Similarly, the religious sceptic challenges orthodox views about God or the church either by explicitly denying and negating these views and by demanding evidence or proof of their truth, or by asserting claims that are the contraries of these orthodox views. For example: "God does not exist." "If God exists there is no evidence of his concern with and intervention in the affairs of the world." "*Clergyman* is just another word for *scoundrel.*"

The same kind of activity makes up at least a part of the other forms of scepticism outlined in section 2. Descartes, for example, can be seen as challenging both ordinary and philosophical beliefs that are or were widely held, or as demanding, so to speak, that all his own opinions come forward with unassailable proof of their truth, or be cast aside, negated, counted as false. More moderately, the Pyrrhonian grants the plain man's view that his honey seems sweet, but challenges the philosophers' attempts to go beyond appearances to tell us that honey *is really* Y (or that X *is really* Y), and that we know this by such and such means (veridical perception, reason, and so forth), or that X *is* Y because such and such an ontological structure (prime matter and substantial form; atoms in the void) prevails. In this regard, one can say that the collection of arguments (the *tropes*) that Sextus has cataloged represent the classical sceptics' arsenal of challenge: The dogmatic philosopher had only to lay claim to some particular piece of

---

can scarcely be what they meant by doubting. Historically speaking, then, it is quite mistaken to claim that doubt is merely an uneasy state of mind or the manifestation of such an uneasy state.

philosophical ground—the *real* nature of honey, the *real* nature of man, the *real* nature of the cosmos—and these argument forms could be utilized to challenge these claims, or to show that the dogmatist in question actually knows considerably less than he has claimed. The ordinary man could well be left in peace, but the philosopher and the ordinary man *qua* philosopher were challenged in their pretension to know and understand things and the world.

If we conceive of doubting activities as lying on a continuum with challenging behavior at one end, then cautionary behavior could be said to lie at the other (and there is considerable overlap). In its purest form such cautionary behavior appears to be nothing more than the utterance of gentle admonitions to be careful or circumspect in intellectual matters: we see things from a necessarily limited perspective and must be careful not to impose idiosyncratic elements onto whatever reality is our concern; our knowledge of any matter is limited, and hence our generalizations must be cautiously drawn; the human understanding is notoriously fallible, and so it will not do to be immodest in our claims. So gentle are these admonitions that uttering them may scarcely seem to be raising doubts. On the contrary, they seem in our time the stuff of common sense and a far cry from scepticism. That these are axioms of common sense—of our contemporary common sense, that is—I grant; nonetheless, to use these axioms is to doubt and to be, even now, (mildly) sceptical. Just as the challenging behavior of the religious and ethical sceptics has in our age become a commonplace, so, too, has the cautioning behavior of certain other sceptics. It is as a matter of course that we now recommend circumspection and claim to be cautious and undogmatic.[73]

Consider again Descartes. In the First Meditation he clearly challenges the veracity of a great many beliefs. However, the fact of these challenges should not be allowed to obscure the motive which underlies them: Descartes's desire to eliminate, once and for all, mistaken beliefs and the uncertainty that derives from

[73] It should not be forgotten that even in Hume's lifetime there were those who claimed that tolerance is a vice, intolerance a virtue.

such beliefs. I shall doubt my beliefs, he says, and eliminate those that do not stand up to the test so that I may be certain that I am not deceived. And then, type by type, his beliefs are eliminated as this hyperbolic caution manifests itself in hyperbolic doubt. The classical sceptics, although possessed of ultimate aims that were very different from those of Descartes, also challenged in order to caution. They attacked the pretensions of the dogmatists because, as the Pyrrhonians believed, that which mankind sought through philosophy, namely, tranquility, peace of mind, could be attained only if the endeavors of the philosophers were abandoned. It was not this or that philosophical system that the Pyrrhonians opposed, but philosophical systems in general, philosophical arguments in general, the entire philosophical enterprise. But to undermine and eliminate philosophy, they thought it was necessary to bring those attracted to it to despair of philosophical success or understanding, to bring them to the point that they would, as had Apelles, throw in the sponge. It was to this end that the sceptical arguments were refined and cataloged, and it was to this end they were used to challenge the dogmatists. Does Democritus claim that the authority of the senses supports his views? Note then the variations which the senses undergo— between times, between places, between men and animals. Does Aristotle then claim the authority of reason as the foundation of his system? Note that this foundation must either regress infinitely or circle upon itself, and proves quite as deficient, quite as variable, as the senses. If you would avoid wasting your time; if you would avoid foolish, sometimes bigoted pretension; if you would live a peaceful, useful life—avoid philosophy for the philosophical life is not worth pursuing. It is this cautionary message that underlies the message of the Pyrrhonians.

Similarly, in place of the claims to validated knowledge made by the Stoic sages, the Academic sceptics recommended a more modest, a more cautious, probabilism, and explicitly suggested that each of our claims is legitimately open to examination. It is perhaps unnecessary, Carneades says, to give to every trivial matter the full attention of our critical faculties, but the more important the matter before us, the more cautiously ought we to proceed. And when the matter is one of the greatest moment, and also one that carries us beyond our ordinary experience, then surely we ought to leave no intellectual stone unturned. Then especially ought our cautioning behavior to rise to its peak; we ought to question, to scruple, to doubt actively and to reserve our judgment until our questions are answered. And even when these scruples are satisfied, we ought to remember that although we may be right, we are nonetheless shooting in the dark, and have not perfect grounds for our beliefs—and hence ought to be cautious and humane in our application of them.

I have argued, to summarize, that *doubt* may refer to a particular psychological state, to a disposition to behave in a particular manner, or to an intellectual activity of a certain character.[74] Further, I have argued that doubting as an activity can be characterized as either challenging, as when the religious sceptic says, "God does not exist," or as cautioning, as when an epistemological sceptic shows the gap between evidence and conclusion, the corrigibility of our evidence or faculties, the lack of a satisfactory criterion of truth, or other deficiencies. In the interim I have also argued that one may engage in these doubting activities without being "in doubt," without, that is, being in an uneasy state of mind or having a hesitating disposition. If these claims are correct, then it seems clear that one could be a sceptic without being either puzzled or hesitant. I would agree, of course, that in order to be a sceptic, or to be justifiably called a sceptic, one must doubt. But, although the manifestation of some doubt be supposed a necessary characteristic of the sceptic, it does not follow that the sceptic must manifest all possible forms of doubt, nor, historically, has he done so. Indeed, the sceptic who is both in doubt and actively doubting may be the exception rather than the rule.

There is a further consequence of my claims: an individual justifiably called a sceptic regarding a particular issue—because actively challenging or cautioning received opinion on that is-

[74] Richard Watson has reminded me that doubting has sometimes taken the form of physical activity, as when Dr. Johnson kicked a stone to challenge Berkeley's views.

sue—may in fact believe the very received opinion which he or
she is doubting. This may sound paradoxical, but it is not. It
would not be supposed strange to say that assertions of belief are
made by those who are in doubt. Surely, countless millions have
repeated one or another creed in such circumstances. It is no
more paradoxical to suggest that a man who believes some fact
or proposition—or creed—can at the same time doubt it. Some
doubting is an activity analogous to asserting, and as such its
performance is not dependent upon being in doubt or upon being
in an uneasy state of mind or of a hesitating disposition. Consequently, it is not logically absurd to suggest that one can doubt
some claim while at the same time believing this claim. Neither
is it psychologically absurd, provided only that we agree that it
is possible to believe something while yet granting that this belief
may be mistaken, and making an effort to test or prove it. Our
beliefs and our actions need not be consistent. Humans are complicated enough to be able to go off in two directions at once,
and many are sophisticated enough to do so intentionally, a claim
that is supported and illustrated by the fact that we not only tell
lies or play poker, but also play the devil's advocate.[75]

To this it may be objected that, if correct, the sceptic then
becomes a milk-and-water figure of little philosophical interest
or consequence. I do not agree. In the first place, nothing I have

[75] I grant that one may never hear even a philosopher say, "I believe that but
I doubt it," or, that is, hear anyone couple belief and doubt in such a bare,
unmitigated fashion. When we are doubting our own beliefs we speak in a more
mitigated fashion: "I happen to agree with what you've said, but I wonder if we're
right. Have you thought about . . . ?" Or, subvocalized, something to the effect
of, "Here I say this, but I wonder if that's right," or "He certainly seems guilty,
but perhaps I'm biased." In some such cases, of course, time and further consideration may weaken an initial assurance and thus make questioning more likely.
We may also want to say that there are degrees of belief or assurance, and that
we are more likely to raise doubts about a belief when our assurance regarding it
is significantly below greatest strength, or when assurance is mixed with doubt.
It may also be found that philosophers who appear to doubt what they also believe
are sometimes doubting only one or another justification of the belief, not the
belief per se. I have no reason to resist these suggestions. They show further the
complexity of our epistemic activities, but they do not show that it is more
difficult to doubt what one believes than it is to assert what one finds doubtful.
(This formulation of my views on these matters owes much to the critical remarks
of Páll Árdal and Wade Robison.)

said makes it impossible for the actively doubting sceptic also to be in doubt, and to find a literary expression of such a combination one need look no further than I, 4, 7 of Hume's *Treatise*. Further, those who prefer what Hume so aptly styled an "easy and obvious philosophy" may continue to refute that colorful, quixotic figure, the sceptic whose doubt has made him incapable of functioning normally, or, that is, a kind of metaphysical lunatic akin to the man of glass or the solipsist of Paris. There will be, one can note, some difficulty in finding a real figure of this sort, but as one is conceivable, the same straw man may continue to be set up and knocked down by those of a superficial bent.

Secondly, to reveal that many sceptics are a kind of devil's advocate, or are, that is, not only sane, but philosophically sane, is by no means to show this stance to be uninteresting or inconsequential. We ourselves live in (relatively speaking) a critical age, an age which has incorporated and even (in some places) made a fetish of the lessons of the classical and modern sceptics. For us, challenging and cautioning—denying, questioning, demanding evidence, reserving judgment, seeking probabilities— just are the milk and water of intellectual life. That this is so is in no small part due to the efforts of these sane, normally functioning believing sceptics, of whom not the least important was David Hume. If such philosophers now seem to be of little consequence, or not sceptics at all, it is, I suggest, because their views and attitudes are no longer striking, and that they are no longer striking because they are so much like our own.

V. As I have shown in chapter 5, Hume recognized that it is one thing to say that one cannot (sometimes) avoid believing a certain X, and quite another to suppose that X is true or objectively certain. He recognized, we could say, the difference between psychological certainty and epistemological certainty.[76] Now

[76] Hume in effect sees doubt as having two forms. In one form it is similar to belief insofar as it arises naturally and is constituted by a certain sentiment or feeling. In the second form doubt is similar to assertion or asseveration insofar as both are intellectual activities that we can consciously decide to engage in or

that we have seen how it is that one can doubt X while at the same time believing X, we can also see one form that Hume's scepticism can and often does take: he engages in doubt, "active doubt" in my terminology, about a number of opinions, some of which he himself generally believes, and which he often enough continues to believe (although perhaps with some moderation of assurance) even while he is engaging in this active doubt. Hume argues, for example, that our belief in body or necessary connection is instinctive, but nonetheless is able to raise questions about these beliefs. In the early stages of such questioning, these beliefs are apparently unshaken—the shift from the perspective of the vulgar to that of the philosopher who is in doubt is a gradual one. In fact, Hume may be unusual among philosophical sceptics insofar as his disposition to caution or scruple sometimes produced a hesitating disposition or an uneasy state of mind. In any event, his report of such a result seems credible enough:

> But what have I here said, that reflections very refin'd and metaphysical have little or no influence upon us? This opinion I can scarce forbear retracting, and condemning from my present feeling and experience. The *intense* view of these manifold contradictions and imperfections in human reason has so wrought upon me, and heated my brain, that I am ready to reject all belief and reasoning, and can look upon no opinion even as more probable or likely than another.

---

forego. Furthermore, given that Hume looks favorably upon the Academic sceptics' call for suspension of judgment when judgment is limited to assertion or asseveration, it is reasonable to suggest that the basic polarities of Hume's position are judgment and doubt, each of which has two forms that create paired opposites in the following way:

Judgment	Doubt
(1) Belief	(1) Affective doubt
(2) Assertion	(2) Active doubt

Belief and affective doubt, I suggest, are psychological aspects of judgment and doubt, while assertion and active doubt are epistemic aspects of them. Further, one can actively doubt while believing just as one can make assertions that run contrary to one's affective doubts. Hume may also have had this in mind when he wrote, "Thus the sceptic still continues to reason and believe, even tho' he asserts, that he cannot defend his reason by reason. . ." (*Treatise*, p. 187).

Where am I, or what? . . . What beings surround me? and on whom have I any influence, or who have any influence on me? I am confounded with all these questions, and begin to fancy myself in the most deplorable condition imaginable, inviron'd with the deepest darkness, and utterly depriv'd of the use of every member and faculty.[77]

Generally, however, Hume's doubt is less dramatic. It is limited to the sophisticated challenging and cautioning inserted into his more mature analyses. His first *Enquiry* constitutes an extended illustration of this approach. Following the three relatively brief opening sections, Hume turns to his "Sceptical Doubts Concerning the Operations of the Understanding."[78] Here he tells us that of the two forms of human reasoning (those concerning either relations of ideas or matter of fact), neither is an adequate foundation for our belief that the future will resemble the past, or that similar effects will follow from apparently similar causes. Neither a rationalistic nor an empirical philosophy can provide a foundation for our causal reasonings. He grants that it is by experience that we arrive at what we call "knowledge" of cause and effect, and to this extent leaves the empiricist unchallenged.

---

[77] *Treatise*, pp. 268-269. This is also precisely what one would expect to happen from time to time given Hume's account of belief. Granted, we cannot directly command ourselves to disbelieve that we are surrounded by independent and continuous objects, but close attention to philosophical argument may on occasion shake our ordinary belief that we are so surrounded. We cannot will to so disbelieve, but our reason, by working underground as it were, can serve as the cause of just such an effect. Belief is natural (caused, not willed), but reason functions as one of its causes. Hume's account of the manner in which he came to doubt received religious opinion is a further example of this phenomenon: "You wou'd perceive by the Sample I have given you, that I make Cleanthes the Hero of the Dialogue. Whatever you can think of, to strengthen that Side of the Argument, will be most acceptable to me. Any Propensity you imagine I have to the other Side, crept in upon me against my Will: And tis not long ago that I burn'd an old Manuscript Book, wrote before I was twenty; which contain'd, Page after Page, the gradual Progress of my Thoughts on that head. It begun with an anxious Search after Arguments, to confirm the common Opinion: Doubts stole in, dissipated, return'd, were again dissipated, return'd again; and it was a perpetual Struggle of a restless Imagination against Inclination, perhaps against Reason" (*Letters*, 1: 153-154).

[78] Pp. 25-39. Section 3, "Of the Association of Ideas," was much longer until 1770.

But when in the second part of this section he asks, *"What is the foundation of all conclusions from experience?"* it is clear that both of the two leading philosophical schools are under sceptical attack, especially as he goes on to say that he has raised a new and more difficult question, and that those philosophers who "give themselves airs of superior wisdom and sufficiency, have a hard task when they encounter persons of inquisitive dispositions, who push them from every corner to which they retreat, and who are sure at last to bring them to some dangerous dilemma. The best expedient to prevent this confusion, is to be modest in our pretensions; and even to discover the difficulty ourselves before it is objected to us. By this means, we may make a kind of merit of our very ignorance."

Heeding his own warning, Hume contents himself first with an allegedly "easy task," a defense of his claim that our causal beliefs (the future will resemble the past or like causes, like effects) are "*not* founded on reasoning, or any process of the understanding." Drawing our attention to the fact that we are unable to connect the sensible qualities of objects with any real powers, for these latter are hidden from us,[79] he then goes on to suggest that his "negative argument" to this effect will in time "become altogether convincing, if many penetrating and able philosophers shall turn their enquiries this way and no one be ever able to discover any connecting proposition or intermediate step, which supports the understanding in this conclusion" that like causes will have like effects. He then rounds out his sceptical challenge by attempting a more difficult task, namely, "enumerating all the branches of human knowledge [in an] endeavour to show that none of them" can provide the required argument or connection. It is sufficient for my purposes to note that Hume is moderately confident of his success in this more difficult task ("If I be wrong, I must acknowledge myself to be indeed a very backward scholar. . . ."), for I intend here only to highlight the challenging char-

---

[79] *First Enquiry*, p. 32. Hume notes that we have sensible ideas of motion, but not the slightest conception of that "wonderful force or power, which would carry on a moving body for ever in a continued change of place, and which bodies never lose but by communicating it to others" (p. 33).

acter of Hume's philosophical behavior in this significant portion of his work. Modestly formulated though it may be, and commonplace though it may have become, section 4 of the first *Enquiry* constitutes a challenge to every philosopher who has thought to explain the basic workings of the world. Explanations, Hume grants, they may surely give. That these ever have been, or ever will be, well-founded explanations, he doubts.

If section 4 is a sceptical challenge to philosophers whose pretensions surpass Hume's, then section 5, "Sceptical Solution of these Doubts," is a cautioning correlative. The opening paragraph makes this clear. Although philosophy, like religion, "aims at the correction of our manners, and extirpation of our vices," it may, says Hume, if imprudently undertaken, only serve to push us more firmly into our biases. We may, as did the Stoics, aspire to the magnanimity of the sage, yet make our philosophy "only a more refined system of selfishness, and reason ourselves out of all virtue as well as social enjoyment." Or turning from the vanity of the world, we may merely indulge our natural indolence. Hume's continuation of this warning is noteworthy in several respects. It is here that he recommends the "Academic or Sceptical philosophy" as being "little liable" to this danger. This philosophy does not, he says, serve to support or increase any of these disorderly passions or "any natural affection or propensity," largely because the Academic sceptics were essentially philosophers of caution.[80] Nor does such a scepticism, he insists, undermine the reasoning and actions of common life along with those of speculation. We cannot carry our academical doubts "so far as to destroy all action, as well as speculation." Nature is too strong for that. In short, Hume can recommend the Academic philosophy above all others because, while still permitting us to carry on as ordinary men, it restrains our predominant inclinations and "the bias and propensity of the natural temper." The Academic philosopher may make no effort to overturn these natural propensities, but he does reveal the wisdom of a certain modesty and diffidence toward

[80] Hume's remark is cited in full at p. 277.

them, and he does reveal how such tempered assurance can be achieved.

Hume was convinced that he had introduced just such a valuable note of caution by showing that our factual inferences have a very modest foundation indeed. Other philosophers had gloried in the reason of man, and had used it as evidence that he is the god-like pinnacle of earthly creation, capable of capturing the innermost secrets of nature. Hume's analysis leads to a cooler assessment. True, we are equipped to "adjust means to ends, or employ our natural powers, either to the producing of good, or avoiding of evil," but this is not due to our god-like reason, but to a "species of natural instincts," to instincts that can prove not only fallacious, but which also regularly lead us to conclusions beyond the evidence available. The wise man, in Hume's opinion, is even a modest empiricist or natural philosopher. Those who have cast scepticism in the narrow mold of Descartes or the allegedly lunatic Pyrrho will perhaps find this an unarresting form of scepticism, but it is nonetheless a significant one.

There are in the *Enquiry*, though, sceptical challenges of a more striking character: the analysis of miracles found in section 10, and the discussion of providence and a future state in section 11. In these sections Hume applies certain aspects of his analysis of our causal beliefs to two crucial and allegedly empirical supports of certain theological claims, and he emerges from them as a religious sceptic *par excellence*.[81] Christianity has been traditionally supported by arguments, of course, arguments which in Hume's scheme would either involve only the relations of ideas (the ontological and cosmological arguments, perhaps), or matters of fact. Hume was too much of an empiricist to find arguments of

---

[81] Although Hume mildly bemoans (in his *My Own Life*) the fact that Conyers Middleton's *Free Enquiry into the Miraculous Powers* . . . upstaged his own *Enquiry*, it is nonetheless true that the sceptical religious tendency of the latter work was very soon noted and responded to. According to Mossner, John Conybeare, Dean of Christ Church, Oxford, induced the Rev. Philip Skelton to read "Of Miracles," and to comment on it. Skelton's comments are found in his *Ophiomaches; or Deism Revealed*, 2 vols. (London, 1749). William Adams, *An Essay on Mr. Hume's Essay on Miracles* (London, 1752), explicitly brands Hume a sceptic.

the former type in need of extensive refutation,[82] but the allegedly empirical evidence for various theological positions he attacks with great and enduring vigor.

The attempt to provide a foundation for a particular religious position by appeal to certain "miracles" can be aptly said to be an empirical argument inasmuch as these putative facts are said to provide justification for particular religious convictions. Hume's attack on miracles as such a foundation is twofold. He argues first that even if the evidence for the occurence of any particular miracle were all that it could possibly be, even if it were perfect of its kind, we would nonetheless still fail to have perfect and certain grounds for a belief that this miracle has occurred. He then argues that human testimony can never be sufficiently strong to prove that a miracle has occurred, and thus that no (allegedly) miraculous event can ever serve as an empirical justification for particular theological beliefs or dogmas.

To develop his first argument, Hume alludes to Archbishop Tillotson's argument against "the *real presence*" (transubstantiation), and preens himself with having found a similar "decisive argument of this kind, which must at least *silence* the most arrogant bigotry and superstition, and free us from their impertinent solicitations." Tillotson, in challenging the Roman Catholics, had in essence claimed that they were being epistemologically inconsistent, and hence were undermining the certainty of Christianity. On the one hand, they were relying on the evidence of the senses as the foundation of their beliefs, while on the other hand, they were claiming that the evidence of our senses is sometimes unreliable. The body of Christian doctrine taught by Christ and the apostles, says Tillotson, was confirmed as divine by the miracles these individuals performed. The assurance we have that these miracles occurred rests ultimately on the evidence of sense (and its subsidiary, testimony), and thus the certainty of Christianity is dependent upon the senses. The doctrine of transubstantiation, however, constitutes in effect a claim that a wafer

---

[82] But what Hume thought of such arguments can be easily deduced from *Treatise*, I, 2, 6 ("Of the idea of existence, and of external existence") and I, 3, 3 ("Why a cause is always necessary").

that to all sensory appearances remains unchanged undergoes a substantial change. Bread becomes flesh, but this change can in no way be detected by the senses. In short, if transubstantiation takes place, we cannot trust our senses.[83]

This, then, is Tillotson's decisive argument. If the doctrine of the real presence is said to be true, the consequence of this assertion is a diminution of the confidence we can repose in the most reliable form of evidence we have, that of the senses, and we are faced with a choice: we may suppose that the doctrine of real presence is false, in which case we may continue to accept the evidence of our senses as reliable. Or we may suppose that the doctrine is true, imagining for the sake of argument that we have the best possible evidence for believing it, namely, a clear assertion of the doctrine in the holy scriptures. However, if we suppose the latter then we undermine the very grounds on which our acceptance of the doctrine rests, for acceptance of the truth of the scriptures depends upon acceptance of the reliability of the senses, while the doctrine in question, if true, shows that the senses are not reliable. Further, if the senses are not reliable, we then have no reason to think the doctrine itself is true, for we no longer accept as reliable the only grounds we have for thinking the scriptures true, while the doctrine rests, by hypothesis, on

[83] Tillotson's argument is found in Sermon 26, "A Discourse upon Transubstantiation," in *The Works of John Tillotson*, 7th ed., 2 vols. (London, 1714), 1: 314-315. He says in part, "Suppose then *Transubstantiation* to be part of the Christian Doctrine, it must have the same confirmation with the whole, and that is Miracles: But of all Doctrines in the World it is peculiarly incapable of being proved by a Miracle. For if a Miracle were wrought for the proof of it, the very same assurance which any Man hath of the truth of the Miracle he hath of the falshood of the Doctrine, that is, the clear Evidence of his Senses. . . . Consequently *Transubstantiation* is not to be proved by a Miracle, because that would be, *to prove to a Man by something that he sees, that he doth not see what he sees.* And if there were no other Evidence that *Transubstantiation* is no part of the Christian Doctrine, this would be sufficient, that what proves the one, doth as much overthrow the other. . . . For a Man cannot believe a Miracle without relying upon sense, nor *Transubstantiation* without renouncing it. So that never were any two things so ill coupled together as the Doctrine of Christianity and that of *Transubstantiation*, because they draw several ways, and are ready to strangle one another: For the main Evidence of the Christian Doctrine, which is Miracles, is resolved into the certainty of sense, but this Evidence is clear and point-blank against *Transubstantiation*."

the scriptures. The doctrine of real presence, then, may be justifiably doubted or disbelieved. It may either be rejected outright (as beyond all evidence), or rejected subsequently, after we have realized that it requires of us an inconsistent assessment of the same form of evidence, that of the senses.

Hume gives this argument a more general application, one that such empirically disposed theologians as Tillotson would scarcely have applauded. A miracle is, says Hume, echoing theological orthodoxy of his time, "a violation of the laws of nature," or, more accurately defined, "*a transgression of a law of nature by a particular volition of the Deity, or by the interposition of some invisible agent.*" He adds to this orthodoxy, however, a conception of the laws of nature drawn from his own analysis of experience. This had shown, of course, that we have no rational grounds for inferring that the future will resemble the past, and thus for Hume a law of nature is no more, strictly speaking, than a summation of a wholly uniform past experience. If our experience of X's has been "firm and unalterable" or "infallible," then we have, in Hume's scheme, a "proof" and are in a position to formulate a law of nature, or a summation of uniform experience. Correlatively, the moment we fail to have a proof, or perfect empirical support for any summation, we fail to have a law of nature. Once the evidence is mixed we have only (at best) what Hume calls a "probability." What was a summation of uniform experience has become a summation of mixed experience, and the result is a very different proposition indeed.

Hume next points out that testimony, or the evidence of attestations, although not apparently dependent upon the causal relation, is subject to the same limitations as our causal reasonings. There is no necessary connection between attestation and fact: the connection of testimony "with any event seems, in itself," he says, "as little necessary as any other," although if there has been a uniform "conjunction between any particular kind of report and any kind of object" we have again a "proof," while a less uniform experience of this sort results in a "probability." Attestations are simply another kind of experience; the evidence of witnesses may be on a par with, and is certainly commensurate with, the evidence of nature.

It is in this context that Hume grants (for the sake of argument, no doubt) that the evidence for a particular (alleged) miracle may be perfect of its kind. But even given this concession, he points out, there would be insufficient grounds for concluding that the event was a miracle, for there would be, contra this evidence, equally perfect evidence that the event has not taken place—the evidence of the uniform experience that is summarized by the (allegedly) violated law of nature. In such cases, as Hume says, "There is proof against proof, of which the strongest must prevail, but still with a diminution of its force, in proportion to that of its antagonist." And although Hume does not spell out the analogy with Tillotson's argument, it is clear that there is a similar kind of inconsistency: the very perfection of the proof that a miracle has occured implies that what has occurred is not in fact a miracle. A miracle is a violation of the laws of nature; a law of nature is established by a firm and unalterable experience. The champion of miracles is arguing, however, that this experience is not firm and unalterable; at least one exception is, he claims, known. From this exception it follows, Hume reminds us, that there is no violation of a law of nature because there is no law of nature, and hence, there is no miracle. Just as the theologian who supports the doctrine of transubstantiation undermines by his very argument the evidential foundation of this argument, so does the defender of miracles, insofar as he produces a fully credible claim for a particular miracle, by this very argument undermine the claim that a miracle has occurred. His conceptions are, to say the least, incompatible, and thus to argue that there are both uniformities and miracles is inconsistent. Hume certainly does not deny that unusual events take place, or that there can be good evidence of these occurrences.[84] But he

[84] Those who have taken Hume to deny that there can be good evidence that an unusual event has occurred include Bishop Richard Whately and Richard H. Popkin. See Whately's *Historic Doubts Relative to Napoleon Bonaparte* (London, 1819), and Popkin's "Hume: Philosophical Versus Prophetic Historian," in *David Hume: Many-sided Genius*, ed. K. R. Merrill and R. W. Shahan (Norman: University of Oklahoma Press, 1976), pp. 83-96.

believes that he has discovered a "decisive argument" that will
serve the wise as an "everlasting check to all kinds of superstitious
delusion," an argument that reveals the inconsistency of calling
a miracle a violation of the laws of nature when in fact there can
be no law of nature unless there is a uniform experience, the very
fact which is denied by the claim that a miracle has occurred.
Hume, much as had many sceptics before him, has granted the
dogmatists their initial premises, and then shown that these lead
to philosophical absurdities. No doubt Hume derived additional
pleasure from the fact that he was able to derive his argument
from such a bastion of orthodoxy as Archbishop Tillotson, and
to expand a Protestant argument undermining a Catholic miracle
into a general argument undermining the pretensions of Protestant and Catholic alike.

Part 2 of the essay on miracles is reminiscent of certain passages
in Sextus Empiricus, those in which the various reasons for doubting the reports of the senses are cataloged, although Hume is
obviously cataloging reasons for refusing to give more than hypothetical assent to the suggestion that the evidence for a miracle
constitutes a proof. For the sake of argument he granted in part
1 the fact of such a proof, but he now withdraws this concession
with the remark that "it is easy to shew, that we have been a
great deal too liberal in our concession, and that there never was
a miraculous event established on so full an evidence." No (alleged) miracle has ever been attested by a sufficient number of
good witnesses, reporting facts so well known, as to insure that
any fraudulent aspects of the event or report are certain to have
been detected. Secondly, we have a natural propensity to be
credulous in the face of prodigies or wondrous tales, a natural
propensity which, when joined to the spirit of religion, puts an
end to common sense.[85] Thirdly, one finds that supernatural
events occur much more frequently among ignorant and barbarous

[85] Those who would represent Hume as well satisfied with man's natural propensities and the beliefs they produce should read again this segment of his
discussion. His view is aptly summed up a few paragraphs further on (p. 126)
when he says, "The *avidum genus auricularum*, the gazing populace, receive greed-
ily, without examination, whatever sooths superstition, and promotes wonder."

peoples, although it must also be granted that the more civilized descendants of these peoples often retain a belief in the prodigious tales bequeathed them by their remote ancestors. Fourthly and last, Hume argues that the presumably definitive evidences (that is, miracles) in favor of one religion are counterbalanced by the allegedly like evidences in favor of additional religions of like exclusiveness. Here again evidence is weighed against evidence—much as Sextus has urged that philosophical arguments be balanced one against the other—and the credibility of each is diminished to the vanishing point.[86] When considerations of this sort are brought to bear on (alleged) miracles of religious significance, it appears, says Hume, that no such miraculous event has ever been shown probable, not to mention proven. There is evidence for some allegedly miraculous events, but as this evidence is no different from other kinds of evidence, its force is subject to diminution as various kinds of contrary evidence are brought forward and placed on the balance. When two pieces of evidence are contrary, we must, says Hume, "substract the one from the other, and embrace an opinion, either on one side or the other, with that assurance which arises from the remainder."[87] Furthermore—and this I submit is the key sceptical conclusion of the entire essay—this subtraction or balancing, "with regard to all popular religions, amounts to an entire annihilation; and therefore we may establish it as a maxim, that no human testi-

[86] Hume actually suggests a fifth reason for doubting the reports of miracles. "The wise," he says, surely savoring the pun, "lend a very academic faith to every report which favours the passion of the reporter."

[87] Hume's suggestion that we proceed by "substraction" has been roundly criticized from the time of George Campbell, whose *Dissertation on Miracles* Hume read before its first publication in 1762. Recently, for example, Antony Flew has suggested that Hume in this particular instance proceeds by a "Wonderland Arithmetic" that permits him to subtract a lesser quantity from a greater and arrive at a zero remainder. But Hume says nothing about a zero remainder, only of "entire annihilation," a result that makes sense outside Wonderland if one understands him to suppose that the greater quantity is subtracted from the lesser—although even then one might want to say that Hume is making his point by means of a loose analogy with subtraction, not by any strict mathematical conceptions. For Flew's remarks, see "The Red Queen at Substraction," *Hume Studies* 5 (1979): 110-111.

mony can have such force as to prove a miracle, and make it a just foundation for any such system of religion."

Those who do see a just foundation for popular religions through empirical reason rely also upon the argument from design, or the claim that our experience of the world is the experience of an ordered state of affairs that can only be the effect of a cause possessed of an equal or greater supply of orderliness or design. Indeed, as commonly formulated, this argument is alleged to show that this cause could be nothing less than a being of supreme intelligence and benevolence, from which facts we can conclude that each aspect of his creation is well designed to fulfill an essentially beneficial function. Hume's attack on this second prop of the empiricist theologians consists, in general terms, in showing that the conclusions of the argument far outstrip the evidence on which it is based, and that this flaw is compounded by some flagrantly circular reasoning. From our experience, Hume insists, and granting that every event has a cause, we can infer only that the world has or had a cause sufficient to produce just those (mixed) effects experienced, and nothing at all about the additional specific attributes (omniscience, omnibenevolence, and so forth) of this cause. Further, as our inference is legitimately limited to what might be called the "world-cause," any attempt to interpret particular items of experience as the consequences of the operation of divine attributes is doubly fallacious. The attributes are, philosophically speaking, completely fictitious; the use of them to interpret objects and events is an exercise of pretentious fancy.

All of this is well known, but the reasons Hume gives for including the analysis are here noteworthy. Philosophy, he reports himself saying to a friend, prospered in the tolerant atmosphere of Greece and with the support of Roman emperors, but how different are the circumstances now, where it suffers from calumny and persecution. Yes, replies the sceptical friend, but that is exactly "the natural course of things." The bigotry which is regretted as detrimental to philosophy is a consequence of philosophy itself, which has been allied with superstition to create an "inveterate enemy and persecutor." The "religious philosophers, not satisfied with the tradition of your forefathers, and the doctrine of your priests . . . indulge a rash curiosity, in trying how far they can establish religion upon the principles of reason. . . ." It is for this reason that they advance the argument from design, and it is for this reason that Hume's sceptical friend challenges the philosopher-theologians. Their vanity and pretension carries them not only beyond experience and just inference, and not only to the persecution of any philosopher who dares challenge their belief in providence and a future state. Even more importantly, they are led to minimize, even overlook, our present existence in favor of some castle in the sky: "But what must a philosopher think of those vain reasoners, who, instead of regarding the present scene of things as the sole object of their contemplation, so far reverse the whole course of nature, as to render this life merely a passage to something further; a porch, which leads to a greater, and vastly different building; a prologue, which serves only to introduce the piece, and give it more grace and propriety?"[88]

Hume subjects the religious empiricists, then, to two perenially significant challenges. He does this because he sees their efforts as uncertain and useless, and even more importantly, as dangerous. Drawing conclusions that are well beyond any just inferences from "the experienced train of events [which] is the great standard, by which we regulate all conduct," they not only discourse dogmatically on subjects that are beyond the reach of human experience, but attempt (and succeed in this attempt) to regulate human conduct on the basis of the uncertain precepts they pretend to have deduced. Not only is the importance of this world minimized, but what is done here becomes no more than a preparation for life in a more grandiose realm—the activities of this life must be directed to the next. As a consequence, those whose thought or behavior fails to conform to the divine ordinances so (allegedly) discovered may be and are persecuted, disposed of in whatever ways *seem* to be justified by these same uncertain precepts. Scepticism may sometimes seem trivial, even absurd, but

[88] *First Enquiry*, pp. 132-140, 141.

underlying what may appear to be mere quibbles there are humanistic considerations, not the least of which are a concern for tolerance, and a concern for man *qua* man. If Hume's commitment to such a scepticism is sometimes only implicit, it is also sometimes explicit and beyond any doubt, as when he says,

> The greater part of mankind are naturally apt to be affirmative and dogmatical in their opinions; and while they see objects only on one side, and have no idea of any counterpoising argument, they throw themselves precipitately into the principles, to which they are inclined; nor have they any indulgence for those who entertain opposite sentiments. To hesitate or balance perplexes their understanding, checks their passion, and suspends their action. They are, therefore, impatient till they escape from a state, which to them is so uneasy: and they think, that they can never remove themselves far enough from it, by the violence of their affirmations and obstinacy of their belief. But could such dogmatical reasoners become sensible of the strange infirmities of human understanding, even in its most perfect state, and when most accurate and cautious in its determinations; such a reflection would naturally inspire them with more modesty and reserve, and diminish their fond opinion of themselves, and their prejudice against antagonists.[89]

VI. In my introductory chapter I suggested that this book may be taken as an extended argument in support of three claims:

1. Hume's philosophy developed in response to two quite distinguishable philosophical crises, a speculative crisis and a moral crisis, or as may be preferable, in response to two kinds of scepticism, epistemological and moral.
2. Hume's responses to these distinct scepticisms, his metaphysics and his theory of morals, respectively, differed significantly in method and substance.

[89] *First Enquiry*, p. 161.

3. Hume was fully cognizant of the differences between his sceptical speculative position and his common-sensical moral theory, and in fact gave reasonably clear (though not always convincing) reasons for supposing metaphysics and moral theory to be distinct and (partially) different philosophical enterprises.

In support of these claims I have discussed the antisceptical moral theories of Cudworth, Shaftesbury, and Hutcheson, and in chapters 1 and 3, Hume's own theory of morals. There it was seen that Hume also attacks the moral sceptics, and that he does in fact make sentiment the fundamental standard of morals—just as his important letter to Gilbert Elliot suggests. In chapter 4 I discussed two philosophers (Turnbull and Kames) who extended the domain of sentiment to include speculative philosophy. Hume, although he readily acknowledges the importance of sentiment (in the form of natural or instinctive belief) as a guide in practical affairs, was not prepared to support the view that sentiment has, de jure or de facto, control in both practical and speculative affairs. Again, the view expressed in the letter to Elliot is found to echo Hume's published writings.

To summarize, I have shown that there are very good grounds for concluding that Hume's philosophy was shaped at a fundamental level by the distinction that he outlined for Elliot. Any remaining doubts about this claim will surely vanish once it is seen that Hume attempts to explain and vindicate the very distinction to which I have drawn attention.[90] His efforts in this latter regard may not convince us that his division of philosophy was entirely well founded, but they do place the burden of proof on those who would challenge my claim that Hume attempted just the division I have described in this book.

Hume, as we saw in chapter 3, argues that reason alone is unable to motivate us to a particular end. Nor is it alone adequate to produce approbation or blame; sentiment, on the other hand,

[90] My claim that Hume attempts this particular division is confirmed by his efforts to explain and vindicate the division, even though these efforts seem less than fully satisfactory.

can motivate us and approbation and blame are themselves sentiments. However, these claims only establish the leading role of sentiment in morals, while leaving unanswered all questions regarding the standard of truth. It is only when Hume goes on to reveal the characteristics of our moral sentiments and to define virtue as "*whatever mental action or quality gives to a spectator the pleasing sentiment of approbation*; and vice the contrary," that we can see why he thought that our moral judgments must necessarily rest upon sentiment.[91] If an action or quality is said to be virtuous or morally good, the test of this claim is whether or not that action or quality produces in the appropriately disinterested observer a feeling of moral approbation. If it does, the claim is correct; if not, it is incorrect.

When we deliberate concerning our conduct, as, for example, whether to help a brother or a benefactor when both are involved in a particular emergency, we must, says Hume, "consider these separate relations, with all the circumstances and situations of the persons, in order to determine the superior duty and obligation." This situation appears strikingly similar to that in which we deliberate "to determine the proportion of lines in any triangle," for then it is also "necessary to examine the nature of that figure, and the relations which its several parts bear to each other." There is, however, an "extreme difference" between the two cases. A "speculative reasoner concerning triangles or circles considers the several known and given relations of the parts of these figures, and thence infers some unknown relation, which is dependent on the former," or, more generally, in the "disquisitions of the understanding, from known circumstances and relations, we infer some new and unknown." In contrast, "moral deliberations" require that we "be acquainted beforehand with all the objects, and all their relations to each other; and from a comparison of the whole, fix our choice or approbation." Or, again, "In moral decisions, all the circumstances and relations must be previously known; and the mind, from the contemplation

[91] *Second Enquiry*, p. 289. See above, pp. 134-147.

of the whole, feels some new impression of affection or disgust, esteem or contempt, approbation or blame."[92]

Thus, although Hume assigns to reason an important role in morals, he views moral judgments or moral decisions as a particular kind of reaction to a complete situation of a certain character; if the situation has this character, and if the objects and relations making it up are comprehended, then and only then do we experience those feelings of affection or contempt, approbation or blame which constitute the moral response. In such cases, our sentiments serve to reveal the character of the situation presented to us. Speculative philosophy, on the other hand, is characterized by its incompleteness, or by its attempts to extend our knowledge from the known to the unknown. In this case, we must rely on reason, for it is reason that "judges" the relations of ideas or matters of fact. "Reason is," Hume says in the *Treatise*, "the discovery of truth or falshood. Truth or falshood consists in an agreement or disagreement either to the *real* relations of ideas, or to *real* existence and matter of fact." In the same section, he goes on to say that "the operations of human understanding divide themselves into two kinds, the comparing of ideas, and the inferring of matter of fact; . . ."[93] Given, then, that the abstruse and speculative concerns of philosophy are efforts to infer the unknown from the known, and given that it is reason or reasoning that both makes and judges such inferences, it is clear that Hume is committed to the view that it is reason, not sentiment, that is the standard of truth in speculative philosophy. As it is reason (the understanding) that can compare ideas to determine their similarity or dissimilarity, or can compare our ideas to matters of fact to determine the adequacy of these ideas, so it is this same faculty of reason that determines the truth or falsehood of the claims made about these relations of ideas or matters of fact. Our passions or sentiments may generally determine what we believe. But they do not, on Hume's theory, determine what it is we call true or false, nor are they beyond all hope of alteration or improvement. As it is by inference that the abstruse and speculative

---

[92] *Second Enquiry*, pp. 289-290.
[93] *Treatise*, pp. 458; 463.

philosopher proceeds, it is only by the justness of its inferences that his work can be judged. Should it ever happen that we become acquainted with all the objects and relations that concern the speculative philosopher, perhaps then we shall find in ourselves an agreeable or disagreeable sentiment which will inform our metaphysical decisions, just as such sentiments (according to Hume) inform our "moral decisions." Until then, however, philosophers must resist the erratic and biased interference of sentiment, in the hope that reason, in the form of an abstruse and difficult philosophy, will refine both our opinions and our temper.

Objections may be posed, however, to Hume's explanation of his position. It may be argued that there are more than a few instances in which we make what to all other appearances are moral decisions even though not all circumstances and relations are known, and other cases in which all the facts will either never be known, or not known before our moral evaluations must be made. Secondly, although the fundamental hypothesis of the sentimentalist theory—that sentiments signal moral reality—is not inherently implausible, it does seem naïve of Hume to suppose that simply because all the facts and circumstances are known we will experience the appropriate sentiment. Leaving aside the question of the manner in which moral perception is alleged to take place, our moral perceptions seem at least as corrigible as any others.

Several things may be said in Hume's defense. He may have realized that there is a sense in which all the facts and circumstances are never in, and simply have meant that, practically speaking, they must be taken to be in just because a decision must be taken, much as in a given legal proceeding all the relevant facts are taken to be before the court. Hume does distinguish between practical and speculative matters, and he may simply have assumed that in practical ones our inquiries must come to an end. Indeed, his answer to the question Elliot poses ("The only question is, where to stop,—how far we can go, and why no farther") might be supposed to imply such a practical limitation, although I do not recall that Hume has been more explicit on this issue elsewhere. Also, in fairness to Hume, it must be said that he tries to meet the second objection by assigning to reason the prior tasks that are necessary for impartiality: gathering facts and providing insights and criticism. It is when these tasks are completed, and only then, that *moral* sentiments arise. This reveals that reason's role in morals is of much greater importance than some of Hume's readers have thought, but that is a fact I have already established.

I would also suggest that Hume had something much more profound in mind. He was, I think, suggesting that the kind of truth available in morals is significantly different from that available in metaphysics. Hence reason, although it has a function in morals, is limited there (and elsewhere) to matters of correspondence, or the agreement/disagreement of ideas or the agreement of ideas and matters of fact, while moral truth or falsehood are not matters of correspondence. He clearly does insist that the truth about nature, for example, is entirely independent of human thought; there is "always a real, though often unknown standard, in the nature of things," he says, and thus no amount of thinking that the earth is at rest will cause the slightest stir in the heavens. On the other hand, he did inhabit the world left by Galileo, Descartes, and Hobbes, and that was a world in which there seemed to be nothing, or nothing extrahuman, to which moral claims could correspond. Some of the rationalists had claimed that *relations* served this purpose, but Hume rejected as morally inadequate that particular attempt to provide an ontological foundation for a correspondence theory of moral claims, just as he rejected as "pretty uncertain & unphilosophical" what seems to have been Hutcheson's attempt to provide such a foundation through the positing of what I have called "extrinsic final causes." Hume tells us that we will not find moral qualities in the world, but in ourselves, and he told Hutcheson that morality "regards only human Nature & human Life."[94] Nevertheless, he propounds a theory in which moral right and wrong are matters neither of mere individual preference nor of group preference. In Hume's opinion, there is some kind of objective moral standard to which

[94] *Letters,* 1: 40.

our moral judgments can be made to conform more or less closely, but he apparently does not think that this standard has an existence independent of human beings or that our moral judgments are right or wrong only as they correspond to some extrahuman reality. I have outlined what Hume does say about these matters, and I have speculated about his moral ontology, but there is certainly room for further analysis. It is at least conceivable that this analysis will vindicate Hume's view that morals and metaphysics have essentially different standards of truth. If so, we will have a clearer understanding of why he thought sentiment the standard of truth in morals, but not in other kinds of philosophy. This in turn will provide further evidence that Hume was neither a purely negating sceptic, nor a complete naturalist, but a critical thinker. He was, in his own words, a philosopher of no particular party who attempted to achieve a proper balance between doubt and belief and who considered man a reasonable being whose understanding could be formed by abstruse thought and profound reasonings, or by what is commonly called metaphysics. As he puts it, "The chief triumph" of philosophy is that it "insensibly refines the temper, and it points out to us those dispositions which we should endeavour to attain, by a constant *bent* of mind, and by repeated *habit*."[95]

[95] *Works*, 3: 224.

List of Works Cited

THE STANDARD BIBLIOGRAPHY of Hume's works is that of T. E. Jessop, *A Bibliography of David Hume and of Scottish Philosophy, from Francis Hutcheson to Lord Balfour* (London: Brown and Son, 1938). Supplemental information about the earliest editions of Hume's works may be found in W. B. Todd, "David Hume, A Preliminary Bibliography," *Hume and the Enlightenment: Essays Presented to Ernest Campbell Mossner*, ed. W. B. Todd (Edinburgh: The Edinburgh University Press, 1974), pp. 189-205.

There is also a bibliography of recent work on Hume, namely, Roland Hall's *Fifty Years of Hume Scholarship: A Bibliographical Guide* (Edinburgh: The Edinburgh University Press, 1978). Supplements to this bibliography for the years 1976-1979 have been published annually in *Hume Studies*, volumes 3-6, and further supplements may be expected there. In view of this valuable bibliographic work by Hall, I have made no effort to list the many additional articles and books that are relevant to any general interpretation of Hume. I should also mention that I have made no effort to take into account two recent and important books on Hume, *Hume's Philosophy of Mind*, by John Bricke (Edinburgh and Princeton, 1980), and *Hume's Moral Theory*, by J. L. Mackie (Routledge & Kegan Paul, 1980).

Adams, William. *An Essay on Mr. Hume's Essay on Miracles.* London, 1752.

Aldridge, A. O. "A Preview of Hutcheson's Ethics." *Modern Language Notes* 61 (1946).

Allen, D. C. *Doubt's Boundless Sea.* Baltimore: Johns Hopkins Press, 1964.

Árdal, Páll S. "Another Look at Hume's Account of Moral Evaluation." *Journal of the History of Philosophy* 15 (1977).

Árdal, Páll S. *Passion and Value in Hume's Treatise.* Edinburgh: The Edinburgh University Press, 1966.

« WORKS CITED »

Árdal, Páll S. "Some Implications of the Virtue of Reasonableness in Hume's *Treatise.*" *Hume: A Re-valuation.* Edited by D. Livingston and J. King. New York: Fordham University Press, 1976.

Austin, John Langshaw. *How to Do Things With Words.* Oxford: Clarendon Press, 1962.

Battersby, Christine. "The *Dialogues* as Original Imitation: Cicero and the Nature of Hume's Skepticism." *McGill Hume Studies.* Edited by D. F. Norton, N. Capaldi, and W. Robison. Studies in Hume and Scottish Philosophy, 1. San Diego: Austin Hill Press, 1979.

Bayle, Pierre. *The Dictionary Historical and Critical.* 5 vols. 2d English ed. London, 1734-1738.

Bayle, Pierre. *Historical and Critical Dictionary.* Edited and translated by R. H. Popkin. Indianapolis: Bobbs-Merrill, 1965.

Beattie, James. *An Essay on the Nature and Immutability of Truth, in Opposition to Sophistry and Scepticism.* 4th ed. London, 1773.

Berman, David. "Francis Hutcheson on Berkeley and the Molyneux Problem." *Proceedings of the Royal Irish Academy* 74 (1974).

Boswell, James. *Private Papers of James Boswell from Malahide Castle.* Edited by G. Scott and F. A. Pottle. 18 vols. New York: privately printed, 1928-1934.

Broad, C. D. *Five Types of Ethical Theory.* London: Routledge & Kegan Paul, 1930. Reprint ed., Littlefield Adams, 1959.

Burnet, Gilbert. Letters, *London Journal,* April 10, July 31, August 7, November 27, and December 25, 1725. Reprinted in *A Collection of Letters.* . . . Edited by J. Arbuckle. London, 1729.

Burton, J. H. *Life and Correspondence of David Hume.* 2 vols. Edinburgh, 1856.

Burtt, E. A. *The Metaphysical Foundations of Modern Physical Science.* London: Kegan Paul, 1925; revised edition, 1932.

Butler, Joseph. *Sermons.* London, 1726.

Butler, R. J. "Natural Belief and the Enigma of Hume." *Archiv für Geschichte der Philosophie* 42 (1960).

Campbell, George. *Dissertation on Miracles*. Edinburgh, 1762.

Capaldi, Nicholas. *David Hume: The Newtonian Philosopher*. Boston: Twayne, 1975.

Cassirer, Ernst. *The Platonic Renaissance in England*. Translated by F.C.A. Koelln and J. P. Pettegrove. Austin: University of Texas Press, 1953.

Cicero, Marcus Tullius. *De natura deorum; Academica*. Translated by H. Rackham. Loeb Classical Library: Cambridge, Mass., and London, 1961.

Clarke, Samuel. *A Demonstration of the Being and Attributes of God. 1705* and *A Discourse concerning the Unchangeable Obligations of Natural Religion. 1706*. Faksimile-Neudruck der Londoner Ausgaben. Stuttgart-Bad Cannstatt: Fredrich Fronmann Verlag (Günther Holzboog), 1964.

Courtines, Léo Pierre. *Bayle's Relation with England and the English*. New York: Columbia University Press, 1938.

Crane, R. S. Review of "Shaftesbury and the Doctrine of Moral Sense in the Eighteenth Century," by William E. Alderman. *Philological Quarterly* 11 (1932).

Cudworth, Ralph. *The True Intellectual System of the Universe: wherein all the Reason and Philosophy of Atheism is Confuted, and its Impossibility Demonstrated, with a Treatise concerning Eternal and Immutable Morality*. Translated by J. Harrison and edited by J. L. Mosheim. 3 vols. London, 1845.

Davie, George. "Berkeley, Hume, and the Central Problem of Scottish Philosophy." *McGill Hume Studies*. Edited by D. F. Norton, N. Capaldi, and W. Robison. Studies in Hume and Scottish Philosophy, 1. San Diego: Austin Hill Press, 1979.

Descartes, René. *The Philosophical Works of Descartes*. Translated by E. S. Haldane and G.R.T. Ross. 2 vols. Cambridge: At the University Press, 1967.

Dewey, John. "Naturalism." *Dictionary of Philosophy and Psychology*. Edited by J. M. Baldwin. 3 vols. Gloucester, Mass.: Peter Smith, 1960; reprint of 1925 edition.

Flew, Antony, "Hume." *A Critical History of Western Philosophy*. Edited by D. J. O'Connor. London, 1964.

313

Flew, Antony. *Hume's Philosophy of Belief.* London: Routledge & Kegan Paul, 1961.

Flew, Antony. "The Red Queen at Substraction." *Hume Studies* 5 (1979).

Foot, Philippa. "Hume on Moral Judgement." *David Hume: A Symposium.* Edited by D. F. Pears. London: Macmillan, 1966.

Frankena, William. "Hutcheson's Moral Sense Theory." *Journal of the History of Ideas* 16 (1955).

Galileo Galilei. *Il saggiatore.* Rome, 1623. Translated by Stillman Drake and edited by C. D. O'Malley and S. Drake in *Discoveries and Opinions of Galileo.* Garden City, N.Y.: Doubleday, 1957.

Gaskin, J.C.A. "God, Hume, and Natural Belief." *Philosophy* 49 (1974).

Gaskin, J.C.A. "Hume's Critique of Religion." *Journal of the History of Philosophy* 14 (1976).

Goudge, T. A. "Emergent Evolution." *Encyclopedia of Philosophy.* Edited by Paul Edwards. 8 vols. New York: Macmillan and Free Press, 1967.

Gouhier, Henri. "Doute méthodique ou négation méthodique?" *Les études philosophiques* 9 (1954).

Harrison, Jonathan. "Ethical Objectivism." *Encyclopedia of Philosophy.* Edited by Paul Edwards. 8 vols. New York: Macmillan and Free Press, 1967.

Harrison, Jonathan. "Moral Scepticism." *Supplementary Volume 41.* London: Aristotelian Society, 1967.

Hearn, Thomas K. "Árdal on the Moral Sentiments in Hume's *Treatise.*" *Philosophy* 48 (1973).

Hearn, Thomas K. "General Rules and Moral Sentiments in Hume's *Treatise.*" *Review of Metaphysics* 30 (1976).

Hearn, Thomas K. "General Rules in Hume's *Treatise.*" *Journal of the History of Philosophy* 8 (1970).

Heineccius, Johann Gottlieb. *A Methodical System of Universal Law: or the Laws of Nature and Nations deduced from Certain Principles and applied to Proper Cases.* Translated and illustrated with notes and supplements by George Turnbull. To which is added *A Discourse upon the Nature and Origin of Moral and Civil Laws*. 2 vols. 2d. ed. London, 1763.

Holland, R. F. "Moral Scepticism." *Supplementary Volume 41*. London: Aristotelian Society, 1967.

Hume, David. *David Hume: The Philosophical Works*. Edited by Thomas H. Green and Thomas H. Grose. 4 vols. Darmstadt: Scientia Verlag Aalen, 1964; reprint of the edition of 1886.

Hume, David. *Enquiries concerning Human Understanding and concerning the Principles of Morals*. Edited by L. A. Selby-Bigge. Third edition by P. H. Nidditch. Oxford: Clarendon Press, 1975.

Hume, David. *The History of England*. Cited from *David Hume: Philosophical Historian*. Edited by D. F. Norton and R. H. Popkin. Indianapolis: Bobbs-Merrill, 1965.

Hume, David. *A Letter from a Gentleman to his friend in Edinburgh*. Edited by E. C. Mossner and J. V. Price. Edinburgh: The Edinburgh University Press, 1967.

Hume, David. *The Letters of David Hume*. Edited by J.Y.T. Greig. 2 vols. Oxford: Clarendon Press, 1932.

Hume, David. *New Letters of David Hume*. Edited by Ernest C. Mossner and Raymond Klibansky. London: Clarendon Press, 1954.

Hume, David. *A Treatise of Human Nature*. Edited by L. A. Selby-Bigge. Second edition by P. H. Nidditch. Oxford: Clarendon Press, 1978.

Hunter, Geoffrey. "Hume on Is and Ought." *Philosophy* 37 (1962).

Hutcheson, Francis. *Essay on the Nature and Conduct of the Passions and Affections. With Illustrations on the Moral Sense*. 3d ed. London, 1742; reprinted, Gainesville: Scholars' Facsimiles and Reprints, 1969.

Hutcheson, Francis. *An Inquiry into the Original of our Ideas of Beauty and Virtue; In Two Treatises. I. Concerning Beauty, Order, Harmony, Design. II. Concerning Moral Good and Evil*. London, 1738; reprinted, Farnborough: Gregg International Publishers, 1969.

Hutcheson. Francis. Letter to William Mace. *European Magazine and London Review*, September 1788.

Hutcheson, Francis. Letters, *London Journal*, November 14 and 21, 1724, June 12 and 19, 1725 and October 9, 1725.

Hutcheson, Francis. "Observations on the Fable of the Bees." *Dublin Journal*, February 4, 12, 19, 1726.

Hutcheson, Francis. *Synopsis metaphysicae, ontologiam et pneumatologiam complectens.* Glasgow, 1744.

Hutcheson, Francis. *System of Moral Philosophy.* 2 vols. Glasgow, 1755.

Hutcheson, Francis. "Thoughts on Laughter." *Dublin Journal*, June 5, 12, and 19, 1725.

Immerwahr, John. "A Skeptic's Progress: Hume's Preference for the First *Enquiry*." *McGill Hume Studies.* Edited by D. F. Norton, N. Capaldi, and W. Robison. Studies in Hume and Scottish Philosophy, 1. San Diego: Austin Hill Press, 1979.

Jensen, Henning. *Motivation and the Moral Sense in Francis Hutcheson's Moral Theory.* The Hague: Martinus Nijhoff, 1972.

Jones, Peter. "Cause, Reason, and Objectivity in Hume's Aesthetics." *Hume: A Re-evaluation.* Edited by D. Livingston and J. King. New York: Fordham University Press, 1976.

Kames, Henry Home, Lord. *Essays on the Principles of Morality and Natural Religion in two Parts.* 2d ed. London, 1758.

Kant, Immanuel. *Prolegomena to Any Future Metaphysics.* Translated and edited by Paul Carus. La Salle, Ill.: Open Court Publishing Company, 1955.

Kydd, Rachel. *Reason and Conduct in Hume's Treatise.* London: Oxford University Press, 1946.

Lewes, G. H. *A Biographical History of Philosophy.* London: George Routledge & Sons, 1902.

Locke, John. *An Essay concerning Human Understanding.* London, 1690.

Loeb, Louis E. "Hume's Moral Sentiments and the Structure of the *Treatise*." *Journal of the History of Philosophy* 15 (1977).

Mackinstosh, Sir James. *On the Progress of Ethical Philosophy Chiefly During the XVIIth & XVIIIth Centuries.* Edited by William Whewell. 4th ed. Edinburgh, 1872.

Mandeville, Bernard. *The Fable of the Bees: or, Private vices, Pub-*

lick Benefits. Edited by F. B. Kaye. 2 vols. Oxford: Clarendon Press, 1957.

Marcil-Lacoste, L. "Dieu, garant de veracité, ou Reid critique de Descartes." *Dialogue* 14 (1975).

McCosh, James. *The Scottish Philosophy, Biographical, Expository, Critical from Hutcheson to Hamilton*. New York: Carter, 1875.

Middleton, Conyers. *Free Enquiry into the Miraculous Powers*. London, 1748.

Mintz, S. I. *The Hunting of the Leviathan*. Cambridge: At the University Press, 1962.

Montaigne, Michel de. *Complete Essays of Montaigne*. Translated by D. M. Frame. 3 vols. Garden City, N.Y.: Doubleday, 1960.

Monteiro, J. P. "Hume, Induction, and Natural Selection." *McGill Hume Studies*. Edited by D. F. Norton, N. Capaldi, and W. Robison. Studies in Hume and Scottish Philosophy, 1. San Diego: Austin Hill Press, 1979.

Moore, G. E. *Philosophical Papers*. London: Allen and Unwin, 1959.

Moore, James. "The Social Background of Hume's Science of Human Nature." *McGill Hume Studies*. Edited by D. F. Norton, N. Capaldi, and W. Robison. Studies in Hume and Scottish Philosophy, 1. San Diego: Austin Hill Press, 1979.

Mossner, E. C. *The Life of David Hume*. Edinburgh: Thomas Nelson and Sons, 1954.

Nethery, Wallace. "Hume's Manuscript Corrections in a Copy of *A Treatise of Human Nature*." *Papers of the Bibliographic Society of America* 57 (1963).

Norton, David Fate. "George Turnbull and the Furniture of the Mind." *Journal of the History of Ideas* 35 (1975).

Norton, David Fate. "History and Philosophy in Hume's Thought." In *David Hume: Philosophical Historian*. Edited by D. F. Norton and R. H. Popkin. Indianapolis: Bobbs-Merrill, 1965.

Norton, David Fate. "Hume and His Scottish Critics." *McGill Hume Studies*. Edited by D. F. Norton, N. Capaldi, and W. Robison. Studies in Hume and Scottish Philosophy, 1. San Diego: Austin Hill Press, 1979.

Norton, David Fate. "Hume's *A Letter from a Gentleman*: A Review Note." *Journal of the History of Philosophy* 6 (1968).

Norton, David Fate. "Hume's Common Sense Morality." *Canadian Journal of Philosophy* 5 (1975).

Norton, David Fate. "Hutcheson on Perception and Moral Perception." *Archiv für Geschichte der Philosophie* 59 (1977).

Norton, David Fate. "Hutcheson's Moral Sense Theory Reconsidered." *Dialogue* 13 (1974).

Norton, David Fate, "Reid's Abstract of the *Inquiry into the Human Mind*." In *Thomas Reid*. Edited by S. F. Barker and T. L. Beauchamp. Philosophical Monographs. Philadelphia, 1976.

Norton, David Fate. "Shaftesbury and Two Scepticisms. *Filosofia*, Supplemento al fascicolo 4 (1968).

Noxon, James. *Hume's Philosophical Development*. Oxford: Oxford University Press, 1973.

Noxon, James. "In Defence of 'Hume's Agnosticism.' " *Journal of the History of Philosophy* 14 (1976).

Oswald, James. *An Appeal to Common Sense in Behalf of Religion*. 2 vols. Edinburgh, 1766-1772.

Passmore, John. "Cudworth." *Encyclopedia of Philosophy*. Edited by Paul Edwards. 8 vols. New York: Macmillan and Free Press, 1967.

Passmore, John. "Hume and the Ethics of Belief." *David Hume: Bicentenary Papers*. Edited by G. P. Morice. Austin: University of Texas Press, 1977.

Passmore, John. *Ralph Cudworth: An Interpretation*. Cambridge: At the University Press, 1951.

Patrick, Mary Mills. *The Greek Sceptics*. New York: Columbia University Press, 1929.

Peach, Bernard. "The Correspondence between Francis Hutcheson and Gilbert Burnet: The Problem of the Date." *Journal of the History of Philosophy* 8 (1970).

Peach, Bernard. "Editor's Introduction." *Illustrations on the Moral Sense*. Cambridge, Mass.: Harvard University Press, 1971.

Peirce, Charles Sanders. *The Collected Papers of Charles Sanders Peirce*. Edited by C. Hartshorne, P. Weiss, and A. W. Burks.

318

8 vols. Cambridge, Mass.: Harvard University Press, 1931-1958.

Penelhum, Terence. "Hume's Scepticism and the Dialogues." *McGill Hume Studies*. Edited by D. F. Norton, N. Capaldi, and W. Robison. Studies in Hume and Scottish Philosophy, 1. San Diego: Austin Hill Press, 1979.

Pope, Alexander. *An Essay on Man*. Edited by Maynard Mack. London: Methuen, and New Haven: Yale University Press, 1958.

Popkin, Richard H. "David Hume: His Pyrrhonism and His Critique of Pyrrhonism." *Hume*. Edited by V. C. Chappell. New York: Doubleday, 1966.

Popkin, Richard H. "Hume: Philosophical Versus Prophetic Historian." *David Hume: Many-sided Genius*. Edited by K. R. Merrill and R. W. Shahan. Norman: University of Oklahoma Press, 1976.

Popkin, Richard H. *A History of Skepticism from Erasmus to Descartes*. New York: Humanities Press, 1964.

Popkin, Richard H. "Skepticism." *Encyclopedia of Philosophy*. Edited by Paul Edwards. 8 vols. New York: Macmillan and Free Press, 1967.

Popper, Sir Karl. *Conjectures and Refutations*. New York: Basic Books, 1962.

Price, Richard. *A Review of the Principal Questions in Morals*. Edited by D. D. Raphael. Oxford: Clarendon Press, 1948.

Randall, J. H. *The Career of Philosophy. From the Middle Ages to the Enlightenment*. New York: Columbia University Press, 1962.

Raphael, D. D., ed. *British Moralists, 1650-1800*. 2 vols. Oxford: Oxford University Press, 1969.

Raphael, D. D. *The Moral Sense*. London: Oxford University Press, 1947.

Reid, Thomas. *The Philosophical Orations . . . Delivered at the Graduation Ceremonies In King's College, Aberdeen, 1753, 1756, 1759, 1762*. Edited by W. R. Humphries. Aberdeen: Aberdeen University Press, 1937.

Reid, Thomas. "Unpublished Letters of Thomas Reid to Lord

Kames, 1762-1782." Edited by I. S. Ross. *Texas Studies in Literature and Language* 7 (1965).

Reid, Thomas. *The Works of Thomas Reid.* Edited by Sir William Hamilton. 2 vols. 7th ed. Edinburgh, 1872.

Robison, Wade. "David Hume: Naturalist and Meta-sceptic." *Hume: A Re-evaluation.* Edited by D. Livingston and J. King. New York: Fordham University Press, 1976.

Robison, Wade. "Hume's Scepticism." *Dialogue* 12 (1973).

Ross, I. S. *Lord Kames and the Scotland of His Day.* Oxford: Oxford University Press, 1972.

Scott, William R. *Francis Hutcheson. His Life, Teaching and Position in the History of Philosophy.* Cambridge: At the University Press, 1900.

Selby-Bigge, L. A., ed. *British Moralists.* 2 vols. Oxford: Clarendon Press, 1897; reprinted, New York: Bobbs-Merrill, 1964.

Sextus Empiricus. *Scepticism, Man, and God: Selections from the Major Writing of Sextus Empiricus.* Edited by Philip P. Hallie. Translated by Sanford G. Etheridge. Middletown, Conn.: Wesleyan University Press, 1964.

Sextus Empiricus. *Sextus Empiricus.* Translated by R. G. Bury. London: William Heineman; Cambridge, Mass.: Harvard University Press, 1933.

Shaftesbury, Third Earl of (Anthony Ashley Cooper). *Characteristics of Men, Manners, Opinions, Times.* Edited by J. M. Robertson. Introduction by Stanley Grean. 2 vols. New York: Bobbs-Merrill, 1964.

Shaftesbury, Third Earl of (Anthony Ashley Cooper). *The Life, Unpublished Letters, and Philosophical Regimen of Anthony Ashley Cooper, Earl of Shaftesbury.* Edited by B. Rand. London and New York: Sonnenshein, 1900.

Shaftesbury, Third Earl of (Anthony Ashley Cooper). *Second Characters, or the Language of Forms.* Edited by B. Rand. Cambridge: At the University Press, 1914.

Singer, Marcus. *Generalization in Ethics.* 2d ed. New York: Atheneum, 1971.

Skelton, Philip. *Ophiomaches; or Deism Revealed.* 2 vols. London, 1749.

Smith, Norman [Kemp]. "The Naturalism of Hume." *Mind.* N.S. 14 (1905).

Smith, Norman Kemp. *The Philosophy of David Hume: A Critical Study of its Origins and Central Doctrines.* London and New York: Macmillan, 1941; reprinted 1964.

Spràgèns, Thomas. *The Politics of Motion.* Lexington: University Press of Kentucky, 1973.

Stough, Charlotte. *Greek Scepticism: A Study in Epistemology.* Berkeley and Los Angeles: University of California Press, 1969.

Stove, D. C. "Hume, Kemp Smith, and Carnap." *Australasian Journal of Philosophy* 55 (1977).

Stove, D. C. "The Nature of Hume's Scepticism." *McGill Hume Studies.* Edited by D. F. Norton, N. Capaldi, and W. Robison. Studies in Hume and Scottish Philosophy, 1. San Diego: Austin Hill Press, 1979.

Stroud, Barry. *Hume.* London: Routledge & Kegan Paul, 1978.

Stroud, Barry. "Transcendental Arguments." *Journal of Philosophy* 65 (1968).

Thyssen-Schoute, C. Louise. "La diffusion européenne des idées de Bayle." In *Pierre Bayle, le philosophe de Rotterdam.* Edited by Paul Dibon. Paris: Elsevier Publishing Co., 1959.

Tillotson, John. *The Works of John Tillotson.* 7th ed. 2 vols. London, 1714.

Trinius, Johan Anton. *Freydenker Lexicon.* Leipzig and Bernberg, 1759; reprinted; Torino, 1960.

Turnbull, George. *Christianity neither False nor Useless tho' not as Old as The Creation: or An Essay to prove the Usefulness, Truth and Excellency of the Christian Religion; . . .* London, 1732.

Turnbull, George. *A Philosophical Enquiry Concerning the Connexion between the Doctrines and Miracles of Jesus Christ in a Letter to a Friend.* 2d ed. rev. London, 1732.

Turnbull, George. *The Principles of Moral Philosophy.* London, 1740.

Van Leeuwen, Henry G. *The Problem of Certainty in English Thought,*

1630-1690. International Archives of the History of Ideas, vol. 3. The Hague: Martinus Nijhoff, 1963.

Vernier, Paul. "Thomas Reid on the Foundations of Knowledge and his Answer to Skepticism." In *Thomas Reid.* Edited by S. F. Barker and T. L. Beauchamp. Philosophical Monographs. Philadelphia, 1976.

Walsh, W. H. "Hume's Concept of Truth." In *Reason and Reality.* Royal Institute of Philosophy Lectures, vol. 5. London, 1972.

Weldon, S. M. "Thomas Reid's Theory of Vision." Ph.D. diss., McGill University, 1978.

Whately, Richard. *Historic Doubts Relative to Napoleon Bonaparte.* London, 1819.

Whitehead, A. N. *Science and the Modern World.* New York: Macmillan, 1926.

Wilson, Fred. "Hume's Theory of Mental Activity." *McGill Hume Studies.* Edited by D. F. Norton, N. Capaldi, and W. Robison. Studies in Hume and Scottish Philosophy, 1. San Diego: Austin Hill Press, 1979.

Wisdom, John. *Other Minds.* Oxford: Blackwell's, 1956.

Wisdom, John. *Philosophy and Psychoanalysis.* Oxford: Blackwell's, 1957.

Wolff, Robert Paul. "Hume's Theory of Mental Activity." *Hume.* Edited by V. C. Chappell. New York: Doubleday, 1966.

Zeller, Eduard. *Stoics, Epicureans, and Sceptics.* Translated by O. J. Reichel. London, 1880.

Index

NOTE: Entries in the index for authors and titles refer to places in the text and footnotes where actual information or comments about a specific author or work appear. There are no entries for footnotes that are merely bibliographic citations of an author's work.

judgments, 103, 118-121, 124, 151, 224, 252; contrary, 261; suspension of, 260-265, 268, 278, 291n; triadic, 117n

Kames, Lord (Henry Home): influence on Hume, 3-5, 153-154, 174-175, 185-191, 193, 305; refutes moral scepticism, 175, 196, 199, 202-205; theories of perception, 181-185; of providence, 180-181, 185, 187-191
Kant, Immanuel, 4, 7, 194n
knowledge, 30-31, 37-38, 49-50, 157-160, 168-172, 190-191, 227-228, 276, 287; moral knowledge, 150-151, 246
Kydd, Rachel, 127n

Language, common, 165-166, 169-170; universal, 139n
Letter from a Gentleman, A (Hume), 4, 44n, 193
Leviathan, The (Hobbes), 88-89
Lewes, G. H., 5
Locke, John, 4-5, 11, 33-45, 56-57, 61, 69, 78n, 85-86, 138, 175, 196
logic, 201n, 211

Mace, William, 79-80n
Mandeville, Bernard, 43, 45, 60-61, 64, 69, 145, 148, 168, 196
Masham, Lady, 27
Meditations (Descartes), 250-252, 287
mental tranquility, 262-263
metaphysics, 9-11, 52-54, 86, 88, 120, 124, 137, 139n, 141, 169, 189, 211-218, 220-221, 241, 242n, 304-305, 308, 310
metaphysical scepticism, 13, 53-54, 154, 196
Middleton, Conyers, 295n
miracles, 295-301
mistakes of fact, 103-104
mistakes of right, 104

Montaigne, Michel de, 267n
Moore, G. E., 280-281
Moore, James, 27n
moral scepticism: and Descartes, 26-27; and doubt, 285; and Hobbes, 33-43; Hume, 3-4, 9-15, 43-54, 134-141, 145-147, 150-151, 241, 244-245, 304-310; and Hutcheson, 58-65, 69, 73, 86-87; and Locke, 33-43; and Turnbull, 160-162, 169
moral science, 157-158, 168-169
moral sense, 12-14, 21, 25-27, 38-43, 45, 64-65, 72-73
moral sentiments, 130-137, 141, 144-146, 148-151, 305-310
moral theory, 154-158, 168-169, 211n, 218; and Hutcheson, 14, 57-59, 61-93, 129; and Kames, 176; and science, 21-23, 26-27, 31, 86-88, 155-160, 228n; and Turnbull, 162-170
motion and rest, 79-81, 87, 293n
motive and morality, 142-143, 148-149

Natural History of Religion, The (Hume), 16, 193, 248-249
"natural furniture," 159-160, 172
naturalism, defined, 15-17, 21; and Hobbes, 23-24; and Hume, 4-7, 10, 14-20, 127n, 149-150, 202-205, 211-212, 217-218, 222, 231-233; and Kames, 179-180, 190; normative naturalism, 19-20; and Shaftesbury, 38-41, 242n; and Turnbull, 154-159, 167-174
necessary connection, 223, 228
negative dogmatists, 264-265, 270
New Academy, 261
Newton, Isaac, 154, 156, 158, 169, 198-199
non-cognitivist interpretations, 57, 60-61, 69, 72, 92-93
non-evidence, 257-259, 264, 268n

recollective signs, 258-259
Reid, Thomas, 4-5, 7, 10, 48-50,
    153, 171-173, 181n, 189-203, 208,
    239, 280n
religious scepticism, 244, 246-249,
    285, 295-303
rest and motion, 79-81, 87
Robison, Wade, 8n, 289n

scepticism: characteristics of, 239-
    241; defined, 8-10; and doubt,
    285-294; and Hume, 3-13, 195,
    219-222, 232, 239, 288-295, 300-
    310; and truth, 272-274. See also
    specific kinds of scepticism
Scholasticism, 21-22, 26, 87-88
science and moral theory, 21-22, 26-
    27, 31, 86-88, 155-160, 228n
Scottish philosophers, 192-203, 206-
    208, 239-241
scruples, 283n, 284-285
"Search into the Nature of Society,
    A" (Mandeville), 64-65
secondary qualities, 80, 85, 87, 113,
    180n, 184
self-interest, 130, 151, 160-163, 165,
    175, 244. See also egoists
self-knowledge, 37-39, 185-186
sensations, 112n, 159, 173, 223, 259
Sense of Honor, 73n, 83
senses, 73-79, 83-84, 129, 159-160,
    177-185, 190-191, 202-205, 232-
    233, 259-260, 263-265. See also
    pain; pleasure
sentiments and morality, 130-137,
    141, 305-310; and reason, 134-
    135, 147-148, 153, 210-212, 305-
    310; subtility of, 133, 141; univer-
    sality of, 137-141, 145-147, 150-
    151. See also subordination thesis
sentimentalists, 9, 49-54, 56, 69n;
    and Hume, 95-98, 101, 109-114,
    117, 123-128, 130, 212n, 215-216,
    220, 232. See also subordination
    thesis

Sextus Empiricus, 255-265, 268, 270,
    285, 300-301
Shaftesbury, Lord, 33-43, 45, 53-54,
    61, 70, 145, 147, 153-154, 160,
    163, 164, 175-176, 196, 241-244,
    277n, 305
sight, 184-185
Singer, Marcus, 12n, 245
Smith, Norman Kemp, 5-10, 14, 17-
    20, 43-50, 54, 56-59, 69, 92, 100,
    127n, 128-129, 151n, 194, 208,
    226-227, 235-237
society and moral sense, 39-41, 64-
    65, 72-73
Socrates, 156
Spragens, Thomas, 23n
speculative morality, 36-37, 43, 50,
    53, 65, 102, 121, 137-139, 145,
    176, 189, 199, 211, 218, 221,
    243, 304-307
Stoics, 261, 270-273, 276, 278, 282,
    284, 287, 294
Stough, Charlotte, 270-275
Stove, David, 6, 194n
Strahan, William, 193-194
Stroud, Barry, 7, 67n, 151n, 210n
subjectivist theory, 92-93, 109-112,
    131, 141-145
subordination thesis, 5-6, 9, 17-20,
    96-131, 134-135, 147-153, 208-
    216, 219-234, 305-310
sympathy, 112n, 136n, 147n
Synopsis metaphysicae (Hutcheson),
    80, 81n, 82
System of Moral Philosophy, A
    (Hutcheson), 81n

taste and morality, 166n, 121, 125
teleological principles, 87-90, 155,
    170-171
Teleological Realism, 170-173. See
    also Providential Naturalism
Theocles (Shaftesbury), 36-37
Tillotson, John, 296-300

Library of Congress Cataloging in Publication Data

Norton, David Fate.
   David Hume: common-sense moralist, sceptical
metaphysician.

   Bibliography: p.
   Includes index.
   1. Hume, David, 1711-1776.   I.   Title.
B1498.N65   192   81-47937
ISBN 0-691-07265-5   AACR2

David Fate Norton is Professor of Philosophy at McGill University. He has published many articles on Hume and other eighteenth-century philosophers and is coeditor of *David Hume: Philosophical Historian* and a critical edition of Hume's works. Professor Norton is also the editor of the *Journal of the History of Philosophy*.

LIBRARY
ST. LOUIS COMMUNITY COLLEGE
AT FLORISSANT VALLEY